THE PSYCHOLOGY TODAY OMNIBOOK

OF

PERSONAL DEVELOPMENT

THE PSYCHOLOGY TODAY OMNIBOOK

OF

PERSONAL DEVELOPMENT

KATINKA MATSON

RESEARCH ASSOCIATE: LYN HORTON

A PSYCHOLOGY TODAY BOOK

WILLIAM MORROW AND COMPANY, INC.

NEW YORK   1977

Printed in the United States of America.

1 2 3 4 5 6 7 8 9 10

Library of Congress Cataloging in Publication Data

Matson, Katinka.
    The Psychology Today omnibook of personal development.

    (A Psychology Today book)
    Includes bibliographical references.
    1. Success—Dictionaries. 2. Psychology—Dictionaries. 3. Psychotherapy—Dictionaries. I. Psychology Today. II. Title.
BF637.S8M34   158'.1'03   77-4966
ISBN 0-688-03225-7

BOOK DESIGN   CARL WEISS

For
Tim Matson,
Hallie Parker,
Jon Matson,
&
Edwin Schlossberg

ACKNOWLEDGMENTS

A project of this scope necessarily involves the participation of many individuals. I wish to express my thanks to the following:

Lyn Horton, my Research Associate, worked with dedication and thoroughness. Her efforts were crucial to the writing of this book.

John Brockman served as the general project consultant and provided me with continued support and guidance.

Edwin Schlossberg suggested the book's conceptual framework and served as a project consultant.

Edward Rosenfeld and Bennett Shapiro offered useful advice during the research and writing stages.

Jim Ellison of Psychology Today Books, Tobi Sanders of Bantam Books, and Jim Landis of William Morrow provided me with all the assistance and editorial guidance that any author could possibly hope for.

Paul Chance and T. George Harris, formerly of *Psychology Today,* provided significant feedback as the book was being written.

Dozens of other individuals replied to research queries with overwhelming enthusiasm and interest. Their responses and support were invaluable and heartening.

PREFACE

During this decade, there has been a remarkable change in the way we perceive ourselves in the world. The 1960's saw a preoccupation with political activism, Vietnam, ecology, be-ins, communes, drugs, etc. Today we are turning inward: we are looking for personal definition, personal improvement, personal achievement, and personal enlightenment.

The Psychology Today Omnibook of Personal Development has been designed for use in several ways:

(1) *Personal Development:*

Each entry in the *Omnibook* will provide you with everything you have to know about a certain subject in order to decide whether to pursue an interest.

(2) *Reference:*

Very few of the entries included in the book are covered in the major encyclopedias now in use. In this sense, you can use the *Omnibook* as a reference work.

(3) *Reality Maps:*

You may also read the *Omnibook* from a philosophical point of view. While the entries all apply to personal development, they can also be considered as maps of reality. The *Omnibook* documents all the different ways you can think about yourself and experience yourself. You may read it as a book about the mind: the one we all share.

K. M.

CONTENTS

THE PSYCHOLOGY TODAY OMNIBOOK

OF

PERSONAL DEVELOPMENT

ACTUALISM was founded by Russell Paul Schofield, a twentieth-century poet, writer, and teacher. It is based on twenty-five years of research and experimentation into *Agni Yoga* ("fire yoga"), which is the primary technique of actualism. The practice of Agni Yoga originated in India and has been traced to Chinese civilization, Polynesian cultures, the Indians of North and South America, and medieval alchemy.

Actualism purports to teach the evolutionary processes and purposes of mankind, whose goal is the realization of an inherently divine potential. Through Agni Yoga, or union by fire, the actual design of man as a cosmic being is illuminated by means of experience, rather than through factual knowledge. According to Schofield, through this yoga technique, the student of actualism ". . . learns to carry the light of his own inner fire into home, business, profession, social life, sports, etc., gradually bringing a growing creative expression into every activity in which he is engaged. He finds his own interior sources of strength, wisdom, good will and love . . . his own immortal individuality, the creator of personality systems."

Agni Yoga is a process of energy transformation based on four principles: thought directs energy; energy follows thought; obstruction to energy causes discomfort, if mild, and pain and dis-ease if strong; energy is concentrated where thought is focused. The underlying principle of Agni Yoga states that the actual design of your personality can be illuminated, and, as a result, the barriers or obstructions which normally impede your way to achieving the totality of consciousness will be eradicated. Agni Yoga considers these barriers to be psychic residue: images and associations which distort your perception of the reality of a situation. Agni Yoga is a step-by-step procedure of bringing light and fire into your system to cleanse it. It has been compared to "the melting of ice on a river." The barriers are frozen energy packets. When they are melted, the flow of energy that will build your immortal self is increased. Agni Yoga augments your ability to deal with the typical defense mechanisms such as repression, suppression, denial, etc., that create false images of the self and are thus destructive. It teaches you how to adopt perceptual, emotional, and mental attitudes and positions that will permit your energies to flow.

Actualism teaches that there are three orders of food: 1) *Third-order food* is what you eat, drink, and breathe or ingest as solid matter. 2) *Second-order food* is comprised of psychological attitudes that you allow to go through your system. 3) *Prime-order food* is the life-light energies that you channel into your system; with light and fire, you can assimilate, digest, and eliminate everything that you take into your system, physically and psychologically.

Actualism teaches that the body has an organizing field that can be polarized as dynamic male on the right, magnetic female on the left, dynamic front, and magnetic back. The dynamic components express themselves through function; the magnetic through structure. The unification of all components is internal; it involves the "balancing and harmonizing of dynamic and magnetic energies between structure and function, right and left, front and back, higher and lower, within the microcosmos and on each level of consciousness." When this unification is achieved, only then are you able to communicate joyfully with others and express yourself fully from both the dynamic and magnetic sides. You will have gotten free of images and realized the goal of actualism: You will allow "radiant light to shine on what actually is" and experience *unity mergence.*

Unity mergence is a psychophysical phenomenon that has two effects: synergy and potentiation, in which present actual experiences are validated by you, apart from images and programmed designs for living. When you discover inner wholeness, you function as an observer of light energies on all levels of consciousness. When you establish joyful communication, you build a stepping stone to cooperation and communion with others on every level of consciousness in a unity that is characteristic of the actual self.

The exercises of actualism require you to think, allow, and observe. They are performed while sitting relaxed in a straight-backed chair, with legs uncrossed, feet flat on the ground, and hands on the legs. One of the main exercises calls for you to think of a point of white light, visualize it six inches above your head, and concentrate on it. Once you have been able to experience this light, your body will be bathed in white-light energy. By focusing on this point of white light and bringing it to the places in your body where there is pain or discomfort from blockages of energy flow, you will "awaken" these areas to light, and increase your total well-being.

Schofield has written both poetry and prose about actualism. He is currently writing a book on the subject, *The Actual Design of Man,* with Ralph Metzner. He has written a book of poetry, *Imprint Unmistakable,* published privately.

REFERENCE

Ralph Metzner, *Maps of Consciousness.* New York: Macmillan, 1971.

ACUPUNCTURE (*acus,* "needle"; *punctura,* "puncture") is an ancient Chinese system of healing that consists of the stimulation of certain specific points on the skin by means of the insertion and withdrawing of needles, the application of heat (moxibustion), massage, or a combination of these methods of treatment.

Acupuncture began in China two thousand years before the birth of Christianity. The earliest known work on the subject is the *Nei Ching,* or *Classic of Internal Medicine,* ascribed to Hunang Ti, the Yellow Emperor (2697–2596 B.C.). In the seventeenth century, Jesuit missionaries, introduced to the practice in Peking, made an unsuccessful attempt to introduce acupuncture to the Western world. It was not until the 1940s with the publication of *L'Acupuncture Chinoise* (5 vols.) by Soulie de Mourant, a French sinologist, that the subject received any serious attention.

The philosophical explanation of acupuncture is based on the Taoist philosophy. The Chinese believe that health is determined by a free and balanced energy flow within the body. This energy, or force, in its basic state is called T'chi and is made up of two complementary forces: yin, a negative force, and yang, a positive force. Yin and yang energy flows through the body from head to foot along channels called meridians, which are represented in diagrams as lines joining a series of specific points. Your body has twelve main meridians. Ten meridians correspond to different organs (lungs, heart, large intestine, small intestine, bladder, spleen, gall bladder, kidneys, and liver). Two meridians correspond to bodily activities (the "triple heater," which corresponds to sexual drive and respiration, and the "heart constrictor," which is related to circulation and the blood vessels). The points on these meridians, of which there are approximately eight hundred to one thousand, are the acupuncture points.

When the energy flow along your meridians is circulating freely and in balance, your health is good. When the flow of energy becomes blocked at any point, or imbalanced because of disease, this imbalance will cause certain areas of your body to become tender. Acupuncture treatment is based on the theory that the stimulation of the proper points on the skin affects the internal organs and other various parts of the body by correcting the imbalances. The acupuncture points on a certain meridian will affect the organ after which it is named. For instance, the heart meridian is made up of a series of points which begins at the chest, runs along the inside of the arm to the little finger. If the heart is unhealthy, the points on the heart meridian will become sensitive.

The first phase of treatment by an acupuncturist is the diagnostic phase to determine the meridians which are affecting either an excess or depletion of energy, and whether this energy is yin or yang. Pulse reading, locating sensitive points on meridians through palpitation of the abdomen, and general observation of your appearance, your facial expression, the tone of your voice, are common diagnostic procedures.

Once the acupuncturist has determined the energy imbalance, treatment can begin. The primary form of treatment is the insertion of needles at the appropriate points to either stimulate or disperse the energy of the meridian. These points are very often on the opposite side of the body, or on the point of the meridian which is farthest away from the location of the symptoms or the affected organ.

The needles are manipulated in a variety of ways. They can be vibrated and twirled. They are usually made of stainless steel, gold, or silver, and vary in shape, length, and diameter. They can be inserted directly or through a guide tube to prevent bending.

Another form of treatment, which is called moxibustion and is especially popular in Japan, consists of burning small cones of wormwood or "moxa" on the appropriate acupuncture points. These cones are left to burn, often to the skin, producing a blister. Many Japanese self-administer this method of treatment.

The third form of treatment is the massaging of the appropriate points with fingers, elbows, or scratching. Massage is often used prior to and immediately after the needles are used.

Research has shown acupuncture treatment to result in several beneficial effects. It has been used in China as a method of general anesthesia, or sedation, on women in childbirth as well as in certain surgical procedures. It is especially effective when used this way because it eliminates the potentially dangerous side effects of drugs. It can be used to control a toxic or hyperactive state of internal organs by having a relaxing effect on them. Acupuncture has also proved successful in treating functional disorders such as obesity, headaches, diarrhea, menstrual disorders, and some forms of color blindness. Acupuncture is most effective as a cure when there is no actual lesion or tissue damage. In the latter case, where there is a functional problem with an organic base, a complete cure is impossible.

The controversies which have surrounded the practice of acupuncture stem from the philosophical explanation the Chinese traditionally gave to it. The idea that there is a "life force" or "energy" that flows through your body, and that this energy is positive and negative, is mystical and nonempirical to the Western mind. The search for an explanation as to why acupuncture works as a cure for certain ailments when Western medical techniques fail (especially as relief for pain) has led to the theory that acupuncture works by affecting the autonomic nervous system somehow, but as yet there is no purely scientific explanation for it.

Presently there are acupuncture associations in over twenty-six countries. In China, acupuncture is an integrated part of the medical system. Japan is engaged in extensive research into acupuncture in its hospitals and universities. In 1974, the United States National Institutes of Health initiated a study of acupuncture as a means of relieving chronic pain caused by cancer, neuralgia, and arthritis.

REFERENCES

Yoshio Manaka and Ian A. Urquhart, *The Laymen's Guide to Acupuncture*. Tokyo/New York: Weatherhill, 1972.

Felix Mann, *Acupuncture*. New York: Vintage Books, 1973.

ALFRED ADLER (1870–1937), the Austrian psychologist, is predominantly known for the founding of the school of Individual Psychology. Adler was born in Vienna, and he received his M.D. from the University of Vienna in 1895. Adler began his association with Sigmund Freud in 1902, as a young practicing physician. During this period, he became a prominent member of the Freudian psychoanalytic circle. At one point, he succeeded Freud as president of the Vienna Psychoanalytic Society and became coeditor of the journal *Zentralblatt für Psychoanalyse.* Adler's relationship with Freud continued until 1911 when he broke away from his mentor, largely because of Freud's emphasis on sexuality. In 1912, he established his own school of Individual Psychology. Adler also differed from Freud in that he did not use a couch in therapy, but rather sat face-to-face with his patient and assumed the role of a teacher rather than the traditional medical role. In 1914, Adler started the journal *Zeitschrift für Individualpsychologie.* In 1920, he established child-guidance clinics in schools in Vienna, Munich, and Berlin, in which both parents and teachers were counseled in the presence of a qualified audience. Adler began to lecture internationally, visiting the United States regularly after 1926. In 1932, he became a member of the Long Island Faculty of Medicine, the first professor of medical psychology in America. Adler died in Scotland in 1937 while on a lecture tour.

Individual Psychology is based on Adler's theory that character is formed in response to an infantile feeling of inferiority in the individual.

According to Adler, the unconscious and the conscious are products of subjective values and interests that are socially oriented, unparalleled in physical reality, and created by the individual. Adler believed that dynamic psychological forces are not rooted in physiological circumstances, but rather that the inner nature of the self is the essential factor determining human nature. The aim of Individual Psychology is to understand how psychological processes proceed from one to another through objective observation. The investigation becomes the examination of the meaning of the individual's goal of superiority, feelings of inferiority, and extent of social interest, with the assumption that the causal relationship among the processes is to be found within the individual.

Adler recognized the one basic dynamic force guiding human activity as the *striving* from a "minus to a plus situation," essentially a drive for power and self-assertion. He called this the *will to dominate*. Striving is specifically directed by your individually created goal or ideal, which is unknown, not understood, and takes the form of the unconscious. For the psychologist, the discovery of this goal becomes essential to the understanding of your personality: It is the end point for the self-consistent organization of psychological processes and builds personality structure. Adler labels this process the *style of life*. Every aspect of your psychology is part of a unified relational system. Any objective determinants particular to biology, your past history, or your *aperceptive schema* (that which is imposed on the world in the early stages of life [ages four to five] whereby "experiences are interpreted before they are accepted and the interpretation always accords with the original meaning given to life") are incorporated into and influence psychological processes in the development of the style of life. Within the context of Individual Psychology, you are never considered separate from your social situation. Furthermore, all your problems that address life and the satisfaction of drives, as well as your values, are regarded as being socially derived. Your *socialization* progresses not as a product of repression, but rather as an innate human ability Adler calls *social feeling* or *social interest* that becomes crucial to your adjustment. Maladjustment to the social environment is rooted in feelings of inferiority, underdeveloped social interest, or an overemphasized goal of personal superiority. In general, thoughts, feelings, and actions stem from your interpretation of the meaning of life;

it is from within this context that problems emanate. This is the essence of Adler's concept of the *life plan*.

Specifically, Adler saw the meaning of life varying between two opposite poles: that which is absolute and that which is absolutely wrong or not "serviceable." The meaning of life is based on the ties which structure your reality: You live on the earth and are thus restricted and must limit your development to meet the requirements that define being on earth; you are a member of the human race and live in association with everyone else; you are either of the male or female sex. These ties reveal three problems: to find an occupation that is coincidental with the nature of earth; to find a cooperative position among others that allows for sharing the benefits of cooperation; and to find a way to assimilate the idea of the sexes in the realization that the continuation of mankind depends upon "love life."

You begin to structure a meaning of life in childhood. Adler defined three situations in childhood in which a faulty structuring of meaning is likely to occur: 1) in the case of a child born with infirmities (physical deformities or disease) whose attention is not directed to others, but who is allowed to dwell on his/her own sensations; 2) in the case of a spoiled child who is the center of attention and later meets difficulties by making demands of others; 3) in the case of the neglected child who is never permitted to know what love and cooperation can elicit. These cases demonstrate the hindrances that can occur in the process of achieving a mature approach to the problems of mankind as cited above, and thus an appropriate meaning of life.

Adler proposed that an appropriate meaning of life is one which stresses cooperation among individuals. This indicates that you, as an individual, must avoid giving "a private meaning to life" and thinking that life exists for you alone. Rather, you should direct your interests to mankind and its welfare, and contribute to the whole. You will be able to understand the problems of love and marriage according to how well you deal with problems in the context of social interest. Love

and marriage should be seen as tasks for two cooper-
ating individuals. Solving the three problems of mankind
will demand that you be "a good fellow worker, a
friend to all other men, and a true partner in love and
marriage." Thus, the true meaning of life is common
to all individuals: "The man who meets the problems
of human life successfully acts as if he recognized, fully
and spontaneously, that the meaning of life is interest
in others and cooperation."

REFERENCES

Alfred Adler, *The Individual Psychology of Alfred Adler*,
ed. and annotated by Heinz L. and Rowena R. Ans-
bacher. New York: Basic Books, 1956.
————, *What Life Should Mean to You*, ed. by Alan Por-
ter. New York: G. P. Putnam's Sons, 1931.
————, *Social Interest: A Challenge to Mankind*, trans. by
John Linton and Richard Vaughan. New York: G. P.
Putnam's Sons, 1964.

AEROBICS   is a physical fitness program developed
in the 1960s by Kenneth H. Cooper, M.D., as a result
of his research while in the U.S. Air Force, into the
effects of exercise on the human body, and the relationship of physical fitness to health, especially as it affected
pilots and astronauts.

Aerobics (from aerobic, pertaining to or caused by
the presence of oxygen) is a system of exercises, whose
main objective is to increase the amount of oxygen that
your body can process within a given time. The goal is
to improve your overall health, and especially the condition of your heart, lungs, and blood vessels, by stimulating them through exercise for a period long enough
to produce beneficial changes in your body.

Cooper's research indicated to him that the nature
of true physical fiitness, when viewed scientifically, was
not simply muscular fitness. Strong skeletal muscles,
which are developed through isometrics, weight lifting,
and a variety of calisthenics, are not a valid measure
of fitness. Neither is the ability to lift hundred-pound
weights. True physical fitness, according to Cooper's re-

search, is endurance fitness, or the working capacity of the entire body. This depends upon the health of your heart, lungs, and cardiovascular system, and other internal organs, as well as your muscles.

The key is oxygen; oxygen is energy. The principal goal of aerobic exercises is to increase your aerobic capacity, the amount of oxygen your body can process within a given time. This is related to your ability to (1) breathe large amounts of air; (2) forcefully deliver large amounts of blood through your body; (3) deliver oxygen to all parts of your body. Laboratory research indicated that the exercises must be of sufficient intensity and duration in order to achieve what Cooper calls the "training effect," which is (1) the strengthening of respiratory muscles and an improvement in the flow of air in and out of the lungs; (2) the strengthening of the heart muscle, enabling it to pump more blood; (3) the general toning up of the muscles throughout the body, an improvement in circulation, and a lowering of blood pressure; (4) an increase in the total amount of blood circulating in the body, an increase in red blood cells and hemoglobin.

The actual exercise program is geared around a point system that derives from laboratory measurements of the oxygen cost of an exercise. The points refer to energy expended. Your ultimate goal is to earn thirty points per week. Exercises included in the program are walking, running, bicycle riding, swimming, and several group games such as volley ball. If desired, indoor exercise equipment can be used, e.g., stationary bicycles, treadmills, or staircases.

Before beginning an aerobic exercise program, you must classify yourself in order to select the proper program for your present physical condition. If you are a conditioned beginner, you can take a twelve-minute test to find out exactly how conditioned you are, and the amount of exercise you must do each week to maintain your physical fitness or improve your level of physical fitness to where it should be. The test consists of finding out how far you can go in twelve minutes, running

and/or walking without straining. If you are unconditioned, you are instructed not to take the test, but to
select an age-adjusted starter program. If you are over
thirty-five, it is advised that you have a physical examination before beginning an aerobic exercise program.

The time you must spend engaged in a chosen exercise depends on the exercise itself. For the first 10–13
weeks, which are designed to get you gradually to a
stage of physical fitness, the time period increases for
each exercise period. For example, if walking is the
exercise, you will eventually spend 56 minutes walking 4 miles, and do this four times a week to earn
your 30 points. If the exercise is running, you will
spend 17 minutes running 2 miles, twice a week, and
11:55 minutes running 1.5 miles twice a week. The
charts are exactly detailed, clearly indicating what you
are required to do, the distance to be covered, the time
goal, and the frequency per week. According to Cooper,
the 30 points represent the minimum number of points
you must earn in order to maintain your physical fitness at a satisfactory level.

The direct result of engaging in an aerobic program
for many participants has been a decreased desire to
smoke, an increase in general energy and diminishing
of fatigue, better appetite, and weight loss.

The physical fitness programs of both the U. S. Air
Force and the U. S. Navy are based on aerobics. The
Royal Canadian Air Force uses a similar program. It
has been adopted by professional athletic teams, and
versions of it are taught in physical-education programs
in colleges and universities. There has been a wide age
range of people who engage in aerobics. People between
forty and sixty years of age use Cooper's age-adjusted
program.

REFERENCES

Kenneth H. Cooper, M.D., *Aerobics*. New York: Bantam
    Books, 1968.
————, *The New Aerobics*. New York: Bantam Books,
    1970.

————, *Aerobics for Women.* New York: Bantam Books, 1969.

AESTHETIC REALISM is a philosophy founded by Eli Siegel in 1941. He published a definitive text on his approach to reality in 1946, *The Aesthetic Method in Self-Conflict,* which was later combined into one volume with his *Psychiatry, Economics, Aesthetics* (1946). Siegel is also a recognized American poet; his *Hot Afternoons Have Been in Montana: Poems* (1958) was nominated for the National Book Award.

Since its founding, Aesthetic Realism has attracted the attention of thousands of people, mainly because of the work of the Aesthetic Realism Foundation in New York City, an independent, educational, nonprofit organization.

The basic tenet of Aesthetic Realism is that all reality is united in an aesthetic union of opposites: This is beauty itself. According to Siegel, reality can be considered in terms of change and sameness, motion and rest, relation and independence, etc. Life can be seen aesthetically, and you, the individual, are "irreducibly specific while being affected every hour by the whole world, the universe of days and lands." The arts and sciences can be viewed aesthetically, showing reality shaped of elements that are both perceivable and invisible. Siegel calls the arts and sciences aesthetic realities; they express the way in which the world works, opposites as one.

Aesthetic Realism defines a way to perceive the world as "all that you can see as different from yourself." At the same time, Aesthetic Realism is a means to "like" the world for the way in which it functions. Liking the world because it consists of opposites, and therefore is beautiful, means liking yourself: "Unless one likes the world, one doesn't like oneself." Liking the world entails viewing it honestly so that you may understand that its most unlikable qualities are integral to it.

According to Aesthetic Realism, contempt makes

you unable to like the world and yourself. Contempt is the prime motivator of fear, anger, and phobias. It causes mental disorder and, in extreme form, insanity. Contempt allows you to deal with what you don't understand. On a large scale, contempt causes wars; on a lesser scale, contempt causes homosexuality, the conquest of the parent who did not demonstrate love properly. Contempt becomes a way to lessen what is external to you and aggrandize the self. All these emotions "are about the world," and their continuous existence has been seen throughout history; they must be accepted in this way.

The recognition and avoidance of failure are also an important part of the definition and concept of Aesthetic Realism. Siegel analyzes what he calls "failures" as personified in the work of certain men, Sigmund Freud and T. S. Eliot, among others. Siegel believes their common failure to be the neglect of seeing "the large continuous purpose of man as good will for everything, animate and inanimate."

Freud "appealed to incompleteness in man." He confined man's possible view of self by emphasizing his sexual anxieties and death instinct as the keys to mental disorder. According to Siegel, Freud entirely avoided man's unconscious desires for good will.

According to Siegel, T. S. Eliot violated poetry through his failure to show how its musicality combines with its meaning. Siegel assumes that Eliot had not seen life honestly or precisely, nor had he shown that he liked life. This is a demonstration of intellectual insanity.

In an early work, Siegel discusses the relationship of imagination to reality and aesthetics. He defines imagination as being based on a known thing outside of the self, the knowledge of which is integrated into the self. The quality of imagination is contingent on this knowledge (or aesthetic state) in relation to your picture of the world, which implies your ethical stance. Pictures of the world are products of the imagination: ". . . beauty and rightness of these pictures depend on how much we can see the world as what it is." Dreams are evidence of the workings of the imagination: They are "criticisms of onself through pictures one earlier was busy in arranging."

Imagination develops within the self, which should be considered in relation to everything else. Imagination becomes a form of concentration of its opposing capacities to expand and be compact at the same time. It consists of fears and hopes regarding what is possible in reality. The quality of imagination describes the quality of your loving of reality. When imagination is corrupted, it functions like contempt, to shape neuroses and insanity. It is the result of your reluctance to see reality using both your unconscious and will at the same time. Discovering where the mind/imagination is not corrupted and does not conceal reality is an aim of Aesthetic Realism. This means discovering that imagination should be based in unity and honest facts; only then can the world's orderliness and beauty be determined.

In an *AR Foundation Newsletter* (1976), Siegel explains that the purpose of Aesthetic Realism is to "encourage people to see the world all through their lives in the best way they can." It teaches that "liking the world . . . is the junction of two opposites: necessity and self-expression." The education offered addresses itself to issues which are essential to liking the world, and seeing yourself and the world as one. Aesthetic Realism education considers subjects such as economics, power, drugs, gambling, sex, alcoholism, crime, etc. For example, power is considered both good and bad. Power comes from food to make you strong, from music to make you feel the continuity of change and sameness, or from a loving relationship. Or, power can cause contempt for someone for whom you have no respect.

According to Aesthetic Realism, religion enables you to focus your thought (ethics, art, and science) in order to see the world. Religion is a union of two opposites, God and self, into a "beautiful whole." To see God is to see reality and life as consisting of relationships between all its elements.

The process of Aesthetic Realism takes the form of seminars, or group consultations, all sponsored by the AR Foundation. The seminars deal with a wide range of subjects: those that are directed toward daily problems and those directed toward the greater problems of life. In seminars, a consultation trio discusses aesthetic solutions to these problems, in terms of music, literature, poetry, painting, history, etc. There are drama workshops concerned with Aesthetic Realism's approach to drama of all periods, and music performance workshops that aim to demonstrate the oneness music creates from opposites in life.

Siegel explains that the reason the arts function as a major part of the education in Aesthetic Realism is because of the pleasure they give people. The arts are a means to find "repose, stir, and meaning" and to see the world as "the simultaneous oneness of sameness and difference." Dance demonstrates continuity and pause; drama approximates the world in showing opposites of expected and unexpected, orderly and frightening; painting allows more meaning to be seen in the world because of the way in which it abstracts the elements of the world, and so on.

Aesthetic Realism publications are produced by Definition Press and distributed by the AR Foundation and the Terrain Gallery in New York City. The literature about Aesthetic Realism includes many articles by Siegel, as well as those written by his followers. The Foundation prints a weekly newspaper, entitled *TRO*.

REFERENCES

AR Foundation, "Contempt Hurts Mind: A Letter to Many People," *TRO*, XXX, No. 29, Oct. 15, 1975.

Reprint from the New York *Times*, August 16, 1976, "The Aesthetic Realism of Eli Siegel Is True," sponsored by the AR Foundation, Greene St., New York City.

Eli Siegel, "Contempt Causes Insanity: Mad at the World," *TRO,* XLVI, No. 179, Sept. 1, 1976.

————, "Contempt Causes Insanity: Aesthetic Realism Itself," *TRO,* XLVII, No. 180, Sept. 8, 1976.

————, "Imagination, Reality, and Aesthetics," Terrain Gallery, New York City, 1965 (orig. copyright 1949; monograph).

————, "Thirteen Is a Good Age to Think about God: A Look at a Real Bar Mitzvah Now: An Aesthetic Realism Lesson of Eli Siegel with the Sobel Family," Terrain Gallery, New York City, 1967 (monograph).

————, "Contempt Causes Insanity: The Three Failures," *TRO,* XLVIII, No. 181, Sept. 15, 1976.

AGING. Human aging is an inevitable degenerative process that involves physical changes as well as behavioral and attitudinal changes. Gerontology, the study of human aging, draws from the biological, medical, social, and behavioral sciences. Evidence reveals that man was interested in the process of aging as long ago as the Sumerian civilization in 2000 B.C. An Egyptian hieroglyph meaning "old" or "to grow old" was discovered in inscriptions dating circa 2700 B.C. An Egyptian medical papyrus dating circa 1600 B.C. prescribes a treatment for aging. Gerontological treatises were composed by Greek and Roman physicians and philosophers. During the Middle Ages, when old age was identified with disease and disability, and warded off with occult practices, Roger Bacon wrote *The Cure of Old Age and Preservation of Youth.* Sir John Floyer, in the eighteenth century, published the *Medicina Gerocomia,* and in 1793, Benjamin Rush published *Account of the State of the Body and Mind in Old Age.* The nineteenth century saw advances in both clinical and social medicine, the latter demonstrating concern for social reform especially with regard to the development of health and welfare programs for the elderly. Gerontology, however, was not viewed in a sociological frame of reference until just prior to World War I. In 1922, behavioral gerontology became established with the publication of *Senescence* by G. S. Hall. In the early twentieth century, scientists began to explore the psychology of human aging. The *Journal of Gerontology* was founded in 1945 by the Gerontological Society, Inc., publishing articles on human aging from a wide range of viewpoints. In 1950, the International Association of Gerontology was founded and, since then, has had regular meetings in various countries.

Changes in body structure, the vegetative functions of the body, and the nervous system are characteristic of the aging process. These changes directly affect behavior. As you grow older, the chemical composition of your bones changes; they become less dense, more susceptible to disease and breakage; your joints become stiff; your teeth and gums may deteriorate because of a decrease in the production of saliva, etc. The skin, muscles, and connective tissues degenerate as the result of change in diet, physical activity, and the inability of the body to assimilate nutrients as efficiently as it could. A decrease in sense of smell and taste, less saliva production, and minor neurotic disorders result in neglect of diet. It becomes difficult to eliminate wastes, and there might be loss of control of this process. Metabolism changes with regard to the assimilation of protein, vitamins, minerals, etc. Cell renewal slows down; blood circulation decreases because of an increase in blood pressure and loss of elasticity of the arteries, etc.; less sleep is required. With the atrophy of brain cells, and lack of oxygen and blood circulation, the functioning of the nervous system becomes less efficient. Sensory functions deteriorate; vocalization becomes difficult because of atrophy of the laryngeal muscles; glandular activity changes, resulting in a decreased capacity for sexual activity.

It has been found that in old age, you can be extremely susceptible to mental illness, the conditions for which are not only the result of the physical process of aging, but also caused by or related to physical illness and emotional stress. There are several psychiatric disorders that have been classified as characteristic of old age: *senile psychosis* which has to do with the deterioration of the intellect and occurs past the age of seventy and more frequently in men than in women; *psychosis with cerebral arteriosclerosis,* the result of disturbed circulation of blood through the brain; *affective psychosis* which is the result of the physical and emotional stresses that accompany aging; and *late paraphrenia* which resembles a form of schizophrenia. These various illnesses affect the ways in which older people behave and invariably shape their attitudes about living. Methods of geriatric clinical psychology are being reseached for use in counseling the elderly.

Also under investigation are therapeutic methods of *revitalization.* Ivan Popov, M.D., the medical director of the Renaissance Revitalization Center in the Bahamas, has devised a process of revitalization for the elderly that has two stages. The first stage entails the examination of your life and its patterns to determine what aspects you would like to change. For example, you may decide to increase your sexual activity, decrease your food intake to avoid obesity, and eliminate the sources of stress that you recognize in your life to prevent hypertension. Popov believes that you must be convinced that the single most important factor in aging, or in youth, is in the mind. If you realize this, you recognize the key to modifying the ways in which the brain affects the nervous and glandular and other organic functions of the body.

The second stage of Popov's method is multitherapeutic, involving specific techniques for changing your life-style. Popov recommends a diet of "live foods," which include yoghurt, fermented cheeses, soybeans, fresh raw fruits and vegetables and juices, raw steak, garlic, honey, yeast, nuts, etc. It is Popov's contention that if you increase the amount of live and natural foods in your diet, you will become more vital. Vitamins, especially those containing enzymes and trace elements such as calcium and iron, are important to your diet; deficiency of them can cause disease.

Other techniques Popov recommends are: 1) *phytotherapy* or *aromatherapy* which includes using plants as sedatives, to treat colds, to treat allergies, and to care for the skin (Popov considers ginseng root to be an important revitalizer); 2) *thalassotherapy* which calls for the use of elements obtained from the sea; and 3) *biofeedback* therapy for relaxation.

Popov has also conducted research into two other therapies in connection with the revitalization process. *Embryotherapy* involves the ingestion of embryonated (fertilized) eggs. The danger with this therapy lies in the possibility that the embryo may be infected. *Cell therapy* involves the regeneration of deficient or degenerated cells of specific organs by the injection of analogous cells taken from young animals or animal embryos. This therapy has been opposed as being extremely dangerous.

REFERENCES

D. B. Bromley, *The Psychology of Human Ageing.* Middlesex, England: Penguin Books, 1966.

Ivan Popov, *Stay Young: A Doctor's Total Program for Youthful Health.* New York: Grosset and Dunlap, 1975.

AIKIDO was created by Master Morihei Uyeshiba in Japan in 1925 after twenty-three years of studying martial arts, religion, and philosophy. Aikido is a synthesis of his study, a unique intermixture of martial arts and ethics. In 1927, Uyeshiba opened a practice hall in Tokyo and taught his art until World War II, when a temporary ban was placed on the teaching of all military arts. It was eventually lifted, and today Aikido is taught throughout the world.

Aikido (*ai,* "harmony"; *ki,* "spirit" or "energy"; *do,* "method" or "way") is a discipline of coordination as well as a method of self-defense. It literally means a method of coordinating or harmonizing your spirit or energy.

Aikido combines practical self-defense movements which Uyeshiba distilled from jujitsu, aikyutsu, sword fighting, and other martial arts, with an emphasis on centralization of thought and action, and the extension of mental energy. The meaning of defense differs in Aikido from other martial arts. In order to practice Aikido, you must learn to develop an Aikido personality.

While supplying you with an extensive practice that will enable you to defend yourself with optimum efficiency against attack, the central philosophy of Aikido teaches that you must take responsibility for not inflicting unnecessary damage upon your attacker. Theoretically, your attacker is operating on a lower level, and you operate from a superior level where it is unnecessary to resort to brutal methods of self-defense because of your confidence, skill, and mastery of technique. This ethical consideration makes Aikido a sophisticated method of self-defense. It is essentially *reflexive*. There is no attack in Aikido and a master of the art will not hurt an attacker unnecessarily.

At the core of Aikido are *ki* and *hara*. *Ki* is the Japanese word for intrinsic or inner energy, which we all possess but rarely develop. This energy is located in the *hara* (or "center"), a point approximately two inches below the navel, our center of gravity: "the spot where your weight reaches its concentration and balance, achieving equilibrium between the central and upper anatomy and the supporting architecture of your hips and legs below." In order to practice Aikido, you must discover and develop this center of power. Your aim is to fuse your mind and body at this central point; your mind represents your means of direction, your body your means of action.

An example of this fusion of the mind and body in the hara is illustrated for beginning students of Aikido in an exercise called the "unbendable arm." The student is instructed to extend his/her arm in front, slightly bent in a shallow half circle, with fingers outstretched. The student is told to remain relaxed, with muscles loose, and to concentrate on a point beyond his/her fingertips. Someone will then try to bend his/her arm. If the student understands the idea of mental extension and does not muscularly resist, the arm will not bend.

The purpose of the practical training in Aikido is to teach you to respond to an attack on a level that is above pure instinct, in a manner that is more subtle and refined. For example, rather than confronting an attacker's force directly, which would be an instinctual reaction, you will learn how to deflect the attack and guide it away from you. The defense in Aikido has three stages which must be developed. They are: perception of the attack; evaluation of the most likely course the attack will take; and reaction. Each of these inner stages must be developed to the point where they happen almost simultaneously. Your body has, therefore, to be prepared and conditioned physically through the practice of certain exercises and movements. Some are designed to develop elasticity, suppleness, and agility; others will improve your coordination and make your actions effective. The overall aim of the practice of Aikido is to integrate your body and mind to respond appropriately to an attack.

Aikido is taught by an instructor in a *dojo,* or practice hall. The name *dojo* was adopted from Buddhism and refers to the hall where monks practice the disciplines of meditation. The exercises are performed on a mat that is often placed on a raised wooden platform. The uniform of an Aikido student is similar to the uniform worn in karate or judo, and consists of a jacket, belt, and pants. Black belt students wear *hakama,* divided pants.

Aikido is practiced by men and women. The students are divided into two classes: *kyu,* students who have not received the black belt, and *dan,* students who have. Within these two classes are subdivisions, or ranks, and each progressive rank requires a number of prerequisite hours of practice and an exam on the techniques that must be mastered for that certain rank.

REFERENCE

A. Westbrook and O. Ratti, *Aikido and the Dynamic Sphere*. Rutland, Vt., and Tokyo, Japan: Tuttle, 1971.

THE ALEXANDER TECHNIQUE is a method of re-integrating the body through reeducation of postural habits, based on the particular dynamic relationship between the head, the neck, and the torso. It was founded by Frederick Matthias Alexander (1869–1955), an Australian actor, whose main interest was recitation, a mode of theatre in vogue before the turn of the century. By the age of nineteen, Alexander had become a specialist in "declamatory thespianism" and had acquired recognition as a Shakespearean recitationist, and status as a professional actor. Having decided to pursue his acting career, he began to experience loss of his voice during recitals. He sought medical help but received only temporary relief from his problem. It was not until 1888, when he lost his voice in a performance that was important to his career, that he began to closely observe the physical activity involved in his recitations. His observation, which continued for a period of nine to ten years, led him to conclude that the cause of his difficulty was the result of a tendency he had to pull his head backward and downward during every movement he made. The means Alexander developed to prevent this habit involved the then unorthodox investigation of the relationship between the body and mind. By the age of twenty-five, teaching his body-mind techniques had become Alexander's main career. Initially only teaching those involved in theatre, Alexander soon found himself teaching his techniques to the medical faculty of the University of Melbourne. Eventually, he moved to London where actors and actresses sought him out for training. By 1914, he was teaching in New York. Among those interested in his techniques were John Dewey, Lewis Mumford, Leo Stein, James Harvey Robinson, Aldous Huxley, and Leonard Woolf. Alexander taught in New York until 1924, attracting vast attention as well as a fair share of criticism. He then returned to London, establishing a school for children which continued until the outbreak of World War II. Alexander returned to the United States and established a new school in Massachusetts where he taught until the age of eighty-six.

The basic procedure of the Alexander technique focuses on the problem of discovering *"a means whereby a reliable sensory appreciation can be developed and maintained throughout an organism . . . brought about in every case by the reliance of the individual, not upon the subconscious, but upon conscious, reasoning guidance and control."* Alexander noted that it is the duty of the teacher of the technique to make you aware of your generally unreliable sensory appreciation, usually prevalent in the processes of normal performance, and to help you prevent your "misdirected activities" which are the cause of your psychological imperfections.

The process is essentially one of *inhibition,* and must be active in all experiences in which coordination of the activities of the mind and body is a primary goal. Inhibition is defined as *"the act of refusing to respond to the primary desire to gain an end."* This act must be transformed into "the act of responding to the conscious, reasoned desire to employ *the means whereby* that 'end' may be gained." The role of the teacher is to instruct you to carry out orders which you, in fact, purposely and consciously do not carry out, inhibiting your desire to carry them out. Thus, through practice, your focus will be on the *means* you use to reach an end, rather than the end itself; and the *means* will enlighten you as to your sensory awareness. For example, if the teacher instructs you to sit down, rather than concentrating on the end (sitting down), you will deliberately inhibit this impulse and instead focus your attention on the physical movements you make on the way to arriving at sitting down. When you do not focus on the means, you reinforce your use of subconsciously developed bad habits which aggravate your psychophysical difficulties. By not working toward an "end," you can respond to orders by *listening* and *waiting,* and then *project* the given orders into a means whereby they connect with the proper coordination of the mind and body.

Misdirected activities are the result of *incorrect conception* and *imperfect sensory appreciation* (feeling). By using a large mirror on a wall or door, you can observe how your body moves. You will also become aware of how important it is to have a clear understanding of the teacher's instructions *before* you attempt to follow them. This allows you to evaluate your conceptions with regard to your interpretation of the instructions, and alter them in order to redefine a method of learning and reasoning.

Procedurally, you learn to move properly through being physically manipulated by the teacher. You will be diverted from the idea of "improving" your movement by first learning how to inhibit yourself from applying *conceptions* of a certain motion to that motion when you execute it. Once accustomed to how it feels to employ these inhibitory devices, you are provided with corrective methods which, with the aid of the teacher's manipulation, will allow you to use your body satisfactorily. You are not taught new exercises and postures to assume temporarily, but rather you are taught how to prevent any faulty use of your psychophysical mechanisms in daily activity. Your subconscious responses gradually become conscious responses. The intended result of these repeated experiences is an overall change in the use of your psychophysical mechanisms, i.e., you will consciously achieve "a satisfactory condition of coordination and adjustment" between the head, neck, and torso. As conceived by Alexander, this technique is especially applicable to breathing, talking, and the intensity of emotional states.

Dr. Wilfred Barlow, a former student of Alexander's, medical director of the Alexander Institute in London, editor of the *Alexander Journal,* has designed a contemporary application of the Alexander technique. He addresses himself primarily to a public concerned with discovering new energy, relief from tension and fatigue, and sees the technique as a means of achieving a rewarding new way of using the body.

Barlow interprets the essence of Alexander's teaching in a simple principle: *Use affects functioning.* Barlow found that in many cases "the basic structure of the personality, at its most minute and intimate level, is fashioned by our body use." As Alexander discovered, "a certain use of the head in relation to the neck and of the neck in relation to the torso . . . constitutes a 'Primary Control' of the mechanisms as a whole." Misuse of the head-neck relationship can be seen in how you may pull your skull back into your neck, for example. Misuse of the head-neck-torso relationship can result in a misalignment of the chest, curvature of the spine, arched-in back, slumping, protruding abdomen, etc. Misuse of the body can begin in childhood as the result of the way parents physically handle a child; it can be the result of a child's emulation of someone whose mechanisms are misused.

The persistent and increasing misuse of the body, according to Barlow, is the result of an inadequate balance, especially as it relates to standing and sitting balance. Dystonic patterns (faulty muscular patterns) evolve into and cause unbalanced resting states, those states of body positioning and posture that exist when you are not in motion. Dystonic patterns also occur when you are in motion, walking, running, jumping, dancing, etc., or when you move the simplest objects. Proper muscular control can be achieved only when you begin motion from a properly balanced resting state and can return to this balanced state of rest after finishing the motion.

Balanced, tensionless, resting states contain no "residue" of an underlying dystonic pattern. They are not the result of temporary means such as tranquilizers, alcohol, nicotine, rest cures, etc., but can be achieved through the Alexander technique in which habits of body mechanism misuse are unlearned, and a new pattern of muscular use is projected. There is a complete grammar of the body which is learned in the practice of the technique. Knowing and implementing the language will enable you to eventually release deeply ingrained, unconscious patterns of body tension and free your psyche. Instruction of the Alexander technique stresses that just as everyone has his/her own unique body, every individual will learn to implement the principles of coordination and adjustment in his/her own unique way; there is no single way.

Since 1969, the Institute of Rehabilitation Medicine in New York City has been using the Alexander technique physiotherapeutically. The American Physical Fitness Research Institute sponsored experimental introduction of the technique in public schools. Barlow recommends that the technique be used in the treatment of patients with rheumatic, orthopedic, neurological, psychosomatic, and mental disorders, and in general as a therapeutic treatment for joint mobility, reflexes, muscular power, and the bodily systems subject to misuse.

REFERENCES

F. Matthias Alexander, *The Resurrection of the Body* (selected and introduced by Edward Maisel). New York: Delta Books, 1969.

Wilfred Barlow, *The Alexander Technique*. New York: Alfred A. Knopf, 1973.

American Center for the Alexander Technique, Inc., 142 West End Avenue, New York, N.Y. 10023.

GORDON ALLPORT (1897–1967), a psychologist, was born in Indiana and educated at Harvard University, receiving his Ph.D. in 1922. He was an English instructor at Robert College in Istanbul, Turkey, from 1919–20. Allport received a Sheldon traveling scholarship and was able to study in Berlin, Hamburg, and Cambridge, England, from 1922–24. From 1924–26, he was an instructor of social ethics at Harvard and then became assistant professor of psychology at Dartmouth. He returned to Harvard in 1930 and became a professor of psychology in 1936, a position he held until 1942.

Allport was director of the National Opinion Research Center, a member of the National Committee of UNESCO, president of both the American Psychological Association, and Society for the Psychological Study of Social Issues. In 1956, he was visiting overseas consultant to the Institute of Social Research at the University of Natal in South Africa. He was a Terry lecturer at Yale.

The goal of psychology, according to Allport, is to increase harmony among the philosophies of mankind, and in doing this set forth standards of truth by which one philosophy can be measured as to its validity against another. This goal is especially relevant to the formation and development of the *personality,* knowledge about which is most uncertain. Allport supports this idea with the opinion that theories of cognition (as found in the phenomenological viewpoints of Husserl, Brentano, Scheler, etc., the American concepts about Gestalt theory, and notions about the valid conceptual framework of a stimulus-response theory) do not offer a strong foundation for a proper psychology of personality or doctrine of motivation "to explain the facilitating, inhibiting, selecting, and vivifying of our cognitive and behavioral systems." The focus of psychology should be to account for the full range of individual organization and growth. Allport contends that the analytical methods of psychology deal with elements which are not "true parts of the original whole," i.e., the individual is considered coincidental, and characteristics which make up the individual are abstracted in such a way that factors of their interrelation, variability, motion, life, duration of time, and uniqueness are not seen as part of a total picture. To understand a personality requires recognizing its unique organization: the unique capacity of an individual to vary biological needs and to create psychogenic needs as reflection of culture and life-style. Studying personality in a purely scientific framework does not allow the problems of individuality to be considered, especially as they arise in an effort to improve personality. What is necessary, therefore, is a psychology of *becoming.*

The psychology of becoming is based on the knowledge of your own uniqueness which, when realized, will allow you to acquire an orderly knowledge of others without basing this knowledge on the imposition of false assumptions. One issue involved in the study of individual personality is *inborn disposition* which Allport considers the "raw material for the development of the personality." Inborn dispositions include: 1) those necessary for survival (*instinctive*); 2) those related to *inheritance* factors (gene-linked characteristics associated with family, stock, race); 3) those related to the capacity to learn and form structures (operating on instinct and inheritance).

Becoming is a process of either incorporating earlier stages of growth with later stages, or a process of dealing with the conflicts that arise between the early and later stages of growth. The study of becoming takes into account the transformation that occurs when you, as an "unsocialized infant," develop a hierarchy of interests which enable you, as an adult, to assume a role in the complex structure of society, aware of your feelings, loyalties, and individual interests. The importance of affiliative needs (i.e., dependence, succorance, attachment) in the early years (three to five) in establishing foundation of character and *freedom to become,* and the conflict that arises between *tribal* instinct and *personal* affinity in the process of development must be considered in order to relate the early stages of growth to the later stages.

In reviewing the importance of self in becoming, a distinction should be made between individual matters of *importance* (that which is vital to the process of becoming) and individual matters of *fact* (that which is peripheral to the essence of being). What is of *appropriate* concern (based on Allport's improvement of William James's scheme) in the early stages of growth are: 1) your *bodily sense* (coenethesis) which functions integrally with the development of self-awareness, allowing you to be aware of your organic sensations; 2) your *self-identity,* which comes out of your separation from the environment (e.g., being clothed), and as the result of social interaction; 3) *ego-enhancement,* which is prompted by self-assertion, self-satisfaction, and pride. Of appropriate concern in the later stages are: 1) *ego-extension,* the process of moving out of the self, rationally designing interests; 2) your *self-image,* which helps you to see the present "in line with" the future; 3) *propriate striving,* whose prime force is motivation, which tends toward the unification of the personality and works both to reduce tension and establish equilibrium, as well as to maintain tension in order to pursue goals. You become a *knower* of a knowledge that is peculiar to you and is a reflection of and intimately bound up with your *propriate self-functions* (i.e., bodily sense, self-identity, self-assertion, rationalizations, strivings, etc.).

The psychological functions of the self are important as data in the scientific study of personality, but these functions do not define the whole personality; they are aspects of the personality. Allport believes that it is valid to employ concepts of self and ego in certain compound forms (e.g., self-knowledge, self-image, ego-enhancement, ego-extension) whose functions fuse and are interdependent in theories of personality. Furthermore, in accounting for the development of personality, the subjective, inner modes of organization created by the self must be investigated along with the activity of stimulus, emotional excitement, association, response. Only part of the uniqueness of the individual develops within the *proprium* as described above; the rest develops in randomness and through opportunity. Allport developed the concept of the proprium in order to separate the philosophy of personality from the psychology of personality.

Allport sees the conscience as "a crucial agent in the growth of the personality" because it "controls transitory impulse and opportunistic adjustment in the interests of long-range aim and consistency with self-image." Consciousness is instrumental in the transformation which takes place between the early and later stages of growth, and the adoption of the proprium. Three changes take place in the transformation: Obedience to external forces is replaced by internally imposed sanction; experiences of prohibition, fear, and the concept of "must" are replaced by experiences of preference, self-respect, and the concept of "ought"; and a schemata of values which are self-guided replace habits of obedience. Despite the fact that you often may be inconsistent in attending to your value system, you develop a personal, individual style of living, working out of your proprium. Your life-style is characteristic of your definite and effective self-image, and can be adapted through rejecting and accepting certain aspects of culture. Freedom, in this respect, becomes an element of mobility and choice, and a question of the limits to possibilities of growth. These limits change according to your ability to reflect, to self-objectify, as well as your efforts and education. Allport believes that the most comprehensive units in personality are *broad intentional dispositions* directed toward the future, whose characteristics are unique, not infinite in number; they are the guiding forces for the lesser aspects of your personality.

To develop a psychology of becoming, Allport finds it necessary to test the viability of abstract ideals before associating the functions of the personality with them. Personality should be examined from the past, looking into the future, rather than examined only in terms of the past.

REFERENCE

Gordon W. Allport, *Becoming: Basic Considerations for a Psychology of Personality*. New Haven: Yale University Press, 1955.

ADELBERT AMES'S (1880–1955) contributions to the field of perceptual psychology influenced the restructuring of psychology as a whole to include the study of man in relationship to the environment. Ames was born in Lowell, Massachusetts. He studied law at Harvard, but because of his interest in art and painting was later drawn into an investigation of *physiological optics*. Ames was research fellow in this field at Clark University from 1914 until World War I. After the war, he went to Dartmouth College as research professor in the Department of Physiological Optics and was at the Dartmouth Eye Institute from 1945 until his death in 1955.

In his later years, Ames corresponded with John Dewey and was closely associated with Hadley Cantril, who was then chairman of the Department of Psychology at Princeton University. Ames wrote articles for the *American Journal of Ophthalmology* and the *American Journal of Psychology,* as well as laboratory manuals and articles for the Institute of Associated Research in Hanover, New Hampshire. Ames's *An Interpretative Manual,* in which he outlines the nature of perceptions, prehensions, and behavior on the basis of his scientific demonstrations in perceptions, was published in 1955 through Princeton University. From 1949–61, Cantril, William Ittleson, and others researched the relationship between problems of perception and human behavior, within Ames's theoretical framework. This research resulted in the development of *transactional psychology*.

Ames concentrated his research in perception in three areas: physical, physiological, and psychological. The model he developed in 1949 is a graphic representation of the interrelationships between man, environment, and time on the basis of perception. He calls his model *Transaction of Living: Analysis of Sub-Phenomena Involved in and Involving Perception.*

Ames considers perception to be that which you are consciously aware of in an actual visual experience. *Perception* is the interpretation of your immediate environment in terms of the significance of your form world. *Environment* is "all other trans-related inorganic and organic functional activities except one's own." Your *form world* is structured by your experience on both the biological level and on the level of inherited patterns of growth, urges, and capacities. It is composed of abstractions, value awareness, and unconscious assumptions. The interaction between perceptual activity and form world takes place in "light and sound wave impingements," stimulus patterns, and higher physiological processes (specifically, the activities of abstracting what you see in the immediate environment according to significances in your form world). That which is unique to you is the perceptual process, the higher physiological processes, and the structuring of stimulus patterns that evolve out of the integration of externality and physiology (e.g., the creation of the microscope or television as means to extend perception of undifferentiated light and sound waves).

Your perceptions direct your action (physiological motor processes) in the environment. Your perceptions are the result of your *reflexive actions* to the *value judgments* you make with regard to your perceptions' usefulness toward *purposeful action*. The reliability of your value judgments will be determined by your interaction with the actual environment. Your actions can be the result of *logical judgments,* which derive from your awareness and your personal responsibility. Logical judgments are most effective "in situations involving conceptualized abstracted processes and frames of reference." Your actions can also be the result of *reflex functioning,* which occurs because of the interaction of higher physiological processes, reflexes, and physiological motor responses. The reliability of your reflexes is determined independent of your perceptual awareness through a constant relationship with the environment. Ames's view includes in a Gestalt-related hypothesis both a framework for form (Euclidean space) and objective time, and a framework for personal time which deals with your past experience and the actions that stimulate your growth, termed *emergence.*

Ames considered behavior comprehensible only from a first-person frame of reference. From this perspective, behavior can be seen as your "desire to bring forth and to experience the value aspects which are potential in every concrete behavioral situation." These value aspects, in turn, determine the what and how of purposing, prehending sequents, perceiving, and acting. According to Ames, behavior occurs within the context of the "here" and "now" that is particular to you as an individual. Ames specifically defined several here-and-now situations: the *inquiry matrix,* in which here and now refer to an objective and abstract "there" and "then" world view (e.g., scientific inquiry); the *perceptual matrix,* in which here and now refer to objects of perception in a subjective-objective world view and become "here-now"; the *sequential matrix,* in which here-now is seen in time; and the *transactional matrix* in which here-now refers to action in a transactional situation toward a *valueful* purpose.

Ames's theories support a psychology in which man's thought and behavior can be understood only as processes of a full situation of organism-environment, i.e., transactional psychology. The implication of this theory is that psychologists cannot divorce themselves from what they are investigating or how they are investigating it; nor can they separate what they are investigating from the process of knowing, from what is known, and from the environment. Moreover, they must not be inhibited by the traditionally used jargon of psychology and field theories which indicate that the environment acts *on* an individual rather than *through* an individual. Transactional psychology therefore becomes a way in which the objectivity of science, along with the exploration of perception, can be applied to psychology.

REFERENCES

Hadley Cantril, ed., *The Morning Notes of Adelbert Ames, Jr.* New Brunswick, N.J.: Rutgers University Press, 1960.
Franklin P. Kilpatrick, ed., *Explorations in Transactional Psychology.* New York: New York University Press, 1961.

ARICA is a mystical school that offers a scientific method for spiritual development and the attainment of full enlightenment and freedom. It is an historical movement, as well, based on recognition of the necessity for the achievement of a universal culture through a scientific understanding of the human psyche and the "Unity," for the survival of humanity.

Arica (which means "open door" in the language of the Bolivian Indians) was founded by Oscar Ichazo (b. 1931), a Bolivian, who after years of studying and seeking the various spiritual paths and disciplines began teaching students in Santiago, Chile. Ichazo completed the method known as the "Arica System" in 1964, and in 1968, he founded the Instituto de Gnoseologia in Arica, Chile, where he taught, developing techniques and researching and testing the Arica methods for internal realization and processing. That same year, he presented the theory and system to a group of professionals and university professors in a seminar given at the Instituto de Psicología Aplicada in Santiago. In 1970, fifty Americans joined Ichazo in Arica for an intensive ten-month training. At the completion of the training, the group decided to continue to work together to impart the theory and system to others. The Arica Institute, Inc., was founded in New York City in 1971, and since then has offered training programs continuously, presenting the Arica theory and system of spiritual development. Ichazo gives courses himself to advanced groups, and actively participates as the guide of the Arica Institute.

The Arica theory is the explanation of the "Unity" through the discovery of a new logic that describes the process and the unity of the whole. This new logic provides the tools by which the human psyche can be systematized and described. With the correct maps and measurements, the entire territory is made known. Thus, the human process can then be approached with complete knowledge of all its parameters and possible variables. The result is that, for the first time, the human process is completely understood and is scientifically systematized and delineated.

There are nine levels of training in the Arica system of which all but the last two may be completed without a guide. Many Arica trainings may be done independently, using separate manuals containing precise and tested indications in order to make the work possible under almost any circumstances. However, professionally trained teachers and group work in certified Arica trainings greatly accelerate the process. Group trainings are usually held at Arica centers; others can be completed at home. Some trainings require special aids such as meditation yantras (wall symbols), training manuals, candles, incense, counting beads, etc. Intensive trainings take from a few hours to forty days. Other trainings are extended over three months and take place on evenings and weekends. Cost varies according to the type and length of training.

The Arica method, according to Arica Institute, is one that influences practically anybody who is exposed to the training. However, the degree and permanence of the influence are related to the type and length of the training. In general, the "40-Day Training" will produce altered states of consciousness that are more or less permanent for most people.

Jerry Rubin describes his experience of the "40-Day Training" (a trip without words) as a combination of physical body work with meditation: "All Arican exercises are geared to bringing energy from the head into the kath, a place four inches below the navel, the midpoint of the body and the key place for Eastern martial arts. A person with consciousness in his kath is in control of himself." According to Rubin, the culmination of the training is "the desert": forty hours to be spent entirely alone, without books, telephone, paper, pencils, or music. The purpose of the sensory deprivation is to "practice self-observation, to observe myself doing what I do without judgment."

The Arica theory and system are practically applied by Aricans toward achieving a metasociety, a society in which relations between human beings are based upon recognition of unity, rather than competition and agreement. Many Aricans live in groups called Arica houses, where the internal work of the school is done, e.g., the "Daily Routine," the "Temple," and "Karma Machines." Arica associations have been formed, as well; these are groups formed for business purposes, e.g., to give trainings, or sell Arica products, etc.

Since 1971, approximately fifty thousand people in nearly a dozen countries have been exposed to some form of Arica training; approximately five thousand have taken the "40-Day Training," which is the basic entry point to the Arica method of transformation. The Arica Institute, Inc., is located at 24 West 57 Street, New York, New York 10019.

REFERENCES

Oscar Ichazo, "We Have No Desire to Strengthen the Ego or Make It Happy," in *Voices and Visions* by Sam Keen. New York: Harper & Row, 1974.

————, *The Human Process for Enlightenment and Freedom*. Arica Institute, 1976.

Jerry Rubin, *Growing (Up) at 37*. New York: M. Evans & Co., 1976.

Adam Smith, *The Powers of Mind*. New York: Random House, 1975.

David Smith, *East/West Exercise Book*. New York: McGraw-Hill, 1976.

ROBERTO ASSAGIOLI (1888–1976), an Italian psychiatrist, developed a system of psychotherapy called *psychosynthesis*. Assagioli was born in Venice, and was educated both as a physician and a psychiatrist of the Freudian school. He first presented his ideas in a doctoral thesis in 1910 which focused on some of the limitations of Freudian psychology. A year later, Assagioli presented a paper to the International Congress of Philosophy in Bologna, outlining his view of the unconscious. Thereafter, he spent his time developing his ideas and putting them into practice through various methods of psychotherapy. This work culminated in the publication of a pamphlet called *A New Method of Healing—Psychosynthesis*. In 1926, the Institute of Psychosynthesis was founded in Rome to develop, apply, and teach techniques of training in psychotherapy toward achieving psychosynthesis. Since 1946, lectures on psychosynthesis have been given in various countries, and many articles and pamphlets have been published. The Psychosynthesis Research Foundation was founded in 1957 in the United States and Italy.

Psychosynthesis is a scientific, psychological/psychiatric approach to the revelation of the self. Methodologically, psychosynthesis focuses on the concept that you are in a constant state of growth, actualizing your hidden potentials in terms of the importance you give to values (ethical, aesthetic, religious), the responsibility you take in making choices and decisions, the importance of the future as founded in the present.

Psychosynthesis emphasizes 1) the function of the will as integral to our choices and decisions; 2) the direct experience of the self manifested in self-awareness; 3) the phenomenologically lived experiences which are positive, creative, and joyous. The process of psychosynthesis concentrates on the transformation and redirecting of psychological energies (i.e., sexual and aggressive) toward creative goals, the development of weaknesses into strengths, and the activation of energies to bring out latent potentialities. In general, it is the conscious and carefully negotiated reconstruction, or re-creation, of the personality either independently or in cooperation with a skilled and competent therapist.

Within the framework of psychosynthesis, all "superconscious" elements, i.e., values formed from experience, intuition, inspiration, mystical consciousness, are considered tangible and observable information. Psychological makeup is viewed in terms of seven parts: the lower unconscious, which directs the fundamental psychological activities of your body, as in primitive urges, highly emotional complexes, phobias, paranoias, etc.; the middle unconscious, where experience is assimilated before reaching consciousness; the superconscious, the seat of your higher feelings: intuitions and inspirations of an artistic, contemplative, or philosophical nature; the field of consciousness, where the analyzable awareness of feelings, thoughts, and impulses lies; the conscious self, the point of pure self-awareness; the higher self, which exists apart from the consciousness of mind and body; and the collective unconscious, which encloses all the aforementioned. This map of the psychological construct aids in reconciling the apparent contradiction between the idea of the existence of two selves (i.e., the personal self and the real self, which is latent), and the idea of the unity within the self, wherein the personal self reflects the real self.

There are four stages involved in the total integration of the selves. The first is to learn about the various elements of your personality. In obtaining knowledge of your personality, it is important to understand that you must not only recognize the formation of your conscious being, but must also get in touch with the depths of your unconscious where images of childhood, fears, and conflict rest. This may be achieved independently or through psychoanalysis (which might not allow you to penetrate regions of the middle and higher conscious). When you look into these areas, you will make contact with previously unknown abilities and potentialities.

The second stage is control of the various elements of the personality. This can be achieved by *disidentification,* which is based on the psychological principle that you are dominated by everything with which your self becomes identified; therefore, you can dominate and control everything from which you *disidentify* yourself. You are dominated by weakness, depression, anger, etc., ruled by complexes and images about which you do not know. To dissolve their causes, the methods of *objectification, critical analysis,* and *discrimination* will create a psychological "distance" between yourself and them. This will free you to redirect the energies which kept them alive into new channels of creative ability, the restructuring of your personality, and your psychosynthesis.

The third stage of integration involves discovering your psychological center, which leads you to establish a unifying and controlling principle by which to live.

This center is discovered through the expansion of your personal consciousness into the real self: projecting your center into an external ideal. Assagioli found that this is a long, slow process, full of intermediate stages, and entails the full use of your strength, stamina, and perseverance.

The fourth stage is *psychosynthesis,* the culmination of your personal self-realization process, as well as the most complicated and arduous phase of integration. Upon discovering or creating your psychological center, you begin to reinforce it with a coherent, organized, and unified personality. Psychosynthesis has its own developmental stages. The first is formulating what Assagioli calls the "inner program," which is geared to reach a specific, clearly visualized goal of being. Once this ideal is established, you can direct your energies, which come from the disintegration of unconscious complexes, to physical, imaginative, or intellectual activities which, in turn, become new emotions, plans, or actions. You will develop those aspects of your personality that do not meet your goal through *evocation, autosuggestion, creative affirmation,* or by training the will, memory, and imagination to function effectively. The last stage of psychosynthesis is coordinating and organizing, as to importance, all your psychological energies and functions.

During the last stage, as cited above, the work of the therapist is complex: to enlighten you to your inner state of affairs, to counsel you to control unconscious drives and not repress them, to teach you techniques of transmutation and sublimation of sexual and aggressive energies, to aid you in recognizing the flow of energy from the real self to superconscious levels, to lead you to develop your personality around a higher inner center, the crux of *spiritual* psychosynthesis.

Assagioli defines technique as "a specific psychological procedure used in order to produce a definite effect on some aspect or function of the psyche." He stresses that the techniques used in psychosynthesis be flexible and modifiable and subordinate to the goal of the therapy, which is to release the energies of the self. The initial techniques used in the process are dream analysis, the use of diaries, and a variety of tests, etc. The biographical material which results is then analyzed in terms of the problems that have been exposed and the tasks of the present existential situation. Thereafter, there are a wide variety of techniques which can be used to focus on developing qualities of the personality desired. In group treatment, working toward interpersonal or social psychosynthesis, methods used are group analysis, psychodrama, cooperative activity, etc., and the emphasis is placed on empathy, friendship, good will, and understanding. Assagioli approves of experimentation with new techniques which can be incorporated into any of the programs dealing with all modes of psychosynthesis.

Since 1960, institutes for the study of psychosynthesis have been established in Greece, England, Argentina, and India. There is a Psychosynthesis Institute and Training Center in California, a center for biopsychosynthesis in Kentucky, and a center for the study of psychosynthesis in education in New Hampshire. There is an Institute of Psychosynthesis in Montreal, and the Psychosynthesis Research Foundation is in New York City.

REFERENCES

Roberto Assagioli, M.D., *Psychosynthesis, A Manual of Principles and Techniques.* New York: Viking Press, 1971.

————, *Act of Will.* New York: Penguin/Esalen Book, 1974.

ASSERTIVENESS TRAINING (AT)   is one of several therapeutic techniques that are an offshoot of behavior therapy. According to Herbert Fensterheim, a behavior therapist and psychologist, Assertiveness Training is based on two premises: 1) what you do serves as the basis for the development of your self-concept; your self-assertion dictates your self-esteem; and 2) behaviors are not isolated events, but interact with each other forming patterns or *psychological organization*. According to Arnold Lazarus, assertive behavior embodies an "emotional freedom" that allows you to stand up for your rights. Assertiveness Training is a means to learn your legitimate rights, defend them, prevent their usurpation, and recognize the rights of others. It can teach you the skills necessary to deal creatively with life and its challenges.

Typical of nonassertive behavior are qualities of timidity and the inability to communicate directly and openly. Communication difficulties take several forms: communication that is indirect, wordy, showing a lack of clearly defined desires; dishonest or pseudoassertive communication; communication that is not properly timed. Nonassertive behavior is demonstrated in the inability to make eye contact or small talk. Fear of rejection, fear of being met with anger, closeness, tenderness, etc. make it difficult to carry through with actions. Furthermore, there is a lack of understanding of the difference between assertiveness and aggression (overassertion implies aggression; behavior that is aggressive or vindictive can defeat your purposes). Nonassertion is also evident when you cannot act properly in a social situation; you worry about worrying; you expect others to always go along with you; you feel as though you should be rewarded for doing the right thing; you keep repeating behavior patterns that you want to change. It has been found that nonassertive behavior can cause actual physical discomfort and psychological disorders ranging from depression to neurasthenia and catatonic schizophrenia to suicidal tendencies.

Developing assertiveness can begin with the procedure of outlining your problem areas. Make a list of questions about yourself, the answers to which will pinpoint areas of your behavior that need work. For example (as derived from the work of Fensterheim, Lazarus, Spencer Rathus, and Joseph Volpe): Are you satisfied with your sex life? Are you spontaneous during sex play and intercourse? Are you satisfied with your work habits? Another step to assertiveness is to list those things that make you feel tense, fearful, disturbed. Rate them on a scale ranging from "very little" to "very much."

Setting assertive goals requires an understanding of and commitment to becoming assertive from the present moment onward. Goals serve as direct means to motivate you and reinforce your self-esteem. Fensterheim recommends that this procedure include the following: 1) Applying the content of the lists you have made, you should be able to recognize that the reasons you are not assertive are only rationalizations that block your actions; the expected ramifications of your rationalizations are not likely to happen and are creative excuses for your being nonassertive; 2) determine in what areas you have problems of a social, personal, or impersonal nature; 3) notice how you activate your fears of rejection, anger, tenderness, and find those specific aspects of your behavior which, if changed, will change your behavior in general (e.g., expressing feelings will lessen your fear of being close to others).

In dealing with your problems, there are some basic principles which, if activated, will help you to become assertive: 1) Reveal your personality as much as is warranted in a given situation; 2) work to express a range of feelings, from anger to tenderness; 3) act in a manner that will improve your self-esteem; 4) continue to notice in what areas you can be more assertive; 5) be sure to know when you are being assertive and when you are being aggresive; 6) work for a balance between your assertive and nonassertive behavior; 7) understand that Assertiveness Training approaches your humanness, not your talents as a manipulator, and that your assertiveness will change as the situations you are in change; 8) realize that *doing* is integral to developing assertiveness.

Assertiveness Training in behavior therapy involves following through on specific behavioral exercises and assignments both in and out of the therapeutic situation. Exercises and assignments guide you in setting your goals and help you to deal with impersonal situations, social interaction, the expressing of negative and positive feelings. AT can help you to be more assertive in a close relationship, in sexual situations, on the job, etc. It can aid you in changing your habits, weight control, avoiding depression; it can help you overcome your role of always being "nice," which can trap you into doing what you don't want to do.

With the recent changes in the status of the female in society, women have discovered that AT is useful in helping them define their relationships to careers, jobs, sex discrimination, husbands, children. It has been found that nonassertive women characteristically use a variety of ways to avoid being assertive. For example, some act as if they are constantly overworked; others are totally dependent on husbands, etc.; they appear to be uninvolved; they are habitually late or forgetful or careless; they procrastinate; they use their powers to be seductive. (Men, families, and society as a whole have been responsible for reinforcing this mode of behavior on the part of women.) Breaking out of these behavioral patterns is a necessary part of Assertiveness Training, which can help a woman stand up for her rights by demanding respect, expressing her feelings, being taken seriously, having priorities and positive wants, and being able to exercise nonassertiveness.

Information about AT is available through the clinical fellows of Behavior Therapy and Research Society, associated with the Eastern Pennsylvania Psychiatric Institute and the Association for the Advancement of Behavior Therapy in New York City.

REFERENCES

George R. Bach, M.D., and Herb Goldberg, M.D., *Creative Aggression: The Art of Assertive Living*. New York: Avon Books, 1974.

Lynn Z. Bloom, Karen Coburn, Joan Pearlman, *The New Assertive Woman*. New York: Delacorte Press, 1975.

Herbert Fensterheim and Jean Baer, *Don't Say Yes When You Want To Say No*. New York: Dell Books, 1975.

Letty Cottin Pogrebin, *Getting Yours: How to Make the*

System Work for the Working Woman. New York: David McKay, 1975.

ASTRAL PROJECTION, *out-of-the-body experience* (OBE), or bilocation, has become a subject of interest to parapsychologists within recent years. Historically, the cultures of Egypt, Persia, India, and China have considered "second body" activity to be a normal occurrence. In Egypt the second body was called *ka;* the Buddhists called it *rupa;* the Hebrews, the *ruach;* the Greeks, the *eidolon;* the Romans, the *larva,* and in Tibet the second body is still known as the *bardo* body.

Research into this psychic phenomenon began in the late nineteenth century under the auspices of the British Society for Psychical Research which dealt with the apparitions of the living and the dead in general, studied people whose bodies had become possessed by invisible beings, studied multiple personalities, etc. In 1920, Oliver Fox, an Englishman involved in psychic research and astral projection, published reports of his experiences. In 1929, Sylvan Muldoon published *The Projection of the Astral Body* which records the OBEs he experienced over a period of years. Robert Crookall, a British geologist, J. B. Rhine, Hornell Hart, and Charles Tart have scientifically investigated this phenomenon. The "life readings" of Edgar Cayce can be read for explanations of second-body activity.

Parapsychologists and technicians associated with the American Society for Psychical Research in New York City study out-of-the-body experiences in the laboratory; the Psychical Research Foundation in Durham, North Carolina, and the Stanford Research Institute in Menlo Park, California, as well as the University of Virginia are engaged in OBE research.

An astral projection, or OBE, is an experience in which your center of perception and awareness shifts to a place that does not coincide with your physical body. This place may take the form of a second body, or it may be a point of consciousness outside your body.

In general, the descriptions of the projection of a

second body have it rotating out of the physical body, through the head, to a horizontal position above the physical body, and then to an upright position. This process is reversed when the second body returns to the physical body. The two bodies are connected by a cord which elongates as the second body moves. The second body can have very little density, or be much like the physical body.

In a projection, the mind is active in the physical body. As has been shown in OBE experiments, a conscious awareness is active in which emotional and intellectual decisions can be made, various modes of perception and sensory experiences can take place, and a series of sequential events can be experienced.

The movement of the second body is guided by thought-action synchronicity whereby the physical body's thought of movement and destination results in the action of the second body.

There are numerous reasons for the occurrence of astral projection. They can be practical or personal, to obtain or give spiritual help, or for other reasons. As has been illustrated by Robert Crookall, projection can occur as the result of drugs such as mescaline. Projection can also be induced through auto- or self-hypnosis.

Robert A. Monroe has recorded his experiences with astral projection in *Journeys Out of the Body*. Monroe believes that the easiest and most natural method to induce astral projection is the "borderland sleep state," one in which the body and mind are relaxed simultaneously. It is essentially a state between sleep and wakefulness. To achieve it, you must first overcome through relaxation any fears of death or the unknown. Monroe's technique utilizes these steps: 1) Lie down, especially when tired or drowsy, close your eyes, and focus your mind on something specific, a single thought, without letting yourself fall asleep. 2) Concentrate on the blackness of your closed eyes. This concentration is achieved fully when there are no longer any images in the blackness, and all nervousness has left you. 3) Deepen your consciousness by systematically shutting out sensory input, i.e., feeling, smelling, tasting, and hearing, in that order. 4) Establish *vibration waves* by concentrating on various points at various angles in the blackness of your closed eyes. *Thought control* is important at this stage: you should concentrate on no thought, or as little thought as possible. 5) To dissociate your second body from your physical body, you must *think* of floating upward or rotating out of your body. According to Monroe, when you initially practice projection, it is necessary to remain in complete control, keeping your second body within close distance of your physical body, and within familiar surroundings. 6) Returning your second body to your physical body is a process of *thinking* your projected body back into the physical one.

The OBE is a completely individualistic experience, of which there are thousands of recorded cases. Herbert B. Greenhouse, a member of the American Society for Psychical Research, who has participated in many OBE experiments, envisions the future of astral projection thusly: "With the rapid advances in electronics, photography, and holography, it may be possible some day to get a clear picture of the double leaving at death. The time of death itself, which is still uncertain, may be pinpointed as the moment when the silver cord breaks off."

REFERENCES

Robert Crookall, *The Study and Practice of Astral Projection*. New York: University Books, 1966.

Herbert B. Greenhouse, *The Astral Journey: Evidence for Out of Body Experiences from Socrates to the ESP Laboratory*. New York: Doubleday & Co., 1975.

Robert A. Monroe, *Journeys Out of the Body*. New York: Doubleday & Co., 1971.

AURA READING. The aura (from the Greek *aure,* which means "breath") is an invisible, colored emanation that surrounds the human body. The idea of the human aura originated in ancient times, and is depicted in the sacred images of Egyptian, Indian, Greek, Roman, and Christian art. The ability to see an aura has been traditionally assigned to clairvoyants and psychics. At the turn of the century, scientific research into the aura began with the work of Baron Carl von Reichenbach, Edwin D. Babbit, and W. K. Roentgen who discovered x-rays in 1895. In the same year, C. W. Leadbeater published a pamphlet called *The Aura: An enquiry into the natural forms of luminous mist seen about the human and other bodies;* the theories documented in this work were of a theosophical nature. In 1903, Professor Blondot of Nancy University in France discovered what he called "N rays" that supposedly were emitted by a variety of substances, as well as by the activity of the human nervous system. In 1908, W. J. Kilner determined that the human aura could be made visible if it interacted with the proper substance. As a result of his experiments with dicyanine, a coal-tar dye, which, when used in conjunction with a viewing screen, made an observer shortsighted enough to be able to see radiation in the ultraviolet band of light, Kilner published *The Human Atmosphere* (1911). The work explained the techniques he had discovered for viewing the human aura, as well as explaining his theories about the structure of the human aura, i.e., an inner component which follows the body outlines and an outer component which is more nebulous. Kilner claimed that an aura changes in appearance according to the state of health of the person, and, therefore, aura reading could be an aid in medical diagnosis. Kilner continued to experiment and publish his findings until his death in 1920. In 1937, Oscar Bagnall, who had developed Kilner's research further, published *The Origins and Properties of the Human Aura.* Bagnall also improved the viewing screen which Kilner had designed. Since then, J. J. Williamson of the Metaphysical Research Group in England, Dr. M. K. Muttic, Dr. W. E. Benham, Dr. H. Baraduc, and others have continued to do research into the human aura.

The human aura is a luminous cloud that radiates out from the body. Its structure and distribution are predicated upon the forces emanating from the body. The aura of a healthy person is symmetrical in size, shape, and texture. According to Kilner's studies, the auras of healthy males, females, and children have their own particular characteristics.

The male aura radiates out around from the head equally with a width that is three or four inches wider than the shoulders. Viewing the aura facing the male, with his arms raised and his hands on top of his head, the outer aura is narrower at the trunk than at the head; it follows the contour of the body, extending out no more than four or five inches. Seen in profile, the aura is broad down the back as it is on the sides, and slightly less in front. It encircles the arms and legs in a similar manner and is broader around the hands and tips of the fingers. The inner aura uniformly extends two to three inches out from all around the body.

The female aura is similar to that of the male, except when viewed from the front. When the female places her hands on her head, her aura extends farther out from the sides of the trunk than the male's, reaching full width at the waist, and gradually narrowing toward the ankles. In profile, the female aura is wider in back than in front, and more distinct around the breasts and nipples. Female auras may change both in width and color because of changes in temperament.

In children, the aura is more masculine. The aura of a pubescent child, however, changes from one similar to the male form to one which is more identifiable with the female. In females, this change occurs at the onset of menstruation. In general, a child's aura will begin to expand between the ages of fourteen and fifteen.

The aura consists of three sections: *the etheric double,* when visible, appears as a dark band that uniformly surrounds the body and extends no farther than one-quarter inch in width; *the inner aura* that appears just outside the etheric double, varies little in width, and is the densest part of the entire aura; and *the outer aura* that begins close to the edge of the inner aura and varies in size around the body. Sometimes the outer aura has been seen to extend for a distance in a fine haze; this is called the *ultra-outer aura phenomenon.*

According to Kilner, the aura becomes visible in dim, diffused light against a dark background. It can be clearly seen when an observer uses screens to sensitize vision to ultraviolet light. The aura cannot be seen in total darkness.

The colors of auras range from blue mixed with gray, to what Kilner called a "peculiar blue." When you are healthy, your aura will have a blue-gray color, which is its natural color.

Given his theory that the aura is connected with and dependent upon the activity of the central nervous system, Kilner determined that the outer aura could be enlarged if influenced by electricity. He observed that permanent changes in the size and shape of the aura could occur because of nervous diseases such as epilepsy. Other nervous disturbances, such as sciatica, can also change the size and shape of the aura temporarily; when the ailment is cured the aura will return to its normal shape. The higher brain centers determine the auric output; any impairment of mental powers will cause the aura to shrink in size and become less distinct. Auras will change in brightness and size as the result of nervous exhaustion. Changes in temperament can change the volume and quality of an aura.

There has been renewed interest in the human aura since the reissue of Kilner's books, *The Human Aura* (1965) and *The Human Atmosphere,* retitled *The Aura* (1973).

REFERENCES

W. J. Kilner, *The Human Aura.* New York: University Books, 1965.

————, *The Aura.* New York: Samuel Weiser, Inc., 1973.

Nicholas Regush, *Exploring the Human Aura.* Englewood Cliffs, N.J.: Prentice-Hall, 1975.

MEHER BABA (1894–1969).

Shri Sadguru Meher Baba (originally named Merwan Sheriar) was born in India. From 1921 until his death in 1969, he was deemed the Perfect Master and Saviour of the day by hundreds of thousands of followers. Meher Baba began a period of silence in 1925, communicating only by means of a small rectangular board on which the letters of the alphabet were painted. He formed words by pointing successively to letters on the board. He was given the name "Meher Baba" by a group of his disciples. In 1927, he established a school for boys of all religions. However, it was shut down in 1929, probably due to the controversial method of teaching through daily meditations. In 1931, Baba went into seclusion and entered a phase of his life he called the Man-o-mash (the annihilation of the mind) that lasted until 1952. That year he traveled throughout the United States leading a "complicated-free" life. This was followed by his experience of a "full-free" life, which was, in turn, followed by a "fiery-free" life in which strength and weakness were "consumed by the fire of divinity." Late in 1952, he returned to India to continue his journeys and teachings. During this time, Baba began to use hand gestures rather than the alphabet board to communicate. He claimed that he would break his silence at his death, and then only to speak one word, the "Word of Words," which would penetrate the hearts of men.

Meher Baba regarded Absolute Truth as transcending all "isms" (e.g., Sufism, Christianity, Vendantism, Buddhism, etc.), and he saw his function to be that of demonstrating the meaning and spirit of all these beliefs. According to Baba, "the unity of All Life is integral and indivisible. It remains unassailable and inviolable in spite of all ideological differences." The goal of mankind should be to realize the Reality and become God in human form, for God can only be lived, not explained. Baba designed a complete system by which to understand the process of achieving the "I am God" state, and systems by which to understand the realm of God and His states. These systems involve numerous schema which Baba describes in his own terminology.

According to Baba, the soul takes many forms which are of God. The confirmation of the soul is based on its *impressions* of 1) the *gross world,* sensory and physiological experiences; 2) the *subtle world,* seeing, smelling, and hearing; 3) the *mental world,* the experience of seeing God. Souls that exist apart from impressions are the infinite knowledge and bliss of the *Over-soul.* Being the Over-soul means losing consciousness of gross, subtle, and mental bodies, and gaining consciousness of the self. "Gross, subtle, and mental bodies are nothing but the *shadows of the soul.* The gross, subtle, and mental worlds are nothing but the *shadows of the Over-soul."* These worlds are products of our dreams. The Over-soul (*Paramatma*) is the soul (*atma*) in Reality. Atma exists separately from paramatma because of self-created ignorance which is the result of gross, subtle, and mental impressions of gross, subtle, and mental worlds.

There are three processes involved in the attainment of Paramatma. The first process, the *evolution of consciousness* of the soul, is completed after the soul has experienced all there is to experience about animal form and human form. This evolution moves through seven stages of experience: from stone to metal to vegetable to worm to fish to bird to animal to human being. When the soul is ready to release itself from the gross world, the second process occurs. It is a process of *reincarnation,* the soul continually trying to balance both unconscious and conscious experience and impressions. When the soul enters a spiritual path, the third process of the *involution of consciousness* begins. This process involves moving successfully out of the six planes of consciousness of the gross, subtle, and mental worlds toward the seventh plane of consciousness where the atma is realized: "Only on the seventh plane does the soul fulfill the *initial urge* for self-knowledge by experiencing its own self as identical with the unchanging, eternal, indivisible, and formless Over-soul, with infinite knowledge, infinite reality (Truth), infinite power, and infinite bliss."

In the process of *evolution* of consciousness, you realize that consciousness of the stone is most crude; in the process of *involution* of consciousness, you realize that consciousness of the human being is most crude.

It is impossible to make the *jump* from the sixth to the seventh plane without aid: To be God-realized, you must be touched directly by a Perfect One, or Sadguru (Meher Baba was kissed by Hazrat Babajan, the Perfect One, in 1914). On the seventh plane, you become God which alone is real. When all mankind is God, all mankind is one. According to Baba, there must be fifty-six God-realized human beings on earth, five of whom must be Perfect Masters; they are ruled by the Avatar who is in an "independent state of God when God directly becomes man without undergoing or passing through processes of evolution, reincarnation, and involution of consciousness."

According to Baba, there are ten states of God where He presents Himself in all roles, real and imaginary. God's purest form is in the first and last state; in all others, God wavers among the extreme forms of His role playing. The first state of God is God in the Beyond the Beyond (*Para-par Parabrahma*). This is the *most original* state. It is the unbounded *Absolute* vacuum state of God including *everything* and *nothing;* it is the state of *God is,* eternally and indescribably. The second state is God in the Beyond (Paramatma). This state differs from the first state in three ways: God neither consciously experiences or uses power, knowledge, or bliss; God consciously experiences but does not use power, knowledge, bliss; God consciously experiences and uses power, knowledge, bliss. The third state is God as emanator, sustainer, and dissolver, His three principal attributes. These attributes are latent in God in the first state, revealed in the second state in God's urge to know Himself, and in the third state God is infinitely conscious and infinitely unconscious at the same time. The fourth state is God as the Embodied Soul, beginning to become conscious, beginning to know Nothingness or the Creation. The fifth state is God as soul in the state of *evolution* of consciousness. The sixth state is God as the human soul in the state of *reincarnation.* The seventh state is God in the state of spiritually advanced souls, in which souls are turning inward from the gross world to the process of *involution*. The eighth state is the state of God's highest divine consciousness, marking the end of reincarnation processes and the end of realization processes through the planes. The mental world soul moves toward the formlessness of the conscious experience of power, knowledge, and bliss. In the ninth state, God is suspended, sometimes conscious of the gross, subtle, and mental worlds and sometimes conscious of the "I am God" state (eighth). In the tenth state, God is in the human body as Perfect Master. Although experiencing the "I am God" state of infinite power, knowledge, and bliss, He is bound by limitations of time, space, and causation. In the tenth state, the soul has finally returned to its original source, the Over-soul, or God.

Man is God's perfect medium. The realization of God is a process of finding Truth, the approach to which is not bound by steadfast rules. The attainment of each step toward being "I am God" depends on individual conscience as it relates to spiritual tendency, physical aptitude, and external circumstances. The "I am God" state does not vanish in death.

Each aspect of Baba's analysis of God, the acting of Man-God, the mechanics of life and the universe, is directly pertinent to Vedantic, Mystic and Sufi philosophies as well as to all religions generally, in keeping with his belief about the discovery of Truth. His teachings have been published in English, as well as in five other languages. These publications are available in India, the United States, Switzerland, England, and Australia.

REFERENCE

Meher Baba, *God Speaks: The Theme of Creation and Its Purpose.* New York: Dodd, Mead & Co., 1955.

THE BATES METHOD is a method of improving eyesight through exercise and without the use of glasses. It is the result of the work of Dr. William Bates, who, nearly seventy-five years ago, began making discoveries that often contradicted standard assumptions of ophthalmology. Bates attended Cornell University, and the College of Physicians and Surgeons in New York City, and he taught ophthalmology at the New York Post Graduate Medical School and Hospital. He is predominantly known for his theory that eyeglasses can do more harm than good, act as crutches for those who wear them, and not cure the essential causes of bad vision. He is reputed to have smashed the eyeglasses of his new patients and, in 1912, he protested against the decision to fit large numbers of New York schoolchildren with glasses. His unorthodox approach to ophthalmology caused the American Medical Association to drop him from membership, although he challenged the association to prove his theories wrong. Since his death in 1931, Bates's theories have still not been proven or accepted, although new techniques have been developed that supplement his original techniques and are geared toward the relaxation of mind and body to reduce the tension which Bates felt to be often the cause of poor eyesight.

Specifically, Bates believed that even though glasses might improve vision and lessen discomfort for many, for others, wearing glasses could be harmful and would not improve vision. He demonstrated the above theories with several facts: 1) When we look at colors, they are less intense when seen through a concave or strong convex glass than if perceived with the naked eye; 2) in order to see through a pair of glasses, the same refractive errors the glasses are intended to correct must be constantly produced; 3) for cases of nearsightedness, vision is further impaired by the use of glasses; 4) glasses contract the field of vision because they cannot be used properly except by looking through the center; 5) glasses get dirty, obstructing vision; 6) glasses reflect strong light, which could be harmful.

In his research, Bates questioned accepted notions of *accommodation* (the eyes' ability to shift focus from distant to nearby points, and vice versa), the fixed shape of the eyeball, and errors of refraction. He believed that defective vision and even diseases of the eye, such as glaucoma, could be the result of emotional stress; that nearsightedness and farsightedness are not permanent but related to the shape of the eyeball, which can be changed. His conclusions centered on the ability of the eyes to cure themselves, with proper treatment.

The fundamental principles of the Bates method are based on several techniques for using the eyes in their natural state, and relaxing both the eyes and the mind. One technique deals with the phenomenon of *central fixation,* which allows the eye to remain unaffected by errors of refraction or functional disturbances. Central fixation occurs when your center of vision, the point of maximum sensitiveness in the retina of the eye, is in operation. To achieve it, you must concentrate on a particular point in your field of vision, and allow the rest of your visionary field to remain unclear and indistinct. The practice of central fixation will allow you to see in a relaxed manner, relieving your eyes of inflammatory conditions or infection. Central fixation requires mental control; the efficiency of the mind is a determining factor in how well the process will work.

Techniques for eliminating errors of refraction are also concerned with relaxation and the elimination of tension and strain. *Palming,* covering the eyes with the palms of the hands for several seconds, relieves pressure on the eyeballs.

Bates also felt that memory and imagination could be useful tools in improving vision. For example, remembering an object perfectly, or imagining what an object looks like with the eyes closed, will later enable you to actually see the object in question more accurately.

Another technique is called *swinging.* It involves moving the head and eyes in coordination with the body, without concentrating on any objects. It is effective in relieving the tension of eyestrain. You can rest your eyes by *sunning* them, blinking your eyes facing the sun for a period of time.

Part of Bates's method entails testing your eyes with the Snellan test card, which measures visual acuity, for five minutes each morning, in order to gauge how much your eyesight has improved.

One of the most famous cases in which the Bates method was used was that of Aldous Huxley, who at the age of sixteen suffered from keratitis punctata which left him nearly blind for eighteen months, and subsequently with one eye capable only of light perception and the other with minimum vision. Huxley's condition was a result of opacities of the cornea, complicated by farsightedness and astigmatism. His doctors advised him to read with a powerful magnifying glass, and later he was fitted with glasses. Even then, his eyes felt strained and fatigued, and his vision worsened rapidly. Huxley finally went to Dr. Bates after hearing about his methods of visual "re-education," and after a few months of treatment, was able to read without glasses and without feeling eyestrain or fatigue. The opacities in the cornea began to clear up after having remained fixed for nearly twenty-five years. Huxley describes his experience in *The Art of Seeing,* which he wrote for the purpose of correlating methods of visual re-education with the discoveries of modern psychology and critical philosophy.

Further studies have been done which relate the Bates method to psychology. Dr. Marilyn Rosanes-Barrett, working with Frederick Perls, the founder of Gestalt therapy, discovered that sight-training techniques fail because people compensate for bad vision by erecting defenses, living with a sense of inferiority, and subconsciously steering themselves away from curing the problem. She concluded that psychotherapy, and specifically the methods of Fritz Perls, can be used for achieving improvement of vision when other methods fail. Rosanes-Barrett is convinced that eyesight can be improved to the point where glasses are completely unnecessary through simple sight-training techniques or, if the tensions are deeply ingrained, through psychotherapy.

REFERENCES

William H. Bates, M.D., *Better Eyesight Without Glasses.* New York: Pyramid Books, 1970.

Aldous Huxley, *The Art of Seeing.* New York: Harper,
1942.
Marilyn B. Rosanes-Barrett, Ph. D., *Do You Really Need
Eyeglasses?* New York: Hart Publishing Co., 1974.

GREGORY BATESON (1904–) is an anthropologist who has also done extensive work in the areas
of psychiatry, genetics, biological evolution, systems
theory, and cybernetics. Bateson was born in England
and educated at Cambridge University. He worked with
Margaret Mead in Bali and New Guinea. In 1942, he
was a participating member of the Macy Conferences
on Cybernetics. He was awarded a Guggenheim fellowship in 1947 for his work on the synthesis of cybernetics and anthropological data. From 1949–62, Bateson held the title of "ethnologist" at the Veterans
Administration Center in Palo Alto, California, during
which time he had the opportunity to study whatever
he thought interesting. He worked with John Lilly as
director of his dolphin laboratory in the Virgin Islands
(1963–64) and then was invited to the Oceanic Institute in Hawaii, to work on cetacean and other problems
of mammalian communication. Bateson has received
grants from the Foundations Fund for Psychiatry and
the National Institutes for Mental Health. He has been
visiting professor at The New School for Social Research (1946), Harvard University (1947), Stanford
University (1951), and now teaches at the University
of California at Santa Cruz.

Bateson is primarily concerned with redefining the
nature of reality, which he sees essentially as a network
of ideas. This redefinition requires the consideration of
the context of the ideas, the context of their meanings,
and the context of the data on which the ideas were
originally founded. Bateson calls this view of reality an
"ecology of mind." When applied, it is a way to unify
the heuristic concepts (which he sees as "so loosely
derived and so mutually irrelevant that they mix together to make a sort of conceptual fog . . .") with
"fundamentals," or the laws of science. This means

bringing the modern concepts of psychology, psychiatry, anthropology, sociology, and economics into contact with scientific principles. By considering these elements from an ecological standpoint, "the constancy of the relationship" between them is ensured.

The major cause of the separation of idea from data is method. Scientists have been trained to observe and test hypotheses inductively (specific to general) rather than deductively (general hypothesis to specific data). Creating a scientific method through which the actual case of situations can be approached, necessitates paying attention to the forms of the changing existence. The forms are the behavior patterns and systems of order to which the elements of existence conform, and vice versa. Scientific thought will advance when we use a "combination of loose and strict thinking," which is characteristic of the domains of the mind. Depending upon how well we structure and widen our observational and analytical scope, we can begin to approach the problems in behavioral and environmental circumstances.

Bateson proposes a theory of communication, based on the assumption that communication is the means through which people interrelate and influence each other. This pertains to culture as well as to the individual. He examines communication as it occurs at the most basic levels of organization, and as it becomes more complex, at the human and cultural levels, where awareness of perception is shared.

One aspect of human communication which Bateson examines is the idea that our lives are based on "propositions whose validity is a function of [our] belief in them." These propositions encompass a wide range of phenomena: learning, character formation, the development of human relationships, the development of religious faith, the activities of art, etc. Bateson calls these propositions *deutero-propositions,* propositions that are valid because we believe in them in the same way we believe those things we have learned to repeat, becoming more skilled at that level of information (*deutero-learning*). Religion, art, and other branches of knowledge (e.g., psychiatry) become the means to consolidate deutero-propositions into epistemologies that concern "our theories of the nature of the reality in which we live and our theories of the nature of our knowledge of this reality." We use these epistemologies as the bases for our action, conceptual and otherwise.

Bateson says these propositions are limiting. They do not refer to a whole circumstance, but only to the observer's frame of reference and the technical capability of observational tools. They are evidence of the dichotomy between the materialistic view and the romantic, mystical view of the universe. The idea that we have control over behavioral and environmental problems because of our epistemological viewpoints of the whole is an indicator of destruction: We think we see the whole, when, in fact, we cannot even see the parts.

What becomes an issue is the aggregation of levels with which we approach totality. At each level, which is a part of the ecology of ideas, we must consider a different logic. From a biological standpoint, "the 'logic' of adaption is a different 'logic' from that of the survival and evolution of the ecological system"; from a psychological standpoint, the logic of our action is different from the logic of the contexts of the action.

The survival of ideas is a matter of how humans interact with the environment: "the unit of evolutionary survival turns out to be identical with the unit of the mind." So, how we exist therefore becomes a matter of dispelling our epistemologies to get to the roots of the problems. Simply regarding them as products of a larger biological, social, or other system of which we are a part is a step in the right direction toward a reconceptualization of the world. Our conception of the world cannot be separate from the world as it works. Our minds interact with the world, and thus should not conceive ideas in an effort to transcend it.

Bateson applies his ideas to the field of psychotherapy and psychology. One of his major contributions is a theory of communication concerning the origin and nature of schizophrenia. He begins with the theory of logical types advanced by Bertrand Russell in *Principia Mathematica,* which addresses the "discontinuity between a class and its members." The distinction between the two is the difference between their levels of abstraction, or logical type. Extended, this means that we do not learn to discriminate between, for example, literalness and fantasy, because we lack the vocabulary to describe the difference in levels of abstraction. Instead, we resort to gesture to indicate the difference. The message signals required to convey progressively more complex levels become inexplicit, and, as a result, we learn to deal with the discrepancies because we have no choice.

Bateson considers the schizophrenic unable to discriminate between such modes of communication either "within the self or between the self and others." This applies to how messages are received from others, how messages are conveyed to others, how a schizophrenic thinks, senses, and perceives. Bateson hypothesizes that a schizophrenic has assimilated from experience the kind of patterning that elicits a schizophrenic response. This patterning creates the internal conflicts with logical typing, i.e., a schizophrenic perceives the world in terms of what Bateson calls the *double bind.*

According to Bateson, the experiences which create the double bind: 1) involve two or more persons; 2) recur, rather than being isolated traumatic experiences; 3) elicit learning to avoid punishment.

Bateson says that "how a schizophrenic talks depends greatly on how another person talks to him . . ." In his research, he observed that psychotherapy submits the schizophrenic to other double-bind situations. However, this "therapeutic bind" evokes responses from a schizophrenic that are unusual in relation to past forms of response. The therapist can create the binds intentionally or intuitively for the purpose of freeing the schizophrenic from inner conflicts.

Bateson studied schizophrenia with regard to genetic

mutation, learning, and change within the family. He concluded that in order to consider the problems of schizophrenia in terms of the idea of logical types, it is necessary to see that "the problem of adaptation and learning and their pathologies must be considered in terms of a hierarchic system. . . ." This system is composed of those levels of existence where change occurs naturally, as well as the contexts of those changes (i.e., environment).

Bateson believes that our most needed venture is to understand the environment. Cybernetics, systems theory, information theory, and related sciences are a means to do this. Using the tools we have invented, we will be able to see the differences between levels of abstraction and levels of existence. We will be able to see where one subsystem stops and another begins within a total context. Most importantly, we will be able to see our own minds as a part of a greater "mind," and ourselves as part of a larger system.

Bateson's philosophy is highly regarded in the academic circles of the Western world. His articles have been published in more than one hundred journals of anthropology, psychiatry, and science since 1926. His books include *Naven: A Survey of the Problems Suggested by a Composite Picture of the Culture of a New Guinea Tribe Drawn from Three Points of View; Balinese Character: A Photographic Analysis; Communication: The Social Matrix of Psychiatry;* and *Steps to an Ecology of Mind.*

REFERENCES

Gregory Bateson, with Margaret Mead, *Balinese Character: A Photographic Analysis.* New York: The New York Academy of Sciences, 1942.

Gregory Bateson, *Naven: A Survey of the Problems Suggested by a Composite Picture of the Culture of a New Guinea Tribe Drawn From Three Points of View.* Stanford, Ca.: Stanford University Press, 1958.

————, *Steps to an Ecology of Mind.* New York: Ballantine Books, 1972.

John Brockman, ed., *About Bateson: Essays on Gregory Bateson.* New York: E. P. Dutton & Co., 1977.

Jurgen Ruesch, M.D., and Gregory Bateson, *Communication: The Social Matrix of Psychiatry.* New York: W. W. Norton & Co., 1951.

BEHAVIOR MODIFICATION (or behavior therapy) is the therapeutic application of the psychology of behaviorism. The roots of "behavior mod," as it is popularly known, lie in the work of several psychologists. John B. Watson first proposed behaviorism as the scientific approach to the modification and control of behavior in 1912. B. F. Skinner is the major contributor to the modern concept of behaviorism. In 1938, with the publication of *Behavior of Organisms,* Skinner proposed that behavior can be measured by its frequency, and in this way, normal, neurotic, and psychotic behavior can be distinguished. Skinner contended that conditioned reflexes (as shown by the Russian physiologist Pavlov in his experiments with dogs) are not the major factor in shaping behavior. Rather, organisms behave to get a reward, an aspect of voluntary behavior.

Another related idea is that behavior can be changed through manipulation of rewards; an aspect of this is the concept of reinforcement. Sometimes behavior can be rapidly changed through a process called *continuous reinforcement,* i.e., following a behavioral act continuously with some kind of reward. Skinner takes issue with this. He proposes a method in which rewards are given in four intermittent patterns: fixed ratio, variable ratio, fixed interval, and variable interval. All are concerned with measuring the frequency with which rewards are given; it is a schedule of rewards. Skinner also proposes the concepts of discrimination and generalization, applicable in situations in which organisms respond to differences and in situations in which organisms respond to similarities. Most of these theories have been tested on animals. Only recently have psychologists begun to use these techniques as an alternative to psychoanalysis.

The purpose of behavior modification is to help you break bad habits, replacing them with different and better habits. This process involves dealing with your existing behavior patterns in order to discover and remove the reinforcement that is causing the adverse behavior to occur. (This approach is in contrast to a psychoanalytical approach that aims at discovering the *reasons* for the behavior patterns, which are often unconscious.) Depending upon the severity of the behavioral problem, modification can be achieved either under the guidance of a professional therapist or independently.

In the mid 1960s, behavior modifiers began to explore the possibilities of the application of behavior modification for weight loss. Since then, nine studies have been done, comparing the effects of behavior mod with other methods of weight reduction (e.g., dieting). In each study, behavior mod has been shown to be most effective. In 1967, Dr. Albert Stunkard, chairman of the University of Pennsylvania's Department of Psychology, claimed the treatment of obesity with behavior mod "the first significant advance in years."

The method for changing a behavioral pattern of overeating with behavior mod is a process of changing actual eating habits. This necessitates: 1) eliminating the reinforcements that support this undesirable behavior; 2) having the motivation to change behavior; 3) having incentive; and 4) being realistic about goals.

An important tool in the process is a notebook, or "behavior diary," in which you faithfully record *when, where, what,* and *how* you are eating. This information should include circumstances, places, etc., and other details of your eating activity. By keeping such a record, you will learn your behavior patterns well enough so that you can isolate them and control them according to your desires. Another tool is a chart on which you graph your weight daily. The last item recorded in the diary is an account of the activities you enjoy doing that have nothing to do with eating. This is a means of getting involved with some kind of physical or creative activity that can't be interrupted by eating.

To give yourself incentive, realistically plan how you want to be at the end of the program. (Dorothy Susskind of the Association for the Advancement of Behavior Therapy calls this your "Idealistic Self-Image.") There are subsidiary techniques you can use to facilitate the process. For example, *chaining*: making a chain of events as long as possible between going to the store to buy food and bringing it back to the table, e.g., buying fresh vegetables instead of frozen, etc.

Within the last ten years, behavior modification has been used in schools in the United States with hyperactive, retarded, delinquent, and other problem children, as well as with normal children, in which case it is geared to controlling troublesome behavior. The normal means of punishment are replaced by a means of eliminating the reinforcement of the bad behavior. Behavior mod is also used at home, as well, as a child-raising method.

Behavior mod has been applied to correct unsatisfactory sexual relations between partners; it has been used in training salesmen and to increase the motivation and efficiency of workers. Behavior modifiers are working on programs for use in prisons. Research on the "operant conditioning of the brain" is in progress in relation to behavior mod (e.g., to aid in voluntary control of blood pressure, etc.).

Currently, those noted for work in behavior modification are Dr. R. Vance Hall of the University of Kansas, Dr. Leopold Walder of the Associates for Behavior Change, Dr. Richard Malott of Western Michigan University, Dr. Barry Lubetkin and Dr. Steve Fishman, codirectors of the New York Institute for Behavior Therapy.

REFERENCES

Philip J. Hilts, *Behavior Mod.* New York: Bantam Books, 1974.

Jhan Robbins and Dave Fisher, *How to Make and Break Habits.* New York: Dell Books, 1973.

ERIC BERNE (1910–1970), a psychiatrist, was the creator of Transactional Analysis. Berne first presented his ideas on this new method of psychotherapy in 1957 at a Western Regional Meeting of the American Group Psychotherapy Association in Los Angeles. Transactional Analysis, however, did not receive great attention until the publication of Berne's *Games People Play* (1964), which sold over three million copies. This book was a sequel to his *Transactional Analysis Psychotherapy* (1961), which outlines Berne's system of analysis. The concept of Transactional Analysis was further popularized by *I'm OK—You're OK* (1976) by Thomas A. Harris, who studied with Berne for ten years, and founded the Institute for Transactional Analysis in Sacramento in the late sixties.

Transactional Analysis is an intellectual tool for the understanding of behavior and emotions. Its scientific nature replaces the vagueness often encountered in many traditional methods of psychotherapy, individual or group. In the development of Transactional Analysis, Berne isolated and defined a basic unit for the purpose of giving the approach an object for study and observation. This unit, called the *transaction,* is a unit of social intercourse, called into play when an individual is involved in relating verbally with one or more persons. The exchange is called the *transactional stimulus.* When the individual responds to the stimulus, either by doing something or by speaking, the *transactional response* occurs.

Transactional Analysis is not only a method of examining transactions, but also a method of systemizing the information derived from the analyses of transactions into words which have established definitions and connotations, and therefore little chance of being misconstrued.

One of the basic theories of Transactional Analysis is that you change the states of your character within any given situation over small periods of time. These states are your psychological realities, and they manifest themselves in terms of your appearance, manner, words, and gestures. Observation has revealed that there are three states of being that make up a personality: the parent, the child, and the adult.

Your parent state exists as recordings in your brain of data concerning external events which were imposed on you early in childhood (birth to age five) and remained unquestioned. Examples of events recorded typical to the parent state are fights your parents had, warnings and rules given to you by your parents, the joy your parents demonstrated (if any), how you were taught to eat, make your bed, brush your teeth, dress, etc. These data are recorded as truth, recalled often, and have a considerable influence on how you live your life.

Your child state exists as recordings of data reflecting the internal events that occurred in childhood (birth to age five). These events took place as acts of seeing, hearing, feeling, and understanding. Your recollections of these events as an adult will produce the same emotions in you that occurred in childhood, whether or not you were experiencing the effects of creativity, the process of discovery, a reprimand, etc.

Within the first year of life, the adult begins to form. The adult state is a result of your taking responsibility to explore and test the environment for the purpose of obtaining information pertinent to your control of it. The adult state performs many functions: It is a filter for new information, it weighs possible outcomes of events, it makes decisions, etc. The adult state is the seat of success in changing behavior patterns.

Transactional Analysis permits you to see the variety of ways in which your parent, child, and adult states of being are activated and why, in the course of your transactions. Clues which help you identify which state of being has commanded the surface of your behavior are of two types, physical and verbal. For example, physical clues which might indicate the child state is working are giggling, pouting, whining, crying, etc.; verbal clues to that state might be phrases such as "I dunno," "I guess," "I gonna," "How come," "I want." When any of these clues appear, and you will know how to recognize them, you will be able to determine which one of your states of being is responding transactionally to one of the states of being of the person(s) with whom you are relating. For example, if you want to give up smoking, your adult state says that to do so would be very good for your health. But, because giving up smoking is so difficult, you will put the responsibility for it on another person, who will play parent and control your access to cigarettes. If you now smoke, you become the object of reprimand, the child.

The goal of Transactional Analysis is to build a strong adult state of being, by learning to recognize the child and parent in you, by being sensitive to the child in others and responding to it, by giving the adult in you time to deal with new information and filter out child and parent in a new situation, and by working out a new system of values on which to rely.

Simple Transactional Analysis is the diagnosis of ego states as they are implemented in transactional exchange. There is a wide variety of possible transaction combinations involving the different ego states. The simplest transactions occur when the adult ego state of the persons involved in the transaction are in operation, both as stimulus and response. These complementary transactions, which usually occur in superficial working and social relationships, allow communication to occur without difficulty, but they can be easily disturbed by crossed transactions. A crossed transaction occurs when the ego states of persons involved are different, and, as a result, communication breaks down. You program your transactions serially from the three sources of parent, child, adult, or more generally, society, material, and idiosyncracy. Transactional Analysis can make it possible for you to achieve *autonomy* by releasing or recovering three capacities in you: awareness, which requires living totally in the present; spontaneity, which allows you the freedom to choose and express your feelings on all levels of your ego states;

and intimacy, which permits you to be spontaneously candid. Your autonomy will steer you away from old and irrelevant methods of social intercourse.

Transactions originally begin in infancy as *stroking,* which designates intimate physical contact and denotes any act which implies the recognition of another's presence. A stroke is a stimulus; the response which occurs is a stroke. This exchange of strokes is a transaction.

According to Berne, in development you experience three kinds of growth: *stimulus-hunger, recognition-hunger,* and *structure-hunger.* Stimulus-hunger develops in response to impending emotional deprivation. As a child, your most favorable forms of stimuli are provided through physical intimacy; as an adult, you are subject to sensory deprivation. Biologically, psychologically, socially, stimulus-hunger affects your survival the same way food-hunger affects it. Stimulus-hunger, especially for physical contact, becomes sublimated as you learn that only in special circumstances can you overtly elicit physical stimulation. This sublimation results in the transformation of stimulus-hunger into *recognition-hunger.* Your need to be recognized in the most common interchange becomes, according to Berne, "highly prized."

Structure-hunger is the result of your need for time structuring and the avoidance of boredom. It results in "programming," a method of structuring time on material, social, or individual levels. Material programming is based on processing data, and is important for the matrix it constructs for stroking, recognition, and other more complex forms of social interaction. Social programming teaches you certain forms of "ritualistic or semiritualistic interchanges" (e.g., proper manners, pastimes like chitchat, etc.). Individual programming is the result of your deeper involvement with others. It occurs as "incidents" which follow definite patterns and can be analyzed through sorting and classification. Berne calls these sequences of inci-

dents *games*. Each level of time structuring (ritual, pastimes, games, intimacy, activity) allows you to obtain
satisfaction from your transactions.

Social contact evolves satisfactorily with regard to
somatic and psychic equilibrium for several reasons:
for tension relief, in order to avoid noxious situations,
for the security of stroking, and to maintain an established equilibrium. Games and intimacy are the most
gratifying forms of social contact. Games are "ongoing
series of complementary ulterior transactions progress-
ing to a well-defined, predictable outcome." Games,
which take many forms, are essentially dishonest in
nature, dramatic in quality, and occur unconsciously
and innocently. You learn to play games as a child.
They function as a means to satisfy the need for intimacy, and are designed so that they culminate in a
"payoff." The structure of a game depends on the
specific advantages to be gained, the flexibility of the
variables within the game, the intensity with which they
are pursued, and the tenacity of the players.

There are three degrees of games. The first degree
includes games that are socially acceptable; the second,
the games played secretly; and the third, the games
that are dangerous and result in damage to the
players. "Alcoholic," "debtor," "kick me" are games
which influence the destiny of the player. There are
marital games such as "frigid woman," "harried," "if
it weren't for you"; party games in which your pastimes
come to the forefront such as "ain't it awful," "why
don't you—yes, but"; underworld games which pervade
prisons and correctional facilities; consulting-room
games which occur in therapeutic situations. These
latter games lead their players into difficulty and are
generally played by disturbed people. Games are
passed down through generations and occur on the
levels of parent, adult, child.

Transactional Analysis is most effective in groups because it functions as a learning tool rather than an exploration of the individual psyche. Transactional Analysis
is being used in group treatment in many state hospitals

in California, in prisons, and in youth authority institutions. It is used by therapists in marriage counseling, adolescent counseling, religious counseling, and family-oriented obstetrical care. Over a thousand professionals have been trained in Transactional Analysis in California, and training centers are appearing in other parts of the United States and in foreign countries.

REFERENCES

Eric Berne, M.D., *Transactional Analysis in Psychotherapy.* New York: Grove Press, 1961.

————, *Games People Play: The Psychology of Human Relationships.* New York: Bantam Books, 1964.

————, *The Structure and Dynamics of Organizations and Groups.* New York: Grove Press, 1966.

————, *A Layman's Guide to Psychiatry and Psychoanalysis.* New York: Ballantine Books, 1973.

Thomas A. Harris, *I'm OK—You're OK.* New York: Avon Books, 1967.

LUDWIG VON BERTALANFFY (1901–   ), a biologist, is the founder of General Systems Theory (GST), which he originally presented in 1937. An Austrian by birth, Bertalanffy later became a Canadian citizen. He was educated at the universities of Innsbruck and Vienna, receiving his Ph.D. in 1926. From 1934–48, he was a lecturer at the University of Vienna, and later professor of biology. From 1949–54, he served as professor of biology and director of research at the University of Ottawa. The Society for General Systems Research was established in 1954 for the purpose of furthering "the development of theoretical systems applicable to more than one of the traditional departments of knowledge." Bertalanffy taught physiology at the University of Southern California and directed biological research at Mt. Sinai Hospital in New York City from 1955–58. He became Sloan Professor and resident associate of the Menninger Foundation in Topeka, Kansas, in 1958. From 1961–69, he served as professor of theoretical biology at the University of Alberta in Edmonton, Canada. During this time, Bertalanffy published a definitive book on the foundations, development, and applications of General Systems Theory. He was a member of the Center for Advanced Study in Theoretical Psychology, and fellow of the American Association for the Advancement of Science and the International Academy of Cytology. He authored books and articles on GST, biology, physiology, etc., many of which were originally published in German.

As early as the 1920s, Bertalanffy stated the necessity for viewing living organisms as organized systems; this was a fundamental premise of the study of what he called *organismic biology:* "The fundamental task of biology is the discovery of the laws of biological systems at all levels of organization." This mode of thinking in combination with his organismic view of life eventually led to him to his General Systems Theory.

General Systems Theory, as defined by Bertalanffy, is an interdisciplinary doctrine that deals with principles and models which can be applied to "systems in general, irrespective of their particular kind, the nature of their component elements, and the relations or 'forces' involved." The purpose of GST is to *un*specialize fields of knowledge, to speak of them in terms of their structural similarities or *isomorphisms,* so that those models, laws, etc. that have been discovered in one field can be transferred and applied to the development of another field: "It seems, therefore, that a general theory of systems would be a useful tool providing, on the one hand, models that can be used in, and transferred to, different fields, and safeguarding, on the other hand, from vague analogies which have often marred the progress in these fields." GST can formulate theories of organization quantitatively which, according to Bertalanffy, is "the basic problem posed to modern science."

GST is a general science of wholeness. Specifically, it aims to concretize the already existing tendencies toward integration of the natural and social sciences, and encourages the development of "unifying principles running vertically through the universe of individual sciences," in a natural move toward unifying science and scientific education.

The general characteristics of systems have been mathematically discovered, given that systems can be defined as "sets of elements standing in interaction." These elements can be observed in terms of number, species, and relations that can be specifically measured by means of a system of simultaneous differential equations. The manipulation of these equations can indicate the trend of growth of a system and the competition between parts of a system; these are two concepts that normally are used to describe living systems, but which are also integral functions of general systems.

There are other formal properties of systems which can be mathematically demonstrated: *wholeness,* in which the changes in every element depend upon changes in other elements; *sum, physical summativity,* or *independence,* in which the variation of the total complex is the physical sum of the variations of its elements; *summativity in the mathematical sense; progressive segregation,* which is characteristic of biological, psychological, and social systems, the interaction between elements decreasing in time; *progressive mechanization,* exhibited by interaction within a system, the action of the elements being dependent on the very elements; *progressive centralization,* particularly significant to biology, relating to progressive segregation to manifest evolution and progressive individualization toward defining the individual as a centered system; *hierarchical order,* systems structured in which the individual elements are systems constituting the next lower level; systems are *closed* (physical) or *open* (living); and *finality,* which is characteristic of *static teleology* in which elements are arranged toward a specific goal or *dynamic teleology* in which processes of a system assume a direction.

These principles of general systems determine the isomorphism in different fields; similarities of the order of general systems could not be discovered if the principles did not exist and hold true. The medium of GST is not only mathematical, however, for the same function can also be served by cybernetics, information theory, game theory, decision theory, topology, and factor analysis.

Since its formulation, GST has elicited new theories concerning those concepts integral to natural sciences as well as those concerning that which has been considered inaccessible to exact formulation. GST has encouraged the application of the theory of open systems to physical theory, kinetics, thermodynamics, population dynamics, ecology, geomorphology, and meteorology. It has enabled the knowledge of simple forms of growth to increase, as well as knowledge about forms of relative growth, both biological and social. It has brought about the observation of the competition and growth principles of population dynamics. It has spirited the creation of systems engineering, theories on personality, and models of history, all in the organismic sense. Attitudes in psychology and psychopathology have been influenced by GST, necessitating a reorientation of the basic psychological principles (e.g., Allport, Piaget, Maslow, Rogers, etc.). In each of these psychologies, man is not considered an automaton, but rather "an active personality system." As Bertalanffy states: "The system concept is a radical reversal with respect to robotic theories, leading to a more realistic (and incidentally more dignified) image of man." The systems concept allows normally disparate physical and psychological phenomena to be viewed in similar terms on the basis of similar principles of structure.

An offshoot of GST is *systems philosophy* propounded by Ervin Laszlo, who describes it as an argument for "a systematic and constructive inquiry into natural phenomena on the assumption of general order of nature." The information gained from the study of empirical sciences can be seen in terms of basic philosophical problems: "By this method scientific findings are used instrumentally, to construct a conceptual framework adequate to the understanding of nature as an integral network of ordered interdependency of which man is a part . . . man is not the center of the universe, nor is the universe built in his image . . . he is part of the overriding order which constitutes the universe."

REFERENCES

Ludwig von Bertalanffy, *General Systems Theory, Foundations, Development, Applications.* New York: Braziller, 1968.

F. E. Emery, ed., *Systems Thinking.* Middlesex, England: Penguin, 1969.

Ervin Laszlo, *Introduction to Systems Philosophy: Toward a New Paradigm of Contemporary Thought.* New York: Harper & Row, 1972.

LUDWIG BINSWANGER (1881–1966), a Swiss psychiatrist, founded the school of existential psychoanalysis known as *daseinsanalyse,* based on the philosophy of Heidegger, especially Heidegger's *Daseins Analytics,* which essentially describes the structure of man's existence as *dasein,* or being-in-the-world (*da* in German meaning "there" and *sein* meaning "being").

Binswanger was born in Switzerland and attended the universities of Lausanne and Heidelberg. He studied with Carl Jung at the University of Zurich and received his medical degree in 1907. He later became a psychiatric intern under the auspices of Eugen Bleuler. In 1911, Binswanger succeeded his father as medical director of the Sanatorium Bellevue in Kreuselingen, Switzerland, a position he held until 1956. Binswanger first established his views on existential psychoanalysis in the 1930s with the publication of "Dream and Existence" and material on studies of mania. His major work, *Grundformen und Erkenntnis menschlichen Daseins* (*Basic Forms and Conditions of Human Existence,* 1942), fully outlines the system of daseinsanalyse. Despite their differing philosophies, Binswanger maintained a close relationship with Freud.

At one point, he was a member of the Vienna Psychoanalytic Society on Freud's recommendation. The group that made up the existential analytic movement was trained in both Freudian and Jungian analysis. A. Storch, M. Boss, G. Bally, and Roland Kuhn in Switzerland, and J. H. Van Den Berg and F. J. Buytendijk in Holland were among the other members.

Binswanger defines existential analysis as a science based on empiricism, or *ontic statements,* which are "statements of factual findings about actually appearing forms and configurations of existence." Its primary concern is what he calls an *anthropological* scientific investigation of the essence of being human. The structure of man's existence is *being-in-the-world,* which Binswanger interprets as meaning a unification of existence, the world, and the activity of transcendence (rather than man, as subject, separated from the environment, as object). Dasein is not equal to the self, but rather acts as a background from which the self emerges; dasein defines the actual existence of a being whose essence is being-in-the-world. The world is taken personally. You are self-aware and take responsibility for your existence. The basic process of daseinsanalyse is the examination of what you are "knowing-feeling-willing."

Mental diseases are considered "modifications of the fundamental or essential structure and the structure links of being-in-the-world as transcendence." The investigation of psychoses becomes a matter of understanding and seeing them as modes of transcendence. They are products of your *world design,* which refers not only to the environment but to the world that includes others and your self. The complexion of your world design determines your mental illness and prevents communication.

The activity of transcendence can be measured in daseinsanalyse, given the phenomenon which you experience within the context of your transcendental structure. Transcendental structure gives meaning to your world design, and within it, you render visible phenomena that are clearly characteristic of all areas (temporal, spatial, personal, social, etc.) of your experiences. Binswanger calls it the *transcendental category*. It must take into account your complete world; one part of your world cannot be explained on the basis of another part of your world.

Binswanger believes that if a therapist understands the nature of the transcendental category, or the a priori structures of human existence, the therapist will be able to make closer contact with the patient's world. The existential analyst does not stop investigating once given "the single fact, the single disturbance, the single symptom"; rather the search continues for the unity of the patient's world design within which facts are seen as partial phenomena. The search is conducted methodologically through the observation of behavior, speech, dreams, writings, free association, etc. In this way, anxiety is not viewed as separate from the world. Anxiety becomes analyzable as a product of an empty, simplified, and constricted world design. The intensity with which you commit yourself to such a world magnifies your anxiety. "The source of anxiety is existence, itself."

Important to the structure of daseinsanalyse is the observation of the *spatialization* and *temporalization* of your existence, and the "lighting and coloring, and the texture" of your world design. Binswanger feels that the way in which you express phenomena is the means to clearly know the *content* of your existence in order to determine the *world content* of your world design.

In daseinsanalyse, the self changes in response to four *existential modes* which define your relationships with others and yourself. The *dual mode* is manifested in the mother-child, brother-sister, and lover-beloved relationships. According to Binswanger, the *dual mode of love,* which transcends space and time, determines the core of the normal existential experience. The *plural mode* defines formal relationships, competition, and struggle. The *singular mode* defines the relationship with yourself and your body. The *anonymous mode* defines the means by which you can live and act externally and, thus, escape coming into conflict with others.

As with Freudian analysis, in daseinsanalyse the *symbol* is considered in terms of its subjective properties, i.e., properties of objects refer to the self. But, furthermore, in daseinsanalyse, the symbol arises from an a priori existence, which is the meaning matrix upon which your particular world is based. Therefore, what is seen to create the conditions of anxiety in Freudian analysis is considered basic to the structure of your world design in daseinsanalyse; you are your world design, including the assimilation of the past into the present. The point that the analysis wants to reach is the *context* of the meanings which can be assigned to symbols; the context, or mode of being-in-the-world, dominates the meanings of events.

Existential analysis essentially denies the principle on which the concept of the unconscious is founded. The unconscious is understood rather to be a source of explanation for one aspect of dasein which is known as *thrownness,* a term derived from Heidegger. Binswanger qualifies thrownness as the transcendental horizon of all that psychiatry studies in terms of body, organism, mood, depression, insanity, compulsion, etc. Thrownness is already a part of the dasein, a part of the self; it expresses your sense of finitude, needs, character, etc.

Neurotic anxiety is produced when you commit yourself to a world that you have created in which you allow yourself no freedom. This activity indicates the *dynamic vicious circle of neurotic anxiety.* The perpetuation of the vicious circle is a sign of your psychosis. The goal of existential analysis is to reestablish your freedom.

REFERENCES

Rollo May et al., eds., *Existence: A New Dimension in Psychiatry and Psychology.* New York: Simon & Schuster, 1958.

Jacob Needleman, ed., *Selected Papers of Ludwig Bin-*

swanger: Being-in-the-World. New York: Basic Books, 1963.

H. M. Ruitenbeek, *Psychoanalysis and Existential Philosophy.* New York: E. P. Dutton & Co., 1962.

BIOFEEDBACK is a technique for the measurement of biological systems, using scientific equipment for the purpose of conscious control through self-monitoring of those systems in order to improve and promote health, both mental and physical. The word "biofeedback," a condensation of biological feedback, was coined by the Biofeedback Research Society at its first meeting in 1969.

The study of biofeedback and its use in *visceral learning,* or control of internal organs, began with the work of experimental psychologist Dr. Neal E. Miller of the Rockefeller University in New York in the 1960s. His studies ranged from an investigation of white rats to college students for the purpose of examining how higher animals learn. In an experiment with white rats whose skeletal muscles had been paralyzed so that these muscles could not be used in any way, Miller proved that rats could learn to control involuntary body functions such as heartbeat, blood pressure, and intestinal contractions. The rats were not only able to learn to manipulate and control their physiologic responses, but also to retain and repeat what they had learned. This research led to the correlation between scientifically investigated human behavioral patterns and the meditative exercises practiced in Yoga and Zen.

In the late 1950s, Joseph Kamiya of the Langley Porter Neuropsychiatric Institute in San Francisco, interested in the control of brain waves, determined that when a person was informed about the electrical activity of the brain through EEG (electroencepthalograph) feedback, he or she could learn to control the alpha rhythms of brain waves, turning them on at will. This type of control correlated with the experiences of Eastern mystics during meditation. Further research

demonstrated the occurrence of "consistent and pronounced physiologic changes" in people practicing
Transcendental Meditation.

Another pioneer in biofeedback research is Barbara
Brown, chief of Experiential Physiology at the Veterans Administration Hospital in Los Angeles, California, and lecturer at the UCLA Medical Center.
Brown has been largely concerned with exploring the
conditions which biofeedback sets up for coordinating
the activity of the mind with the activity of the body.
She has researched the full range of these coordination
processes, from the ways that the mind can even influence the skin to the mental processes that occur in
altered states of consciousness. Brown describes the
biofeedback process as "a new mode of communication" between the physical self and the mental self
that can be extremely useful. She suggests that the
future of biofeedback lies not in its capacity to control
behavior, but in its potential as a means to explore the
energy of the mind as a directive for voluntary control
of autonomic internal body processes; physical and
psychosomatic and emotional illnesses; psychic phenomena; and even death.

The EEG is one of the instruments used in biofeedback. It records brain waves through electrodes
which are attached to the scalp. Brain waves are the
result of electrochemical impulses occurring in the
cells of the brain as they send out information to various parts of the body. Four different kinds of brain
waves have been pinpointed: alpha, beta, theta, and
delta. Alpha waves occur more smoothly and slowly
than beta waves; they are indications of a relaxed and
peaceful state in which there is no deliberate thought,
although the individual is alert. Beta waves occur in
rapid, jerky form and are associated with alertness, concentration, and normal daily activity. Alpha and beta
waves occur alternately in the brain and have been
recorded as operating in different halves of the brain at
the same time: alpha in one half and beta in the other.
Theta waves are slower than alpha waves and are char-

acteristic of the state of mind before the onset of sleep, as well as of the creative state of mind, hallucinatory activity, and perhaps anxiety. Delta waves are the slowest recorded waves and are characteristic of the state of deep sleep.

Other biofeedback instruments are: 1) EKG (electrocardiograph), which is used to measure heartbeat; 2) EMG (electromyograph), which is used to measure the electrical activity in muscles or muscle tension; 3) GSR (galvanic skin response), which is used to measure the electrical resistance of the skin.

The development of biofeedback as a science and a tool for self-awareness is in the experimental stages. However, there are several important known uses of biofeedback. For example, working with EEG feedback, you can determine your state of mind and, as shown by Kamiya, learn how to enter, maintain, and increase your alpha state. Alpha activity is produced in significant amounts by yogis and Zen monks during meditation; it has been shown that meditation has a marked and probably beneficial effect on the metabolic processes of the body.

In laboratory situations, biofeedback training has been used to control blood pressure in advanced cases of obesity in which the effects of weight reduction and regular exercise would not necessarily influence a change in hypertensive conditions. Biofeedback training has been used to relieve migraine headaches by controlling blood flow. Eventually, physicians may be able to use biofeedback as a diagnostic tool. Biofeedback could replace tranquilizers, anesthetics, and drugs that produce so-called pleasurable states (alcohol, for example).

Essentially, research into biofeedback has revealed that living organisms can modify seemingly involuntary body functions if guided by external signals that tell them what is happening in their bodies from moment to moment.

Universities and colleges throughout the United States are doing biofeedback research and often need subjects for their experiments; it is recommended that if you want to experience biofeedback training, you should offer yourself as a subject in this research context.

REFERENCES

Barbara Brown, Ph.D., *New Mind, New Body*. New York: Bantam Books, 1975.

Gerald Jonas, *Visceral Learning: Towards a Science of Self-Control*. New York: Pocket Books, 1974.

Gary Null, Steve Null, et al., *Biofeedback, Fasting and Meditation*. New York: Pyramid Books, 1974.

BIORHYTHMS. The discovery of the theory of biorhythms was the result of the work of Dr. Hermann Swoboda (1873–1963), a professor of psychology at the University of Vienna, and Dr. Wilhelm Fliess (1859–1928), a physician in Berlin. Essentially, the theory of biorhythms is the result of the application of mathematics to the biological scheme of life; mathematics is used as a tool to predict behavior and experience.

Swoboda was involved with his initial research into this phenomenon between 1897 and 1902, after he discovered periodicity in fevers, in the outbreak of illnesses, and in heart attacks. He determined that our dispositions and resultant actions were influenced by the regularities and rhythms of changes which occur in the biological structure, and that these rhythms could be precalculated. He labeled this science *bionomy*. He published *The Periodicity in Man's Life* (1904), *Studies of the Basis of Psychology* (1905), and *The Year of Seven* (1917). The latter contains mathematical analyses of the rhythmical repetition of births through generations. Swoboda also designed a slide rule with which the so-called critical days of biological rhythms, given the birth date of the subject, could be determined.

Simultaneously, in Berlin, Dr. Wilhelm Fliess was engaged in research in order to confirm his discovery of the twenty-three-day and twenty-eight-day rhythmic periods he had diagnosed in his patients. Fliess believed that each individual inherits both male and female characteristics, and that everyone has bisexual characteristics. He concluded that the rhythms he had observed, as well as evolution, the creation of organisms, and life itself, were all interrelated. In the publication of his formula for describing biorhythms, Fliess stated that the twenty-three-day rhythm is masculine, affecting physical conditions, and the twenty-eight-day rhythm is feminine, affecting emotions and sensitivity. He recorded his discoveries in *The Rhythms of Life: Foundations in Exact Biology* (1906), which gained him the support of Sigmund Freud. Freud helped make the book a success, believing that Fliess had made a significant step in the science of biology. Between 1909 and 1925, Fliess published *Of Life and Death* (1909), *The Year in the Living* (1918), and *Theory of Periodicity* (1925).

It has been determined that there are three different kinds of biorhythms: *Physical rhythm:* This is a twenty-three-day cycle which originates in the cells and fibers of the muscles, according to Fliess's discoveries. Changes in the rhythm affect physical strength, endurance, resistance, as well as physical confidence. It has been demonstrated that in the first half of the cycle (eleven and one-half days), which is called the ascending or discharge period, you are vigorous and have optimum vitality and endurance, and can perform physical tasks easily. The second half of the cycle, called the recharging period, finds you with less energy and capacity for endurance, and more apt to tire easily. *Sensitivity rhythm:* This is a twenty-eight-day cycle which affects your nervous system. During the first fourteen days of this cycle, you tend to be cheerful and optimistic, attitudes which affect your creativity, feelings of love, cooperative tendencies, and the coordination connected with the nervous system. In the last fourteen days of this cycle, you experience negativism and irritability. *Intellectual rhythm:* This thirty-three-day cycle was discovered by Alfred Teltscher in Switzerland during the 1920s as a result of his work with students in high school and college. During the first sixteen and one-half days of this cycle you think clearly, your memory functions well, and your thought response operates spontaneously. This time period enables you to delve into new subjects, to study, to think creatively. During the last sixteen and one-half days, your thinking capacity is reduced and you are better off practicing, reviewing, and storing knowledge subconsciously.

Biorhythms are not supposed to predict specific future behavior or accidents. You can judge the importance of your biorhythms in terms of what happens to you and how your environment influences you. The *critical days* of the biorhythmic cycles are considered switch points when you are in a state of flux, moving from one half of a cycle into the other. During this period you might be unstable and prone to creating uncomfortable, even critical, situations for yourself with regard to your physical, emotional, and intellectual states. It can be helpful to recognize when these critical days occur in order to be conscious of the effects they may have on your life.

The importance of the theory of biorhythms has been carried over into the study of biological time. *Body time* is in evidence in the day-to-day activities of sea creatures, insects, animals, and in man. Physical behavior during the day and night has been found to correspond to time cycles. This temporal physical behavior is called *circadian rhythm,* and it can be measured in man by body temperature, urine flow, blood and hormone constitutions, protein metabolism, as well as changes in sense of taste, smell, hearing, etc. Circadian rhythms also cause changes in brain waves. Reactions to drugs, stress, pain, the symptoms of allergy or disease are partially determined by circadian rhythms. Knowledge of these rhythms can indicate when you are most vulnerable to disease. However, it is necessary to know more about the variety and range of human circadian rhythms before accurate medical diagnoses can be made on this basis. Knowledge of seasonal body time structure can be a significant factor in how you live and control your life.

REFERENCES
Gay Gaer Luce, *Body Time: Physiological Rhythms and Social Stress.* New York: Bantam Books, 1971.
———, *Biological Rhythms in Human and Animal Physiology.* New York: Dover Publications, 1970.
George S. Thommen, *Is This Your Day? How Biorhythms Help You to Determine Your Life Cycles.* New York: Crown Publishers, 1973.

RAY BIRDWHISTELL (1918–   )   is the anthropologist responsible for the development of the science of *kinesics,* or body communication. The study of kinesics has been largely supported by research done in a linguistic framework at several institutes and universities, and by individuals such as Edward T. Hall, Albert Scheflen, Margaret Mead, Gregory Bateson, Erving Goffman, Henry Smith, and George Trager.

Birdwhistell was born in Cincinnati, Ohio. Until 1959, he, along with Bateson, a fellow anthropologist, Norman McQuown and Charles Hockett, linguists, Henry Brosin and Freida Fromm-Reichmann, psychiatrists, participated in compiling data on the way in which verbal communication and body motion interact during conversation. This work was done at the Center for Advanced Studies in the Behavioral Sciences.

In the development of kinesics as a science, Birdwhistell found it necessary to create a methodology which could be used to analyze communicative behavior of the body beyond the structural analysis of linguistics. His work in viewing body motion in detail, often with the use of film, led him to examine German, French, Italian, Spanish, and American gestural behavior.

A background study of body language in these many cultural environments led Birdwhistell to challenge the idea that imitation is the reason for all communication carried out by means other than speech, and that body motion is an artificial appendage to speech. Birdwhistell was, in fact, unable to discover any kind of body motion, facial expression, or gesture which has universal meaning. In different cultural situations, there are as many contexts for gestural response as there are functions for the gesture. For example, the smile in one society may express joy, while in another, embarrassment. A smile, which is a facial activity involving more than the movements of the lips, can carry much more meaning than is standardly accepted. Birdwhistell concluded that dictionary-type compilations of data which bestow general absolute meanings to gestures in the literature of signs and symbols are ill founded. The idea of "natural" gestures within a culture should be dispensed with in the light of the fact that the ways various societies organize body behavior into communicative forms are as variable as the structures of their verbal language.

The isolation of gestures and the effort to understand them as they are used in context have led to the most important discoveries of kinesic research. Studies have shown that the kinesic system has forms within it that parallel the spoken word. In studying American, German, and English kinesic systems, Birdwhistell found that there are body behaviors which act like meaningful sounds and combine to form simple and sometimes complex units similar to words; and extended forms of body behavior can function as sentences or even paragraphs. Such kinesic systems require analysis within the proper context.

Communication should be regarded as a structural system of significant symbols which allow for human interaction; analysis must be contained within a situation, defined as an ordered matrix whose structure allows for the comprehensible delineation of communicative acts. In this light, it would be inappropriate to examine a military situation where body motion already has specific meaning, or a therapeutic situation where body motion may be symptomatic of mental illness. Rather, kinesic research aims at discovering the precise social meaning of an interactional situation whereby judgments can be made regarding the social background of already defined body motion, how these body motions are standardized (or not) in terms of their performance, the quality of their performance, and their influence on the communicative acts of others within a society. In order to see how body motion is used to pass information among participants in a communicative interaction, and how that information affects them (either educationally or therapeutically), and how the effect holds within other situations in the same culture, it is necessary to have sufficient knowledge of the social context in which such types of communication are occurring.

The development of systems which annotate body movements along with field work done by anthropologists, which concluded that body motion and facial expression result from a biological socialization process within the culture, led to the basic assumptions which are the basis of kinesic research: 1) No body movement or expression lacks meaning in the context in which it appears; 2) body posture, movement, and facial expression are patterned like other aspects of human behavior, and can be systematically organized; 3) the systematic body motion of members of a community is a function of the social system to which the group belongs, unless biologically limited; 4) visible body motion and audible acoustic activity influence the behavior of other members of a particular group, and this behavior is examinable communicational material; 5) the meaning given to such behavior is functional, both in terms of the behavior as well as the way in which the behavior is examined; 6) analysis of an individual's behavior will provide information as to idiosyncrasy and will simultaneously contribute to the larger social kinesic system under investigation.

In kinesics, each possible aspect of behavior is defined and assigned a name or symbol which makes it possible to record regularities and inconsistencies, and incorporate them into a total kinesic system. The *kine* symbolizes a body movement, the degrees of which may change from one person to another within the same interaction. The *kinemorph* is an assemblage of *kines,* or movements, within a specific area (e.g., head, neck, shoulders, trunk, etc.). The kinemorph is analyzed in terms of complexity and is called a *kinemorphic construction.* Kinemorphic constructions pertain to motion on levels from the *microkinesic* (gesture) to the *macrokinesic* (posture, pose, demeanor). The dynamics of a given body movement, muscular tension, duration, range, are symbolized in motion qualifiers. Action modifiers, interaction modifiers, and motion markers further classify the ways in which body motion can operate.

Interpretation of the language of kinesics is structured on what Birdwhistell has established as four methodological canons: Establish and maintain a given level of analysis; isolate the units observed for manipulation; establish the independent identity of body movements as demonstrated by individuals through constant analysis; and weigh the analytic value of newly discovered units of body motion by examining the contexts in which they do or do not appear. These canons are applicable in the analysis of the social significance of any set of body motions. The method of contrast by which body motion is analyzed allows the inconsistencies and incongruities to be seen. The total kinesic picture of a society depends upon the analysis of each segment of the society; the complete pattern of communication depends upon the separation of the linguistic and kinesic structures in order to see how they interact.

Birdwhistell's work has been sponsored by the University of Louisville, the University of Buffalo, the Center for the Advanced Study of Behavioral Sciences. He received a research fellowship award from the National Institute of Mental Health and the Commonwealth of Pennsylvania's Eastern Psychiatry Institute. Since 1954, he has had many articles and essays published on the development of kinesics. His books focus on communication, science, linguistics, and psychotherapy. He is the author of *Introduction to Kinesics* and *Kinesics and Context.*

REFERENCES
Ray L. Birdwhistell, *Introduction to Kinesics.* Louisville, Ky.: University of Louisville Press, 1952.
————, *Kinesics and Context.* Philadelphia: University of Pennsylvania Press, 1970.
————, "The Kinesic Level in the Investigation of the Emotions," *Expressions of the Emotions of Man.* New York: International Universities Press, 1963.

BODY LANGUAGE, technically known as kinesics (developed by Ray Birdwhistell), is a relatively new science, originating within the last fifteen years. Julius Fast, working with Arnold Buchheimer, psychologist and professor of education at the City University of New York, and Dr. Albert E. Scheflen, professor of psychiatry at the Albert Einstein College of Medicine, has studied how body language communicates as effectively as, and often as a substitute for, verbal communication.

The study of body language encompasses all body movements ranging from the very deliberate to the entirely unconscious, and from those that are unique to one culture to those that are utilized in all cultures. The origins of nonverbal communication can be seen in experiments done with animals. Birds, for example, communicate with each other by singing; recently it has been discovered that bird songs are learned and not inherited, and that the learning of them is directly linked to the mating process. This revelation raised questions concerning how much of any means of communication is inherited and how much is learned.

Studies done in Brazil, New Guinea, Borneo, and the United States proved that social nonverbal gestures are recognized despite different cultural orientation. This indicates that basic physical reactions to emotion can be inherited along with a typical mode of expressing them nonverbally. Nevertheless, there are gestures which are means of nonverbal communication that must be learned. Therefore, it can be concluded that nonverbal language is partially instinctual or inherited, partially learned, and partially imitative.

Nonverbal communication constitutes a means by which you map out and command your individual spaces. How you regard your territory and how you move into territories of others are essential functions of relating to others. Edward T. Hall defined four zones in which most people operate: *intimate distance, personal distance, social distance,* and *public distance.* Using these zones, it can be seen that you move within a range of distance patterns, the least intimate distance being the most distant. These distances are defined by your body reactions. Intimate distance occurs between two people in a very close relationship, two people making love, and between parent and child. When intimate distance is realized, you are unmistakably aware of the closeness of your partner. Personal distance allows for exchange between partners at a close, but comfortable, distance. Social distance necessitates the occurrence of a transaction of personal distance; it is a dominating factor when visual contact is the only relational tie. Public distance concerns such situations as the place a teacher holds in the classroom, or situations in which distance is a safety or security factor.

Space is handled in terms of the territory or zones set up according to these distances; the handling of space, however, varies from country to country. What is done in the Western world, considering cultural variations, is distinctly different from what is done in the Eastern world. When your territory is invaded, body language becomes a means of specifying the kind of aggression or nonaggression that you expect to perform or respond to within a given situation.

Body language signals describe how you wish to relate in certain situations. These signals are important in the study of the design of sexual encounters. Spoken language often deters the exposure of the truth about a relationship and confuses it. The coordination of tactile communication with visual communication enriches a love relationship. The signals a man sends to a woman to initially attract her take a variety of forms; his stance, his easiness of motion, complemented by gestures which can be interpreted as implicit sexual messages. When a man invades the personal space of a woman, he usually begins to exercise certain facial expressions. He narrows his focus in order to place only one woman in his range. In turn, a woman, using the same general tactics as the man, concentrates on emphasizing the aspects of her body which can do the work of attraction.

You learn how to read the messages conveyed by body language in order to determine their content. The use of body language becomes a means of manipulation and explanation of genders. A therapist uses body language as an aid in a psychological situation: how he sits, where he sits, how he uses his eyes, etc. A businessman uses it to keep certain relationships in perspective. A teacher uses it as an aid to teaching.

There are different postures for different occasions. An individual's body language can convey a warm and friendly image, creating a charismatic aura about him. Political and public figures use body language in this manner to manipulate audiences. In a family group, body language is a determinant for demonstrating filial respect. A son many imitate the motions and attitudinal positions of his father; a daughter may imitate her mother in the same way. The understanding of how body language functions within the family context can be important in understanding how it applies in larger social and cultural situations.

The value of body language is demonstrated in how nonverbal communication blends with verbal communication: Body language becomes a complement to words. If you understand the meaning of different motions, you can create situations in which motions alone are sufficient to communicate a message without the necessity of words. When body language is incorporated into methods of self-confrontation in psychiatric situations, you can become aware of what your body is doing, and how that might totally contradict what you are saying.

REFERENCES

Ray Birdwhistell, *Kinesics and Context.* Philadelphia: University of Pennsylvania Press, 1970.

Julius Fast, *Body Language.* New York: Pocket Books, 1971.

NATHANIEL BRANDEN (1930–), writer, researcher, and psychologist, has been practicing psychology since 1956. Branden was born in Brampton, Ontario, Canada. He acted as consultant in psychology at the Neuro-Physiology Biophysics Research Unit for the Veterans Administration Hospital in Boston. From 1962–68, he cofounded and coedited *The Objectivist,* a journal, with Ayn Rand. In 1969, he became prominent in academic circles for his new approach to the study of human nature, which focused on the importance of personal autonomy and the development of self-esteem to the establishment of personal well-being. Branden labels his approach *biocentric psychology.*

Essentially, biocentric psychology looks at the individual from a biological standpoint. Man's psychological nature can only be understood through the study of his nature as a living organism, with very specific needs. This approach helps clarify the uniqueness of the individual's accomplishments, as well as the uniqueness of his problems. Crucial to it is the idea that inherent in man's psychological nature is the need for self-esteem. To satisfy that need, he must recognize its nature, the conditions necessary for its fulfillment, how it influences values, goals, and interactions, and the consequences of ignoring it. Branden contends that psychologists have failed to explore the need for self-esteem and the causes of the relationship between degrees of self-esteem and corresponding degrees of mental health.

We are living organisms constructed as systems of component parts which function to preserve the integrity of the system and to keep the system alive. When we take materials from the environment and process them to suit our needs, we are exercising self-preservation. We do this according to our immediate goals, carrying out the actions necessary to realize them. According to Branden, self-preservation as instinct is a myth; instinct does not supply enough information for our ability to discover our inherent capacity for performance. Just as we see how we operate biologically, we can see how our ability to reason operates. Rationality is the result of our capacity to comprehend reality on the conceptual level of consciousness and springs from the practice of differentiation, classification, and symbolization in an easily accessible language. When we integrate conceptualization with consciousness, we become self-aware; self-awareness allows us to monitor, reflect on, and criticize our mental activity. We confront ourselves in the face of how we, as individuals, perceive reality. Our ability to regulate our basic needs for food, shelter, etc. is inbred; but our ability to control the activity of the mind, and our conscious self-awareness is a learned process. We focus our minds for the purpose of *active cognitive integration,* and do so voluntarily. This choice is the key to maintaining a psychological state of well-being. We *can* know how our minds function because we choose to know; we are not forced into knowing.

Experiencing emotions is a response to the values which we set for ourselves in a given situation. Although we cannot escape their impact, we can choose to act on these emotions as we see fit. Nevertheless, it is very difficult to define the effects of emotions on our consciousness for several reasons: 1) We must acquire introspective ability; without it we will not be able to understand why we feel a certain way; 2) we are not able to understand our values and beliefs clearly enough so that we can articulate them verbally; 3) we cannot untangle the intensity of emotions as they exist on different levels, universally oriented emotions versus individually oriented emotion; 4) we respond emotionally to peripheral occurrences; 5) we cannot recognize the truth behind emotional reactions since we tend to repress their essential causes.

To facilitate our pursuit of a satisfying psychological state, it is essential to develop an incentive to exercise our capabilities for realizing self-responsibility, self-confidence, and self-esteem. Self-esteem implies a conviction that we are competent to live and worthy of living. We require self-esteem in order to deal with reality, to understand it, to maintain a balance in it, using all our mental faculties. In doing so, we must have confidence in the capability of mind; we must have respect for our ability to exercise it. Authentic self-esteem lies in our determination to be rational and willing to open the mind completely. If we believe in false values that obviate our need to be mentally active, we will never have the self-esteem which sparks motivation. The absence of self-esteem subjects us to anxiety, depression, and guilt. Feelings of conflict and defeat interrupt our perception of the real situation and steer us away from clear thinking, objectivity, and responsibility.

On a metaphysical level, we must think, act, and create the values which our lives require. It is our duty to see the facts of reality as they are and construct our values through dedication to thinking. Introducing an idea unsupported by judgment causes uncertainty to overwhelm the remainder of our convictions. Faith in an idea attests to the idea's validation through rationalization. To take pride in our capability to think and to reward that pride with self-esteem is to create a strong foundation for the realizing of our own individual potential.

Branden's intervention in the mainstream of contemporary psychology has generated much excitement in the field. He lectures frequently on the philosophical bases of biology and psychology in academic institutions in the United States and Canada. His books, *The Psychology of Self-Esteem, Breaking Free,* and *The Disowned Self,* are used as textbooks in colleges and universities throughout the United States and Canada.

REFERENCES

Nathaniel Branden, *The Psychology of Self-Esteem.* New York: Bantam Books, 1971.

————, *Breaking Free.* Los Angeles: Nash Publishers, 1970.

————, *The Disowned Self.* Los Angeles: Nash Publishers, 1971.

G. SPENCER BROWN was born in England, educated at Trinity College in Cambridge, and did postgraduate work with Bertrand Russell and Ludwig Wittgenstein. He holds degrees in philosophy and psychology. He received a Perrott studentship in psychical research, and studied and practiced psychotherapy under R. D. Laing. He worked as an electronics engineer and consultant, was a sports writer for the *Daily Express,* and founded a publishing house. In a professional capacity, he served as philosophy don at Oxford University.

Brown's philosophy stems from his knowledge of mathematics, which he finds provides a key to understanding the world beyond the ordinary means of words. The laws that relate similar universes and the forms within them create a reality independent of the universes as they appear. According to Brown, mathematics supplies the law of that reality, and through mathematics we can see symbolically how the forms of the universe intercept, diverge, and mingle with each other.

In inventing a new reality, we must understand that the manipulation of the mathematical language can reach an impasse if the injunctive nature of mathematics is left unaltered by further description in another context. (The injunctive nature of mathematics is its ability to relate processes in models and ideas of the universe or universes.) Yet, in order to maintain a purely mathematical mode of presentation, we must confine ourselves consistently to the subject at hand, i.e., mathematics. Thus, only the spirit of the injunctive laws should be attended to; whoever uses mathematical tactics in an effort to describe the universal situation must learn to be flexible and weigh the importance of all possible relationships and methods of relating among elements set out in the mathematical structure. The use of certain mathematical rules to guide the functions of the invented system is often unconscious. When we have reached what we have set out to do, we can review the process and find that these unintended gestures work to our advantage. In this way, we can refine our methods of application. But first, all new principles set out in a mathematical system must be defined or justified in terms of already defined principles in order to be used clearly and properly.

The form of a means of mathematical communication develops in response to its author. Given the system, the names of its parts, and the symbols which represent the names, forms of expression (a, b, x, etc.) are then created. The proofs of theorems become increasingly formalized the further we go from the original givens.

In the midst of the creation of our mathematical structure, we find that what we have conceived can be already familiar to us, i.e., we have externalized our internal knowledge of the world and have intuitively imposed a discipline upon it which governs the new reality we have constructed. Mathematics provides a way of reassuring us that we do know the extent to which the elements of the universe interact. Mathematics falls into a pattern by natural consequence. A mathematical form is an archetypal structure.

The nature of our awareness of the universe is such that we are versed in distinguishing elements as we learned to do by controlling our environment. Judging from one part of the universe, we learn of the manner in which the parts operate and recognize the parts, judging from the manner in which they operate without hindrance of laws, theorems, etc. Mathematical logic, for example, can only supply the groundwork for understanding one part of a more generalized form in a process which is never ending. The mathematical treatment of this form gives us access to a way of talking about ordinary experience. Creating laws of mathematics is much easier than devising a way of communicating them. Brown devised a mode of operation which tends to separate the algebras of logic from the subject matter of logic, and puts them back into focus in the field of mathematics, i.e., the realignment of commonly known Boolean algebra so that its arithmetic application is distinct from how it is interpreted.

The approach Brown takes to illustrate the external world begins with the theme that the universe is born through an original act of severance (i.e., like the skin of an organism which separates inside from outside). According to the state of this boundary, the act of severance can be represented by the form created in conjunction with the laws of that form. Form, by graphic definition, is form in terms of distinction (one form cannot reach another form without crossing the boundary that separates them), and it is that which is contained in the space that is distinct from any other space. The value of the content of the form follows set patterns of motion defined by the flexible borderline of definitions, axioms, canons, theorems, and consequences.

G. Spencer Brown began work in the exploration of form in its mathematical context in late 1959. In 1963, he held a position of staff lecturer in physical sciences at the University of London, where he gave a course and lectured on the mathematics of logic. This same course, somewhat extended, was later given annually at the Institute of Computer Science at Gordon Square, London. Brown's book, *Laws of Form,* is a statement of his philosophy.

REFERENCES

G. Spencer Brown, *Laws of Form.* New York: Bantam Books, 1973.

————, *Probability and Scientific Inference.* London and New York: Longmans, 1957.

NORMAN O. BROWN (1913–), a philosopher concerned with the psychoanalytic meaning of life and history, was born in El Oro, Mexico. His father was a mining engineer. Brown was educated at Oxford University, the University of Chicago, and the University of Wisconsin, where he received his doctorate in 1942. He served for three years as research analyst for the Office of Strategic Services and was professor of languages at Nebraska Wesleyan University, and the Wilson Professor of Classics and Comparative Literature at the University of Rochester. From 1953–54, he worked in psychology and anthropology under a Ford Foundation grant from the Fund for the Advancement of Education. He wrote while on sabbatical leave from Wesleyan and the University of Rochester (1958–65), working under grants from the Guggenheim Foundation, the Center for Advanced Study in the Behavior Sciences, and the Yaddo Foundation.

The premise underlying Brown's philosophy is a rethinking and reappraisal of the nature of politics, the political character of human nature, and, more specifically, Freud's conception of the nature and destiny of man. Brown considers Freud's analyses applicable to a degree, but feels that the total thrust of Freud's thinking cannot satisfy the need to shape psychoanalytic theory into a more general theory including human nature, culture, and history.

Brown's intention is to reexamine the Freudian conception of neurosis. According to Freud, neurotic symptoms are a meaningful exposure of our involuntary purposes, our "unconscious ideas"; these unconscious ideas conflict with conscious ideas and resist exposure. Freud contended that all humankind suffers from repression (the keeping of a purpose or idea from consciousness, and/or the refusal to recognize the realities of our nature). Repressed purposes, ideas, and desires can be discovered in dreams and unconsciously made mistakes ("Freudian slips"). However, according to Brown, this theory does not support the idea of the unconscious. Freud's premise that all mankind is sick, or "repressed," is problematical in application to a total picture of human beings in society. If we consider psychoanalytical consciousness coupled with a general historical consciousness as a higher state of the general consciousness of mankind, we can reveal those origins of thought that have been a subject of study for so long. We can begin to live, instead of being conscious of making history; we can enjoy, instead of reverting to the past; we can begin to become.

Brown sees Freud's concept of Eros and death as energies which create human culture. If these concepts are recognized, human culture can be reevaluated. Eros is the bodily sexual instinct. It instigates the pursuit of pleasure. Pleasure is sought by children in the playful exploration of their bodies; this drive develops into normal sexual activity in adulthood. Eros speaks of our love of objects; it affects our view of the self, our view of others, our concepts of art and literature. To unify Eros, as life and death, we must see how death is as vital as life. Acceptance of death and its reunification in consciousness with life cannot be accomplished through art and philosophy alone. Acceptance of death can only occur through the destruction of repression. We repress Eros (life) in terms of sexuality, aggression, the pleasure principle. We flee from death as we flee from life. We build our culture around immortality and history in order to ward off death. In repression, we return to the past, to childhood, disrupting the instinctual biological unity of life and death. On the biological level, death occurs as a function of life. On the human level, the repressed death instinct cannot affirm life; it affirms death. Life cannot affirm death because life is repressed; death can only affirm itself by becoming the force which denies life.

We must consider the concept of sublimation to be the link between psychoanalysis and human culture. Sublimation can be seen as the force which commands us to relate the human spirit to the body and to grasp social phenomena in medical and scientific terms. Sublimation is the desexualization of the sexual instinct.

The subject matter of sublimation is the denial of the body. Throughout history, we have practiced sublimation to quell neuroses, overthrow the pleasure principle, and desexualize ourselves supposedly in order to return to reality. The practice of the reality principle reveals the falseness of dualism. In modern times, science diverts our attentions away from our bodies and our instincts. Science has created a world of intelligence and rationality. In order to unify the world of intelligence and the world of instinct, we must develop a new consciousness that will embrace and affirm Eros. Because the culture of intelligence has taken us away from our bodies, we have been forced to use psychoanalysis to rejoin the mind and body. Psychoanalysis aims to help us avoid repression and bring the unconscious into consciousness. Eros eliminates the sterility of intellectualism and gives us humility. It returns us to the state of childhood where we were "polymorphous perverse," i.e., gaining pleasure through any invention of our body/mind.

Brown sees the political problem as a failure to unify all of mankind in Eros. An erotic sense of reality would reveal the inadequacy of fraternity. Fraternities exist as parts of a whole where the "body" of the world is divided. The parts are assigned as property, and a system of property develops, marked off by boundaries. The boundaries are false; they exist as divisions between the self and the external world and have no relation to reality. The essence of fraternity is the personality, the success of the individual, and, more generally, theatricality. In fraternity, we project ourselves into our government or representative. We split ourselves, alienating ourselves mentally and physically. Psychoanalytic consciousness, consciousness of the whole, returns us to the body and spirit of the present: we burn the boundaries; we eliminate the representative; we come to believe in anarchical freedom, which is the culmination of the consciousness in mind and body. We break through the barrier of the reality principle.

Brown's psychoanalytic view is recognized as an

important contribution to recent intellectual history. His first book, *Life Against Death,* examines Freud's thought in terms of history and the existent cultural situation. *Love's Body* details more specific applications of his viewpoints.

REFERENCES

Norman O. Brown, *Life Against Death, The Psychoanalytic Meaning of History.* New York: Vintage Books, 1959.

————, *Love's Body.* New York: Vintage Books, 1966.

————, *Hermes the Thief.* Madison: University of Wisconsin Press, 1952.

MARTIN BUBER (1878–1965), the Jewish religious philosopher, was born in Vienna. He studied philosophy and art at the universities of Vienna, Zurich, and Berlin. In his twenties, he practiced Zionism, working with Theodor Herzl and Chaim Weizmann. He taught philosophy and religion at the University of Frankfurt-am-Main. Through his book *Tales of the Hasidim* (Vol. 1, *Early Masters* and Vol. 2, *Later Masters*), he was largely responsible for the renaissance of interest in the stories of the great Jewish masters. His interest in Hasidism, which permeated East European Jewry during the eighteenth and nineteenth centuries, as well as the Christian existentialism of Kierkegaard, led Buber to develop his own religious philosophy. From 1938–51, he was professor of sociology of religion at the Hebrew University in Jerusalem.

Buber's philosophy is centered around the question: How may I understand my experience of a relation with God? He examines this question undogmatically and in the context of its inner nature. He wants to go beyond mere concepts and feelings, toward a vision of a direct and immediate relation with God. The distinctions of "I" and "Thou" which Buber makes are secondary to the intricacy of the human situation. "I" and "Thou" are only a means of talking about the characteristics of humanity without reducing it to unyielding terminology.

According to Buber, we should consider the world as

twofold, and speak of it in the terms "I and Thou" and "I and It." These are primary word combinations that are indications of relationships and not intended to signify things. "I" is not to be interpreted singly; "I" should always be taken in relation to some one, or as experience with some thing. These relations arise in three categories: our life with nature, where words are not expressed; our life with others, where speech is an integral part of relationships; and our life with spiritual beings, where speech is induced within our beings and not aloud.

The relation to "Thou," a form of the Eternal Thou, is direct and in the present. The original relation goes back to primitive experience where speech indicated a wholeness of a relation, the true original unity. The world image of primitive man was based on the concept of a magical power (a Thou) from which all human power derived. Causality, therefore, is seen in a continuous sequence of regeneration of the magical power. The "I" in primitive experience is included in the relational event, not on a level of conscious self, but on a level of cosmic self. The realization of the self-conscious I comes through the external Thou. We understand the nature of this process in our growth from childhood, where aspects of primal experience occur.

We experience what surrounds us as perceptions of things, beings, events as actions, things of quality, events of moments, things in their place, events in time, and things and events bounded and measured by, and compared with, other things and events. The organization of all things and events is always with us; it is our "truth," and only through it can we be understood in relation to others. We deal with what exists over us as a single being, God. The qualities of this being are intangible and immeasurable. The justification of its reality lies deep within our soul. Mutual giving connects us with this being. We address it as Thou and give of ourselves to it. It addresses us as Thou and gives of itself to us. We are alone with it, and it means our connection with eternity. We see the world of It in space and time. The world of Thou does not exist in this context, although the specific Thou, relationally viewed as thing or being, becomes an It. It is the world in which we have to live, where our activity and grasp of knowledge occur. The I of "I and Thou" is different from the I of "I and It." The former is a person who is conscious of himself without a dependent relation. The latter is a person who is conscious of himself as the subject of experiencing and using.

Contact with the Thou is the goal of relation for it means eternal life. The more we are in contact with the Thou, the more fulfilling is the act of sharing, which constitutes all reality. The reality of the I stems from the fullness of its act of sharing. Individuality only differentiates the I from others, and combines it with the It. In this way, the I is unreal and nonexistent. The stronger the I of I and Thou, the more the I's are persons, not individuals.

Buber contends that the I and Thou relationship has strong cultural foundations and is definite in its structure. The relationship is not mystical in nature. Although it might be necessary to break with our daily habits of thought to comprehend the relationship, we do not have to break with the general patterns of human thought which have led us to the reality as God. God is an absolute person; we dedicate ourselves to God and our I and Thou relations to others. Conversation with God is our ever-present means of instruction to carry on in the world around us.

Buber's ideas have become well-known in a variety of fields, education, medicine, politics, sociology, poetry, theology, and philosophy, since the publication of his book *I and Thou* in Germany in the 1920s.

REFERENCES

Martin Buber, *I and Thou*, trans. by R. G. Smith. New York: Charles Scribner's Sons, 1958.

————, *Between Man and Man*. Boston: Beacon Press, 1961.

————, *God and Evil*. New York: Charles Scribner's Sons, 1953.

————, *Tales of the Hasidim* (Vol. 1, *Early Masters* and Vol. 2, *Later Masters*). New York: Schocken Books, 1947, 1948.

CARLOS CASTANEDA (19??–   ), an anthropologist, has become famous for his recording, analysis, and explication of his five years as a pupil of don Juan, a Yaqui Indian shaman, in a series of four books: *The Teachings of don Juan, A Separate Reality, Journey to Ixtlan,* and *Tales of Power.*

Born in Brazil, Castaneda attended UCLA and received his B.A. in 1962, his M.A. in 1964, and his Ph.D. in 1970. While an anthropology student at UCLA, in 1960 Castaneda encountered don Juan while doing research on the medicinal properties of plants in the Southwest and Mexico. He began serving his apprenticeship to him in June 1961, first in Arizona and then in Sonora, spending time with don Juan at irregular intervals that became more frequent during the summer months of 1961–64. Castaneda took notes, at first covertly, relying on his memory to reproduce his conversations with don Juan, until don Juan permitted him to openly record what went on. According to Castaneda, no photographing or tape recording was ever allowed. Castaneda ended his apprenticeship in 1965 voluntarily, returning in 1968 for a second cycle of apprenticeship, which ended in 1971.

Throughout his first years with don Juan, Castaneda had difficulty understanding the concepts of which don Juan spoke. He found that the only way to understand the wisdom that don Juan was trying to impart to him was to examine it in terms of how don Juan understood it: "Only in such terms could it be made evident and convincing." This entailed giving order to don Juan's conceptualizations in light of the fact that don Juan emphasized the uses of hallucinogenic plants as a means to perceive his knowledge. Castaneda records that "don Juan used, separately and on different occasions, three hallucinogenic plants: peyote (*Lophophora williamsii*),

Jimson weed (*Datura inoxia* syn. *D. meteloides*), and a mushroom (possibly *psilocybe mexicana*). Castaneda found that don Juan used the Jimson weed and the mushroom to acquire power, or what he called an "ally," and the peyote to gain "wisdom, or the knowledge of the right way to live." Castaneda calls the states which don Juan experienced via the use of these plants *states of nonordinary reality,* "to mean unusual reality versus the ordinary reality of everyday life." Don Juan considered these states to be the only means to pragmatic learning and to power.

Through a procedure of thought based on a specific order both in relationship to its operation and conceptualization, don Juan taught Castaneda a coherent belief system by means of a pragmatic and experimental method. The primary goal of the operative order of thought is to become a *man of knowledge.* Castaneda analyzes this process in terms of several givens which he considered integral to all of don Juan's teachings: that becoming a man of knowledge requires learning, strenuous labor, and entrance into a process that is never ending; that a man of knowledge does not deviate from his intent, possesses clarity of mind, is a "warrior" and has an "ally." These themes related to a way of behavior that functioned inherently from experiences of nonordinary reality. Who is to become a man of knowledge is a decision that is made by an impersonal power. Undergoing the strenuous labor involved in the pursuit of knowledge, according to Castaneda, means having the ability "to put forth dramatic exertion, achieve efficacy, and meet challenge." Being intent in this pursuit means being existentially frugal, sound in judgment, and not pursuant of that which is not a part of the established knowledge. Being clear in mind gives one freedom to "seek a path, knowledge of the specific purpose, and being fluid." Being a warrior implies having respect, fear, awakened sensibility, self-confidence, awareness of intent, and of the possible changes therein. Being engaged in the never-ending process that is becoming a man of knowledge (which is a goal essentially unattainable because of man's impermanency) means continually gaining control over the self, recognizing that man is subject to death and that dedication to knowledge is a means of fulfillment and satisfaction in life. The ally has the power that allows one to transcend ordinary reality. The allies of don Juan are Jimson weed and the mushroom. An ally as a concept is formless, perceived as a quality, is tamable, and has a rule. Don Juan called the rule the law; it was passed on from teacher to apprentice verbally; it was "the rigid organizing concept regulating all the actions that had to be executed and the behavior that had to be observed throughout the process of handling an ally."

At the end of his first apprenticeship with don Juan, Castaneda had personally adopted two "units" of the system don Juan was teaching him: the idea that there is a separate reality or separate world, and the idea that the separate reality is as utilizable as ordinary reality.

According to don Juan, a common-sense view of reality cannot be final; a world view is only an interpretation. What becomes a sensible interpretation, of which don Juan was a practitioner, is explicable only in terms of the system which reveals the sensible interpretation. A sorcerer like don Juan exists on the basis that all that is known of the world is description. As don Juan explains it, the only way to see beyond ordinary interpretation and ordinary description is by "stopping the world." In order to stop the world, "one had to learn the new description in a total sense, for the purpose of pitting against it the old one, and in that way break the dogmatic certainty, which we all share, that the validity of our perceptions, or our reality of the world, is not to be questioned."

REFERENCES

Carlos Castaneda, *The Teachings of Don Juan: A Yaqui Way of Knowledge*. New York: Ballantine Books, 1968.
————, *A Separate Reality: Further Conversations with Don Juan*. New York: Pocket Books, 1972.

————, *Journey to Ixtlan: The Lessons of Don Juan.* New York: Pocket Books, 1974.

————, *Tales of Power.* New York: Simon & Schuster, 1974.

EDGAR CAYCE (1877–1945), famous psychic healer and clairvoyant (called the "Sleeping Prophet"), was born in Kentucky and raised in a rural and religious environment. During his schooling, which lasted only through the seventh grade, he was said to have slept on his books and developed a photographic memory that helped him in his studies. Throughout his youth, he talked about experiences which indicated that he possessed a certain kind of mystical power, although he was not taken seriously. At twenty-one, Cayce suffered from a paralysis of the throat muscles. Doctors could not find a physical cause for the condition and treated him unsuccessfully with hypnosis. In 1901, Cayce, through the suggestion of a friend, entered a self-induced trance in which he determined the medication and therapy necessary to cure his problem. According to his son Hugh Lynn Cayce, from that point on, Cayce was invited by several Kentucky physicians to use his ability to diagnose illnesses and recommend treatment for their patients, which he did successfully. In 1910, the New York *Times* reported on this "Wonder Man" and his "unorthodox procedures." From that point on until his death in 1945, Cayce gave readings throughout the United States, diagnosing and prescribing treatments for thousands of people. The records of these readings, which number somewhere between nine thousand and fourteen thousand, are kept at the Association for Research and Enlightenment (ARE) in Virginia Beach, Virginia. This association, created to preserve Cayce's readings, also conducts research and experiments, and sponsors conferences, seminars, and lectures about psychic phenomena.

Cayce gave readings that covered a wide range of categories, the majority of which concentrated on understanding one's self and one's relation to God and fellow men. (Cayce could never remember what he said in the "sleep state" he entered to give the readings.) He gave physical readings that focused on specific ailments; life readings that dealt with psychological problems and took the form of marriage counseling, vocational counseling, etc.; Cayce gave dream interpretations; he gave readings which concerned mental and spiritual questions, especially what he called "the purpose of the soul's entrance on earth"; he gave readings about spiritual laws, prayer, and meditation for the purposes of healing. Not all of Cayce's readings were successful. However, the large percentage of them that were have been the subject matter for study.

In an effort to understand Cayce's powers, it has been said that he got his information from two sources in the mind: the *subconscious,* which consists of innumerable impressions from physical consciousness that are often not consciously known, and the *superconscious,* which is the seat of spirituality. It has been theorized that Cayce received information from his psychic perception of *unconscious memory* (which has been shown to exist in recent experiments whereby people remembered entire childhood events when certain exposed brain tissue was electrically stimulated); from *clairvoyant observation* of physical data, a kind of out-of-body experience in which Cayce was able to move his mind to the location of the person who had requested the reading; *telepathic communication* between subconscious or superconscious mind and that of living or dead persons; and a world of *thought forms* which Cayce often defined through dream interpretations.

It has also been concluded that the thoughts to which Cayce was "attuned" and the sources from which he drew the information for his readings were determined by the *suggestions*—the motives, attitudes, and desires—from the person requesting the reading, and Cayce's own physical, emotional, and mental state at the time.

In 1933, Cayce gave a reading on his own powers. According to his sons, in this reading Cayce revealed that "in previous reincarnations the entity known as Edgar Cayce developed the ability to function 'in the realms of psychic or mental forces' . . . and that spiritual development related to such abilities had taken place on the various planes between incarnations." Cayce described those factors which prevent activity "through the channels that pertain to psychic or mental or spiritual influences in the realms about the entity" as "unwillingness of the body-conscious to submit to the suggestions as pertaining to the information desired at that particular time. Or the activity of the physical in such a manner as to require the influence or supervision of the superconsciousness in the body, or ill health, at such a period. Or the mental attitudes of those about the body that are not in accord with the type, class, or character of information sought . . . Or there may be many variations of the combination of these, influencing one to another, as to the type, class, or real activity of the entity or soul that seeks the information." Cayce believed that being with God should be the ultimate goal for everyone, and that those who wish to better their relationship with God would be aided by their "spirit-mind," which "may give that as may be helpful in the experience of those who seek to know better their relationship to their Maker."

REFERENCES

Edgar Evans Cayce and Hugh Lynn Cayce, *The Outer Limits of Edgar Cayce's Powers.* New York: Harper & Row, 1971.

Hugh Lynn Cayce, *Venture Inward: A Quest for Spiritual and Psychological Insight Based on the Psychic Discoveries of Edgar Cayce.* New York: Harper & Row, 1964.

Hugh Lynn Cayce, ed., *Edgar Cayce on Diet and Health.* New York: Paperback Library, 1969.

Thomas Sugrue, *The Story of Edgar Cayce: There Is a River.* New York: Dell Books, 1942, 1945, 1970.

CHANGE OF LIFE. At a certain age both men and women experience what is commonly called a change of life: in the case of women, menopause; in the case of men, male climacteric.

Menopause is the phase in a woman's life during which menstrual periods gradually lessen, and finally stop altogether, because of a decline in the functioning of the ovaries. The human female is the only animal to experience menopause, which usually occurs between the ages of forty-eight and fifty-two. Currently, there are approximately twenty-seven million women who have reached the age of fifty and are experiencing, or will experience, this change of life. In essence, menopause signifies the conclusion of a woman's ability to conceive and bear children.

There are different kinds of menopause. Premature menopause occurs when menstruation ceases before the age of forty; in most cases, this occurs because of a late pregnancy. Late menopause occurs with irregular vaginal bleeding after the age of fifty-two; it can be the result of diabetes, or a tumor in the ovary, or an inherited tendency. Some doctors feel that late menopause increases the incidence of cancer of the uterus. Artificial menopause occurs as the result of the surgical removal of the uterus, ovaries, or both.

In 1967, a study done in Holland of more than 6,500 women between forty and sixty years of age revealed that menopause occurred at the average age of 51.4 years. The study revealed trends in the complaints women have from menopausal symptoms. For example, women who started menstruating at a late age complained more than women who started early; women who had pregnancies after the age of forty complained less than women who had their last children earlier; women from higher income groups and women of higher education complained less than other women; unmarried women complained less than married women.

Physiologically, menopause is the result of a decrease in the functioning of the ovaries, and, as a result, the production of the hormone estrogen. It has been discovered that although the ovaries might have totally ceased producing estrogen, the pituitary gland continues to produce gonadotrophins to induce the ovaries to produce estrogen. The result is large quantities of gonadotrophins in the blood, which might account for some of the symptoms of menopause.

Menopausal symptoms are characteristically hot flashes and the atrophy of the genitalia. Although hot flashes differ in women, typical are sensations of warmth in the neck, face, and upper body. This can be accompanied by a visible blush. The flashes can last for as long as two minutes and can occur up to ten or twenty times a day. At night, they might be manifest in profuse sweating. There are other vasomotor symptoms of menopause such as numbness, tingling of the hands and feet, heart palpitations, headaches, dizziness, and fainting. These symptoms are more rare than hot flashes and are caused by hormonal changes. They usually cease after one or two years. The menstrual pattern changes in quantity of flow, duration of flow, and length of time between periods; a six-month interval between periods is a sign that menstruation is going to stop. The genital organs deteriorate: The labia of the vagina become thinner, less elastic, and fatty; the vagina itself becomes drier and less elastic; the uterus and cervix shrink. Other menopausal signs might be thinning hair, growth of hair on the upper lip and chin, lack of elasticity and fullness of the breasts, increase in the size of the buttocks and hips, weight gain, headaches because of tension and anxiety, depression, and a possible lessening of sexual desire as a result of psychological stress, or, on the other hand, an increased sexual appetite because of the freedom from fear of conception.

Medical treatment for menopause involves correcting estrogen deficiency in order to relieve the symptoms caused by a lack of this hormone in sufficient amounts in the body. Oral dosages of estrogen are usually prescribed, in an amount that will correct the vasomotor malfunctions and relieve vaginal problems without causing vaginal or uterine bleeding. The treatment can last for three years, with gradually smaller amounts of estrogen prescribed.

Estrogen must be used discriminately, however, and it should not be prescribed if the woman suffers from blood clots, sickle-cell anemia, severe hypertension, liver disease, or cerebral vascular disease. Recent studies have also linked estrogen with cancer.

Treatment for the psychological disorders which might accompany the physical symptoms of menopause usually take the form of mild sedatives or tranquilizers to reduce tension. A well-balanced diet, exercise, and education and reassurance regarding menopause can be extremely helpful in preventing severe anxiety, tension, or depression.

Male climacteric (climacteric, derived from the Greek word meaning "the rung of a ladder") is very similar to the menopause in women. The climacteric usually occurs between the ages of forty-five and sixty, and can result in major physical and emotional changes which can be disruptive to health, career, and private life. In many cases, the climacteric male is not aware of the changes occurring in him, and therefore dealing with the resulting problems can be difficult.

There are numerous symptoms associated with the male climacteric, which are similar in nature to the symptoms of menopause, and generally affect the male body-mind relationship. The illnesses are frequently psychosomatic and can occur intermittently, singly or in numbers (i.e., stomach cramps, asthma, peptic ulcers, headaches, heart palpitations, etc.). It is important, however, not to dismiss such symptoms as being simply psychosomatic, as they may be related to a more serious disorder.

Many of the nonsexually related symptoms of the male climacteric are such that together they signify one essential problem stemming from an external source. Typical symptoms are 1) an enlargement of the prostate gland, causing a problem with urinary regulation; 2) fluid retention in the tissues of hands and feet (a symptom more common to middle-aged women); 3) hot flashes, often followed by chills, then sweating, because of temporary loss of coordination between the autonomic nerve fibers and their control of blood circulation; 4) *paroxysmal tachycardia,* or irregular heartbeat, causing the heartbeat to accelerate, the result of chronic mental or emotional stress; 5) *pseudoangina,* a sharp pain in the center or left side of the chest, a symptom of anxiety (vs. a defect in the heart); 6) peptic ulcers caused by an excessive production of hydrochloric acid in the stomach; 7) itching and formication, a sensation of stinging under the skin, the result of disturbances in the autonomic nervous system, the duration of which is completely subjective; 8) air hunger, the subjective feeling of not having enough air to breath, which can result in hyperventilation; 9) liver spots on the surface of the skin (not to be confused with freckles or moles, which are not signs of aging); 10) headaches, usually the result of hormonal disturbances and emotional tension in veins, arteries, cranial nerves, muscles; 11) *osteoporosis,* the increased porosity of the bones (more common in middle-aged women).

There are several sexually related symptoms of the male climacteric which are the result of *secondary impotence.* This condition results in a decline in potency (not to be confused with sterility), and the acquired inability to produce an erection. It can take four forms: permanent loss of potency which occurs when a male accepts the fact that former sexual capacity is gone and does not seek help to remedy the problem; temporary or periodical impotence; weak or short-lasting erection, the result of a variety of psychological factors; and premature ejaculation. These symptoms are all related to the essential fear of erectile failure, which increases its probability. When the symptoms of the male climacteric are severe, some men have been driven to extremes such as seeking a sex change through surgery or becoming homosexual. The climacteric male can also lose all interest in sexual activity, which is not necessarily related to impotency. The accompanying mental and emotional symptoms manifest themselves in marked irritability, insomnia, moodiness, abnormal fatigue, weakened mental acuity, loss of confidence, and change in behavioral patterns.

The middle-aged man is faced with an entire spectrum of realizations regarding his habits, his familial circumstances, his fears, which often have been suppressed for a long time and suddenly come to the surface (fear of aging, fear of women, fear of fathering more children, fear of impotence). In order to ease the climacteric condition, middle-aged men can reassess their activities within their family and business by paying specific attention to emotional habits, which can be restructured, how their leisure time is spent, ways to reduce obsessive work habits. By avoiding the circumstances which can create tensions, the rate of occurrence of some psychosomatic illnesses, and the inability to have sexual relations, can be decreased. The climacteric male is free to explore new possibilities for achieving a satisfactory sex life. Although the climacteric can be medically treated, it is crucial that the middle-aged man face up to the situation first, without feeling ashamed or embarrassed to seek help.

Middle-aged men and women should recognize the similarities of the unavoidable problems and difficulties they may experience at this stage of their lives. In this way, they can openly support each other, and transform the experience into a more positive one, reaping the rewards that this period of life can offer.

REFERENCES

Sheldon H. Cherry, *The Menopausal Myth.* New York: Ballantine Books, 1976.

Wendy Cooper, *Don't Change: A Biological Revolution for Women.* New York: Stein and Day, 1975.

Madeline Gray, *The Changing Years: What to Do About the Menopause.* New York: Doubleday & Co., 1973.

Helmut J. Ruebsaat, M.D., and Raymond Hull, *The Male Climacteric.* New York: Hawthorn Books, 1975.

SRI CHIMNOY (1931–) is a master of Yoga. Born in Bengal, he began practicing meditation at a young age. In 1964, he came to the United States to work for the Indian consulate. During the past ten years he has acquired a number of disciples, among them Santana, the recording artist, John McLaughlin, the guitarist, and Peter Serkin, the pianist. He has established meditation centers in Europe, Canada, the United States, the Far East, and the Caribbean, and visits these countries annually to lecture. Since 1970, he has held weekly meditations for the delegates and staff of the United Nations, and has delivered the monthly Dag Hammarskjöld lectures. His daily meditations and morning services are broadcast on several radio and television stations.

According to Sri Chimnoy, the way to discover your inner reality is through spirituality, which is the uniting force between you and God. It embodies an infinite freedom from the troubles which arise in the course of life. Spirituality directs you to find reality on earth. Spirituality can grow aided by the discoveries of science which make the fulfillment of practical needs possible. Spirituality, if sincere, can bring God to you quickly and fully.

Sri Chimnoy believes that there should be no fear in self-knowledge, for in knowing yourself and living your inner life, you become closer to God. When you experience your soul, you conquer fear. Knowing how your inner world functions permits you to see, understand, and experience the outer world with clarity. You have to understand yourself as "infinite, eternal, and immortal consciousness."

Sri Chimnoy considers Yoga to be the Universal Truth and the most important experience of life. Yoga provides the way to self-knowledge. It demands that you be self-disciplined, accepting of the world, and master of your senses. Pure reasoning can only lead to frustration and away from the Infinite Wisdom which comes only from God. You must be dedicated and aspiring to God. In that way, life will become your experience of both wisdom and faith.

Your goals should be discovering Truth, Peace, and Bliss in the love of God. Sri Chimnoy recognizes false

goals as human love, physical beauty, and material
wealth. The Supreme Duty is loving God through realizing God and loving mankind. When you aspire to God,
you must have faith in yourself, faith in the living Guru;
only then can you perform the Supreme Duty, the duty
of self-discovery, the realization of God.

For Sri Chimnoy, God is Love, Joy, and the Eternal
Giver. God shapes you in his image; you are God's
dream, reality, pride, and the embodiment of God's
Existence-Conscious-Bliss. To please God, you should
never underrate your inner capacity or exaggerate your
self-imposed responsibilities, nor should you believe that
to realize God is futile. Denying the existence of God
is to deny yourself the path to fulfillment of faith, reality,
and oneness. You must offer yourself to God. This
process demands a self-control that is achieved through
continual self-examination, and a discovery of inner
joy. Inner peace comes from spirituality in your access
to the soul, in inner silence, in aspiration, in God's
grace. The secret of inner peace lies in the truth which
God has given you on earth and which God sustains
with love.

Sri Chimnoy bases his ideology on the attainment
of self-knowledge through meditation. In meditation,
you strive for the Infinite Real, the Eternal Real, the
Absolute Real. The key to meditation is achieving conscious and constant oneness with God. In order to
meditate, you require inspiration from the scriptures
as well as the aid of a spiritual teacher to awaken your
aspirations, which will bring you to self-realization and
God-realization.

Meditation is a means of self-discipline. Meditation
"purifies the heart." It is a way to transcend human
understanding and reach immeasurable infiniteness.
Meditation shows you the way to perfection of human
life. It takes you beyond frustration and toward the
Supreme which is "the Person, higher than the unmanifest."

Perfection exists on the level of your inner world and
the level of your outer world. In the inner world, per-

fection comes through realization; in the outer world, through manifestation. To live spontaneously and in constant oneness with God is the achievement of perfection. To speculate about perfection is only to demonstrate your ignorance.

Your consciousness teaches you how to find perfection and realize God. Sri Chimnoy describes it as Power and Light working together: as Light, your consciousness becomes one with inspiration and aspiration that are deep within your inner world; as Power, you are allowed to overcome your ignorance of the external world.

There are several kinds of consciousness, each one being symptomatic of your will. The ultimate consciousness, that of Existence-Consciousness-Delight, is Infinite, Eternal, and Immortal. Living in Existence, consciousness allows you to receive the offerings of Divinity. Living inside its own domain, Consciousness allows you to share experience with Divinity. Living in Delight, consciousness allows you to realize your humanity and fulfill the realization of Divinity.

The end of all knowledge is the knowledge of God; the beginning of Divine knowledge marks the end of human knowledge. Divine knowledge carries you to Immortality; it is fulfilling and "illumining." In the pursuit of Divine knowledge, you must learn to know the living embodiment of Peace, Light, Bliss, and Power, which are Divine qualities. The end of all knowledge is the beginning of self-knowledge. With help from a spiritual teacher, you find self-knowledge, you make your self-discovery, you have God knowledge.

There are three ways to see God, according to Sri Chimnoy. You can see God "through a window"; this can be done by concentrating on God six hours a day. You can see God "through an open door"; this can be done by meditating for twelve hours a day. You can see God "face-to-face"; this can be done by meditating twenty-four hours a day. When you constantly see God face-to-face, you begin to have transcendental knowledge.

You should share your knowledge of God with mankind, and not hoard it. You should make a promise of dedicated self-service to yourself and mankind. Your function on earth is to practice your inner teaching, which is loving for love's sake and loving for God's sake. Science will take care of discovering truth of the earth on earth; spirituality, in the practice of Yoga, will take care of discovering truth of the universe on earth. When you shake away doubts of God by purifying your nature through knowledge of God, you will see that the discoveries of science, spirituality, and of your oneness with God will work together moving toward the Eternal God. When you satisfy your Divine Duty in aspiration, you will be rewarded with God the Realization, God the Liberation, and your "eternal ever-transcending journey."

The Inner Promise is a series of lectures given by Sri Chimnoy from 1968–70 in the United States, England, the Philippines, and other countries.

REFERENCES

Sri Chimnoy, *The Inner Promise, Paths to Self-Perfection.* New York: Simon & Schuster, 1970.

————, *The Goal Is One.* Jamaica, New York: 1974.

————, *Songs of the Soul.* New York: Herder & Herder, 1971.

————, *The Supreme and His Four Children.* New York: Fleet Press Corp., 1973.

CHIROPRACTIC (from the Greek *cheiro* and *praktikos,* meaning "done by hand") is a method of medical treatment, based on the theory that disease is the result of a disturbance in the normal functioning of the nerves, that involves the manual manipulation of the structures of the body (e.g., the spine) in a variety of ways. No drugs or surgery are used.

Although practiced for centuries as a natural healing method, chiropractic was officially founded by Daniel David Palmer in 1895. Palmer had studied with Paul Caster, a practitioner of magnetic healing, and had practiced this method of treatment himself for ten years.

(Magnetic healing derived from the work of Anton Mesmer, an Austrian physician who had determined that cures of seemingly organic disorders could be effected through manual contact with specific areas of the body.) In order to answer questions he had about the causes of various diseases, Palmer began to experiment. In 1895, he performed an experiment which involved correcting the positioning of a vertebra of a deaf man. The result was an improvement in the man's hearing ability. This led to a formal investigation into the effects of chiropractic medicine. Fifteen years later, Palmer published *The Science and Art and Philosophy of Chiropractic* in which he outlines the first principles of chiropractic relating the physical structure of the body to its functions. In it he states that ". . . disease is not a thing, but a *condition* . . ." and that "disease is a disturbed condition . . . an abnormal performance of certain functions . . ." According to Palmer's theory, the abnormal performance was the result of pressure from a displaced vertebra or another bone on the nerves causing them to "become excited, irritated and more or less inflamed . . ." resulting in nervous tension which could be relieved by the realignment of the bones in question. The modern theory of chiropractic is that body tissue is maintained and controlled by nervous impulses; when these impulses are disrupted, the result is disease.

According to Dr. Julius Dintenfass, a practicing chiropractor for more than thirty years, chiropractic care maintains the "stability of self-regulating systems of the body to allow the recuperative powers of the body to function normally." A chiropractic diagnosis requires knowledge of your medical history, as well as analysis through the examination of the mechanics of your body by means of inspection, palpitation, mobility tests, muscle tests, x-ray, measurement of the effects of gravity on your body. It also includes an examination of your posture to locate *subluxations* (or displacements) of the spine, muscle spasms, and tissue and organ malfunctions, etc.

Treatment procedure involves the use of specialized manipulative techniques and *adjustments,* which are aimed at correcting the mechanical disorders of the spine and other areas of the body. These techniques include the use of electrical devices, traction, the application of heat or cold, muscle stimulation, ultrasound, and basic exercises for your posture and normal body function.

Chiropractic is used in treating both somatic and visceral disorders. Of somatic disorders such as arthritis, bursitis, neuritis, sciatica, the recovery or improvement is high. Of visceral disorders such as simple colitis, simple hypertension, migraine headaches, and constipation, many of the cases treated have been reported as relieved or cured through chiropractic.

Although legally recognized in the United States (and other countries), the practice of chiropractic has met with a great deal of opposition from the American Medical Association. As of 1968, it was excluded from the Medicare program, in an action recommended to Congress by the Department of Health, Education, and Welfare. However, this order was rescinded in July 1973, and chiropractic is now part of the Medicare program in certain treatments. The scientific foundation of the practice has been generally disputed, as well as the use of x-ray in a chiropractic examination. Public research funds have been denied to chiropractic training institutes. Despite these controversies, over thirty million Americans have been treated chiropractically, as reported by the International Chiropractic Association in 1969, and there are more than twenty-three thousand licensed practitioners of chiropractic.

REFERENCES

Julius Dintenfass, D.C., *Chiropractic: A Modern Way to Health.* New York: Pyramid House, 1970.

Ralph Lee Smith, *At Your Own Risk: The Case Against Chiropractic.* New York: Trident Press, 1969.

ALEX COMFORT (1920–), editor of *The Joy of Sex* and *More Joy of Sex,* has brought to the public's attention an honest, forthright treatment of sexual intercourse and methods in which sexual activity can be improved and enhanced.

Comfort was born in London and was educated at Trinity College in Cambridge, and is the recipient of several degrees including a Ph.D. in biochemistry. He has been a physician, a lecturer in physiology, a research fellow in gerontology, and the director of the Medical Research Council Group on Aging. He is a poet, novelist, essayist, playwright, and author of texts on aging and sexual behavior. In 1962, along with Bertrand Russell and others, Comfort was jailed for efforts to organize a protest against nuclear arms in England. Comfort calls himself "a medical biologist, writer, and pamphleteer, dividing time equally between science, literature, and politico-social agitation of various kinds, chiefly connected with anarchism, pacifism, sex law reforms, and application of sociological ideas to society generally."

Comfort chose to edit *Joy of Sex* because the premise on which the book is based—a gourmet guide to lovemaking—was unique. The book is the result of work done by a couple, one of whom is a practicing physician, and has been elaborated upon by experts in sexual behavior. Comfort contributes biological explanations, while the authors furnish explanations of sexual foreplay and modes of sexual intercourse, emphasize various means to make sexual activity more exciting, and define terminology connected with sexual behavior. The authors also discuss problems that might hamper sexual activity such as age, bisexuality, the climacteric, etc. Comfort defines *The Joy of Sex* as "the first explicitly sexual book for the coffee table."

One of the basic intentions of *The Joy of Sex* is "to cure the notion, born of nondiscussion, that common sex needs are odd or weird." Comfort considers sex the safest of all human activities. Enjoying sex and wanting to be adventuresome and uninhibited in sexual behavior are, by nature, a product of loving. Sex becomes a means to express all of the self. In this way, it is important for you as an adult to be less self-conscious and not deny yourself the pleasure of fulfilling your sexual needs. According to the authors, "bed is the place to play all the games you have ever wanted to play, at the play-level. . . ." Sex is play, an expression of love, and an activity that is enhanced by your creative imagination.

The Joy of Sex proposes two rules for good sex: Don't do anything that you cannot enjoy; and find out about your partner's needs so that you can satisfy them. These "rules" are guide lines for a satisfactory give-and-take relationship; partners in a well-founded sexual relationship should not only enjoy their own individual satisfaction but also gain pleasure in seeing the other respond. In this context it is important for you to be able to respond sexually. The exploration of your adventurous sexual nature is a healthy one provided you engage in nothing "silly, antisocial, or dangerous," for "finding out someone else's needs and your own, and how to express them in bed, is not only interesting and educative but rewarding, and what sexual love is about."

The theme of *More Joy of Sex* stresses the development of relations that go beyond the physical aspects of sexual activity. Comfort explains that development is a major factor in the activity of making love; you have sex not only for pleasure but to measure the understanding and growth that evolves between you and your partner. Sexual activity helps to strengthen relationships. Partners should realize that the expression of sexuality should not be feared. Improving your sexual identity is a way of getting in touch with yourself. Furthermore, a physical relationship is a means by which to tap the source of "self-comprehension." The ramifications of the physical aspect of sexual behavior between two people can be "warm feelings of identity and concern, more complicated feelings of dominance and hostility, and tensions between wanting to be possessed by another and not wanting to be wholly possessed." Surmounting the problems that accompany the myths about how sexuality is supposed to be expressed is a way of breaking down barriers, and allowing two people to be together and enjoy each other apart from specific genital excitement. This means learning that "people aren't dangerous, that the body isn't shameful, and that no rewarding sexual sensation is abnormal or bad unless it's antisocial in some way."

More Joy explores how you can increase your sensuality, particularly by means of body language. Your sensuality can be increased by focusing on other means of body stimulation, for example, massage, masturbation, touching the skin, etc., or sharing the lovemaking experience in the company of another couple by watching them and enjoying their sexual experiences. Therapy can also be helpful for learning more about your sexual capacity and dealing with sexual problems that you cannot solve simply by reading a book.

REFERENCES
Alex Comfort, ed., *The Joy of Sex: A Cordon Bleu Guide to Lovemaking.* New York: Simon & Schuster, 1972.
————, *More Joy of Sex: A Lovemaking Companion to the Joy of Sex.* New York: Simon & Schuster, 1974.

DANCE THERAPY is the psychotherapeutic use of movement as a process which furthers the emotional and physical integration of the individual, according to Claire Schmais.

Dance therapy was founded by Marian Chace, a dancer with the Denishawn Company in the late thirties. Chace had studied the dance forms of other cultures, and choreographed, taught, and performed her own works as well. In her dance school in Washington, D.C., Chace's approach focused on the individual student. As a result of her unique techniques, her students felt her classes to be more than traditional dance classes; they described feelings of emotional well-being and release. The therapeutic aspects of movement eventually aroused the interest of the psychiatric community. In 1942, Marian Chace was invited to work at St. Elizabeth's Hospital by psychiatrists interested in exploring new approaches to group therapy. Her work with patients was so successful that a dance therapy program was formed, and it became an integral part of the over-all treatment plan at the hospital.

After World War II, dance therapy was used in the treatment of soldiers, both for mental illness and relief of tension. During the 1950s, the introduction of the use of tranquilizers on mental patients, although render-ing them more approachable, did not necessarily make them more communicative. In this regard, dance therapy was used as a means of nonverbal communication by which patients could express their feelings individually and collectively through movement. The sensitivity training movement of the 1960s explored the use of dance therapy for the neurotic patient on a one-to-one basis, and it gained status as a viable primary therapy. The American Dance Therapy Association was founded in 1966 to create professional standards and to set up a communications network for dance therapists in the country.

Dance therapy is based on the concept of body-mind integration, and the belief that a realistic and positive body image is a fundamental part of a healthy indi-vidual. All body movement has a psychological com-ponent, and the body is a reflection of internal feeling states. The body holds our kinesthetic memory and is the sum of all our experiences; it contains our history. Awareness of the body leads to awareness of feelings.

The role of the dance therapist is one of facilitating movement. The therapist seeks to widen the patient's range of movement in order to 1) increase behavioral choices; 2) increase feelings of self-worth by develop-ing a more positive body image; 3) create an awareness of body parts, their use and capabilities; 4) put a patient in touch with his or her feelings by relating them to their movement components; 5) increase the patient's ability to socialize through a group experience; 6) encourage the sense of self by permitting the patient to initiate group movement. In working toward these goals, the therapist will pick up cues from the patient and reflect the patient's movements, as well as feeling tone, in order to promote self-awareness in the patient and a feeling of acceptance by the therapist.

Dance therapists work in individual and group situations, adjusting their goals and methods according to the specific needs. The length of a therapy session, which can range from fifteen minutes to one hour, depends largely upon the attention span of the individual or group. Sessions are usually much shorter with groups of small children than with an adult group. Some therapists will use music or props such as balls or mats as an aid in therapy.

A dance therapist is generally trained in dance, movement observation, anatomy, psychology, and group process. Formerly, all dance therapists were self-taught or taught by another dance therapist. Now, five universities in the United States offer graduate degrees in dance therapy. The American Dance Therapy Association has five chapters across the country, with approximately 950 members and 350 dance therapists working actively in the field.

Movement therapies have become an acceptable part of the psychiatric field, although the psychiatric community considers dance therapy to be an adjunctive therapy rather than a primary therapy. The awareness of the body as a reflection of feeling, a consideration furthered by such schools as bioenergetics, has strengthened the credibility of dance therapy. Educators of autistic and retarded children, geriatric institutions and organizations, and mental hospitals have set up programs of treatment using dance therapy, having had positive results with it in initial experimental stages.

REFERENCES

Claire Schmais, "Dance Therapy in Perspective," *Dance Therapy Focus on Dance VII*.

The American Dance Therapy Association publishes monographs of their meetings: American Dance Therapy Association, Suite 216, E Century Plaza, Columbia, Md. 21044.

DIVORCE. Four hundred thousand couples were divorced in the United States in 1963. Ten years later, the number of divorces nearly doubled. When more closely examined, these statistics also reveal that one out of every nine adults in America has gone through the divorce process, that many divorces occur in the seventh year of marriage, that seemingly successful marriages of fifteen years or more are being terminated, that many people are simply dissolving their marriages informally. Because of this increasing divorce rate, the literature and counseling programs aimed at ameliorating the emotional and legal problems that often accompany the process have flourished recently. The overall psychological approach is essentially to make divorce acceptable.

Mel Krantzler, author of *Creative Divorce,* has established himself as a popular divorce expert. According to Krantzler, divorce is a crisis that elicits three types of response: a new kind of behavior that must be adopted once you have been forced out of your daily routine; the expressions of feelings that evolved in the past but were left untapped and, if resolved, could have resulted in your happiness in marriage; and the expression of emotional energies. Dealing with these responses can become a serious problem unless divorce is seen as a *process* rather than a punishment.

Considering divorce a process implies 1) recognizing the death of a relationship; 2) accepting the emotions which accompany it; 3) understanding that, as a result of divorce, a new and independent you can emerge. Easing the initial pain in the separation that precedes divorce at first can be a matter of adopting new attitudes: facing your children as a single human being, understanding that you alone can deal with the responsibilities formerly designated for your partner, enjoying your free time, and acquiring positive feelings. If these attitudes can be put into practice, Krantzler believes they will lay the groundwork for a pattern for personal growth.

A couple contemplating divorce will normally have

a difficult time coming to grips with their emotions. This can result in concealing the reality of the situation, an act which Krantzler feels will only make the process of overcoming the divorce trauma more drawn out and agonizing than necessary. In order to avoid the fantasies, hostility, anger, or withdrawal which can be the result of what Krantzler has labeled *separation shock,* he recommends several rules to follow which will help you to commit yourself to your real feelings. He recommends that each individual make an effort to "stick to business" when dealing with those inevitable meetings concerning finances, children, etc.; "be alert to double signals" coming from either partner which might be misconstrued; avoid blame; respect your former partner's independence and make your own evident; avoid expressions of superficial friendship toward your former partner.

Your status and personal growth as a single individual can be considered well-established when the bitterness and resentment toward your former spouse is depleted, surfacing only in occasional flashes of anger; you are more interested in solving your problems than complaining about them; you are not ashamed to get in touch with old friends or make new acquaintances; you take the responsibility of satisfying your interests and pleasures; you no longer judge other men and/or women in the same context in which you judged your former spouse; you realize that your situation is not unique and that divorce is simply the means to end a marriage that is self-destructive.

According to Krantzler, there are certain traps that you can fall into on the way toward reestablishing yourself emotionally on firm ground, i.e., making unwarranted generalizations, which prevent you from tending to yourself; expecting to be self-fulfilling; expecting the occurrence of ideal situations; overaccepting an unsatisfactory life; being overly defensive; living vicariously through others; expecting that you can be "whole" again only with the help of another person.

At the core of Krantzler's solution to the problems

inherent in the divorce process is his idea of creative living. After coming face-to-face with your feelings of guilt, anger, anxiety, etc., you reach a point where you recognize the challenges and excitement that are part of your new life as an individual and that, in life, you are dealing with *choices,* not inevitabilities. In making this effort, you will discover qualities you never knew you had. You will be able to reassess your values, build new sets of priorities, make new friends, have new relationships with other men and women, cope with your children, etc. Divorce essentially sparks a new kind of self-knowledge. You can see your real feelings in contrast to society's expectations; you can take risks and make mistakes that supplement your growth; you can set realistic goals and move ahead in life, self-confident and self-assertive; and when you need it, you can seek help either professionally or from a friend.

New Horizons, a counseling service in which Krantzler is an adviser, has been effective along the above guide lines. A practical handbook such as *Dealing With Divorce* can give you the information necessary regarding the divorce laws of a particular state, divorce counselors in the United States, and the practical implications of divorce, financial and other.

REFERENCES

Edmond Addeo and Robert Burger, *Inside Divorce: Is It What You Really Want?* New York: Chilton, 1975.

J. Epstein, *Divorce in America.* New York: E. P. Dutton & Co., 1974.

Mel Krantzler, *Creative Divorce: A New Opportunity for Growth.* New York: New American Library, 1974.

Robert K. Moffet and Jack F. Scherer, *Dealing With Divorce.* Boston: Little, Brown & Co., 1976.

DREAMS are a product of the seemingly undirected functioning of the brain while you sleep. The interpretation of dreams has been a matter of study for over a thousand years. In the second century A.D., Artemidorus Daldianus compiled a manual of dream interpretations called the *Oneirocritica,* which was still popular in the nineteenth century. Many ancient interpretations of dreams have been incorporated into modern-day interpretations.

Dreams have become integral to psychology and have been used to unlock the recesses of the mind. Freud was the first in modern times to delve into the interpretation of dreams, working to find their causes, the determinants of their occurrence, as well as a scientific method of interpreting them. Freud recognized that dreams are expressions of the unconscious, and that they are a channel into which the suppressed thoughts of waking life are routed. According to Freud, dreams were the primary substance of psychoanalysis.

Carl Jung, an early associate of Freud's, took another view of dreams. Jung believed that the content of dreams demonstrated the "secrets of inner life and reveal to the dreamer hidden factors of his personality." Dreams contain aspects of human nature, symbolized in universal and primordial terms, i.e., archetypes. According to Jung, interpreting dreams was a matter of considering them as "true symbols—that is to say, as expressions of something not yet consciously recognized or conceptually formulated." Jung believed that dreams should be analyzed, not by means of association but by a method of *exegesis;* dreams should be considered in terms that would clarify the situations of real life that they expressed; dreams and dream images should be considered real and not fantastic.

Erich Fromm, a prominent voice in modern psychology and psychiatry, defines the activity of dreaming using Freud's concepts as a base. However, he takes issue with the question of how sleep affects general mental activity. Fromm regards sleeping and waking as two modes of existence, characterized respectively by the unconscious and the conscious. The unconscious should be judged relative to consciousness, and vice versa. The subject matter of dreams is not necessarily distinctive of the absence of time-space; for in waking states we are able to transcend time-space in thinking. Rather, dream content is a product of thinking and feeling apart from the "acting" of waking existence. Therefore, how we interpret and understand dreams should not be in terms of waking-state conditions. They should be seen as existing in relation to the state of existence in which they occur (either sleeping or waking). Fromm observes that dreams often counteract the way in which we are influenced by the external world in that, in dreams, we often have qualities superior to those of our waking state. This observation calls into question the "exclusive truth" aspect of Freud's analysis of dreams. Fromm contends that Freudian analysis neglects "the paradoxical fact that we are not only less reasonable and less decent in our dreams but that we are also more intelligent, wiser, capable of better judgment when we are asleep than when we are awake."

Much of the reanalysis of dream interpretation has occurred as a result of the physiological studies made of dreaming within recent years, since the experiments conducted by Nathaniel Kleitman, E. Aserinsky, and W. Dement in 1953, in which sleep was electrically monitored. These experiments correlated dreaming to the state of sleep known as REM (rapid eye movements). They revealed that dreams can be measured by the tracings of brain waves that occur during REM sleep. Kleitman's studies also revealed that dreams can be in color; they can occur in split seconds; dreams disappear rapidly from memory; life circumstances affect dreams; if problems are suggested before sleep, they can be solved during sleep; external sounds and sensations can be incorporated into dreams. At the beginning of a night's sleep, REM dream periods last from ten to twenty minutes and dreams are usually about recent events. At the end of a night's sleep, REM dream periods last longer and the dreams are usually more bizarre. Overall, approximately 20 per cent of sleep time is spent dreaming.

There are several people who have been recognized for reviewing the interpretation of dreams with the new information available for dream study. Montague Ullman's theories relate to the Kleitman studies and the idea that dreams should be recognized for what they reveal rather than what they hide. Calvin Hall, who has documented and interpreted dreams at his Institute of Dream Research for twenty-five years, believes that dreams have a language of their own and do not necessarily avoid reality. Thomas French uses a clinical method of interpretation and deals with focal conflict of interpersonal relations as the prime instigator of dreams. George Klein and Robert White approach psychoanalysis with a method that includes a psychology of dreaming.

Elsie Sechrist, whose association with Edgar Cayce led her to become seriously interested in dream interpretation, theorizes that dreams emanate from several sources: your multileveled subconscious; the subconscious of another person with whom you can communicate; the superconscious; and extremely high planes, i.e., God. According to Sechrist, physical dreams originate in the upper levels of the subconscious and are stimulated by sounds, feelings, or pressures in the external surroundings that affect your body and senses. This same level of the subconscious also deals with day-to-day problems. From a deeper level come dreams about diet, exercise, and physical health; at an even deeper level, mental and emotional dreams originate and often contain warnings of emotional tensions as well as factors of encouragement pertaining to your life. The superconscious is the seat of extrasensory-perception dreams, inspirational, and creative dreams. According to Sechrist, dreams, visions, and experiences that relate to the meaning of life, the nature of the high spiritual plane, and the interrelationship between the two are received through the superconscious.

Sechrist believes that dreams can be an important source of information in numerous ways: for understanding yourself; for guidance in practical matters; for encouragement and inspiration; for stimulating creativity; as record of psychic sensitivity and experiences;

for realizing responsibility to immediate relationships; for developing your spiritual nature; for gaining inner peace and awareness of your inner being.

The most efficient way to recall your dreams is to keep a dream diary. Have paper and pencil at your bedside so that you can write down your dreams as soon as you wake up. You can also train yourself to wake up in the middle of sleep to record a dream. The more you practice this, the more material you will have to work with for the purpose of eventually interpreting your dreams. You will be able to recognize a vocabulary of symbolism that does not necessarily correspond to the interpretations of dreams commonly found in dream glossaries. Sechrist suggests that you pay attention to the settings of dreams, the people involved in your dreams, the activity of the dreams, colors, feelings, and words.

Interpreting your own dreams is a matter of discovering techniques which satisfy you. According to David Graham, "Dream interpretation is not easy. . . . It requires time and much patience, but the old adage is true when it says that nothing worthwhile is easy, and the purpose . . . is to help you to help yourself in finding the path to happiness and awareness through your dreams."

A process called *creative dreaming* has been advanced by Patricia Garfield who believes that you can learn to "shape" your dreams and make them useful by controlling their subject matter. Garfield has studied the dream processes of yogis, the interpretation of dreams by the Senoi people of Malaysia, the ways in which the American Indians and ancient Greeks used dreams, and the ways in which dreams have been used by writers, artists, and other creative people. This research yielded much information that she has incorporated into her theories of creative dreaming.

Creative dreaming is the result of acquiring certain abilities which will enable you to give yourself feedback in order to observe yourself and unify your personality. In order to dream creatively it is necessary to accept dreams as a meaningful part of life and accept the fact that it is possible to consciously influence the content of your dreams. You should be eager to experience as much as possible in your waking life so that you can later apply this material in dreams. Choose a subject that you want to dream about, concentrate on that subject, as in a meditation. Expose yourself in waking life to the things that you fear so that you will not have fearful dreams. Expose yourself to positive elements in your environment that you want to dream about. Dream control will result from increasing your capacity for concentration and attention so that you realize the subject you have chosen to dream about. Practicing dream control will expand your consciousness into an awareness of your dream states. You will, according to Garfield, be able to understand yourself more completely and discover the uniqueness that lies within the structure of your personality.

REFERENCES

Edward Frank Allen, *The Complete Dream Book*. New York: Warner Paperback Library, 1966.

Erich Fromm, *The Forgotten Language: An Introduction to the Understanding of Dreams, Fairy Tales and Myths*. New York: Grove Press, 1951.

Patricia Garfield, *Creative Dreaming*. New York: Ballantine Books, 1974.

David Graham, *Dream Your Way to Happiness and Awareness: A Guide to Remembering and Deciphering Your Dreams*. New York: Warner Paperback Library, 1975.

Richard M. Jones, *The New Psychology of Dreaming*. New York: Viking Press, 1970.

Gay Gaer Luce, *Body Time: Physiological Rhythms and Social Stress*. New York: Bantam Books, 1971.

Elsie Sechrist, *Dreams: Your Magic Mirror*. New York: Cowles Education Corp., 1968.

DRUGS AND THE MIND. Different drugs have different effects on the brain. In general, drugs can alter the functioning of the brain's chemical transmitter-receptor system which carries messages for nervous impulses. Drugs can act similarly or as a substitute for the naturally existing chemical substances present in the brain; drugs can speed up the process of message transmission or they can stop it.

Within recent years, confusion about the use of drugs has contributed to their abuse and has given rise to criticism of their use. This confusion can be attributed to the lack of information made available to the general public about the components of drugs and the lack of documentation concerning the effect that drugs can have, both physical and psychological.

There are five kinds of drugs: *narcotics, sedatives, tranquilizers, stimulants,* and *hallucinogens,* all of which affect the chemistry of the brain and induce some form of behavioral change, the intensity of which depends upon the dosage.

Narcotics, which include morphine-like drugs (e.g., heroin) are called opiates. Used medically, opiates serve as pain killers. Their manufacture and distribution are controlled by law. The physical effects of opiates are drowsiness and a decrease in physical activity. Psychological effects are reduced sensitivity to all stimuli, reduced tension and anxiety, and feelings of euphoria. The result of their regular use to the point where a tolerance is developed and the dosage must be increased to achieve the same physical effects is addiction. Narcotics withdrawal often results in severe symptoms, including nervousness, sleeplessness, muscle twitching, vomiting, increase in respiration and blood pressure and temperature, and even death. Some drugs, such as paregoric, contain small amounts of opiates and are available over the counter.

Sedatives, which include barbiturates, are medically used in the treatment of epilepsy, high blood pressure, insomnia, and some psychological problems. Barbiturates can be taken orally, intravenously, or rectally. When overused, the effects are dulled reaction ability, emotional instability, irritability. Like narcotics, they produce a tolerance, and, therefore, a physical and/or psychological dependence on them can occur. Withdrawal results in symptoms of nervousness, nausea, headaches, insomnia, a drop in blood pressure. If severe, there can be convulsions, which are sometimes fatal, delirium, and hallucinations.

Alcohol is considered a drug, despite its social acceptance. It acts as a depressant on the central nervous system, and its effects are similar to those of barbiturates. An overdose of alcohol acts in the same way as an overdose of narcotics or sedatives, inhibiting respiration and depriving the brain of oxygen. Alcohol can be addictive, causing alcoholism.

Tranquilizers are classified as either major or minor. Major tranquilizers are used to treat psychoses, and are not prone to abuse. Minor tranquilizers are used in the treatment of emotional disorders, anxiety and tension, and are muscle relaxants. Minor tranquilizers if overused can result in a physical and psychological addiction. Their effects are similar to those of barbiturates, and withdrawal from them is similar in its symptoms.

Stimulants directly affect the central nervous system. Some stimulants are caffeine, synthetic amphetamines (pep pills), and cocaine. Caffeine is found in coffee, tea, colas, and other beverages, and produces symptoms similar to those of amphetamines. Amphetamines are used therapeutically to treat narcolepsy, to balance the effects of sedatives or depressants, to aid in weight loss, and to relieve mild forms of depression. They are sometimes used in the treatment of hyperactive children. The physical effects of large dosages of amphetamines are an increase in blood pressure, diarrhea, and dilated pupils. Amphetamines also increase alertness and eliminate fatigue. The dependence resulting from abuse of amphetamines is psychological as well as physical. Excessive dosages can cause excitability, restlessness, insomnia, excessive perspiration, hand tremors, and frequent urination.

Cocaine, from the South American coca bush, is a white powder which has effects similar to large doses of amphetamines. Its aftereffect is depression. If overdosed, it can result in respiratory disorders, and heart-function disorders which can be fatal. Cocaine can cause psychological dependence; withdrawal from it does not result in physical symptoms, but rather depression and a continuation of hallucinations.

Hallucinogens (or psychomometics, psychedelics, dysleptics) include marijuana, mescaline, psilocybin, DMT, and LSD.

Marijuana (grass, pot) consists of the dried flowers of the female hemp plant, *Cannabis sativa*. Hashish is also a derivative of the hemp plant, consisting of the resin that coats the flowers. Both marijuana and hashish have a long history of use in the cultures of India, Iran, and American Indians. Although occasionally used for medical purposes, their more common use has been for their hallucinogenic powers. The effects of marijuana are rapidly felt if it is smoked; it can be eaten or sniffed, as well. The hallucinogenic effect is mild. It acts on the central nervous system. Large doses may elicit psychoses, as found with the effects of LSD. A dangerous effect of marijuana is the slowing down of reflexes. Other effects are reddening of the membrane of the eyes, rapid heartbeat, muscular incoordination, unsteadiness, drowsiness, distorted perception of space and time, and hunger, especially for sweets. Marijuana is not physically addictive, but excessive use can result in a psychological dependence. The behavioral changes that can occur are a loosening of inhibitions and a heightening of suggestibility as a result of its intoxicating effect. The long-range physical effects of marijuana use are being investigated.

Mescaline is derived from the Mexican cactus, peyote; it is also easily synthesized, usually as a crystalline powder in capsule or liquid form. It can be taken orally, or it can be injected. The effects of mescaline are intoxication and hallucinations. Psilocybin, also an hallucinogen, is derived from a mushroom native to Mexico, and has a history of use by Mexican Indians in religious ceremonies similar to that of mescaline. It is usually in the form of a liquid or powder. Research has found that psilocybin can damage chromosomes.

DMT (dimethyltryptamine) is a synthetic drug,

which can also be found in the seeds of certain South American and West Indian plants. The powder of the seeds is said to have been used as snuff during the time of Columbus.

LSD (or acid) was originally isolated from a fungus that grows on rye and later synthesized. It is the most powerful hallucinogen known to man. Usually taken orally, it comes in the form of a small white pill, a powder in a capsule, or a liquid. LSD directly affects the nervous system. Psychological dependence may occur, as well as a tolerance for it, but it has not yet been found to create a physical dependence. Because of its powerful effects, LSD is most often used as a mind-expanding agent. LSD causes changes in perception, mood, thought, and activity. Spatial relationships are distorted, colors seem more vivid, sensitivity to sound increases, hallucinations of voices or music can occur, sense of touch is altered, and time may be distorted. On an LSD "trip," your ideas may become strange and unfamiliar. You may feel a creative urge to record the thoughts and sensations you are experiencing. You may have a "religious" experience which manifests itself in feelings of unity, brotherhood, egolessness. Your mood changes come from intense feelings of aloneness, anxiety, or fear. Your actions may become impulsive. Physically, you may feel as though you are floating, and you may perceive the environment in a constant state of flux. You may experience lightheadedness, fogginess, or emptiness.

The immediate effects of LSD can last for several hours. The long-range effects of the drug have not been determined. Good or bad trips are unpredictable. It has been said that LSD may induce psychoses, regardless of the state of psychological health prior to taking the drug. Also, recent controversial research has indicated that LSD may result in physiological changes. To date, this research is inconclusive.

REFERENCES

George Andrews and Simon Vinkenoog, eds., *The Book of Grass: An Anthology of Indian Hemp.* New York: Grove Press, 1967.

Robert S. DeRopp, *Drugs and the Mind.* New York: Grove Press, 1960.

Erich Goode. *The Drug Phenomenon: Social Aspects of Drug-Taking.* New York and Indianapolis: Bobbs-Merrill Co., 1973.

Richard Horman and Allan Fox, eds., *Drug Awareness.* New York: Avon Books, 1970.

Brian Inglis, *The Forbidden Game: A Social History of Drugs.* New York: Charles Scribner's Sons, 1975.

EGOSPEAK is a word coined by Edmond G. Addeo and Robert E. Burger to describe a modern-day phenomenon of noncommunication. Addeo received a Bachelor of Science degree from the University of California at Los Angeles. He was a feature writer for the Los Angeles *Citizen News,* and West Coast editor of *Electronics* magazine. He received the Jesse Neal Award for his editorship of a series on computers in education. Robert Burger received a Bachelor of Arts in classics and an M.A. in philosophy from the University of California. He founded and is copartner of an advertising agency in San Francisco.

Egospeak, defined by Addeo and Burger, is an art of ego boosting which occurs when we talk about what *we* want to talk about, and fail to pay attention or listen to what anyone else has to say. It is a psychological disease to which we all are prone. It causes the death of meaningful conversation, the success of which depends upon the cooperation of two or more individuals. We play egospeak expressly for our own satisfaction, to work out problems and frustrations, as well as to be impressive.

Egospeak seems to be related to a desire for recognition. Addeo and Burger surmise that it could be the result of the vast amount of information that bombards us from both the printed and electronic media, as well as the threats society imposes on individuality.

There are different levels on which egospeak can be performed. Each level pertains to our psychological peculiarities as they reveal themselves in our speech.

The most basic form of egospeak is "jobspeak." While playing jobspeak, we will refer to our boss, our job title, our secretary, fellow workers, the difficulties of the job, etc., in an effort to impress a listener (who probably isn't listening), and feel confident, secure, and unapproachably important. We will talk about how much more important we are to our job than anyone realizes, point up the mistakes of fellow workers, and tend to overuse the terminology or jargon identifiable with the job. The latter habit increases the distance from the person with whom we want to "communicate."

"Babyspeak" is another form of egospeak. In it, we constantly praise our children for what they do, whether we believe in their activity or not. We inflate their egos to the extent that to satisfy them, we must deliver more and more praise. As a result, our children grow up and follow through on the egospeak games which we, as parents, taught them.

"Businessspeak" is a form of egospeak unto itself. The incapability of people to listen on all levels of the business hierarchy nurtures it. Trainees do not listen to instructors, secretaries don't listen to bosses, executives don't listen to their associates, and on up the scale. These individual weaknesses are compounded by the fact that committees and boards have replaced individuals, and these business entities develop an egospeak all their own. Committees and boards are not structured to listen; they function unidirectionally, in terms of output. The subsets of businessspeak ("phonespeak" and "letterspeak") attest to the promotion of the idea that accompanying every move made within the business construct there is an invisible power, whether it be on the secretarial level, the executive level, or a committee report.

There are further subcategories of egospeak, i.e., "easyspeak," the overindulgence in the use of jargon to affirm our identities; "sexspeak," played by males to boost their egos; "namespeak," or name-dropping. Egospeak is a game of one-upmanship; we are so intent on "speaking" that little or no significant information is conveyed. The communication of information is facilitated only when we mean the words we say.

Talking embodies power to influence others. Talking attracts attention and establishes rank. Talking releases tension. Talking acts punitively. Talking imposes our "best" characteristics on others. We talk in these ways out of insecurity or a lack of direction. We fail to listen because listening takes discipline, time, and appreciation of the conversational situation.

According to Addeo and Burger, the cure is listening. It is much easier to indulge in egospeak; it takes much less self-confidence than to be able to keep silent and listen.

REFERENCE

Edmond G. Addeo and Robert E. Burger, *Egospeak, Why No One Listens to You.* New York: Bantam Books, 1974.

ALBERT ELLIS (1913–), a psychologist, is the founder of Rational Emotive Therapy (RET). Ellis was born in Pittsburgh, Pennsylvania. He received a Master's and Ph.D. in clinical psychology from Columbia University, and taught at Rutgers and New York University. He was chief psychologist of the New Jersey State Diagnostic Center and the New Jersey Department of Institutions and Agencies. Ellis is a fellow of the American Psychological Association and president of its division of Consulting Psychology. He is a fellow of the American Sociological Association and the American Association for the Advancement of Science. He is president of the Society for the Scientific Study of Sex, and a member of the Executive Committee of the American Academy of Psychotherapists, the American Association of Marriage Counselors, Psychologists in Private Practice, the New York Society of Clinical Psychologists, and chairman of the Marriage Counseling Section of the National Council on Family Relations. Ellis was associate editor of *Marriage and Family Living, International Journal of Sexology,* and *Journal of Sexual Research.* He has a private practice in psychotherapy, marriage, and family counseling in New York City. In 1961, the Institute for Rational Living published *A Guide to Rational Living* by Albert Ellis and Robert A. Harper, which outlined a new view of psychotherapy, later expanded in *Rational Psychotherapy*, and a multivolumed *Handbook of Psychotherapeutic Techniques*.

Ellis and Harper believe that self-analysis can be useful for a large percentage of people who are capable of self-evaluation and self-questioning. Their method, based on clinical discoveries, is called *Rational analysis*, and is a method by which you can get to the source of your emotional problems without becoming involved in a long, drawn-out process of psychoanalysis with a therapist. Nevertheless, it is important to realize that self-analysis is a serious and time-consuming process in which you must act as your own guide, and guard against the incorrect application of the stated methods.

Rational analysis is based on Ellis and Harper's premise that you can live a self-fulfilling, creative, and emotionally satisfying life if you "intelligently organize and discipline [your] thinking." Your behavior is the result of four interconnected processes: sensorial perception, action, emotion, and thinking (or reasoning). These processes contribute to your functioning as an organism and do not occur apart from one another. The source of your problems, and your neuroses and psychoses is your emotional process.

Emotions happen in a three-way process: through physical stimulation of the emotional center of the brain and the body's network of nerves; through the activities of moving and perceiving; and through thinking and desiring.

Control of the emotions has been achieved through electrical and biochemical means. However, through the techniques of Rational analysis, emotionally disturbed people can help themselves with methods that are not self-limiting, and can be used whenever necessary.

One principle of rational therapy is that your thoughts and the emotions linked up with them can be controlled and changed if you formalize them into essential "sentences" and then change the sentences. You can eliminate depression, guilt, anger, by thinking straight and taking effective action in response to your spoken thoughts. Rational therapy allows for the release of inhibitions and apathy, resulting in a fuller realization of emotional feelings.

You can suffer from neuroses and emotional instability without recognizing the source of your problems and, as a result, indulge in self-defeating behavior without being aware of it. Temporary diversions (e.g., alcohol, sex, drugs, etc.) are familiar avenues of escape from such problems. In order to see your problems, you must gain insight into yourself. It is important to recognize and understand the unrealistic and illogical thoughts which you have been taught, and which have become indoctrinated into your thinking patterns and mode of life. The next step is to dispense with them by changing these notions which lie at the root of your disturbances.

You must be careful to use your reasoning power sensibly because rationality, when carried to extremes, becomes irrational. A totally reasoned-out life can be dull, cold, and machinelike, taking you away from activities which are pleasurable such as art, music, literature, hobbies, etc. In a psychological sense, the rationalization and intellectualization of neurotic behavior only perpetuates it; people tend to make excuses for and overemphasize their problems to the degree that they deny them and avoid acting to correct them. Rationality can allow you to think and act more logically to avert the unpleasantness of irrational behavior. If you reason your way out of emotional problems, you are acting sanely and sensibly. You can train yourself to avoid long periods of misery by consistently trying to be mature, thinking, and reflective.

There are many irrational ideas which are obstacles to rational thinking. Since you are part of a social group, you become accustomed to the idea that it is necessary to be loved and approved of by almost everyone for practically everything you do. You *enjoy* satisfying your physical and mental drives, but you do not *need* them to be satisfied. It is illogical to want approval from those who are important to you. You create unattainable goals in the *number* of people you want to love you, in trying to get approval from *everyone,* in the *duration* of loving that is expected, and in attempts to be loved in all circumstances by doing what *others* want rather than what *you* want to do.

The idea that you should be competent, adequate, and achieving in *all* respects is another concept which blocks clear thinking. It results in an unreasonable drive for perfection, or the need to accomplish certain goals simply in order to be superior. Because of so-called inbred ethical systems, people have the idea that certain people are bad and should be punished. You can obviate this idea by discovering how you blame yourself and others through an examination of the language used to describe the activity.

Other ideas that become obstacles to our healthy existence are the following: It is catastrophic when things are not going right; happiness is externally caused, and you do not have the ability to control your sorrows or rid yourself of negative feelings; it is easier to avoid difficulties and responsibilities than to discipline yourself to take care of them; the past is so significant that certain events have affected you permanently; perfect solutions to problems should be found immediately; people should be different than they are, and happiness is found in "passive" enjoyment.

These ideas should be replaced by ideas that are realistic and rational and relate to you as you really are. This requires a reworking of thinking habits, behavioral habits, a restatement of preferences, and self-discipline in order to recognize real priorities, and involve yourself in something or people other than your own self. Devotion to others should occur because you enjoy involvement. Involvement in something should fulfill your desires. Morality should be based on enlightened self-interest and individualism. Your powers to reason can help you achieve a satisfying emotional existence.

REFERENCES

Albert Ellis, *An Introduction to the Principles of Scientific Psychoanalysis.* Provincetown, Mass.: Journal Press, 1950.

Albert Ellis and Robert A. Harper, *A Guide to Rational Living.* North Hollywood, Ca.: Wilshire Book Co., 1975.

————, *Creative Marriage.* New York: Lyle Stuart, 1961.

Robert A. Harper, *Psychoanalysis and Psychotherapy: 36 Systems.* Englewood Cliffs, N.J.: Prentice-Hall, Inc., 1959.

ERIK ERIKSON (1902–   )   is a leading figure in the field of psychoanalysis and human development, and has been a training psychoanalyst for many years. He was born in Frankfurt-am-Main, Germany. After graduating from the Vienna Psychoanalytic Institute, he began his career in clinical psychology, with the treatment of children. Since then he has researched the phenomenon of growing up in many different cultures and societies. He was on the senior staff at the Austin Riggs Center, and professor of human development and lecturer on psychiatry at Harvard University. He has been involved in research at the Harvard Psychological Clinic, the Yale Institute of Human Relations, and the Western Psychiatric Institute in Pittsburgh. He won both the Pulitzer Prize and the National Book Award. His first book, *Childhood and Society* (1950), is regarded as a classic work on the social significance of childhood. In his studies of Luther and Gandhi, he pioneered in the genre of psychohistory and psychobiography. Since 1963, Erikson has been involved with the Center for the Advanced Study of Behavioral Sciences at Stanford, California.

The premise upon which Erikson bases his psychological viewpoints is that people are beset with *human anxiety* which, when clinically observed, seems closely related to three processes of organization: the process of organization inherent in our organism; the process of the organization of the experience of our individual egos; and the process of social organization. Erikson places an important value on clinical observation and therapy as a means by which human crises may be understood, and he thinks it important that the training focus on the above-mentioned processes of organization. In this way, a "relativity of human existence" is revealed; the evidence arising from one process will give relevance and significance to another process, and so on. It will become evident how the processes change simultaneously, and where breakdowns occur in each. The processes operate in a continuum and when a catastrophe occurs, it is a decisive event in the continuum. Clinical research begins in the postcatastrophic situation and the clinician can never know what an individual's life was like before therapy. Clinical observation deals with a given item in a case history, and how it relates to and makes other items more meaningful. The accessible sets of observable changes in the three organizational patterns are studied by: 1) beginning with one process and observing how those changes affect other processes; 2) reviewing the data of all the processes to see how each variation in the ego, for example, relates to the developmental stages, the state of the organism and its history of social associations; 3) reconstructing family history and changes in social life which are derived from and influence body changes and ego development.

The biological basis of psychoanalytic theory is contained in Freud's timetable of the development of the libido, which begins in childhood and goes through various pregenital stages (oral, anal, etc.) before becoming fundamentally genital. In this growth, the ego becomes distinct in accordance with sex and organized in terms of existence, feeling, and anticipation. Genitality in relationship to tradition guides the patterns of our drives, the way in which we construct space relations, etc. How we experience situations is grounded in our body structure. Given that the biological, cultural, and psychological penetrate our growth, Erikson sees psychoanalysis as a means of revealing the integration between the psychosexual and the psychosocial, and their effects on society.

In his study of the American Indian society, past and present, Erikson determined that there are several distinct ways in which a primitive society operates efficiently and avoids anxiety and social panic: 1) Early physical and personal experiences are given specific meanings and the correct combination of ways is provided for the satisfaction of biological urges, with a proper emphasis placed on how the process affects society; 2) the energies involved in organizing organismically are carefully and systematically channeled into the intricate patterns of everyday life; 3) the anxieties characteristic of the infantile structure are given a supernatural nature. In this way, a strong societal ego is developed, whose core is firm, though flexible enough to handle the complexities and contradictions within the society. It can integrate individual differences, accomplish a sense of identity and a viable concept of integrity, and protect society from achieving an unfeasible "ideal" state. Understanding the "instinctive blueprints" within society allows us to see that mankind, as a whole, is continually adapting, both rationally and consciously, toward a more universal equilibrium.

Society develops in eight stages, which are parallel to our growth as individuals from infancy to mature adulthood. At each stage we, as individuals, acquire personality characteristics which indicate our preparation to be driven toward, become aware of, and interact with a steadily enlarging social radius. Collectively, in terms of society, we tend to structure ourselves so that we may confront, encourage, and safeguard the changing range of our potentialities for interaction. The eight stages of the society's growth are in a constant state of jeopardy to hazards of existence, just as its members are subject to metabolic decay.

Erikson describes the development of societal consciousness in each stage of growth in terms of opposites:

1) In the oral and sensory stage, basic trust or mistrust is developed, drive and *hope;* 2) in the muscular-anal stage, autonomy or shame and doubt, self-control and *willpower;* 3) in the locomotor-genital stage, initiative or guilt, direction and *purpose;* 4) in the latency stage, industry or inferiority, method and *competence;* 5) in puberty and adolescence, identity or role confusion, devotion and *fidelity;* 6) in young adulthood, intimacy or isolation, affiliation and *love;* 7) in adulthood, generativity or stagnation, production and *care;* 8) in maturity, ego integrity or despair, renunciation, and *wisdom.* Erikson views these eight traits (hope, willpower, purpose, etc.) as the basic virtues of human development that are transferred from generation to generation and are significant to the functioning of all other changeable systems of human values.

Strong ego and identity are crucial to the nature of a society. In gaining identity, we use our energy to maintain a vision of numerous cultural trends. In this way, we adopt a humanistic universal view and are less susceptible to the dilemma of social integrity which technology poses. When the strength of our identity can be based on the experience of social health and cultural solidarity, a sense of humanity is achieved. When we lose this sense, when integrity gives way to despair, generativity to stagnation, etc., we revert back to our infantile fears and fail to build the "patrimony" of strong cultural identity which "produces a workable, psychosocial equilibrium." According to Erikson, it is important "to perfect methods which, in given situations, facilitate the elucidation of such prejudices, apprehensions, and lapses of judgment as emanate from infantile rage and from the adult's defenses against his latent infantile anxiety."

REFERENCES

Erik Erikson, *Childhood and Society* (second edition). New York: W. W. Norton & Co., 1963.
———, *Insight and Responsibility.* New York: W. W. Norton & Co., 1964.

————, ed., *Youth: Change and Challenge*. New York: Basic Books, 1963.

————, "The Problem of Ego Identity," *Journal of the American Psychiatric Association*, 4:56–121.

————, *Young Man Luther*. New York: W. W. Norton & Co., 1958.

————, *Gandhi's Truth*. New York: W. W. Norton & Co., 1969.

est (Erhard Seminars Training), *an educational corporation*, was founded by Werner Erhard in October 1971. Erhard (1935–   ) was born John Paul Rosenberg in Philadelphia, Pennsylvania. He changed his name to Werner Erhard in 1960 after he left his wife and children. Erhard settled in Spokane, Washington, and worked for Parents' Magazine Cultural Institute (1962–69), eventually becoming vice president, and for Grolier Society (1969–71) as division manager. During this time, seeking enlightenment, he studied and participated in a wide variety of disciplines, including Yoga, Dale Carnegie, Mind Dynamics, Scientology, Subud, Gestalt, Encounter, and Zen. According to Erhard: "Then I had what I call a catalytic experience. I experienced the source of perfection in life . . . and after I had this transformation, things began to work for me in an incredibly simple yet powerful way." Erhard developed the *est* training so that he could share his experience of transformation with others. Since his founding of *est,* he has lectured to educational, psychological, and philosophical associations including the American Psychological Association, the Association of Humanistic Psychology, the National Alcoholism and Drug Abuse Conference, the Department of Correction of the State of California, the Lindau Psychological Congress, the University of Munich, the May Lectures, and Kings College Hospital, London.

   est is a "practically-oriented philosophical educational experience," created out of Erhard's personal experience into a four-day (sixty hours) "Standard Training." The *est* training is concerned with transformation: "To transform is to alter fundamentally the context in which experience is held. *est* is not about content. *est* is about altering the context in which one views and experiences everything in life." According to Erhard: "The purpose of the training is to allow you to see that the circumstances of your life, and your attitudes about them, are held in a particular system of knowing—an epistemology, a context—and that it is possible to transform that context. . . . It's possible for you to choose the context for the content of your life."

est is concerned with three branches of philosophy: *epistemology, ontology,* and *ethics.* Epistemologically, the *est* training offers you the chance to observe how you know what you know, by realizing yourself as the source of your experience. Ontologically, the training has you consider what is reality and what is unreality in order to discover and experience what it means to be. Ethically, the training helps you to consider the implications of who you are and the way in which you know reality and unreality with regard to personal integrity and personal responsibility.

The *est* Standard Training is held on two consecutive weekends, usually in a hotel ballroom or conference room, large enough to accommodate 250 participants. The room is arranged in theatre style, with chairs facing a raised platform on which there are a stool, a lectern, and chalkboards for the trainer's use. On the first Saturday, the training begins at 8:30 A.M., 9 A.M. the other mornings; it continues until late that night or into the next morning. On the first day, the training supervisor reads a list of rules concerning such things as "smoking, drinking, eating, talking, staying in your seat, and other agreements." Then the trainer explains what will be done in the training, as well as answering questions.

According to *est,* there are three things which happen in the training: 1) *Presentation of data* that "allows trainees to look at, become aware of, and examine their established beliefs." 2) *Training "processes"*: "A process is a state of awareness in which you are not thinking about or figuring out or looking at your experience, but actually are *experiencing* your *experience* toward the source of the experience." A training process is intended, among other things, to result in your increased spontaneity. 3) *Group communication:* During the training, you are permitted, on a voluntary basis, to ask questions and/or "share" any insights or realizations you may experience.

During the *est* training, you are given the chance to "realize a transformation (not merely a change or enlargement)" of your experience of self, of experiencing, of knowing, of others.

According to *est,* some results of the transformation reported by graduates are: 1) the ability to begin a job, relationship, or other pursuit satisfied, rather than trying to become satisfied; 2) the experience of barriers to satisfaction at their source, thereby dissolving them; 3) the realization of personal responsibility for one's life experience; 4) the acceptance of direct experience; 5) an expansion of the experience of love, happiness, health, self-expression, as well as personal effectiveness and the ability to "make life work."

est is emphatic regarding the fact that it is not psychology or therapy, and that if you are interested in the latter kind of service, you should consult an appropriate source.

Since *est* was founded, over eighty-four thousand people have graduated from the *est* Standard Training, which is offered at *est* centers in thirteen cities in the United States, current cost, $300. The main office of *est* is located at 1750 Union Street, San Francisco, California 94123.

est offers teen and children's trainings. To be eligible, the child must live with an *est* graduate parent at least 50 per cent of the year. In addition, *est* has a Graduate Participation Program made up of eight seminar series created by Werner Erhard to provide graduates with a common environment in which they can "participate in their own and each other's growth." The seminars cover subjects such as sex, the body, self-expression, etc. *est* has also conducted Standard Trainings for the inmates and staffs of Lompoc Federal Prison and San Quentin.

Several scientific investigations have been done on *est*. Dr. Robert E. Ornstein, faculty member of Langley Porter Neuro-Psychiatric Institute, headed a retrospective "*est* Outcome Study" of 1,400 random members of the *est* graduate population in 1974. The survey of 680 items was designed to identify changes related to health and well-being reported after taking *est* Standard Training. According to Ornstein and Charles Swencionis (project director): "Respondents reported strong positive health and well-being changes since taking the *est* Standard Training, especially in the areas of psychological health and well-being and those illnesses with a large psychosomatic component."

REFERENCES

est, Public Information Office, 765 California Street, San Francisco, Ca. 94108.

Adelaide Bry, *est: 60 Hours That Transform Your Life.* New York: Harper & Row, 1976.

Carl Frederick, *est—Playing the Game* the New Way.* New York: Delta, 1976.

Robert Hargrove, *est—Making Life Work.* New York: Dell/Delacorte, 1976.

Luke Rhinehart, *The Book of est.* New York: Holt, Rinehart and Winston, 1976.

EXISTENTIALISM is a philosophical movement that culminated in Europe in the 1940s and has since had a major influence on literature, art, ethics, theology, education, and psychology.

Existentialism has been described as more a way of thinking than a set doctrine. In general, philosophical existentialism places man at the center of the universe as an existent subject, free to choose and responsible for his life, not a thinking subject. According to Sartre: ". . . man first of all exists, encounters himself, surges up in the world—and defines himself afterwards. If man, as the existentialist sees him, is not definable, it is because to begin with he is nothing . . . will not be anything until later, and then he will be what he makes of himself," i.e., existence precedes essence.

The predominant themes in existentialism are ontological, rooted in the investigation of the meaning of personal being toward the attainment of selfhood, apart from the objective nature of the external world, yet always in tension with it. Existentialism is concerned with the function of freedom, decision, and responsibility as the crucial determinants for personal being and the effects of the individual's realization of finitude and death, manifested in feelings of guilt, alienation and despair. The existentialist believes that man's emotions play a critical role in the perception of the objective world. Existentialist themes address other problems in man's existence such as those of language, history, and society; these become circumstantial in relation to the central concern of being.

Sören Kierkegaard, the nineteenth-century Danish philosopher, is considered the father of modern existentialism. His two major works are *Philosophical Fragments* (1844) and *Concluding Unscientific Postscript* (1846). Kierkegaard had an intense Christian background which he eventually rejected in his search for a philosophy that would define the individual's relationship to God. Christianity was a paradox in which intellectualism became a doctrine and only served to change the individual's will. Kierkegaard concluded that Christianity supported a speculative philosophy that distorted the reality of man's existence in illusion, becoming the residue of pure thought: merely an abstraction of existence, not existence itself. The only object of thought is one's personal being, within which lies the potential of a supreme ethical choice which can only be determined by thought. The reality of such a choice is predicated upon the individual's ability to believe in the idealism of the choice, while remaining uncertain about the objective nature of the choice.

Kierkegaard questioned the idea that one can think absolutely, make such a choice, and yet live unabsolutely. As interpreted by H. J. Blackham, Kierkegaard's impact upon philosophy was his "protest against 'pure thought' and irrelevant knowledge and his recall to the permanent basis of human living in the ethical isolation of the existing individual."

Edmund Husserl, the German philosopher, founded *phenomenology,* a philosophical school that established the basis for existentialism. Husserl was concerned with an analysis of consciousness which endeavored to discover the structure of experience. In his approach, all naturalistic presuppositions and preconceptions are eliminated. The main point is that consciousness has no life apart from the objects it considers.

Martin Heidegger, called the father of German existentialism, and a student of Husserl, developed his method of existential analysis in his work *Being and Time* (1927). The focal point of Heidegger's philosophical investigations was not the human condition as molded by personal existence and ethical stances, but the problem of being. He rejected the label "existentialist." His metaphysical questions addressed the meaning of being, total and unified.

Heidegger believed that man contains the potential of being; man is not originally invested with absolute being. The *Dasein* (mode of existence of the human being) has a structure which is *being-in-the-world,* a necessary state of self that is constantly relating to the state of nonself within a world of other human beings and things, tools to be used to understand that world. The Dasein is also *being-in-common,* which explains the individual's existence as shared with the existence of others. It is the nature of the Dasein to explore its existence and thus confirm its meaning in a mode of becoming.

Heidegger believed that personal existence was made authentic through a conscious acceptance of death, without willingness to overcome it, apart from any ethical convictions. Once one's personal existence was understood, so was the totality of personal existence, or of the world.

Jean-Paul Sartre, a student of both Husserl and Heidegger, is the major spokesman of modern existentialism. His philosophical work, *Being and Nothingness,* published in 1943, develops his system of thought and his philosophy of being.

At the core of Sartre's existentialism is his theory that existence precedes essence. According to Sartre, there is a single constant being that consists of two distinctions: being-in-itself (*en soi*) which is unconscious being, and being-for-itself (*pour soi*) which is conscious being. Being-in-itself is the basic condition for being-for-itself. "Being-in-itself is never either possible or impossible. It *is*. . . . Uncreated, without reason for being, without any connection with another being, being-in-itself is *de trop* for eternity." Being-for-itself, consciousness, is free to choose how to be, and free to create its own significance or meaning of being. Consciousness causes things to be, through its original nothingness. Nothingness is a positive determination; it is the denial of objects and yet depends upon those objects in order to exist.

According to Sartre, there can be no God. God is a representation of the ideal which is the synthesis of in-itself and for-itself. For *en-soi* to unite with *pour-soi* requires justifying both being and nonbeing, and that is a contradictory activity. Therefore, Sartre holds that man is free; he is responsible; there is no God or myth of God which causes man to act. Man creates his own meaning and must make the choices that he is faced with by himself. Man is free to acquire knowledge of himself and by himself. "Man is a useless passion": He comes into the world, accepts it with full responsibility in ethical isolation, becomes active in it through relation and projects, and thus gives it meaning. This is man's destiny.

Other figures associated with the development and influence of existentialism are Nietzsche, Dostoevsky,

Karl Jaspers, Gabriel Marcel, Albert Camus, Martin Buber, Miguel de Unamuno, and José Ortega y Gasset.

REFERENCES

H. J. Blackham, *Six Existentialist Thinkers: Kierkegaard, Jaspers, Nietzsche, Marcel, Heidegger, Sartre.* New York: Harper & Row, 1959.

Martin Heidegger, *An Introduction to Metaphysics.* New York: Doubleday & Co., 1961.

Edmund Husserl, *Ideas: General Introduction to Pure Phenomenology.* London, 1931.

W. A. Kaufmann, ed., *Existentialism from Dostoevsky to Sartre.* Magnolia, Mass.: Peter Smith, 1969.

John Macquarries, *Existentialism.* Baltimore: Penguin Books, 1972.

Jean-Paul Sartre, *Being and Nothingness.* New York: Pocket Books, 1971.

————, *Nausea.* New York: New Directions, 1964.

EXTRASENSORY PERCEPTION. The phenomenon of extrasensory perception (including telepathy and clairvoyance) has been the subject of experimentation since the 1880s, especially in connection with the Society of Psychical Research in England. It was not until the 1930s with the work done by J. B. Rhine, associate professor of psychology at Duke University, that ESP was explored scientifically on a large scale. With the publication of *Extra-Sensory Perception* in 1934, Rhine introduced the field of parapsychology as a science to be taken seriously, into the realm of university research. Rhine is responsible for the term "extrasensory perception." At first designated to mean "perception without the functions of recognized senses," as more evidence accumulated, it was determined that ESP was "fundamentally different from the sensory processes, lacking a sense organ, apparently independent of recognized energy forms, non-radiative but projectory, cognitive but analyzable into sensory components . . ." Within the context of Rhine's early studies, the term developed to mean "perception in a mode that is just not sensory," although it is a means of perception that has a natural function integral to mental processes.

In the first experiments conducted at Duke University, over ninety thousand "trials" were run. The research had two objectives: to measure the occurrence and range of ESP, given the "mathematically indisputable evidence that ESP could occur," and to understand how ESP related to "other mental processes and to the essential physiological and physical conditions." The original tests involved trance-telepathy experiments in which hypnotized subjects demonstrated telepathic abilities in identifying numbers, in matching the hand raised by another person, and in picking out a section of a circle from the circumference upon which an agent was gazing. Experiments were done testing the ESP of clairvoyant types using numeral cards, alphabet cards, and ESP cards containing symbols. Experiments were done which proved pure clairvoyant perception (ESP of objective facts) and clairvoyant perception of playing cards. Other experiments measured the effects of caffeine on the subject, while long-distance experiments measured pure clairvoyant perception and pure telepathy (ESP of the mental processes of another person).

To disprove the validity of hypotheses opposing the theories of how ESP functioned, Rhine did experiments with the chance guessing of cards, which tested the actuality of ESP occurrence judging from the honesty, general competence, and reliability of the subjects being tested and the investigators doing the testing. He did experiments which focused on the possibility of unconscious sensory perception through the unconscious transferring of information to a subject. He tested the Hypothesis of Rational Inference, in which a subject could determine the position of cards in a deck, for example, through logical reasoning.

The evidence of Rhine's studies supported their original intention. It was found that ESP could be explained physically, physiologically, psychologically, psychically, or parapsychologically, and in a wider context, biologically.

On the physical level, *demonstrable energy,* or energy which although not necessarily measurable by instruments does work, effects change, and influences the processes that govern overt behavior, is manifest. Given the way in which the senses intercept energy (light rays, molecular vibration, etc.) in their functioning, Rhine and others proposed that ESP could be explained physically as a spaceless function with the proper language of such a physics. It followed logically that in perceiving extrasensorially, a subject was intercepting some kind of energy, but as to how was unknown. Yet, it was determined that ESP requires a controlling mechanism that originates in the higher functions of a well-integrated (unaltered by drugs or the like) nervous system.

A psychological condition for successful ESP was found to be volitionally controlled concentration in which attention is withdrawn from the sensory mode of perception and directed elsewhere. This attention could be measured in the subject's ability to adopt states of detachment, abstraction, and relaxation, as well as the subject's alertness and exertion to perform ESP tasks. Rhine concluded that ESP is less resistant to disassociation than sensory perception and reasoning. It is similar to creative intellectual and/or artistic synthesis. It is capable of being speeded up. It is not learned, developed, or analyzable on an introspective basis. It is interoperative with other forms of cognition, visual and auditory perception, rational judgment and recall. According to Rhine, ESP was an inherited means of parapsychological activity. He speculated that the phenomenon could be of "tremendous value to the species" because it is "a fairly dependable and persistent capacity," given the proper conditions.

Since the publication of Rhine's studies in 1934, new methods have been devised for mathematically appraising the results of ESP experiments as well as testing ESP events, e.g., using two experimenters, providing good psychological conditions, observing spontaneous parapsychical occurrences. Experiments have also been done on the phenomenon of psychokinesis (PK) in which mind appears to control matter.

Louisa Rhine, herself a contributor to the modern development of parapsychology as a science, has documented much of the experimentation that indicates that psychic ability is potential in everyone. A psysich experience can take several forms. In general, it is a process in which you receive true information which you did not or could not know in an ordinary way. It has been proved that psychic experiences happen unconsciously and that the unconscious mind can *know* aspects of the external environment apart from the senses. This information reaches the conscious mind the same way it would if perceived sensorially.

Testing in school situations has suggested that certain psychological conditions create an atmosphere conducive to the success of ESP; that ESP may be connected with mental characteristics linked to sex; that ESP effects can occur when subjects are not aware of the possibility of their occurrence. Controlled experiments have also confirmed that ESP effects can be measured in the dreaming state, not only in the telepathic sense, but in a way that dream content can be influenced by the thoughts of an agent.

Psychic experience can be considered a product of various states of consciousness (e.g., out-of-body experiences, automatic writing, automatic muscular action demonstrated in Ouija board motion) and some altered states of consciousness (sleep and hypnosis). According to Louisa Rhine, the review of the various mental states has not offered sufficient evidence as to how mental states fit into the realm of psychic experiences. A psychic phenomenon cannot be dealt with in the "physical materialistic-mechanistic scheme of research," according to Rhine, because it does not come into contact with any of the physical properties or characteristics of the person demonstrating it. Rather, "it connects the personality to the world around it without a mechanism" observable in a physical context. Thus, what has been shown is that there operates in a human being some phenomenon that is "free from mechanics," and will not disappear when subjected to the intellectual test.

In 1967, the Society for Psychical Research in England sponsored experimental research in telepathy. Alister Hardy, a marine biologist and director of the Religious Experience Unit in Oxford, designed an experiment involving 200 people. Twenty people at a time sat in individual "double blackout" cubicles at the rear of a large hall. In front of them sat the remaining 180 people, watching photographs, drawings, and pictures of symbols flashed on a screen. These people acted as the "agents" (or senders) for the twenty "percipients" (or receivers), who were instructed to describe in some way, either in words or by a drawing, what they thought was being viewed by their "agents."

The results of this experiment (there were 140 test situations, and each person had a chance to be both percipient and agent) afforded that there was no way to measure what had been *unexpectedly* expressed by percipients in any one instance as being evidence of telepathy or simply chance.

Robert Harvie, a graduate of London University in psychology and trained in statistics, designed a new set of controlled experiments. In these, of which ninety were conducted, a randomizing procedure was followed to obtain the control group of percipients and to select their responses. Nevertheless, the results were as surprising as in the original experiment. Hardy and Harvie tried to explain the results, using theories of mathematical probability, although they questioned the validity of such an analytical approach in the light of so much "coincidence" of the percipients "hitting the targets."

The study of ESP and related phenomena had been relatively neglected and criticized in the United States until 1969 when the American Academy for the Advancement of Science accepted the study of parapsy-chological phenomena. The questions that had been and still are frequently raised pertain to the validity of the investigations.

A recent study that has received attention was con-ducted by Dr. Harold Puthoff and Russell Targ of Stanford Research Institute. Their experiments dealt with the psychic abilities of various subjects, one of whom was Uri Geller. Other studies include those conducted by E. Douglas Dean, using a plethysmograph (for measuring blood volume changes), Dr. Charles Tart, and researchers at the Maimonides Hospital in Brooklyn, New York. Credibility has been given to precognition to the degree that Central Premonitions registries have been established in New York and Cali-fornia. These organizations screen any premonitions that psychics communicate to them about disasters.

Several theories have been put forth in the United States to explain ESP. In 1903, Frederick Myers pre-sented his theory that psychic phenomena related to the workings of the subliminal self whose manifestations were most prominent in states of hypnosis, trance, dreaming, etc. More recently, Dr. Rex Stanford of St. John's University in Jamaica, New York, has con-cerned himself with how psi can and is being used in everyday life. He has suggested the idea of psi-medi-tated instrumental response (PMIR) to explain psychic occurrences that happen unintentionally. Stanford also suggests that we use both our normal senses and ESP to filter necessary information out of the environment, a process which utilizes our subliminal mind to re-spond to psychically perceived needs.

Sheila Ostrander and Lynn Schroeder, members of the American Society for Psychical Research, studied the psychical research being done in the U.S.S.R. within the last ten years. According to Ostrander and Schroeder, Russian scientists have been exploring sev-eral theories: 1) that ESP is related to both the sun and moon with regard to its functioning; 2) that ESP occurs when there is a biological harmony between sender and receiver (heartbeat, brain waves); 3) that ESP is related to magnetic and electrical force fields; 4) that ESP is affected by "cosmic static," the interception of a third party between sender and receiver.

Dr. Edward Naumov, a Soviet biologist, believes that ESP should be explored in relation to PK, psychic photography, and dowsing to detect sensitivity to radiation, eyeless sight (for example, the ability to "see" with fingers), precognition, "biorapport" (the influence of one individual in a group over the others), and the psychological aspects of psi. Some of this is being explored. In addition, scientists have investigated cases of artificial reincarnation, which is a form of active trance in which a subject will take on the knowledge or talents of a figure of the past.

Ostrander and Schroeder pointed out that the Soviets' attitude toward the study of parapsychology is very serious. They intend to discover ways in which ESP can be technologically applied. ESP is studied in universities, technological institutes, and colleges in the Soviet Union. The government allots funds for its investigation. ESP studies are also being conducted in Russia's satellite countries, Bulgaria, Czechoslovakia, Rumania, Hungary.

Today, in the United States there are several organizations which are concerned with parapsychological phenomena. The Academy of Parapsychology and Medicine, in Los Altos, California, is one such group. Founded in 1970, it has several thousand members, over six hundred of whom are medical doctors. The organization is basically concerned with discovering alternatives to traditional medical healing techniques.

Ostrander and Schroeder have put together a *Handbook of Psychic Discoveries* (1974) to aid the individual in discovering psychic energies. It outlines experiments that can be done with plants, describes how to build a Kirlian photography device; it describes how to develop telepathic powers and how to make and use a dowsing rod, etc. The authors call their hand-book "an unfinished map" for the individual to com-plete toward developing a "new biology of thinking."

REFERENCES

Alister Hardy, Robert Harvie, Arthur Koestler, *The Chal-lenge of Chance*. New York: Vintage Books, 1975.

Jeffrey Mishlove, *Roots of Consciousness: Psychic Libera-tion Through History, Science, and Experience*. New York: Random House, and Berkeley, Ca.: The Book-works, 1975.

Sheila Ostrander and Lynn Schroeder, *Handbook of Psy-chic Discoveries*. New York: Berkley Publishing Corp., 1974.

————, *The ESP Papers: Scientists Speak Out from Be-hind the Iron Curtain*. New York: Bantam Books, 1976.

————, *Psychic Discoveries Behind the Iron Curtain*. New York: Bantam Books, 1971.

J. B. Rhine, *Extra-Sensory Perception*. Boston: Branden Press, 1964.

Louisa E. Rhine, *ESP in Life and Lab: Tracing Hidden Channels*. London: Collier Books, 1967.

————, *PSI: What Is It? The Story of ESP and PK*. New York: Harper & Row, 1975.

FACE READING, or physiognomy, is an ancient sci-ence of divination which originated in China. It is based on the theory that facial features, or facial signs, are a map of the personality as well as a source of information about the future. Master Lu was a pop-ular face reader who lived during the third century B.C. Chen Po, another physiognomist of note, became famous for his prediction that General Chao Kuan-Yin would become a member of royalty; ten years later, the general became the first emperor of the Sung dynasty (960–1276). Although not a formally prac-ticed art in the West, Aristotle's analysis of the features of the face can be found in his *History of Animals*. More recently, Timothy Mar, a student of physiognomy since 1929, when he began studying with Master Wang Fa-shen in China, published *Face Reading*, introducing the art into Western culture on a popular level.

At the core of the Chinese system of physiognomy lies the model of the ideal face which is well proportioned and balanced, and on which the facial features are well placed and without defects. The more balanced and proportioned your face is, the more apt you are to have a strong character and a favorable fate. Any feature that is proportionately too large or small is interpreted in this light. The way the skin covers the face, whether it is firm or fatty, soft, flexible, wrinkled, etc., is also analyzed.

The Chinese divide the face into three zones, which are read horizontally. The *upper zone,* from the hairline to the eyebrows, is interpreted as an indication of your intellectual capacities and the conditions of your family life during childhood. The *middle zone,* from the eyebrows to the tip of the nose, indicates your adventurous spirit and personality strengths, as well as tendencies toward mediocrity. It is especially significant regarding the years between thirty-five and fifty, and if the zone is well shaped can mean a long life. The *lower zone,* from the tip of the nose to the tip of the chin, denotes your capacity for affection, as well as success potential. It is significant for the later years, i.e., fifty-one to ninety-nine.

The shape of the head is analyzed according to five basic patterns. The oblong-shaped head denotes intelligence, sensitivity, judiciousness, calmness, and often success. The triangular-shaped head, which is wide at the forehead and pointed at the chin, denotes supersensitivity, introspection, high intelligence or jealousy, lack of affection, and incompatibility. This shape can indicate an interest in philosophy, science, art or, at the opposite pole, a traitorous nature. The semitriangular head that has a wide forehead but lacks a pointed chin, denotes intelligence or artistic nature but also the lack of "fighting spirit." The square-shaped head denotes masculinity, hot temperament, leadership qualities, but also stubbornness rooted in persistence and determination. A woman with a square-shaped head will be the dominant figure in a marriage. The round-shaped head denotes an enjoyment of the pleasures of life and lack of ambition. At the same time, if the cheekbones are prominent, this will indicate a quick efficient mind. It is likely that you will have the qualities of two or more of the five basic patterns.

The features of the face which are most important are the eyebrows, the eyes, the nose, mouth, and ears. In ancient Chinese literature on physiognomy, these are called the Five Vital Organs. Each feature tells of a specific aspect of your personality and a specific quality of your destiny. According to ancient texts, if any one of these features is ill formed, then there is some point of failure or weakness in your personality. The basis of interpretation of these features is the concept of the ideal. For example, the ideal eyebrows are broad, long, and elegant. They are shaped like a crescent over the eyes. Any deviation from this reveals the degree of your disharmony with society, family, and friends. The ideal eyes are elegantly shaped, long and narrow, or large and round, with well-matched upper and lower lids. The irises are centered, clear, and steady, with a certain "glitter" which denotes your inner vitality and well-being. Deviations from this model indicate varying degrees of instability and weakness, as well as unluckiness, in your personality and destiny.

In Chinese physiognomy, positions of your face are charted and numbered from 111 to 130. These positions are distinctive of a certain age and tell of aspects of your fate and personality.

In a face reading, the physiognomist will take these various factors into account in order to judge how your basic features (forehead, eyebrows, eyes, cheekbones, chin, ears) meet the requirements of any of the standard face patterns (noble, superior, resourceful, standard, workaday, lowly), taking your age and maturity into account as well. There are certain positions of the face which the physiognomist will pay special attention to with regard to coloration, size, formation, etc. before making any judgments.

Some original sources for face reading can be found

in *Ma Yi Physiognomy* by Chen Po, written in the tenth
century; *Liew Chuang Physiognomy* by Yuan Liew-
chuang, published in the fourteenth century; *Tieh Kwan
Dao* by Yun Ku Shan Jen, fifteenth century; and *Shui
Chin Chi* by Fan Wen-yuan, seventeenth century.

REFERENCES
Timothy T. Mar, *Face Reading.* New York: New Ameri-
can Library, 1974.
Robert L. Whiteside, *Face Language.* New York: Pocket
Books, 1974.

FAMILY THERAPY. The practice of family therapy
began in the 1950s in response to the concept that the
individual, in a social context, is a product of the environment. There are two contemporary approaches to
family therapy: *structural family therapy,* developed by
Salvador Minuchin, a child psychologist; and *conjoint
family therapy,* developed by Virginia Satir, who was
trained in psychiatry and is a practitioner, consultant,
and teacher.

Structural family therapy was inspired by the ideas
of Ortega y Gasset and Gregory Bateson, as well as by
the evidence obtained in experiments with monkeys conducted by José Delgado. The thrust of this information indicated that the human brain develops in relationship to its activity as it processes and stores *input,*
from both internal and external sources. It therefore
can be assumed that information, attitudes, and modes
of perception are "assimilated and stored" as part of
the development of our approaches to an environmental context. In the investigations conducted by
Minuchin and others, it was found that the family (or
social group) becomes instrumental in the creation of
the structure of input. According to Minuchin, "the
interdependence between the individual and his family
. . . is poignantly demonstrated in the experimental
situation in which behavioral events among family
members can be measured in the bloodstream of other
family members."

Structural family therapy is based on three axioms:

1) Your psychic life is not a strictly internal process, but plays an active and passive role in the context of interaction. Because you are a part of a social system, or family, your actions are controlled by the characteristics of the system, the system itself having been affected by your past actions. You respond to the system, adapting to stresses and creating stresses, and you are, in effect, a subsystem of the whole. 2) Changes in the family system influence you behaviorally and psychically. 3) The behavior of the family therapist becomes an integral part of the behavior of the family involved in therapy.

These axioms illustrate the differences between family therapy and other forms of psychotherapy in which you are treated individually, apart from the context in which you operate. Structural family therapy focuses on a process of feedback which changes the relationship between the individual and the family context so that subjective experience is altered. The therapist and family work together toward reorganizing the family so that experience, in general, will change, and the changed experiences will be reinforced, thus validating the appropriate changes in the individual family members.

The function of the therapist in family therapy is to facilitate the process of modifying behavior in the *present* situation (which, by nature, is based on the past) by joining with the family and working within a framework rooted in theory to the properties of the family system. By joining with the family, the therapist is able to transform its structure to the degree that change is possible. The therapist aids the family in completing tasks which revive its functioning in terms of providing mutual support, regulation, nurturance, and socialization for its members (e.g., actualizing transactional patterns, manipulating space, creating stress situations, assigning specific tasks to be done at home or in a therapy session, manipulating moods, etc.). The changes which the therapist initiates are generally maintained because the structure of the family has been altered, and the new feedback process is therefore justified. The therapist in essence helps the family cure itself of its problems.

As seen in the theoretical framework of structural family therapy, family structure is based on an invisible set of functional demands which organize the means of interaction among family members. The behavior of the members of a family is based on *transactional* patterns which are maintained by two systems of *constraint*: that which lies with parental authority, and that which is *idiosyncratic,* involving the mutual expectations of individual family members. Families operate in conjunction with their subsystems (individual members) which have boundaries that allow for differentiation in the total system so that the functions of and demands on the family members are clearly defined.

There are three basic characteristics to a healthy family structure: A family should change, over time, by adapting and restructuring itself to sustain its functional capability (if it does not change appropriately, it will be subject to developmental stress); the strength of a family should lie in its ability to be flexible, especially with regard to the boundaries existing among its subsystems; and a family should meet stress situations without rigidity, otherwise "dysfunctional" patterns may lead to a need for therapy. According to Minuchin, "the effectively functioning family is an open social system in transformation, maintaining links with the extrafamilial, possessing a capacity for development, and having an organizational structure composed of subsystems."

Conjoint family therapy differs from structural family therapy by focusing on the problems of the individual member which are transferred to the other members of the family. This approach reveals the relationships between individuals and their families, and exposes "family pain." It has been found through clinical observation that the most crucial relationship in the family is the marital relationship. Obviously, it affects the way in which the parents function and influences the stresses which create family dysfunction.

Therapeutic work begins with the therapist's attempt to discover how the individual (e.g., parent), who has sought help, affects the family of which he or she is a member. In dealing with the entire family, the therapist creates a setting in which the family members can observe themselves and their actions objectively. Satir believes that it is necessary to work with the whole family, even though some members (e.g., children) may not show abnormal behavior. Working with the whole family, demonstrates the individuality of all, the differences in the way family members behave, the roles and responsibilities of the parents and children as well, communication gaps, etc. The goal is to induce and encourage the parents to restructure the family around a well-defined marital relationship. According to Satir, the therapist may conclude treatment when the family can operate as a whole; when family members can be honest about their feelings, their disagreements, their expectations of each other; and when the parents have reached a point where they are direct and clear with each other, recognizing each other's individuality.

Although new methods of family therapy are always emerging, they are all based upon aiding and designing future human relationships beginning with the psychological health of the individual, his or her self-image and self-concept. In this sense, it is necessary to be aware of how you interact, not only with your immediate family, but with people in general. It is important to understand how your behavior and self-concepts are surrounded by and affected by family or other social systems. Therapeutic experience will help you to see this, as well as to learn ways in which you can create new interactional behavior patterns.

There are family therapy institutes in California, Idaho, Washington, and other states. Satir's methods for treating families have been adopted by training programs throughout the United States. Minuchin's book,

Families and Family Therapy, is used as a textbook in courses dealing with the subject.

REFERENCES

Gregory Bateson, *Individual and Familial Dynamics* (panel review ed. by J. H. Masserman). New York: Grune and Stratton, 1959.

José Delgado, *Physical Control of the Mind: Toward a Psychocivilized Society.* New York: Harper & Row, 1969.

Salvador Minuchin, *Families and Family Therapy.* Cambridge, Mass.: Harvard University Press, 1974.

José Ortega y Gasset, *Meditations on Quixote.* New York: W. W. Norton & Co., 1961.

Virginia Satir, *Conjoint Family Therapy* (revised ed.). Palo Alto, Ca.: Science and Behavior Books, 1967.

FASTING, the complete abstention from food consumption, has a history that reveals its practice has been a ritualized part of practically all ethical and religious systems throughout the world. In Judeo-Christian religion, fasting was a means of disciplining the body in order to improve it spiritually and abstain from evil; Moses and Jesus were fasters. In Islam, fasting is required for certain occasions, for example, before entering a sanctuary, before prayer, to atone for sins, and at harvest time. Fasting has meaning in primitive ancient religions with regard to the supernatural power of food; food was both dangerous and powerful, and thus its consumption became a sacramental act; food was a means of acquiring extraordinary power and the ability to convene with supernatural forces. Prophyrius, the ancient Greek philosopher, believed that one could enter a God-like state through fasting. The Egyptians believed that fasting was a cure for syphilis. Plato fasted regularly for ten days at a time to improve his mental and physical capabilities. Pythagoras believed that fasting endowed him with prophetic powers and divine knowledge. Plutarch, Hippocrates, and Paracelsus found that fasting remedied illnesses even in their most critical stages.

Research into the effects of fasting did not begin until the early twentieth century with the work of T. H. Huxley, a British biologist, and C. M. Childe, with a group of researchers at the University of Chicago, which included investigation of the effects of fasting on earthworms; it was observed that a process of rejuvenation in the cellular tissues occurred. Research with human subjects was later conducted to see if a similar process of rejuvenation occurred; it was found that significant changes in the chemistry of the tissues occurred during fasting (a decrease in the metabolic rate), as well as a decrease in noticeability of wrinkles, a clearer complexion, brighter eyes. Early twentieth-century advocates of fasting regarded it as a means of ridding the body of toxins and undigested matter. C. C. Clemensen, a Danish physician, in 1932, discovered that fasting for four or five days could effectively prevent epileptic attacks in a majority of 155 test cases. It has only been in the last fifteen years, though, largely because of the therapeutic use that has been made of fasting for the treatment of obesity, that medical research has begun to unravel the exact biochemical and physiological changes which occur in body and brain during a fast.

Fasting does not technically begin until you have stopped food consumption altogether for two or three days. At this point your body begins to rest physiologically, i.e., the metabolism slows down. The calories in your system have been all used up, and your body is dependent upon internal sources of energy to maintain its metabolic equilibrium. As the result of the cutoff of external energy sources, your body will show signs of marked decrease in respiration, circulation, body temperature, blood pressure, bowel movement. The body, in order to fuel itself for the activities of its system, will begin to rely on internal sources such as fat deposits. Triglycerides (fats) are broken down chemically and released from fatty tissues into the blood. Much of this broken-down fat will go to the liver to be processed. The excess fatty acids in the liver will then be transformed into a substance called Acetyl CoA (abbrev.). This substance is broken down further and is crucial to the synthesizing of two other acids, collectively known as ketone bodies, which are later oxidized by the muscles. These substances become major sources of fuel for your body during a fast. Your "ketonic diet" begins when your body has exhausted the glucose energy supply obtained for the chemical conversion of carbohydrates. Normally the only nutrient used by the brain is glucose; when the glucose supply is gone, the brain will also go on a ketone diet. Thus, the body is using fuel which has been stored, sources which are not tapped in normal circumstances. The body, during a fast, will also tap excessive food materials in muscle tissue, the nonvital cells of the organs, the reserves of blood and water, and the protein stores. After all these energy sources are exhausted, the fasting process has been completed. If food is not then consumed, starvation will begin.

The recognizable side effects of fasting are: 1) a coated tongue, which when it has cleared will signify the end of the fasting process; 2) mucus in urine or bowel movements; 3) offensive body odor and breath (the last two are especially prevalent if you are not in good health when you fast); 4) giddiness, nausea, vomiting; 5) possible drops in temperature and erratic pulse rate (if your temperature stays abnormally high or low for a few hours and your pulse continues to be erratic, the fast should be concluded). During a fast, you may require more sleep than normal, and your sexual desires may be reduced or disappear altogether. Usually by the fifth day of the fast, your body's enzymes will have adapted and your stomach will have shrunk, and feelings of hunger will disappear (anorexia). Weight loss in fasting depends on the length of the fast, the diet you had before beginning the fast, your weight, and metabolic rate. As far as can be determined, about one-third of weight loss is attributable to fat loss, one-half to body water loss, and the rest to the elimination of material consisting of proteins, carbohydrates, and skeletal tissue. Psychological effects will show up at first in a

190 / MOSHE FELDENKRAIS

mild euphoria, because of the change in the brain nutrition; irritability and childlike behavior; mild depression and self-centeredness. Recent studies on obese men who were fasting showed, however, that despite these psychological factors, fasting improved overall physical and mental conditions of the subjects.

To prepare for a fast, you should cut down gradually on your food consumption, eating low-calorie meals including fresh, raw fruits, and avoiding acid-forming foods like meat or fish. During the fast, there are certain rules you should follow, such as: Drink two to three quarts of water daily; limit exercise; abstain from any drugs, including aspirin and alcohol; limit sexual activities; and check with your doctor if you intend to fast for more than two or three days.

Fasting can be done for several reasons: to clean out your body, to lose weight, as a spiritual exercise, to experience the fasting high, to acquire self-knowledge. If regularly performed, fasting can eliminate obesity. There is evidence however that fasting to "cleanse" your body can be dangerous because of the sudden release of insecticides and additives which have been stored in fatty tissues into the bloodstream that can cause severe illness and perhaps death. This can be prevented by drinking juices during the fast to dilute the concentration of toxins being eliminated. You should not fast if you have diabetes mellitus, liver problems, poor kidney function, heart disease, or psychiatric disorders, if you are under sixteen or over fifty-five years of age, or if you are pregnant. If you are in good health, you can undertake a fast for the first two or three days, until the actual effects begin, after which time you should only continue under medical supervision.

REFERENCE

Shirley Ross, *Fasting: The Super Diet*. New York: Ballantine Books, 1976.

MOSHE FELDENKRAIS, with the publication of *Body and Mature Behavior* in 1949, laid the groundwork for his approach to the coordination of body and mind. In recent years, Feldenkrais has created rehabilitation programs which involved hundreds of exercises, the purpose being to create the conditions for the realignment of the individual's relationship to the physical environment. He is active as both a teacher at the Feldenkrais Institute in Israel, and lecturer at the University of Tel Aviv. His techniques have become popular in Europe. Among those who have practiced his methods are David Ben-Gurion, former Prime Minister of Israel, and Yehudi Menuhin, the violinist. Feldenkrais' *Awareness Through Movement,* published in 1972, explains the specific exercise techniques he has developed and the philosophy on which they are based.

Feldenkrais views man as a creature unique in his or her capacity to learn. He defines "learning" as "the formation of new patterns out of the elements of total situations of earlier personal experience." In his approach to the treatment of emotional instability and behavior disorders, his perspective is one of teaching and learning, rather than patient and doctor. "Many of our failings, physical and mental, need not be considered as diseases to be cured, nor an unfortunate trait of character, for they are neither. They are an acquired result of a learned faulty mode of doing. The body only executes what the nervous system makes it do."

Feldenkrais distinguishes between the mature individual and the immature individual. The *mature* individual has learned to deal with present circumstances with only those parts of previous experiences which are necessary. The *immature* individual cannot avoid "restoring the whole situation where only an element of it is associated with the present." In treating the immature individual, he feels that the use of psychiatry alone is hopeless, and that reeducation must come about as the result of a radical change in the nervous and body patterns: "The whole self, diet, breathing, sex, muscular and postural habits, must be tackled directly and concurrently with the emotional reeducation."

A basic principle integral to Feldenkrais' work is the establishment of self-image. Three factors contribute to this process: heritage, education, and self-education. You inherit the physical structure that provides the experiential substance upon which your identity is based. Education becomes a means by which you shape concepts, reactions, and essentially "plug into" society. According to Feldenkrais, education "determines the direction of self-education." Self-education begins in childhood with the development of individual and inherent tendencies. Among these determinants, self-education alone provides the means to maintain the "organic contentment" that society only superficially supports. Feldenkrais considers the important question to be how and to what extent can you help yourself? Self-help, because it is a product of will, is the only way to take hold of your development, apart from the influences of society, and tap the power within you.

According to Feldenkrais, the first step toward self-improvement entails the recognition of your value as an individual. This discovery, however, is secondary to the development and change of the action which comprises your experience. This implies the establishment of awareness in as many parts of your body as possible. Such a total awakening can take place given a program of systematic correction, rather than a plan for correcting single actions and flaws in your behavior pattern, which Feldenkrais feels is less useful. A systematic mode of development can enable you "to find ways of behaving and acting that are in accordance with . . . personal and inner needs, ways that [you] might not discover naturally, because circumstances and outside influences may have led [you] in other directions in which continual progress is impossible. Systematic study and awareness should provide man with a means of scanning all fields of action so he can find a place for himself where he can act and breathe freely."

Awareness is the focal point of Feldenkrais' theory of self-improvement. The state of awareness is a waking state in which you know exactly what you are doing and in which you can learn. The waking state has four interacting characteristics: sensation, feeling, thinking, and movement. Feldenkrais believes the correction of movement to be the most viable means for self-improvement for several reasons: 1) It is part of the activity of the nervous system; 2) its quality is easy to judge; 3) you have a greater capacity for movement than for thought and feeling; 4) the ability to move well enhances self-esteem; 5) movement is primary to muscular activity; 6) movement reflects the state of your nervous system as well as your breathing capacity; 7) it is the basis of your awareness of what you can change; 8) most importantly, it is a means of changing the pattern-directing function of the motor cortex of the brain which, by influencing thought and feeling, can change patterns of existence.

Feldenkrais' exercises utilize the entire body and its essential activities. They are "designed to improve ability, that is, to expand the boundaries of the possible . . ." so that they become a part of your habitual existence. The exercises are aimed at improving posture; relieving tension; developing paths of ideal action (movement from one posture to another); developing the capacity to breathe, using the ribs, diaphragm, and abdomen; developing coordination of the flexor and extensor muscles; improving the alignment of the spine; increasing conscious attention to the commonest movement; recognizing that the movement of the eyes is a key to the control of body movement; becoming conscious of activities of the body of which you are not ordinarily conscious.

Feldenkrais stresses the importance of making awareness the goal of everyday living. He believes that improving and expanding awareness are preferable to attempting to overcome instinctive drives: "For the more nearly complete a man's awareness becomes the more he will be able to satisfy his passions without infringing on the supremacy of awareness . . . every action will have become more human."

REFERENCES

Moshe Feldenkrais, *Awareness Through Movement: Health Exercises for Personal Growth.* New York: Harper & Row, 1972.

————, *Body and Mature Behavior.* New York: International Universities, 1959.

FEMINISM, a movement for the equality of women, socially, politically, economically, educationally, sexually, has existed in the United States since the eighteenth century. The first important document to come out of the feminist movement was *The Vindication of the Rights of Women* by Mary Wollstonecraft, published in 1792. In 1848, a group of women, including Susan B. Anthony, Lucy Stone, Elizabeth Cady Stanton, and Lucretia Mott, held a convention at Seneca Falls, New York, at which they demanded independence and equality for women. They demanded that women be granted the right to vote, the right to collect wages, the right to compensation, etc. However, suffrage was not granted women until 1920. In 1946, the United Nations Committee on the Status of Women was established to investigate the status of women throughout the world.

In the 1960s, there was a strong renaissance of feminism in the United States. In 1966, the National Organization for Women (NOW) was founded, and has since become the largest feminist organization in America with over forty thousand members (men included) in both state and local chapters.

In March 1972, the Equal Rights Amendment was proposed and passed by Congress. This amendment was conceived to provide that the "equality of rights under law shall not be denied or abridged by the United States or by any State on account of sex." By April 1975, the amendment had been ratified by thirty-four of the thirty-eight states required for it to become law. Currently, the legislatures of the remaining states are being pressured by both pro-amendment and anti-amendment groups to make a decision. The amendment will go into effect two years after it is ratified by all thirty-eight states.

The renaissance of feminism is also responsible for the legalization of abortion in America during the first three months of pregnancy.

In the 1940s with the dissemination of the theories of Freud in the United States, women were reconsidered in terms of Freud's psychoanalytical model: passive, masochistic, narcissistic, modest, and jealous. These characteristics all stemmed from what Freud invented and labeled *penis envy:* the inferior position of a woman was dictated from the moment she realized that she was missing a penis. Freud regarded childbearing as a woman's primary goal and accomplishment. According to Betty Friedan, the feminist activist, Freud's invention of the feminine mystique placed the woman in a male world and influenced the basic perspectives of sociology, psychology, education, the media, etc., to regard and deal with women primarily as biological and sexual entities.

Within the last fifteen years, feminism has been revitalized as a political force. With the publication of such books as *The Feminine Mystique* by Betty Friedan, *Sexual Politics* by Kate Millett, and *The Female Eunuch* by Germaine Greer, women have been newly exposed to the oppression that has been the status quo throughout history. Friedan points out that the major issue which afflicts the contemporary woman is her desire for more than a husband, children, and a home. This desire comes out of the female will to destroy myths and creatively extend herself beyond the barriers that have been hindering her growth for so long: "the only way for a woman . . . to find herself, to know herself as a person, is by creative work of her own." Friedan contends that female creativity need not be filtered into a job. She discovered in her investigations over a period of years that education for women must be directed toward inspiring them to make a commitment to ideas and work that is socially influential. Her point is that women have to be taken out of the housewife mold and gain respect and recognition for their talents, intelligence, and general capabilities.

A form of consciousness raising for women has become part of the feminist movement as a means by which women can get together to discuss and work out their mind/body, external/internal struggles. Women have turned to feminism as a kind of therapy, or healing process for the wounds that have been inflicted upon them by society.

One of the outgrowths of this consciousness-raising effort can be seen in the interest in maintaining physical health and psychological well-being. This has been channeled into efforts to expose women to information on subjects such as reproduction, sexuality, birth control, abortion, menopause; access to health care; diseases of the reproductive system; lesbianism, etc.

In particular, consciousness raising is concerned with the development of female sexuality by women and for women; more generally, it is concerned with the development of self-awareness, self-responsibility, and a new self-consciousness on the part of women.

Assuming responsibility for your body is a result of your consciousness about your female sexuality. Treating your body properly by having regular examinations by your physician and gynecologist is one of the most important aspects of body therapy. Liberating yourself sexually is an aspect of liberating yourself personally. Working with other women toward sexual liberation is a way to break emotional ties and destroy cultural taboos, in order to gain new freedom as a woman.

Feminism has become a reexamination of the woman's role in a male-oriented society; this entails reviewing politics, media, history in terms of female influence, and language to discover viable alternatives for female expression. Feminism has created an atmosphere in which women can convene and determine what changes they want to make in order to stress their independence and destroy the socially inbred concepts of inferiority and inability to fend for themselves.

The psychological adjustments that women have to make in order to assert themselves are important to their entry into the world in a social context. The primary concern of women, according to Phyllis Chesler, a psychologist and feminist, should be to relocate their egos, withdrawing from all the socially contrived institutions that do not support "their survival and achievement of individual power." This way, sexism will disappear, and women can dedicate their energy to rendering themselves indispensable to the workings of society.

REFERENCES

Lonnie Garfield Barbach, *For Yourself: The Fulfillment of Female Sexuality*. New York: Doubleday & Co., 1975.

The Boston Women's Health Book Collective, *Our Bodies, Ourselves, A Book By and For Women*. New York: Simon & Schuster, 1971, 1973.

Phyllis Chesler, *Women and Madness*. New York: Avon Books, 1972.

Betty Dodson, *Liberating Masturbation: A Meditation on Self-Love*. New York: BodySex Designs, 1974.

Betty Friedan, *The Feminine Mystique*. New York: Dell Books, 1963.

————, *It Changed My Life: Writings on the Women's Movement*. New York: Random House, 1976.

Germaine Greer, *The Female Eunuch*. New York: Bantam Books, 1972.

Anica Vesel Mander and Anne Kent Rush, *Feminism As Therapy*. New York: Random House/Bookworks, 1974.

Kate Millett, *Sexual Politics*. New York: Doubleday & Co., 1970.

Anne Kent Rush, *Getting Clear: Body Work for Women*. New York: Random House/Bookworks, 1973.

Mary Wollstonecraft, *A Vindication of the Rights of Women*. New York: W. W. Norton & Co., 1967.

FISCHER-HOFFMAN PROCESS (the name coined by Claudio Naranjo, a Chilean psychiatrist), a therapeutic process that has been called "emotional surgery," evolved out of the experiences of Bob Hoffman, a onetime successful businessman in Oakland, California. In 1961, under the guidance of spiritualist Rose Strongin, Hoffman discovered that he had psychic powers and could "tune into the living minds of people whose bodies had ceased to exist." As he developed these abilities, they assumed more importance in his life. In 1967, Hoffman had a vision of Dr. Siegfried Fischer, a neurologist and psychiatrist and friend, who had died six months earlier. Hoffman clairaudiently heard Fischer say that he had discovered the key to solving emotional problems. In a five-hour session, Fischer explained Hoffman's own familial problems. Hoffman was so strongly convinced by what Fischer had told him that he began to teach psychic development to others so that they could discover about themselves what he had learned about himself through Fischer. In 1969, Hoffman's efforts began to attract the attention of doctors, psychiatrists, and psychologists. Since then, he has established himself as a psychic therapist, and is refining the Fischer-Hoffman process continually because of suggestions coming from Fischer.

When Claudio Naranjo learned about the process, he integrated it into his group sessions for spiritual and psychological development, known as Seekers After Truth (SAT). The Fischer-Hoffman process has become known throughout the United States, in Chile, Spain, Israel, and India, with the help of Naranjo and his two associates, Rosalyn Shaffer and Kathleen Speeth.

The main goal of the Fischer-Hoffman process is the discovery of self-love. Hoffman describes love as a "feeling and a state of being and it comes from the spiritual essence within ourselves." Theoretically, we should learn how to love when we are children. But, according to Hoffman, "Our parents' failure to teach us to love ourselves and others (including even them!) is the emotional cancer in our lives." Our parents teach us *negative love,* which becomes the primary source of neurotic behavior patterns and of negative characteristics which we have adopted from our parents. Our ability to live positively and lovingly, and even our ability to love at all, is stifled.

Hoffman explains that we adopt negative traits in childhood because we want to be loved by our parents. More often than not, we wind up imitating them to get their attention, being punished, and becoming more un-stable and insecure. Sometimes, we become rebellious. The consequential anxiety that builds up does not help our original struggle. Later on, in mature life, because we have acquired the same negative traits as our parents, our ability to love genuinely is thwarted. Our sexual capacities reflect how we were taught *not* to enjoy sex, but to fear it. Hoffman concludes that this is the source of impotence or homosexuality in men, frigidity or les-bianism in women, sadism, excessive sexual desires, etc.

The key to dispelling these "negativities" is the will to change. Changing is a process of *programming* our-selves with positive love attitudes: "The negative love syndrome is a destructive form of mind programming. Mother's and Father's negative traits, and the rebellion against them, are adopted, not genetic. Not loving your-self and others is like any bad habit. You can learn to love by demolishing the negative love programming and replacing it with positive programming that frees you to be your true self."

According to the Fischer-Hoffman process, our being is a fourfold *Quadrinity*. It is composed of the physical being (brain as well as body), the spirit, the intellect, and the emotions. (The latter three are the nonphysical mind *Trinity*.) Negative love is first bred in your child-hood emotions. As you mature, your intellect and spirit grow and are not able to coordinate with the emotions that you retain from childhood. The process aims to integrate these aspects of your maturity with newly found emotions: "When this newly-mature Trinity merges with the physical self and becomes a total Quadrinity, the individual is free to act, think and feel, and most of all, to love as one with no conflict or inhibi-tion." We become "the way we were meant to be."

These negative childhood emotions are revealed through *mind revelations*: "They are the key to finding and experiencing your own positive reality . . . with deep emotional force." Mind revelations call into action our *natural sensory perception* (NSP), that ability to see clairvoyantly and hear clairaudiently, the potential for which, Hoffman believes, exists in everyone. NSP becomes a tool for reprogramming childhood emotions beyond the intellect.

Activating your NSP requires a certain amount of preparation. It should be allowed to occur easily, without force. Hoffman has devised a relaxation and visualization program to do this. The mental/spiritual activity you experience involves imagining a guide and a sanctuary where you divest yourself of "the negative crud that has blighted you from the psychic side of life." The NSP process is a way to affirm your positive side in your mind. You can refer to this mental place, or sanctuary, often, while finding your self-love.

The complete "mind cleansing" of negativities is done in six stages. Hoffman calls the first and second stages, *Prosecution of the Mother and Father*. They entail ridding yourself emotionally of all the angry feelings you have harbored for your mother and father since childhood. The second and third stages are called *Defense of the Mother and Father*. In these stages, you recall the positive traits of your parents, and you replace their negative traits with the positive. In the fifth stage, you resolve the conflict between your intellect and your childhood emotions and prepare for the sixth stage when you reintegrate the Quadrinity. Hoffman calls this *closure*. It is "the ultimate goal towards which the entire process is directed." Each stage employs your NSP and mind revelation abilities which enable you to psychically receive the events of the past in order to consciously shed their residual negative effects and enforce their positive aspects.

Hoffman believes that it is necessary to experience the process two or three times in order to change the attitudinal patterns you have been practicing all your life, and thoroughly rid yourself of negativities. As a result of experiencing the Fischer-Hoffman process, your capacity to love yourself and to love others will change your living patterns. You will no longer experience neurotic behavior. You will be able to love your parents deeply and genuinely. You will see loving-ness in others and, if not, at least understand the reasons why they are not loving. You will be able to tackle those areas in your life that you have feared encountering before.

The process, carefully guided throughout, takes thirteen weeks, during which time you meet in groups with others for seventeen sessions, and attend lectures; the focus of both is catharis of feelings. During the process, you are given written assignments, aimed at exposing the negative emotion programming learned in childhood. The assignments are read by a teacher and given a taped response. The cost of the thirteen-week course is currently $1,500. The follow-up sessions after the first course are free and are intended to help make your emotional adjustments permanent.

The Quadrinity Center in San Francisco, California, is a religious, nonprofit organization, where the Fischer-Hoffman process is given and qualified teachers are trained.

REFERENCES

Bob Hoffman, *Getting Divorced from Mother and Dad: The Discoveries of the Fischer-Hoffman Process*. New York: E. P. Dutton & Co., 1976.

————, "The Fischer-Hoffman Process: An Alternative to Therapy," monograph published by the Quadrinity Center, San Francisco, Ca., 1976.

VICTOR E. FRANKL (1905–), a European psychiatrist, born in Vienna, is the founder of logotherapy, which he developed during and as the result of three years in Auschwitz and other Nazi concentration camps. He is also responsible for the development of the Third Viennese School of Psychotherapy (preceded by the Freudian and Adlerian schools). He is professor of psychiatry and neurology at the University of Vienna, professor of logotherapy at the United States International University, and visiting professor of psychiatry at Stanford University. In 1961, Frankl was visiting professor at Harvard University summer school. Since then he has lectured frequently in the United States.

Frankl's work has been disseminated largely through the work of Gordon W. Allport, who was a professor of psychology at Harvard University.

Logotherapy (the word derives from the Greek word *logos,* meaning "meaning") is a modern form of existential analysis focusing on the "meaning of human existence as well as on man's search for such a meaning," which Frankl believes to be man's primary motivational force. In contrast to other psychoanalytical methods, logotherapy does not emphasize retrospection and introspection. By focusing on becoming fully conscious of the tasks and meaning to be fulfilled in the future, it diverts you from the development of neuroses by breaking up rather than reinforcing the typically developed self-centeredness. In contrast to the pleasure principle of Freudian analysis and the power principle of Adlerian analysis, logotherapy stresses what Frankl calls *the will to meaning.*

Frankl believes that the search for meaning is not " 'a secondary rationalization' of instinctual drives." Meaning confronts your existence and is not the subject matter of value systems or mere self-expression. Your basic instincts do not conform to moral or religious drives; such drives are products of your decisions. Meaning can become satisfactory and significant only when it is detected and fulfilled by you alone. When your search for meaning is interrupted, you are "existentially frustrated."

Existential has three connotations in terms of logotherapy: existence itself, the human mode of being; the meaning of existence; and the process of striving to discover concrete meaning for personal existence. Existential frustration creates neuroses on the noological level (rather than on psychogenic or psychological levels), which pertains to the nonreligiously spiritual essence of your personality. Noogenic neuroses derive from moral conflicts or spiritual problems, and can be treated logotherapeutically, i.e., treated in terms of their spiritual origins as opposed to being examined with regard to unconscious sources. Frankl contends that existential frustrations are generally not the products of disease, nor should they be treated as such. The duty of a logotherapist is to guide you through your existential problems without recourse to medication.

Frankl found that a widespread phenomenon of the twentieth century is the "existential vacuum" which is demonstrated by a lack of instinctual motivation, the lack of traditional direction, an inability to know choices, career, what to do, and, most basically, in the idea that life is meaningless. You relieve the discomfort of this vacuum through conforming or allowing others to make decisions for you. The form of boredom which often manifests itself as a result of the existential vacuum can result, for example, in alcoholism, juvenile delinquency, or suicide, the final escape.

Logotherapy functions analytically and is distinct from other forms of analysis in that it does not restrict itself to dealing with the consciousness revealing of instinct, but rather focuses on your "will to meaning" and the potential meaning of your existence. It concentrates on the ways to fulfill meaning, rather than the ways to gratify needs and drives, or to resolve the conflicts of the id, ego, and superego, or to adjust to society. According to Frankl, mental health is based inherently on the tensions which are the result of the polarity between what you have accomplished and what you have further to accomplish, how you are and how you should be. You should be in a *noodynamic* state (vs. a homeostatic state) in which spiritual dynamics occur "in a polar field of tension where one pole is represented by meaning to be fulfilled and the other pole by the man who must fulfill it."

One of the techniques of logotherapy is to confront those fears which result from *anticipatory anxiety*. Fears are products of *hyperintention* (excessive intention), or *hyperreflection* (excessive attention). Your fears make what you fear happen, and your forced intention makes what you wish for impossible. A goal of logotherapy is to allow these two characteristics to be "deflected" or refocused in the proper direction. Another technique, called *paradoxical intention,* involves your temporarily intending exactly what you fear. This calls into action your capacity for self-detachment (i.e., the ability to put a distance between yourself and your neuroses) and your sense of humor. The method of paradoxical intention is a short-term therapeutic device useful in treating obsessive, compulsive, or phobic conditions symptomatic of anticipatory anxiety. The method allows you to reinforce your neurotic symptoms to the point where you begin to ridicule them rather than fighting them to make them disappear.

Logotherapy is a process of widening your visual field so that you become conscious of a complete realm of meaning and value. You see your responsibility to yourself and have the option to decide what course of action you will take to fulfill that responsibility. In general, you find meaning in life through experiencing nature, culture, or love, a phenomenon which is both spiritually and sexually primary. Specifically, you can discover meaning in three ways: by doing a deed, by experiencing a value (both are means of achieving), or by suffering. Frankl regards the meaning of suffering as the deepest meaning; it justifies the meaning of survival. The true meaning of life is to be found in the world around you, and you should aim, not for self-actualization, but for *self-transcendence.* Self-actualization is inherent in your commitment to fulfill the meaning of life.

Frankl is the author of *Man's Search for Meaning,* which is an autobiographical account of his experiences in concentration camps, and outlines the basic concepts of logotherapy.

REFERENCES

Viktor E. Frankl, *Man's Search for Meaning: An Introduction to Logotherapy.* New York: Pocket Books, 1974.

————, *The Doctor and the Soul: From Psychotherapy to Logotherapy.* New York: Vintage Books, 1973.

————, *The Will to Meaning: Foundations and Applica-*

tions of Logotherapy. New York and Cleveland: World Publishing Co., 1969.

SIGMUND FREUD (1856–1939)   was an Austrian psychiatrist who founded the system of therapy known as *psychoanalysis* which permanently altered the course of treatment of mental disturbances and disorders. Freud's theories also have had a far-ranging impact on other fields, e.g., art, literature, education, etc.

Freud was born in Pribor, Czechoslovakia, and moved to Vienna, Austria, with his family at the age of four. He was to remain in Vienna until the age of eighty-two when the Nazi occupation drove him to London. Freud received his M.D. from the University of Vienna in 1881. While at the university and the Institute of Cerebral Anatomy, he became interested in neurology. He studied physiology with E. W. von Buerke and brain anatomy with T. H. Meynert. In 1885, Freud went to Paris to study under Jean Charcot, a French neurologist interested in the phenomenon of hysteria. As a result of this association, Freud also became interested in hysteria from a psychical point of view. Upon his return to Vienna, Freud began his collaboration with Josef Breuer, who was investigating a treatment for hysteria using hypnosis which he called the "cathartic" method. In 1893, Freud and Breuer published a paper, "On the Psychical Mechanism of Hysterical Phenomena," and two years later, *Studies in Hysteria,* an elaboration of the paper. The medical profession took a dim view of their work, and Freud and Breuer soon parted ways because of fundamental disagreements.

Freud soon stopped using hypnotism in his treatments, replacing it with a method he devised called conscious *free association.* He published his *Interpretation of Dreams* in 1900, and *Three Contributions to the Sexual Theory* in 1905, which included his theories on *infantile sexuality* that caused a great stir. During this period, Freud began to meet with a group of men including Alfred Adler, Carl Jung, and Eugen Bleuler. In 1908, this group met as the First International Congress of Psychoanalysis, which in 1910 became the International Psychoanalytical Association. (Jung was president.) By 1913, the group had broken apart; Jung and Adler left to form their own schools, the major point of contention being Freud's emphasis on his theories of the Oedipus complex and infantile sexuality. Freud received the Goethe prize in 1930, and in 1936 he was elected to the Royal Society. He left Vienna for London in 1938, where he died a year later.

With the publication of *The Interpretation of Dreams,* Freud laid the foundations for the development of his method of psychoanalysis. As a result of his work with Breuer, Freud came to believe that understanding dreams was the key to understanding "abnormal psychical phenomena" (e.g., phobias, obsessions, delusions). Within the context of the psychological technique that he created to interpret them, Freud defined the dream as a "psychical structure which has a meaning and which can be inserted at an assignable point in the mental activities of waking life." Dreams are derived from life experiences which may or may not be recalled as having happened in a waking state. Thus, dreams become a function of memory. Dreams also originate in various sensory excitations, and biological and psychical stimuli during sleep.

Freud concluded that dreams are of a distinctly psychological nature in their hallucinatory qualities because they are structured of situations that are foreign to us, and they are seemingly nonsensical, transcending time and space. Dreams can be interpreted as the fulfillment of wishes. According to Freud, this theory "is not based on a consideration of the manifest content of dreams but refers to the thoughts which are shown by the work of interpretation to lie behind dreams." The interpretation of dreams becomes a means to discover in detail those "involuntary ideas" which hint at the dreamer's neuroses.

Freud's principles of psychoanalysis operate on the basis of two propositions: 1) Mental processes are essentially unconscious; conscious acts are isolated, constituting part of a whole psychic entity. 2) Impulses, "which can only be described as sexual in both the narrower and wider sense," are the cause of nervous and mental disorders. In Freud's terminology, *unconscious* implies a dynamic mental activity; *preconscious* refers to the unconscious in its latent state, which is closer to the *conscious* than the unconscious. The difference between a preconscious and unconscious idea is that the former is connected in some way with verbal images, the latter with that which "remains unrecognized." In Freud's description of the interrelation of these systems, he compares the unconscious to a large anteroom "in which the various mental excitations are crowding upon one another, like individual beings." Consciousness resides in a smaller apartment or reception room which adjoins the anteroom. Between the two rooms stands a doorkeeper whose job is to examine the various mental excitations seeking admission into the reception room, censoring some, and permitting others over the threshold. Once an idea manages to get over this threshold into the room where the conscious resides, it has entered the *preconscious system*. However, it must manage to catch the eye of the conscious in order to be recognized.

There are two states of the unconscious: that which is *latent* and can become conscious, and that which is *repressed* and unable to become conscious "in the ordinary way." Repression is essentially the rejection of something in order to keep it out of consciousness. Freud defined two phases of repression: *primal repression* in which the idea of an instinct is not allowed to come into consciousness (this idea, which is unalterable, becomes a *fixation*); and *repression proper* in which any ideas associated with the first idea of an instinct become repressed.

Freud determined that in every person "there is a coherent organization of mental processes" which he calls the *ego*. The ego is, in part, conscious and rules the way in which you display excitations to the external world. The ego also censors dreams and so, in part, is unconscious, functioning to stop ideas from becoming conscious, and to activate *resistances* which prevent you from getting closer to what you have repressed.

The *id* is your unknown and unconscious mind; the ego rests on the surface of the id. While the ego represents reason and sanity, the id contains passions. The *superego* (or *ego ideal*) is an unconscious level to which the ego directs its tendencies. It is shaped in the transformation of the infantile ego from the context of narcissism into the activity of sexual aggrandizement of objects (the libidinal cathexis of objects). The activity of sublimation allows that repression does not occur in some cases: "sublimation is a way out, a way by which the claims of the ego can be met without involving repression."

According to Freud's theory, *neuroses,* which result from the conflict between the organized ego and what has been repressed are substitutes for sexual gratification or defenses against it. Their symptoms develop by means of resistance and repression. Freud categorized several types of neuroses: 1) *transference neurosis,* which evolves in the process of recollecting what has been repressed from the past and bringing it into consciousness; it can take the form of *anxiety hysteria, conversion hysteria,* and *obsessional neurosis;* 2) *traumatic neurosis,* induced after a life-threatening event and resembling hysteria; 3) *actual neurosis,* which takes the form of hypochondria, anxiety neurosis, neurasthenia, etc.

Freud's theory of infantile sexuality focuses on the sexual interest in children that derives from their attempt to solve the problem of their birth. Freud describes the force through which this sexual interest occurs as the *libido*. In a child, sexual gratification is achieved initially in activities involving the mouth or lips (*erotogenic zones*) from which the *oral impulse* evolves. This impulse directs the ego to an object in the external world (i.e., the mother's breast); sucking that object becomes a means to gain pleasure. This oral impulse eventually becomes *autoerotic:* the child seeks pleasure from its own body parts, especially the genitalia.

The libido development in children has several phases: 1) the *pregenital period,* in which sexual organization is not defined, sadistic and anal instincts are predominant, the mother is the *love object,* and the *Oedipus complex* develops; 2) the *latency period,* which delays sexual development; 3) *puberty,* in which sexual organization begins to take place to survive through adulthood. Repression occurs in the child when the superego begins to dominate the ego; activities that seem natural to the child are regarded as improper by the parents and censored. This process of repression, manifested as the tension between basic libidinal drives and the superego, can create anxiety, melancholia, etc., and affect a much larger context, i.e., civilization itself. Man's cultural, artistic, and social achievements, according to Freud, are the products of repression.

As Freud developed his theories, he gave birth to new terminologies and new subtheories that served to clarify the process and aims of psychoanalysis. In *A General Introduction to Psychoanalysis,* Freud describes his method of treatment: "In psycho-analytic treatment nothing happens but an exchange of words between the patient and the physician. The patient talks, tells of his past experiences and present impressions, complains, and expresses his wishes and emotions. The physician listens, attempts to direct the patient's thought-processes, reminds him, forces his attention in certain directions, gives him explanations and observes the reactions of understanding or denial thus evoked."

REFERENCES

Sigmund Freud, *A General Introduction to Psychoanalysis,* trans. by Joan Rivere. New York: Simon & Schuster/ Touchstone, 1969.

————, *The Interpretation of Dreams,* trans. and ed. by

James Strachey. New York: Avon Books, 1965.
John Rickman, M.D., ed., *A General Selection from the Works of Sigmund Freud*. New York: Doubleday/Anchor Books, 1957.

ERICH FROMM (1900–), a leading figure in both psychiatry and psychoanalysis, was born in Frankfurt, Germany. He received his Ph.D. in 1922 from the University of Heidelberg and studied at the Psychoanalytic Institute in Berlin. From 1929–32, he lectured at the Psychoanalytic Institute in Frankfurt and the Institute for Social Research at the University of Frankfurt. From 1934–39, he was a fellow at the International Institute for Social Research in New York City, and a guest lecturer at Columbia University from 1940–41. From 1941–50, he held a teaching post at Bennington College, during which time he was also the Terry Lecturer at Yale University. In 1951, he was appointed a professor at the National University of Mexico. From 1957–61, he was a professor at Michigan State University, and became adjunct professor at New York University in 1962.

Fromm's major concern is with the character structure of society, which is measured in terms of the common personality structures of the members of the society, or social group. *Social character* is composed of a selection of the traits of the personalities of individuals within a group, i.e., "the essential nucleus of the character structure of most members of the group which has developed as the result of basic experiences and mode of life common to that group." The concept of social character is necessary for the understanding of social process and functions as an aid to understanding how human energy is channeled and works as a productive force. In a psychoanalytical framework, character is "a specific form in which human energy is shaped by the dynamic adaptation of human needs to the particular mode of existence of a given society." Character is the crux of the shape of thoughts, feelings, and actions. Ideas have an emotional matrix which is the key to understanding the spirit of a culture. In this respect, ideas exert a powerful influence, but only to the extent that they satisfy the needs which are specific to the individual in a given social character. The function of character is to guide individuals to act in a way that is both practical and psychologically satisfying. If the social character adapts dynamically to the objective tasks that the members of society perform, then the collective energies of the society are molded into productive forces indispensable to the functioning of the society. Social character changes responsively to changing social conditions, resulting in new needs and new ideas. New ideas determine the actions of the members of society which, in turn, realign social character.

Fromm maintains that we are no longer one with nature, as we would be if we were animals, but instead have been turned out into a world of reason and self-awareness, which emphasizes our separateness from and helplessness against the forces of nature and society. As a result, we are subject to anxiety which produces feelings of shame and guilt. Our deepest need is to overcome our separateness and achieve union, or "at-onement."

Fromm is concerned with how we analyze both our cultural and individual patterns of existence. He contends that we should see ourselves in terms of our specific natures, rather than how we fit into a general behavioral scheme, so that we can become more concerned with our drives rather than with our behavior. We would then judge ourselves in terms of our passions rather than our instincts. Fromm defines passions as an attempted means to understand and experience life in the most intense and eventful way. He considers passions more active than instincts since they elicit the basic trends in our activity—the manifestations of our culture. They are the aspects of our unification.

In this context, Fromm believes that we have neglected to consider cultural constituents as distinctly human products of a universal language that is both individualized and, most importantly, unified through its symbolism. Understanding this symbolic language (specifically through myth and dreams) would bring us closer to "one of the most significant sources of wisdom, that of myth," as well as to the depths of our personalities. The closures and limitations imposed upon our thoughts about these matters by past schools of psychoanalytic thought would be transcended.

Fromm conducted an extensive study of destructiveness as a meaningful pattern of existence in modern society. He interprets it as man's passion for "drama and excitement." Although it takes the form of the destruction of life, paradoxically it becomes "man's attempt to make sense out of life and to experience the optimum of intensity and strength he can (or believes he can) achieve under the given circumstances." According to Fromm, "All human passion, both the 'good' and the 'evil,' can be understood only as a person's attempt to make sense out of life and transcend banal, merely life-sustaining existence." Destructiveness is the "only true perversion"; its cure lies in the readjustment and "radical change" of social conditions which nurture it.

According to Fromm, aggression is genetically manufactured to ensure man's survival. However, destructiveness (the ability to eliminate one of man's own kind for no ostensible reason) has evolved from the growth of civilization, power, governmental divisions of society and culture, etc. Fromm believes that the tide of destructiveness is rising because of our tendency to lock into automatism.

Present Western society has created so-called solutions to separateness in ways completely antithetical to achieving states which are morally condoned. The first solution is based on conformity and pertains to the mind, not the body. It occurs in the routinization and "prefabrication" of our activities in daily life. The second solution is found in creative activity or productive work, and is not interpersonal. We unite ourselves with a process of creating. For many, who cannot see that their work is productive, their union is only in conformity. Fromm contends that the unity that finds its basis in these states (conformity and productive work) is only a partial answer to the problem of separateness.

The key to solving problems of separateness and the essential key to existence in society is love: "the active concern for the life and growth of that which we love." Love is an inner activity inducing the giving of ourselves genuinely and productively through our joy, interests, understanding, humor, sadness. Our loving of others enriches them. Our ability to love depends on the development of our character in terms of certain basic elements: care, respect, responsibility, and knowledge. These elements are interdependent and characteristic of the maturity which evolves because we have productively developed our powers, we want only that for which we have worked, we have rid ourselves of the narcissistic longing for omnipotence and omniscience, and we have acquired humility rooted in our inner strength. The practice of love depends upon our practice of faith in ourselves and others, and the practice of courage to judge our values.

Attitudes of loving occur on many levels other than the universal one. In a biological sense, loving happens between male and female. The male-female polarity is a basis for interpersonal creativity and penetrates all of nature. Our capacity to love develops from childhood and, for this reason, is a necessary function of the parent-child relationship. Motherly love is selfless, making us secure to grow and develop; fatherly love guides and teaches us in growing. Brotherly love is a fundamental source of different kinds of love. It is the activation of our characteristic sense of care, respect, responsibility, and knowledge of others, and our will to further the lives of others. Brotherly love is rooted in oneness.

Fromm believes that the most deceptive form of love is erotic love, or "the craving of complete fusion" with another. Erotic love, not universal in nature, is based on feeling, rather than decision, judgment, or promise. In this way, erotic love can indicate a relationship which is easily dissolvable. The self is as much an object of love as the other person.

The affirmation of life in terms of happiness, growth, and freedom is a basis of our capacity to love. Selfish people are not capable of loving others because they cannot love the self, are only concerned with themselves and not willing to give. If we love ourselves, we can love others fruitfully.

Loving God is a function of how we conceive of God. In Western religion, we love God because we believe in God, God's existence, God's justice, God's love. In Eastern religion, the love of God is the experience of oneness and linked with its expression in every facet of life. Loving God performs the same function as loving our parents. The quality of our love of God corresponds to our love of man, which is directly connected to our relations with family and determined by the structure of our society.

In contemporary Western society, loving, in the sense of brotherly, motherly, and erotic love, is disintegrating and being replaced by forms of "pseudolove." We are transformed into automatons, routinized in work and amusement, and incapable of loving. We "love," instead, neurotically. Fromm separates this neurotic love into three different categories: 1) *idolatrous love,* which is seen in the tendency to idolize persons we love in the belief that they possess everything we lack; this kind of love only demonstrates our hunger and despair at not having realized our own identity and powers; 2) *sentimental love,* the essence of which "lies in the fact that love is experienced only in phantasy and not in the here-and-now relationship to another person who is real"; examples of this form of love are provided by our experience of movies, magazine love stories, love songs, and our thinking about how we have loved in the past and will love in the future; 3) love in which we use "projective mechanisms" to avoid and ignore our own problems by becoming involved with the loved one's weaknesses.

Because we have become automatons, we can no longer love God. Our image of God is anthropomorphic; our idea of God is idolatrous. Our lives do not depend upon the principles of God. God has become a "Director of the Universe, Inc.," and a "partner in business."

The realignment of human principles is in the interest of future generations. By this, Fromm does not mean advocation of specific schools of thought or doctrine. Rather, he means having faith in our ability to free ourselves from the ties which the latter create in order to see our intention as the embodiment of our most precious quality, the love of life.

REFERENCES

Erich Fromm, *The Anatomy of Human Destructiveness.* Greenwich, Conn.: Fawcett Publications, 1973.

————, *The Art of Loving.* New York: Harper & Row, 1956, 1965.

————, *Escape From Freedom.* New York: Rinehart, 1941.

————, *The Forgotten Language.* New York: Grove Press, 1951.

————, *Man For Himself.* New York: Rinehart, 1947.

————, *Psychoanalysis and Religion.* New Haven: Yale University Press, 1950.

————, *The Sane Society.* New York, Rinehart, 1955.

R. BUCKMINSTER FULLER (1895–), famous for his invention of *comprehensive anticipatory design science,* is a worldwide legendary figure in the fields of design, architecture, science, philosophy, and literature. He was born in Massachusetts and educated at the United States Naval Academy and Harvard. He has been the recipient of numerous honors, honorary doctorates in design, science, art, and humanities, and in 1968 he was awarded the Royal Gold Medal for Architecture by the Queen of England, and the Gold Medal

Award of the National Institute of Arts and Letters. Fuller was appointed research professor at Southern Illinois University in 1959, and in 1961 he instituted the World Design Science Program at the Congress of the International Union of Architects. The program is based on Fuller's conviction that the world's resources, which presently only serve 44 per cent of humanity, can be made to serve 100 per cent of humanity through competent application of anticipatory design science. In 1966, he inaugurated the "World Game" at Southern Illinois University, a computer game to be used to see how the world works so that the needs of all can be satisfied without one section of humanity infringing upon another. Recently, Fuller became World Fellow in Residence at the University of Pennsylvania where he has made himself available as a resource of comprehensive anticipatory design science to the academic institutions in the Philadelphia area. Fuller invented the Dymaxion house in 1929, the Dymaxion car in 1935, the Dymaxion bathroom, the Dymaxion projection of the world, and is inventor-discoverer of energetic/synergetic geometry, geodesic structures (the U.S. Pavilion at the 1967 EXPO in Montreal is the most famous), and Tensegrity structures.

Comprehensive anticipatory design science encompasses the utilization of all our intellectual powers to understand the universe in terms of the generalized principles which govern it, rather than through intellectual specialization. Intellectual specialization is a form of learning which is contradictory to our nature. History shows that we have struggled to understand the world isolated from and ignorant of what exists on the total planet; throughout history 99.9 per cent of humanity has lived on only 10 per cent of the entire earth's surface. The first world-oriented men, Fuller says, were the men of the sea who recognized in their ventures that the integration and distribution of resources obtained from all over the world were advantageous. They were proficient in dealing with the sea, storms, celestial navigation, economics, biology, geography, history, and science. They practiced anticipatory strategy. Unfortunately, they became outlaws, living in secrecy, wallowing in wealth, not sharing their talents as world men.

Our intellectual capabilities can help us anticipate the consequences of the ever-growing number of ways in which we can extend both our physical and metaphysical survival and growth. To use our intellect to the greatest advantage, we must see where we stand in the course of evolution, how the generalized principles which we have extracted from the universe (i.e., leverage, gravity, $E=mc^2$, etc.) apply to the total picture, and how we think of the universe in terms of our experience.

Fuller defines the universe as "the aggregate of all humanity's consciously apprehended and communicated experience with the non-simultaneous, non-identical, and only partially overlapping, always complementary, weighable and unweighable, ever omni-transforming event sequences, which experientially defined, both physically and metaphysically, is finite." The universe is subdivided into systems; what lies outside the system is macrocosmic, what lies within the system is microcosmic. Nature works economically and synergetically, synergy being "the behavior of whole systems unpredicted by the separately observed behaviors of any of the system's separate parts or any subassembly of the system's parts." Furthermore, a corollary of synergy is that "the known behavior of the whole and the known behavior of a minimum of known parts can lead to the discovery of the values of the remaining parts." If we do not adopt a synergetic viewpoint, we will find that our thinking patterns, as established by history, are inadequate to comprehend the universe and its dynamics as a whole.

We are moving away from the state of "discontinuous man," who is illiterate, temporally and geographically bound, and whose uncommunicated experience restricts him to inventing tools in isolation. The emerging "continuous man" is gradually accumulating total world experience, total literate knowledge concerning all the discovered physical resources and generalized patterning principles. Continuous man's intellectual capability multiplies geometrically as his experiences accumulate, and their observed data are transformed into methodologies of anticipatory planning. The laws continuous man has made are universal in scope and only comprehensively applicable in terms of the ever-growing world and its resources. If we directed our attention toward utilizing energy in all its various forms, we could begin to master the environment dynamically and create an Energy-Bourn Commonwealth of Humanity. Our attitudes toward materials used in producing housing, cars, etc. would be transformed: We would be more concerned with actualizing an enriched form of life through scientific design rather than mass production.

Fuller's architecture is based on *geodesics,* which he believes embody the structural integrity of the geometry of natural form. A geodesic is the shortest distance between two points on a curved surface. A geodesic on a sphere is an arc of a great circle, a circle on a sphere whose plane passes through the center of the sphere. Geodesic domes are structures of total equilibrium based on the structural integrity of tetrahedrons (solids of four faces), octahedrons (solids of eight faces), and icosahedrons (solids of twenty faces). A geodesic dome can be constructed out of almost any material and enlarged to great dimensions. In 1961, Fuller designed a two-mile-wide hemispherical dome to span New York City.

Fuller's Dymaxion inventions are based on the maximum utilization of energy and material with minimum consumption. His Dymaxion map is a "comprehensive projection." In contrast to the Mercator projection, the distortion of land mass is at a minimum. The Dymaxion projection, in terms of an infinite number of great circle continuities, makes possible the grouping of whole continents in any of the arrangements in which they occur relative to one another on the globe. Fuller believes that this projection is "unique in that the continental contours are transferable in unbroken integrity from their spherical disposition to a flat map representation without perceptible deformation or modulation of size and with uniform scale measured in great circle arc segments bounding each component section."

Fuller has lectured on his theories, experiments, explorations, and experiences throughout the world. He is the author of numerous books, each one being an exposition of a total thought process. *The Dymaxion World of Buckminster Fuller* by Robert Marks contains a complete review of Fuller's discoveries, inventions, and practiced philosophy.

REFERENCES

R. Buckminster Fuller, *Nine Chains to the Moon.* Carbondale, Ill.: Southern Illinois University Press, 1963.

————, *Operating Manual for Spaceship Earth.* Carbondale, Ill.: Southern Illinois University Press, 1969.

————, *Synergetics.* New York: Macmillan, 1975.

————, *Ideas and Integrities.* Englewood Cliffs, N.J.: Prentice-Hall, 1963.

ERVING GOFFMAN (1922–), a sociologist, was born in Canada and attended the University of Toronto (M.A. 1949) and the University of Chicago, receiving his Ph.D. in 1953. He served as assistant in the Division of the Social Sciences at the University of Chicago in 1952, and became resident associate in 1953. From 1954–57, he was visiting scientist at the National Institutes of Health in Bethesda, Maryland. Goffman was assistant professor at the University of California at Berkeley from 1958–59, associate professor (1959–62) and professor of sociology (1962–68). Since 1968, he has been the Benjamin Franklin Professor of Anthropology and Sociology at the University of Pennsylvania.

Goffman concentrates on an area of sociology which he defines as "face-to-face interaction": the interaction which occurs in social situations where relationships begin and where we are in the immediate presence of others (e.g., weddings, family meals, services, crowds, lines, etc.). Goffman's theory is that the patterns of behavior which we follow and the behavioral routines which have been established with sets of ground rules are the basis of *social order*. To study social order, it is necessary to study modes of social organization, which Goffman finds based on "the interest . . . in the norms and practices employed by any particular participant in the channel of mutual dealings and not in the differentiation and integration of participants." *Ground rules,* one part of total social organization, are a way of regulating these mutual dealings when other modes of organization are lacking; ground rules supply the premises for normal public order (e.g., traffic codes). Within the social context, the individual can be considered in two ways: as a *vehicular unit,* subject to the ground rules of "safe transportation" applicable to a pedestrian traffic system, and as a *participation unit,* presenting himself in public, either singly or with others in interactional units. This condition of the individual demonstrates the activity involved in what Goffman calls the *daily round,* the *service stop,* the *expedition* (making stops which are not part of a routine). The individual can be a "co-participant in an encounter" or "someone reckoned simply as present in a setting or social occasion." The status of an individual will change according to conditions; these labels simply indicate the different roles the individual plays within the social order.

According to Goffman, the "concept of claims" is the center of social order, an idea which he supports with the following terminology: 1) The claim is the qualification to possess, control, use, or dispose of a desired object or state; 2) the claimant is the individual on whose behalf the claim is made; 3) the *impediment* is that which threatens the claim; 4) the *author* (or *counterclaimant*) is the individual on whose behalf the threat to claims is intended; 5) the *agents* are the individuals who act for and represent the claimant and counterclaimant in the situations involving claims. Claims imply *territory of the self,* "a field of things," the boundaries of which the claimant "patrols and defends." According to Goffman's analysis of public order, territories can function in terms of claims which are not necessarily spatial. For example, one kind of territorial situation is that of *personal space*: "the space surrounding an individual, anywhere within which an entering other causes the individual to feel encroached upon, leading him to show displeasure and sometimes to withdraw." This kind of territorial situation can be seen among those waiting in line or using an elevator. Another kind of territory described by Goffman is the *stall,* to which an individual can "lay temporary claim," and possession becomes an all-or-nothing proposition. Examples of this situation can be observed at beaches, parties, in public transportation. The *use space* is the territory surrounding us which we use in our activity, i.e., looking at a painting in a museum. Nonspatial territories are *egocentric;* they include how we protect our bodies, how we protect our possessions, how we protect information about ourselves in the presence of others, how we protect the right to converse. These territories of the self are subject to the conditions set by social circumstances, the ways in which we *mark* them as existing, and the way we manipulate them, offensively and defensively. Goffman believes that territories of the self have two functions; one involves our personal will and determination with regard to how we use our claims, and the other, how our usage of territories establishes bases for the creation of "ritual idiom."

Social rituals are performed so that we may relate with others, either negatively or positively. *Positive relation* illustrates *supportive ritual,* which can occur in two ways: in terms of a shared similar intention within a relationship, or in terms of specialized intention. In the latter case, we can see how we accommodate changes in others by the ways in which we show our support conversationally. On the whole, the exchange of information and the practice of specialized rituals are ways to reveal the relational structure of our individual roles.

Social contact occurs on three levels, each level having its own distinct ritual based upon connecting and relat-

ing: on the business level, by chance, and by appointment. On an interpersonal basis, social contact when
observed reveals various forms of conversational or
physical behavior, and particular exchanges which are
engaged in the supportive or *remedial* sense. The function of remedial work is "to change the meaning that
otherwise might be given to an act, transforming what
could be seen as offensive into what can be seen as
acceptable." This entails the use of *accounts* applicable
in a legal sense; *apologies,* the common form of expression of embarrassment, disavowals, etc.; and *requests*
made in the context of violation of personal rights.
Social rituals provide ways for us as individuals to
move within and without the structures of society, engaged in taking care of matters at hand, either in a
routine manner or for a specific purpose. Within our
Umwelt, the egocentric area which is fixed around us,
there are sources of communicable alarms with regard
to that which we perceive as abnormal, unnatural, or
dangerous, within a specific situation. The transitions
that occur in our actions are determined by how we
perceive the situation at hand, and then shape and apply our attitudes, defenses, offenses, etc., which we
transmit through ritualistic means or specialized roles.

The form of society, including the forms that exist
within it (economic, etc.), determines our course of
action in any given circumstance. We can manufacture
ways to appear unconnected or connected, given the fact
that we have judged how we will affect the circumstance,
or vice versa. We design our motion through circumstances in accordance with our knowledge of or suspi-
cions about the situation. This dynamic makes our Umwelt constantly vulnerable, and can render "normal
appearance . . . broad cover[s] under which persons
and agencies may try to monitor [us], approach [us]
for attack, conceal things vital to [us], attempt to make
contact with [us]," etc. Thus, the most common situation is subject to immediate alteration and a kind of
disorder; the common situation is only one part of the
identifiable "surface character" of public order.

Goffman has written several books which focus on the analysis of behavior within society; among them are *Relations in Public; Strategic Interaction;* and *Interactional Ritual.*

REFERENCES

Erving Goffman, *Relations in Public: Microstudies of Public Order.* New York: Basic Books, 1971.

———, *Interactional Ritual.* New York: Anchor Books, 1967.

———, *Strategic Interaction.* Philadelphia: University of Pennsylvania Press, 1969.

———, *The Presentation of Self in Everyday Life.* New York: Doubleday & Co., 1959.

GRAPHOLOGY is the study of handwriting for the purpose of character analysis. In several countries, France and England in particular, the testimony of a graphologist is accepted as legitimate case evidence in court. Graphology is taught in some universities in Europe and in the United States. It has become a subject of investigation in psychological research centers to determine how it can be applied to personality guidance. Raymond Trillat, associated with the Psycho-Pedagogic Center of the University of Paris, is a practicing graphologist who collaborates with businesses in personnel selection through handwriting analysis, as well as experiments with handwriting therapy for the treatment of emotionally ill children.

Psychographology is a new science which applies psychological principles to graphology. In this context, handwriting is analyzed as an index of strength of character, willpower, judgment, passion, physical and mental condition, as well as characteristics of present and past development. The analysis of different types of handwriting reveals a variety of personality types. By discovering your personality type as revealed by your handwriting, and the weaknesses and strengths characteristic of that type, you can become aware of the changes you would like to make in yourself.

Handwriting is the product of the movements and

gestures which the brain translates through your nerves and muscles. Ostensibly, your handwriting will change according to your mood changes; however, this does not alter your basic handwriting movements (*sign types*) as revealed by pressure, size, letter shapes, style, spacing, etc. In handwriting analysis, personality types are judged on the basis of the similarities or dissimilarities of these characteristics.

There is a progression that can be seen in handwriting from childhood to mature adulthood, from slow, awkward, rather large letters to the gradual acquiring of a set rhythm and set patterns which demonstrate life experiences and personality idiosyncrasies which have been developed. The key to analyzing samples of handwriting lies in noting the differences among certain graphological characteristics. Spacing of writing can indicate your state of mind; speed of writing, the amount of energy you have; the slope of writing, the degree of your affections; the size of writing, your disposition; terminal strokes or spacing between words and letters measure your generosity; capital letters reveal personal tastes; small letters indicate mental development; your signature is a clue to your individuality; the flourishes in your handwriting indicate superficialities in character; a style in your handwriting reveals sharpness of mind; margins demonstrate your sense of proportion; pressure is a key to your emotional state.

Robert Holder, a psychographologist who has studied thousands of handwriting samples, has determined certain characterisics which can determine graphologically specific personality types. For example, an introvert's handwriting will have a vertical or slightly back-slanted flow. It will have a broken rhythm, and the writing will be small, have clipped or short ending strokes, and will contain simple or printlike capitals. The signature of an introvert will be enclosed with a sweeping curve. The handwriting of a moody person will have uneven pressure, the small letters will vary in size, the capital letters will be sharply formed; t's will be crossed in a variety of ways, i's will be carelessly dotted; the handwriting will be generally angular. An "ideal housewife" will write simple capital letters; the g's and y's will have full loops; the stems on d's and t's will be looped. The rhythm on the writing will be slow and steady, generally rounded or mixed, and large and legible. A lover of fine arts will write vertically, with balanced and well-proportioned margins. There will be breaks in words, letters will be disconnected, simple, graceful capital letters, light down strokes, and small letters will be formed with originality. A person who is goal oriented will write with a fast rhythm, many letters will be half formed. The intellectual will write with harmonious proportions, a fast rhythm, small letters, and many upper projections. A nervous person who is extremely inhibited will have a handwriting in which the distance between letters is significant in judging psychic difficulty. Capital letters will be large, lines will be widely spaced, and the ending strokes will point straight upward.

According to Holder, there is a procedure which should be followed in the analysis of handwriting: 1) Examine two or three handwriting samples, preferably written a few months apart; 2) use a sample written in ink; 3) do not use a sample written especially for analysis; 4) do not use samples of writing from envelopes which are usually made purposely legible and clear; 5) use samples that are written on unlined paper in order to judge style and spacing; 6) the samples should include all letters of the alphabet, have many capital letters, enough lines of writing to judge style and spacing, and many examples of i's and t's; 7) use samples that have been written recently; 8) do not look for graphological characteristics which fit a preconceived idea of the writer; 9) in doing a quick handwriting analysis ask for full name in a signature, a sentence about the weather, a personal sentence (i.e., I like . . .), the alphabet in capital letters, and numbers 1–10; 10) be objective.

Handwriting analysis can indicate what you can do to improve your relationships, the kind of job that is right for you, the kind of person with whom you are compatible. It can aid you in understanding your children, and generally help business and family relationships. Handwriting can also reveal your unhealthy practices such as overeating, excessive smoking or drinking, fears, anxieties, and tendency to worry. Although handwriting analysis cannot point out the *exact cause* of any existing problem, it can warn you of your personal tendencies and characteristics, and give you clues to the fact that you should make an effort to ameliorate the shape and content of your actions and attitudes.

REFERENCES

William Leslie French, *Graphoanalysis: Your Handwriting and What It Means*. Hollywood, Ca.: Newcastle Publishing Co., 1974.

H. Hartford, *You Are What You Write*. New York: Macmillan, 1973.

Robert Holder, *You Can Analyze Your Handwriting*. New York: New American Library, 1969.

————, *Handwriting Talk*. New York: Farnsworth Publishing Co., 1974.

Manfred Lowengard, *How to Analyze Your Handwriting*. New York: Cavendish, 1975.

P. de Sainte-Columbe, *Graphotherapeutics*. New York: Popular Library, 1972.

GEORG GRODDECK (1866–1934), a psychiatrist, was born in Germany. In his early years, he wrote a novel, poetry, and a book of art criticism. Later, he became a doctor and worked in the field of psychology. Until his death he has the director of a clinic in Baden-Baden where he worked with patients using a combination of diet, deep massage, and analysis in their treatment. He continued to write, applying his theories of psychology to all aspects of knowledge. His writings were influential and attracted many patients and pupils. Groddeck is often mistaken as a disciple of Freud, especially with regard to his theory of the "It," which, in fact, he had structured before he met Freud. Although Groddeck admired Freud, he did not share his views on the nature of the forces in human beings which control health and sickness.

Groddeck believed that the whole psyche, including the conscious and unconscious, is controlled by an unknown and unknowable entity which he labeled the *It*. He considered "It" to be a definitive term which could be assigned to the human being as a physical, mental, and spiritual organism without emotional or intellectual associations. He used the theory of the It not as a principle (the It was not a thing), but as a means by which he could see through and penetrate reality. Groddeck disclaimed the It hypothesis as truth; rather, the term was a useful tool in medical work and experimentation.

The underlying assumption of his hypothesis is that: "Man is animated by the It which directs what he does and what he goes through and that the assertion 'I live' only expresses a small and superficial part of the total experience 'I am lived by the It.' . . . Of the It we know only as much as lies within our consciousness. Beyond that, the greater part of its territory is unattainable, but by search and effort, we can extend the limits of our consciousness and press far into the realm of the unconscious, if we can bring ourselves no more to desire knowledge, but only to fantasy."

Groddeck structured his overview of psychoanalysis on the idea that it magnifies our mysterious background as manifested in the It-self, a composite of our behavior, size, shape, our beliefs, and desires. Psychoanalysis precipitates cures to all our sicknesses, both mental and physical; through the analysis of the unconscious, the influence of psychoanalysis can be directed toward our injuries. According to Groddeck, there is a reason behind everything that happens to us which works in correspondence with the It, and often is the It, itself. The It creates the brain and the intellect through which it can express itself. The "ego" and the "I" are tools, not masters, of the It. Each individual cell, as well as each organic system, possesses the consciousness of individuality; carry this idea a step further and every It-unit can "deceive" itself into thinking it is an individual, a person, or an "I." The I of the cells, organs, systems, and the general I, or our ego awareness, are not the same entities as the It, but are produced by the It as modes of expression in our thoughts, gestures, actions, etc. This polarity between the ego and the It is the foundation of Groddeck's philosophy.

In contrast to Freud's belief that the pattern of the whole world would become clear if the first cause of it could be ascertained, Groddeck believed that the whole is essentially unknown and unknowable, and demonstrates itself by means of our functions. There is liberation, rather than cure, in attaining self-knowledge. Philosophical, rather than rational, Groddeck maintained a metaphysical view of the problems of health and disease, avoiding a dogmatic system into which everything could fit.

The It utilizes its expressions of health and sickness simultaneously: We are never either completely well or ill. Groddeck dealt with illness in the same manner he would analyze handwriting, trying to trace what the It was trying to express through the disease. Healing the disease is the result of the exchange which takes place between the doctor and the patient: the patient, in his effort to gain enough self-knowledge to cure the It of its "maladjustments"; the doctor in his effort to free himself from his purpose, the desire to cure. Groddeck believed the language of the It to reside in the patient. Illnesses are created for the specific purpose of aggrandizing woes and amassing feelings of guilt. The ego becomes an instrument by which we can interpret the motivations behind our actions and reactions. The ego does not separate us from participation in the world.

The aim of medical treatment is to gain some control of the It, to get rid of the causes of the disease rather than the symptoms. There are two different causes for every illness, accidental or otherwise: the *causa interna,* which we contribute on our own, and the *causa externa,* which comes from the environment. Groddeck focused on treating disease causally, believing that the symptoms of all illnesses are in the I, whose unconscious complexes can be made conscious. The I develops within our minds as the result of a learning process; we are symptoms of the It.

Groddeck applied his theory of the It to other realms of knowledge, expanding on its poetic nature, as well as its philosophical importance. We live in a continual effort to symbolize our It through art, music, and language. The artist is the agent for and translator of the "extracausal" forces which overpower us. Yet the artist's situation is no different from that of the common man: The artist describes or expresses his dilemma through his art, the common man, through disease. The language of art is part of the language of It. We create the world in our image, and our activities and inventions reflect the nature of our primitive experience.

Groddeck discusses the It in several books, and most specifically in *The Book of the It,* published in England in 1949. It is comprised of thirty-three fictional letters, explaining his theories, with examples of their application. *The World of Man, The Unknown Self,* and *Exploring the Unconscious* are other works by Groddeck, composed of essays and papers. *The World of Man* contains an unfinished exploration of the nature of pictorial art, general art criticism, and an essay, "Unconscious Factors in Organic Processes," which pertains to his views of massage and a description of anatomy in terms of psychological processes.

REFERENCES

Georg Groddeck, *The Book of the It*. New York: Vintage Books, 1961.

———, *The Unknown Self*. London: Vision, 1967.

———, *Exploring the Unconscious*. London: Vision, 1966.

———, *The World of Man*. International Publications Service, 1951.

GEORGES I. GURDJIEFF (1877–1949) is an important contributor and significant force in con-

temporary philosophy. Born in Russia, Gurdjieff spent twenty years of his early life traveling throughout Central Asia and the Middle East in search of answers to his questions about man's existence. In Moscow, prior to World War I, Gurdjieff began to gather a following of students with whom he toured to the Caucasus, Tiflis, Constantinople, Berlin, London, and finally Paris, where he ran the Institute for the Harmonious Development of Man in 1922. From 1924–35, Gurdjieff devoted his time to writing. From 1935 until his death in 1949, he worked with his students and secured the posthumous publication of his first series of writings, *Beelzebub's Tales to His Grandson,* which traces the universe from its creation to modern times. Originally published in Russian and Armenian, this series was later translated into other languages according to Gurdjieff's instructions.

In order to understand Gurdjieff, it is necessary to examine his writings as well as the talks with his students which have been recorded, often from fragmentary notes jotted down by his students. It is also necessary to understand that much of his effectiveness stemmed from the immense personal presence of the man. Gurdjieff was very much oriented in the Islamic Sufi tradition. He was also a living example of his philosophy, and taught and inspired with any means at his disposal—confusion, contradictions, insults, etc.

Gurdjieff was interested in synthesizing Christianity and the concepts of Reciprocal Maintenance and Universal Hazard taught in the Sarman Brotherhood with his own questions about man's condition in the universe. According to Gurdjieff, God, or the Creator, is not omnipotent for He cannot control the entropic process of time. God has unlimited being, is all merciful and wise, and elicits an attitude of love, worship, and confidence in response to His goodness. The universe, according to Gurdjieff, is nondualistic; it consists of everything that is material and energy and undergoing transformation. Creation does not arise dualistically or monistically; it gives forth a world whose basis is the continual interaction among all its spiritual and material levels. These levels exist in all experiences and do not halt the process of transformation on the physical plane but further transform in the strata of thought, feeling, love, union, and creativity.

Gurdjieff's teachings are concerned with the evolution of man. His approach is that its process is the result of individual inner growth, not mass influences. Furthermore, inner knowledge, the goal of all religions, can only be achieved through a direct and precise knowledge of the qualitative changes in inner consciousness, the consequence of intense self-study and experience. Thus, the primary question which permanently fixed itself in Gurdjieff's mind from his youth was: What is the sense and significance of life on earth in general and human life in particular?

Gurdjieff's answer to the first part of the question is that the universe experiences a status called *Reciprocal Maintenance:* The universe has an inherent structure or pattern which allows every group of living beings to produce energies or substances necessary for the survival of other groups. He describes this process in terms of *involution* and *evolution.* Involution is an entropic process in which high level energy systems transform lower energy systems through a specific apparatus designed for the purpose with regard to the proper environment and conditions for the transformation. Examples of such an apparatus are the human body, other living organisms, and on a larger scale, the earth. Evolution is a process which acts against probability, producing high level energy from lower level energy sources. Life is an example of evolution.

Gurdjieff believed that none of this could happen without the guidance of a higher power. The "accidental" stage of transformations of energy falls within the realm of possibility as set forth by natural law. Any stages beyond creation depend upon supernatural power to succeed, which means that each entity within the energy transforming system must maintain the existence of other entities. Therefore, each class of entities has an energy that functions significantly in the cosmic process.

Gurdjieff believed that man assumes the role "for maintaining something great or small in the world." Man is an apparatus that produces energy, voluntarily and involuntarily, that is sensitive, conscious, and directed toward the maintenance of a balanced larger system, i.e., the solar system. Voluntary production of energy takes the form of "working on oneself" or "striving for perfection"; involuntary production of energy takes the form of dying. Evolution comes about integrated with the process in which higher level energy, generated unconditionally at a certain level of being, corrects the entropic or involuntary process in keeping with the law of nature. According to Gurdjieff, everything in the universe "exists and is maintained exclusively on the basis of what is called the common-cosmic trogoautoegocratic process . . . actualized by our Endless Uni-Being, when our Most Great and Most Holy Sun Absolute had already existed, on which our All-Gracious Endless Creator had and still has the chief place of His existence; this system which maintains everything arisen and existing was actualized by our Endless Creator in order that what is called the exchange of substances or the Reciprocal-feeding of everything that exists might proceed in the Universe and thereby that the merciless Heropass might not have its maleficent effect on the Sun Absolute."

Another concept Gurdjieff originated is *Iraniranumange,* implying the universal exchange of energies. This concept answers the second part of his question (i.e., what is the sense and significance of human life?). It indicates that evolution led to the birth of conscious and intelligent activity the personification of which is man. Man is capable of furthering evolution in three ways: through concern with his own welfare as related to his immortality; through the commitments he must make in order to establish his place in nature; and through the commitment he must make in a supernatural context to fulfill the purpose of his existence. Man takes part in the Iraniranumange not only by contributing to the reciprocal maintenance process but also by transforming higher energies to render his soul immortal. Thus, the significance and sense of human life are found in man's *decision* to transform energies of the most basic level and on higher and higher levels until he becomes a free, immortal soul. The immortal principle is only satisfied when man transforms his nature by means of "conscious labors and internal suffering." Man, and every other living system, depends upon what Gurdjieff calls the *Okidanokh,* an omnipresent cosmic substance, the Universal Will, that is essential for the creation and maintenance of every aspect of existence. Gurdjieff's conclusion was that man's will alone, not God's, predicates his liberation, the ultimate goal, that is arrived at through transcendence of all lesser goals.

Man is capable of entering different states of consciousness, discovering new ways of understanding, and living beyond an earthly existence. Gurdjieff saw man's potential development as encompassing movement from the physical body to ultimate liberation (a rare occasion), operating within the laws of threefoldedness that governs thinking, feeling, and instinctual experiences. The currency for the stages of development is the Omnipresent Okidanokh, which is invisible and independent of being.

In his talks and private lectures, Gurdjieff explored concepts of language and the necessity for its precision in dealing with knowledge; concepts of the plurality of man; man's ability to wholly experience; the relationship between body, essence, and personality, etc., all within the context of his comprehensive view of the world and the universe. He also wrote aphorisms which were inscribed upon the walls of the study house in his institute in Paris. P. D. Ouspensky's book *In Search of the Miraculous* is considered the most authoritative work on Gurdjieff's philosophy.

REFERENCES
J. G. Bennett, *Gurdjieff: Making a New World.* New York: Harper & Row, 1973.

G. I. Gurdjieff, *Views from the Real World.* New York: E. P. Dutton & Co., 1975.

————, *All and Everything: Beelzebub's Tales to His Grandson.* New York: E. P. Dutton & Co., 1973.

P. D. Ouspensky, *In Search of the Miraculous.* New York: Harcourt, Brace & World, 1965.

EDWARD T. HALL (1914–), an anthropologist and writer, was born in Webster Groves, Missouri. He received his Ph.D. from Columbia University in 1942. During the 1950s he directed the State Department's Point Four Training Program which was created to select and train Americans to work in business and governmental capacities in foreign countries. From 1959–63, Hall directed a communications research project at the Washington School of Psychiatry. He has taught at the University of Denver, Bennington College, Harvard Business School, and the Illinois Institute of Technology. He is a member of the American Anthropological Association, the Society for Applied Anthropology, and the Building Research Advisory Board of the National Academy of Sciences. Hall has done field work with Spanish-Americans in New Mexico and Latin America, and with the Navajo, Hopi, Western Mediterranean Arabs, and Iranians. He collaborated with George L. Trager, professor of anthropology and linguistics at the University of Buffalo, on a theory of culture. Hall is the author of three major works: *The Hidden Dimension; The Silent Language;* and *Beyond Culture.*

Hall's concern is how man relates to the environment, how man creates culture, and communicates within that culture. Hall's premise for his work was his perception of the "great need to revise and broaden our view of the human situation, a need to be both more comprehensive and more realistic, not only about others, but about ourselves as well. It is essential that we learn to read the silent communications as easily as the spoken or printed ones. Only by doing so can we reach other people, both inside and outside our national boundaries. . . ." The "silent communications" are the languages of culture which are specifically found in gesture and *spatial experience*. Analysis of the languages particular to a culture reveals that culture itself is a form of communication specifically about those individuals who make up the culture.

Hall studied various cultures within the context of the science of *proxemics,* which he defines as "the inter-related observations and theories of man's use of space as a specialized elaboration of culture." Proxemics is manifested on three levels: 1) The *infracultural* level is behavioral and has its roots in man's biological past. Hall studied the experiments done with animal behavior, specifically how space is regulated according to function. Revealed in this study is the development of the *behavioral sink* (a term created by the ethologist John Calhoun to describe what occurs in the behavioral process when animals [e.g., rats] collect in crowds) wherein the natural processes of nest building, sexual activities, reproduction, territoriality, and social organization are affected by crowding. Crowding, given the evidence of experiments done by Hans Selye and others, produces biochemical reactions in animals that can be labeled stress. Hall believes that stress has positive value illustrated in the evolution of man by the development of special sensory apparatus, e.g., the development of man's distance receptors.

2) The *precultural* level of proxemics is found in the creation of these distance receptors (sight, hearing, and sense of smell, to a certain degree), which are evidence of how man used his sensory apparatus in different behavioral, environmental, and necessarily experiential situations. Sensory apparatus, and how it is conditioned to respond, controls the way in which man relates to the environment and acquires a sense of space. This sense of space, according to Hall, reflects man's sense of his visual, kinesthetic, tactile, and thermal self. Visual development, as the last to occur, is the most complex with regard to the information-gathering and information-disseminating function of the eyes necessary for the

perception of space. Hall suggests that the physical structure of the eye determines how man designs space. The history of visual development, as it relates to the structuring of space, is found in art. Art gives clues to how man has become aware of himself, his environment, his perceptual relationship to the environment, and aware of the transactions that take place between man and the environment. Literature is another source of information about the development of perception of space, if analyzed in terms of structure rather than content.

3) Proxemics are clearly observable on the *micro-cultural* level in three ways: a) In terms of *fixed-feature space* which measures territoriality; it is "one of the basic ways of organizing the activities of individuals and groups." It is seen in the ways people of different cultures structure their internal space (e.g., houses) and in this way becomes a mold for behavior. b) *Semi-fixed-feature space* is that which is transitional and is as much sociofugal as sociopetal. Hall claims the desirability of such space is its "flexibility and congruence between design and function" so that out of one space can be created a variety of spaces in which people can choose to be involved given the proper situation. c) The characteristics of *informal* space are "unstated" and fluctuate; it is the product of an individual's spatial experience of which the individual is not necessarily aware. Participation in informal space occurs on different levels: that of *intimate distance,* ranging from a close phase (e.g., lovemaking) to a far phase (six to eighteen inches); that of *personal distance,* in which a protective space is maintained between the individual and others; that of *social distance,* in which domination of one individual over another can be observed; and that of *public distance,* in which communication between individuals exists in periphery.

Hall believes that it is important to recognize these specifically cultural "zones of involvement" in order to create environmental situations (e.g., houses, buildings) that will cater to their existence. Knowledge of spatial needs is necessary to avoid the occurrence of over-crowding and the physiological and psychological rami-fications of it. Hall sees that "the relationship of man to his extensions as related to communications, structuring of cities, transporation, etc., is simply a continuation and specialized form of the relation of organism to environment." Therefore, "because extensions are numb . . . it is necessary to build feedback into them so that we can know what is happening, particularly in regard to extensions that mold or substitute for the natural environment." All cultural crises (urban, ethnic, educational) are results of a cultural dimension which, because it is hidden, is neglected.

Communication within culture is demonstrated in what Hall calls primary message systems which are means to establish the patterns and values for the rela-tionships and interactions that occur on various levels within the culture. Hall feels that culture must be recog-nized as a process involving persons which changes in terms of shifts between *levels* on which people operate: the *formal* level in which the norm becomes firmly em-bedded on both an individual and social basis; the *informal* level in which a social or individual pattern is established that is flexible; the *technical* level in which that conformity which is occasionally deviated from sets precedence for a complete cultural transformation. The interrelationship among the members of this "major triad" is such that formal activity tends toward informal which, in turn, tends toward technical. Studying culture becomes a process of taking the indeterminacy in ob-serving it and the relativity of experience that creates it into account, and making clear the equality of value in the events that occur in any compared cultures. The formation of a truly constructive attitude toward culture becomes a result of the observations of its foundations that are rooted in the cultural language of the people who comprise it.

Hall observes that Americans have taken their culture for granted and are not conscious of it. They cannot see that what they have seemingly arbitrarily created is taking them over. Retrieving those aspects of human nature (the silent language of culture) that have been lost means returning to or creating those cultural situations which complement and support them, "because people cannot act or interact at all in any meaningful way except through the medium of culture."

REFERENCES

Edward T. Hall, *The Hidden Dimension*. New York: Doubleday & Co., 1966.

——, *The Silent Language*. New York: Doubleday/ Anchor Press, 1973.

——, *Beyond Culture*. New York: Doubleday/Anchor Press, 1976.

HIGH-FIBER DIET. According to recent statistics from the American Cancer Society, colon and rectum cancer has become the most common form of cancer in the United States. There are over ninety-nine thousand new cases each year, forty-nine thousand of which are fatal. The fiber diet is one of the results of the growing concern of doctors with this form of cancer and how it relates to the average American diet.

Prior to the formulation of fiber diets, a study was done on the bowel movements of African villagers. The findings were later compared with similar studies done in England. The cumulative results when compared to the population of the United States revealed the following information: 1) Coronary heart disease, which causes one third of the deaths in the United States, is unknown in rural Africa; 2) cancer of the colon and rectum, the number-one fatal cancer in the United States, is rare among rural Africans; 3) appendicitis, the most common cause of abdominal surgery in the United States, is rarely experienced by rural Africans; 4) hemorrhoids are rare among Africans who consume a traditional diet; 5) Africans rarely contract diverticulosis, a disease of the colon common in the United States; 6) varicose veins are rare among rural Africans, whereas 10 per cent of Americans have them; 7) phlebitis is rare among rural Africans; 8) obesity is rare in Africa if a traditional diet is followed.

Medical research has revealed a correlation between the rising trends of the above-mentioned diseases and dietary habits in recent years. Studies have shown that those accustomed to high-fiber diets, when introduced to a habitual low-fiber diet, become increasingly susceptible to the diseases which have become identifiably characteristic of low-fiber diets. Scientists have confirmed in studies that people who consume little roughage acquire two types of bacteria in the colon which, in combination with two specific bile acids that are normally present in digestion, can create carcinogens (cancer-causing chemicals). Furthermore, with a low-roughage diet, less acid was passed in bowel movements because the acids had broken down to contribute to the carcinogenic compounds. In contrast, the colons of those people consuming high-fiber diets developed bacteria that do not attack and break down acids to form carcinogens.

When food of a high-roughage diet is consumed, upon entering the stomach it encounters hydrochloric acid and enzymes that precipitate digestion. When the food reaches the small intestine, it is further broken down by bile acids from the liver. Once the food material reaches the colon, it mixes with bacteria (streptococcus and lactobacillus), and is later eliminated in a bowel movement that contains 20 per cent bacteria and bile acids that are intact. The bowel movement is soft, odorless, bulky, and in a large amount.

Changing your diet from low fiber to high fiber necessitates the elimination of such foods as instant potatoes, instant rice, cake mixes, puddings, stuffing, gravies, bread, pastry, and other commercially baked products that contain ultrarefined flour. Replace these foods with a diet that contains bran, whole-grain products, fresh fruits and vegetables which are consumed raw or minimally cooked. The roughage level in your diet should be increased from six grams, which is average, to twenty-four grams.

A high-fiber diet can be considered preventive medicine in relation to several specific conditions. The primary cause of heart attack has been related to large amounts of cholesterol which deposits itself on the arteries of the heart. A high-fiber diet can decrease the amount of cholesterol in the blood by creating a condition in which the liver converts cholesterol to bile salts in an amount significant enough to be passed in the bowel movement. Diverticulosis, which is the result of internal pressure of fecal material on the colon, is a condition most likely to occur with a diet that is high in sugar and ultrarefined carbohydrates (junk food). The slow motion of low-roughage foods through the intestinal tract, which can cause the appendix to become plugged up with fecal concretions, can cause appendicitis. A high-roughage diet can eliminate constipation. Lignin, cellulose, and hemicellulose, the components of fiber, work together to produce enough natural laxatives to allow for regular, easy-to-pass bowel movements. A high-fiber diet can prevent obesity: High-fiber foods require chewing and are therefore more satisfying; the foods are bulkier, and chewing produces more saliva and gastric juices which give a full feeling; the food induces bowel movement release of excess body fat; chances of constipation are greatly decreased.

David Reuben, M.D., has been instrumental in bringing the benefits of fiber in the diet to the attention of the American public. After intense study, Reuben concludes that a high-fiber diet can become a means of disease prevention as well as treatment. In *The Save Your Life Diet,* he outlines high-fiber diets and recipes, and lists foods of high-fiber content that can be incorporated into a weight-reducing plan.

REFERENCES
Lawrence Galton, *The Truth About Fiber in Your Diet.* New York: Crown Publishers, 1976.

David Reuben, M.D., *The Save Your Life Diet.* New York: Ballantine Books, 1975.

HOMEOPATHY (from the Greek words *homeos,* meaning "similar," and *pathos,* meaning "suffering") is a system of medicine that treats a disease with an agent, or drug, that will produce the same symptoms as the disease itself in a healthy organism, the fundamental principle being that *like cures like*.

Homeopathy was conceived in terms of its practical application by Samuel Hahnemann, a German physician of the early nineteenth century, who formally set down the laws and principles of the practice as 292 aphorisms in *Organon of the Art of Healing*. It was Hahnemann's claim that cure through medicine only operated within the boundaries of certain laws of healing that exist in nature; since illness is dynamic in quality, so must be the cure. He arrived at this conclusion after observing the results of his experiments with drugs; the evidence caused him to understand that a remedy cures a disease because it creates symptoms similar to the disease. Hahnemann hypothesized that illness was a disorder with an energy factor of the same intensity as the energy governing the order of being. There exists a dynamic life force, which he called the *vital force,* invisible and immeasurable, governing the transition from life to death. This vital force, observable only through its qualities, is deranged in illness. In order for a cure to be successful, this vital force must be acted upon.

A homeopathic diagnosis is particular to the patient, and the specific symptoms the patient exhibits. The goal of the diagnosis and treatment is to discover what drug will cause the same symptoms as the illness and, theoretically, cure it. (This is in contrast to the *allopathic* school of medicine, which treats a disease with a drug producing effects that are different from the disease.) As Hahnemann states in *Organon:* "Symptoms alone must constitute the medium through which the disease demands and points out its curative agent . . . the totality of these symptoms . . . must be the chief, or only means of the disease to make known the remedy necessary for its cure, the only means of determining the selection of the appropriate remedial agent." It has been suggested that the reason homeopathic remedies work is that the homeopath is careful to select the remedy or remedies that will match the dynamic nature of the symptoms of the illness. Given that the disease is created as the result of an organism's defense against the morbific agents which penetrate it, homeopathy becomes a means to strengthen an organism's natural defense by contributing to its resources and energy. In this way, homeopathy works with the vital force, in contrast to allopathy which works to suppress it.

When the remedial medicine is initially administered, the symptoms are aggravated; this aggravation might take the form of sudden diarrhea or excessive perspiration. The persistence of the aforementioned works in proportion to the seriousness of the illness. This is called the *curative crisis:* It occurs when the remedy gives sufficient strength to an organism to combat disease.

J. T. Kent, who has done research on the effects of homeopathy and originated cures that have been described as spectacular, determined that there are twelve possible reactions to the first dose of a selected remedy, some of which may result in the disappearance of symptoms in the following ways: 1) from the center of the body to the circumference; 2) from above downward; 3) from more vital to less vital organs; 4) the above three patterns in reverse order, i.e., the first symptom to surface will be the last to disappear.

Since Hahnemann, homeopathy has been used to treat epilepsy, infantile paralysis, uremic convulsions, cancer, diphtheria, pneumonia, arthritis, spinal meningitis, and diabetes. Homeopathy has been effective in curing functional diseases in which there is no pathological tissue damage or changes. Dr. W. H. Schwartz in *Homeopathy* (vol. 5, 1936), states: "Perhaps the greatest field for achievement for homeopathy is in correcting the child's inherited dyscrasiae—the inherited syphilis and sycosis; the tendency to tuberculosis, cancer, insanity, Bright's disease, etc." In the case of advanced chronic illness, though, the relief is only temporary. As documented in homeopathic journals, many conditions such as asthma, allergic conditions of lungs and higher respiratory tract, anemia, skin diseases, heart disease, etc. have been completely cured.

Although medical schools and medical practice in the United States do not widely advocate the homeopathic approach, there is an American Board of Homeotherapeutics in Washington, D.C., and other national and international organizations which operate out of that city and New York City. The International Society in the Propagation of Homeopathy is based in Athens, Greece.

REFERENCES

Samuel Hahnemann, *Organon of the Art of Healing,* trans. by C. Wesselhoeft, M.D. Philadelphia: Boericke and Tafel, 1917.

Brian Inglis, *Fringe Medicine.* London: Faber and Faber, 1964.

James T. Kent, *Lectures on Homeopathic Philosophy.* Calcutta: Sett Dey and Co., 1961.

George Vithoulkas, *Homeopathy: Medicine of the New Man.* New York: Avon Books, 1971.

KAREN HORNEY (1885–1952), a pioneer in psychoanalysis, was born in Hamburg, Germany. She studied at the University of Berlin and received her medical degree in 1913. From 1914–18, she studied psychiatry at Berlin-Lankwitz, Germany, and from 1918–32, taught at the Berlin Psychoanalysis Institute. Horney came to the United States in 1932 and was associate director of the Psychoanalysis Institute in Chicago for two years. She became a member of the teaching staff at the New York Psychoanalytic Institute in 1934. In 1941, she participated in the founding of the Association for the Advancement of Psychoanalysis and the American Institute of Psychoanalysis.

Early in her career, Horney departed from Freudian forms of psychoanalysis. Although the bases for Horney's psychoanalytic theories and suggestions for therapy are rooted in the work of Freud, she believed that adhering to Freudian theories would lead to a stagnation of interpretation of actual neuroses.

Horney defined neuroses as both culturally and individually oriented from childhood. Freud had neglected to take the former aspect into account. According to Horney, neuroses present themselves as deviations from "recognized behavior patterns of our time." In her early studies, she observed that there are certain attitudes which are characteristic of the *neurotic personality,* and which specifically indicate neurotic trends.

Neurotic trends originate in early life and are the result of unfavorable environmental and/or cultural factors (vs. biological) which cause the development of certain patterns of behavior to allay fears, avoid loneliness and feelings of insecurity. Neurotic trends are characteristically compulsive: their objectives are pursued indiscriminately, regardless of reality and self-interest, creating anxiety because of their ineffective nature. They force you to seek solutions for the relief of tensions through a variety of emotional attitudes, i.e., self-effacement, dependency, resignation. You begin to devise ways to manipulate others, to shut others out, to refute every suggestion, demand, or expectation presented to you. Neurotic trends, usually hidden, lie at the center of our psychic disturbances. They are a unique form of development which opposes healthy growth.

Horney describes neurotic trends as follows: the neurotic need for affection and approval, for a "partner" to take over one's life; the neurotic need to restrict life within narrow confines; the neurotic need for power, the need to control the self and others through "intelligence," and a belief in the overpowering will; the neurotic need to exploit others and to get the better of them; the neurotic need for social recognition and prestige, for personal admiration (narcissism), for personal achievement, self-sufficiency, independence, perfection, and unassailability. Neurotic trends determine the image of how you want to be, or how you think you should be, but do not necessarily encompass the substance of your character or influence your life.

Horney's departure from Freud is explicitly seen in her discussion of feminine psychology in which she points out that the mental development of women had been specifically viewed in a subjective framework, thus contributing to its misconstruction and narrow definition. An example of this was Freud's theory that women typically suffer from a castration complex due to penis envy. Horney raised the question: How can such a complex be "invariably typical" in women when there is no ostensible reason for women to feel disadvantaged because they are not men? Horney took a factual, often biological standpoint in her interpretations of the problems of women (frigidity, premenstrual tension, etc.). For the most part, she examined female neuroses in nonsexual terms, addressing the neurotic tendencies of both men and women.

Conscious of the interest in self-analysis (as opposed to analysis in conjunction with a therapist), Horney believed that guide lines for a procedure should be set down in specific terms, incorporating the principles of psychoanalysis, making use of the psychoanalytic discoveries of Freud, and citing the intricacies involved in the process itself. The process of self-analysis should not appear simple. It is usually long and arduous for anyone who chooses to undertake it, and it is important to have sufficient incentive to make it feasible. Setting goals for self-realization is realistic only when you have incentive to grow, develop your faculties, realize given potentialities, and maintain consistent strength to endure the psychological hardships. This incentive will come most easily after you have shed your "narcissistic" self, and made contact with your real self.

There are obviously certain differences between the procedures used by a professional therapist in treating a patient, and those that can be used independently in self-analysis. The professional *analyzes* a patient. This requires a considerable knowledge of the nature of the unconscious and all its possible manifestations, as well as the skills needed to bring the unconscious to a conscious level. A therapist must deal with the patient with sensitivity and confidence. However, in self-analysis, you are only dealing with yourself. You can observe and use your observation to gain access to the world, which is your own. Your difficulties can be overcome if you surmount the emotional obstacles which block your ability to recognize them. Because you are with yourself all the time, you have the opportunity to observe your behavior in all circumstances. Self-analysis is desirable for those who, because of money, time, or location, cannot undertake therapeutic treatment. It can also be a means of increasing the intensity of psychoanalysis under professional guidance.

Questions have been raised as to the possible dangerous effects of self-analysis which might make coping with problems impossible, and even inspire extremely self-destructive behavior. Horney, judging from cases of self-analysis which she observed, felt the danger to be minimal. By undertaking self-analysis, you begin to *recognize* your self-destructive tendencies, and it is probable that you will be strong enough to maintain your incentive to deal with these problems and support your will to live.

In the process of self-analysis, the functions of analyst and patient are performed simultaneously. As patient, you have three major tasks: 1) To express yourself as completely and frankly as possible through free association, verbalizing everything that passes through your mind irrespective of content. This will enable you to see how your mind works, and eventually how your personality is structured. 2) To become aware of the forces of the unconscious, and how these forces influence your life. This involves facing problems squarely, and possibly revealing repressed factors which contribute to your problems, thus relieving yourself and gaining insight into your true feelings. 3) To develop the capacity to change attitudes which disturb your relationship both to yourself and to others. These changes, when implemented, will free you and allow for your fullest development. The changes involve gaining a more realistic attitude, dispensing with the mercurial nature of self-aggrandizement and self-degradation; gaining the incentive to be active, assertive, and courageous; being able to plan rather than drift from one thing to another; finding your center in the self rather than in others; being able to be more friendly and understanding of others rather than cultivating defenses and modes of hostility.

As analyst, you must function in behalf of the patient, helping yourself to recognize and restructure your life as much as is thought necessary. An analyst uses knowledge and intuition to understand the patient's character, searching for clues in dreams, and in contradictions or repetitive themes, which occur as the patient reveals what is on his mind, that will lead to the revelation of problems.

The active combination of the duties of the patient and the analyst will allow self-analysis to occur. However, you must also confront your resistance to gain self-knowledge in the process and recognize the limitations which might occur if satisfaction is found in resignation, boredom, tendencies toward self-destruction, and a belief in the unalterability of everything.

Horney understood that no form of analysis can be absolutely complete, but it can lead to freedom and self-understanding which will improve the nature of the struggle for development and growth.

REFERENCES

Karen Horney, *Self-Analysis*. New York: W. W. Norton & Co., 1968.

———, *New Ways in Psychoanalysis*. New York: W. W. Norton & Co., 1968.

———, *The Neurotic Personality of Our Time*. New York: W. W. Norton & Co., 1937.

———, *Our Inner Conflicts*. New York: W. W. Norton & Co., 1945.

————, *Feminine Psychology*. New York: W. W. Norton & Co., 1967.

HYPNOSIS. The term "hypnosis" first came into use in the 1880s as a result of the work of James Braid, an Englishman, who brought hypnosis under the umbrella of scientific inquiry. Subsequently, Jean Charcot, a French neurologist, created interest in hypnosis in Europe with his theories suggesting that hypnosis was pathological and connected with hysteria. Simultaneously, Hippolyte Bernheim advanced another scientific interpretation of hypnosis which stated that hypnosis affected persons psychologically, and that a person did not have to have neurotic tendencies to be influenced by it.

Hypnosis was first used therapeutically by Freud and Breuer in the treatment of hysteria. Medically, it was used as a method of anesthesia on patients undergoing minor surgery. In World War II, after a lull in the interest and use of hypnosis, it was revived to treat "war neuroses" and also applied in dentistry, and later obstetrics. The British Medical Association in 1955 and the American Medical Association in 1959 awarded hypnosis the status of "adjunctive tool in medicine" to be used with proper precautions.

The Society for Clinical and Experimental Hypnosis was established in 1947, and in 1957, the American Society for Clinical Hypnosis. In 1960, the American Psychological Association recognized the American Board of Examiners in Psychological Hypnosis which was set up to carry on research in both experimental and clinical application of hypnosis. Thus, hypnosis, for a long time associated with the occult, has become the subject of legitimate scientific exploration, as well as a therapeutic tool.

Hypnotism is a process of *induction,* the techniques for which are varied, and may be carried out either by a hypnotist or on your own. The tools for induction are *suggestions,* which may be verbal or physical. A hypnotist may ask you to concentrate on the motion of a pendulum or metronome, etc., and then ask you to close your eyes. This is a method for detaching you from the influence of the external environment. The hypnotist may continue to give suggestions after you have reached a hypnotic state in order to increase, or deepen, it.

When you are in a hypnotic state, you are in a non-waking (not necessarily sleeplike) trance state in which you are said to have no initiative to function of your own accord. You are not deprived of the ability to function, however. Research has shown that in a hypnotic state, your attention is selective beyond its normal capacity (e.g., you may only hear the voice of the hypnotist). Another aspect of the state is the ease with which you are able to visually experience your past and fantasize in a way that is similar to hallucinating. You may experience reality distortions to the extent that time is warped, memories are falsified and yet accepted. According to suggestion, you can also change behavioral patterns or habits. You may increase your susceptibility to suggestion. Sometimes, after being in a hypnotic state, you can forget that you have experienced it.

There are three levels of the hypnotic state: light, medium, and deep. In a light hypnotic state, you are so relaxed that you do not move; your closed eyelids flutter; your arms and legs feel heavy; you experience limb catalepsy in which your muscles are either so rigid or so loose that they tend not to move; you experience partial age regression. In the medium state, your body is completely cataleptic; you may have partial amnesia on awakening if suggested; any part of the body can be anesthetized; some organic functions such as salivation or bleeding can be controlled. In the deep hypnotic state, you experience complete age regression; you can open your eyes without awakening; you are completely anesthetized; you have complete amnesia; you have complete control of body functions, positive and negative hallucinations of the five senses; you experience time distortion. These basic responses differ among individuals, and fluctuate as the hypnotic state fluctuates during the trance.

One of the uses of hypnosis is in conjunction with psychotherapy and is called *hypnotherapy*. At issue are the aftereffects of hypnosis. Research has revealed that there have been frequent cases in which the hyno-therapeutic treatment of physical symptoms, although initially successful, has triggered psychological ills of a severe degree (e.g., paranoid psychosis, schizophrenic psychosis). In a research study done with a group of university students, hypnotherapy was used differently: Hypnosis was induced separately from therapy, and there were no posthypnotic suggestions given. The aftereffects in this case were mild and infrequent. The following conclusions were drawn: In the case of those who have suffered illnesses for a long time, hypno-therapy must be administered by or in the company of a professional, because the experience of the subject during the hypnotic state can be traumatic. The presence of a trained professional to handle such experiences is therefore necessary.

Self-hypnosis is a process of mentally suggesting to yourself to go into a trance and concentrating on a single thing, e.g., a lighted candle. There are progressive levels of the hypnotic state. Initially, your eyelids become heavy, your muscles relax, breathing slows down. A deeper state can be achieved by slowly counting backward while imagining yourself riding down an escalator, for example. Measuring the depth of your hypnotic state can be done in your mind only. To awaken youself entails thinking about it or, alternatively, giving yourself the suggestion that you will awaken after a certain period of time before you go into a trance. Other methods of self-hypnosis deal with techniques of conditioned responses that involve formulating your suggestion and then imagining symbols that will at first cause your eyes to close, your body to relax, your emotions to be at peace, imagining certain other symbols that put you into a deeper trance.

Self-hypnosis can be used as a means to condition

your internal response to situations, as well as decondition, adjust, and strengthen your responses. A primary goal in using self-hypnosis constructively is to understand the specific sources of your problems, whether they be vested in the general characteristics of your personality and behavior patterns, or in an emotionally caused illness.

According to Leslie LeCron, a clinical psychologist and therapeutic hypnotist, by using hypnosis the subconscious mind which houses the origins and causes of psychological difficulties can be contacted and its contents illuminated. There are several different methods for communicating with the subconscious in a hypnotic state, for example, *automatic writing:* questions are asked and either you write out your responses, or you are told to imagine a blackboard on which your subconscious writes the answers in white letters for you to read.

The use of suggestion in self-hypnosis can be beneficial in changing patterns of behavior. The suggestions should be positive, result-oriented, and repeated three or four times. You should not overload yourself with suggestions. They can be permissive or of a commanding nature, the latter being more effective than the former.

There are many theories which try to explain the phenomenon of hypnosis. Several deal with a description of the hypnotic state, how it is created, and its immediate effects on the subject; others consider its behavioral manifestations; others associate hypnosis with the larger scope of psychoanalysis, learning and habit formation. Current theories are beginning to focus on the differences between individuals as to their susceptibility to hypnosis. According to Ernest Hilgard, one of the leading investigators of hypnosis, the various theories "provide essential instruments and background knowledge, through which, eventually, by appropriate further studies, understanding hypnosis will be made possible."

REFERENCES

Ernest R. Hilgard, *The Experience of Hypnosis.* New York: Harcourt, Brace & World, 1968.

Leslie M. LeCron, *Self-Hypnosis: Its Technique and Its Use in Daily Living.* New York: New American Library, 1964.

Laurence Sparks, *Self-Hypnosis: A Conditioned Response Technique.* North Hollywood, Ca.: Wilshire Book Co., 1962.

The *I CHING (Book of Changes),* which originated three thousand years ago, is the basis for both Taoist and Confucian philosophies and one of several ancient works of divination that has survived into modern times.

Its authorship is credited to four people: Fu Hsi, a legendary emperor (2900–2800 B.C.), is credited with the invention of the original eight trigrams, which were inspired by the markings on the back of a tortoise; King Wan (1100 B.C.) is credited with the creation of the sixty-four hexagrams that constitute the core of the *I Ching* currently known; King Wan's son, the Duke of Chou, is credited with authorship of the texts which accompany the individual lines of the hexagrams; and Confucius (551–479 B.C.) is said to have written the first Commentaries (on the Decision and the Image) that are interpretations of the structural nature of the hexagrams, with philosophical explanations. The so-called Ten Wings of the *I Ching* are fragments from the commentary literature that was written as it became increasingly popular after the time of Confucius.

The *I Ching* has undergone much interpretation as well as many different usages. Because of changes in Chinese culture through the centuries which, according to Richard Wilhelm (a translator of the *I Ching*), are manifested in the "vicissitudes of centuries, and the change in the system of writing," the *I Ching* has changed from its original form. During the time of the tyrant Ch'in Shih Huang Ti, who ordered the burning of books, the *I Ching* was established as a book of divination and magic. With the introduction of yin/

yang principles by Tsou Yin in the fourth century B.C., the *I Ching* either as a book of wisdom or a book of divination became the subject of debate among Chinese scholars.

The *I Ching* has been translated several times: in 1889, by Charles de Harles; in 1882, by James Legge; in 1950, by the Master Yuan-kuang; in 1965 by John Blofield; and in 1950 by Richard Wilhelm, with an introduction by Carl Jung. Wilhelm worked with the Chinese scholar Lao Nai-hsuan. This translation is intended to make it easy for the lay person to understand and use the *I Ching*.

The text and major part of the *I Ching* is composed of sixty-four hexagrams, each composed of two primary trigrams. A trigram is a lineal figure of three lines; each line is either whole or divided. A hexagram is composed of six lines. Interpretation of a hexagram is determined on the one hand by position and nature of the lines, and on the other, by the position of the two trigrams, which can be read as being one over another, or as overlapping.

Each hexagram represents a situation called the *time,* which determines how the hexagram as a whole, as well as the individual lines, are interpreted. The four middle lines of each hexagram signify the activity of the situation; the lowest line, the status of the beginning of the situation, the highest line, the status of the end. The denotation of the middle lines depends upon the time, although a line must hold a specific position before the meaning of the hexagrams is indicated. In general, the lines are interpreted in terms of their position and nature; undivided lines are firm, divided lines are yielding. Each hexagram also has a complement.

The text of the *I Ching* is structured thusly: Each hexagram has a name describing the situation to be dealt with, e.g., the Creative, the Receptive, etc. Each trigram indicates an image which, when combined, represents the image of the whole hexagram. The meaning of the hexagram is contained in the statements of the judgment, the image, and the meanings of the in-

254 / I CHING

dividual lines. The commentaries of the Ten Wings and those by Confucius further the original interpretations of the hexagrams.

Each hexagram indicates a future state of affairs and counsels you as to the perseverance or the withdrawal from a course you intend to take to reach your future. In order to discover your fortune or fate, you must find your hexagram. In ancient China, this was done using yarrow sticks. Eventually, bronze coins were substituted for the yarrow sticks. Today, any coins may be used.

To illustrate: Three pennies are thrown down together, six times in a row. Each throw indicates the state of one line of the hexagram, the six lines of which are drawn from the bottom up. Heads are assigned a value of two; tails, a value of three. Adding the values of the three pennies after each throw gives the state of a line, e.g., if the first throw shows all heads, the value is six, and the first line of the hexagram is solid, ———; if the second throw shows two heads and a tail, the value is seven, and the second line of the hexagram is divided, — —; etc., until all six lines have been drawn.

There are three predominant themes running through the *I Ching*. The first theme concerns the Tao, the universal law of change. Change is viewed as the transformation of one force (e.g., firm) into another (e.g., yielding), and the cycle of complexes of phenomena (e.g., day and night). The second theme is that of image. Image is an idea in the unseen world; thus, what happens in the visible world is only a reproduction of what happens in the world that cannot be perceived. The third theme is judgment. Judgment allows the possibility for making a decision about a course of action, as found in the image. This course of action may or may not be harmful, as the *I Ching* can indicate.

Since the time of Confucius, the *I Ching* has been used by scholars, statesmen, and private individuals. It has never lost its importance in the formation of Chinese thought. According to Wilhelm, "The Book of Changes opens to the reader the richest treasure of Chinese wisdom; at the same time it affords him a comprehensive view of the varieties of human experience, enabling him thereby to shape his life of his own sovereign will into an organic whole and so to direct it that it comes into accord with the ultimate tao lying at the root of all that exists."

REFERENCE

Richard Wilhelm, *The I Ching or Book of Changes,* trans. by Cary F. Baynes. Princeton, N.J.: Princeton University Press, 1967.

ISOMETRICS is a system of exercise which results in an increase in muscle tone and strength through the contraction of opposing muscles.

During the 1920s, scientists conducted experiments to measure the effects of inactivity on the muscles. One experiment consisted of binding the legs of live frogs for certain periods of time. When the bindings were removed, it was discovered that the muscles of the frogs had increased in size and strength, proving that the strain exerted in the muscles in contraction and tension movements while bound up developed muscles. In 1953, two German physiologists, Hettinger and Muller, began to apply a technique of exercise for healthy people, based on the principles of contraction and tension used by physiotherapists in physical rehabilitation programs. They discovered that when muscles were contracted against a static object once a day for six seconds, muscle strength increased by 5 per cent. Research conducted by other doctors confirmed this evidence. This mode of exercise became known as *isometric contractions* (or isometrics).

An isometric contraction (as defined by Henry Wittenberg, a former Olympic team wrestling coach) is "the action of a muscle or group of muscles against an immovable object or against each other, creating *tension without motion.*" When muscles are contracted in this manner, the oxygen in the muscle fibers as well as calories are used up. The contracted muscle expands, constricting blood vessels, and inhibiting fresh oxygen from reaching the muscle.

You are expending a *maximum effort* when you increase the tension in the muscle to a point where you are unable to increase the force of the contraction, and the muscle begins to quiver. Maximum effort is a sign of the *overload principle* of exertion; overloading causes a depletion of oxygen in your muscles and the result is fatigue. The benefits of isometric exercises are achieved when you reach this overload state, which means that your muscles are rebuilding themselves to take the tension. The general effects of isometrics can be seen in an improvement in the strength of tendons and ligaments, an improvement in posture, body tone, and overall body structure.

In contrast to isometric exercises are *isotonic* exercises, which involve motion. They are valuable in warming-up periods and for the development of the heart and circulatory system. A good program to increase your physical fitness should include a combination of both isometric and isotonic exercises. According to Wittenberg, the results of such an exercise program are increased cardiovascular efficiency and endurance, increased body strength and vigor, improved muscle tone and contour, and, when used in conjunction with a reducing diet, weight loss.

There are several factors to take into account when designing an isometric-isotonic exercise program. One essential factor is age; you should not extend the limits of exercising beyond what your age will permit. Therefore, you will try to increase your efficiency and strength gradually, beginning at a certain level of exercise that you will execute daily. If you are unable to complete the entire program daily, an alternate isometric exercise period that solely involves muscle contractions can be substituted. The latter exercises can be done anywhere, anytime, and will increase strength and tone up flabby muscles.

Wittenberg has created a general isometric-isotonic fitness plan on primary, secondary, and peak levels.

Each level is comprised of a warm-up period, an isometric period and an isotonic period. Time is an important factor in the effectiveness of the exercises: Isometric contractions last ten seconds; the duration of isotonic exercises changes according to your physical condition. A daily workout should last for no more than twelve minutes.

The primary level of the fitness plan includes stretches, bends, twisting, etc. in the warm-up phase; palm pushes, hip presses, triceps pushes, etc., in the isometric phase; jumping jacks, knee push-ups, etc. in the isotonic phase. The plans are to be followed for two weeks, with a change in the third week consisting of an increase in the time period of the isotonic phase.

The secondary level is a more vigorous program, to be followed after mastering the primary level. On this level, the isotonic phase includes more repetitions; the warm-up phase is the same; the isometric phase involves more work, although remaining the same in exercise and time duration.

The peak level is achieved after mastery of the secondary level. The peak level is primarily for athletes. At this level, three isotonic exercises are changed and the number of repetitions increases.

In a fitness plan for women, isometric exercises are important for strengthening specific areas of the body. They can be beneficial for women after childbirth. These exercise plans combine the warm-up and isotonic periods. The isometric period, which is most effective after the technique of maximum effort in muscle contraction is mastered, is designed to increase strength, vitality, and eliminate flabby tissues. The program takes ten minutes per day. Isometric exercises can be used to condition facial muscles. These exercises, when done twice a day, will show results after two weeks.

Isometrics are extremely beneficial for improving performance in sports because they allow you to exert maximum effort exactly where you want and need it. General body strength should be built up initially, and then those isometrics designed for your particular sport can be applied.

REFERENCES

E. J. Waltis, *Isometric Exercises for Figure Improvement.* Englewood Cliffs, N.J.: Prentice-Hall, 1964.

Henry Wittenberg, *Isometrics.* New York: Award Books, 1975.

CARL GUSTAV JUNG (1875–1961), a Swiss psychologist and psychiatrist, was the founder of *analytical psychology.* In his early years, Jung was interested in archaeology; later, he turned to medicine, which he studied at the University of Basel, receiving his degree in 1902. He continued his studies in Paris with Pierre Janet. From 1900–13, Jung was a physician in the psychiatric clinic and lecturer at the University of Zurich. In 1906, he began the development of word association tests to use with his patients. Jung's relationship with Freud began in 1907 and continued until 1912 when Jung broke away from the circle of Freudian disciples, mainly because he disagreed with Freud's theories of the libido, the unconscious, and infantile sexuality. Jung resigned his post as president of the International Psychiatric Society, founded his own practice in Zurich, and began lecture tours of the United States. From 1933–41, he was professor of psychology at the Federal Polytechnical University in Zurich. In 1943, he became professor of medical psychology at the University of Basel. Jung died in Zurich.

The major part of Jung's work was his effort to understand and define the constitution and activity of the human psyche: "The psyche is distinctly more complicated and inaccessible than the body. It is, so to speak, the half of the world which comes into existence only when we become conscious of it." Jung saw the psyche as possessing an organic structure and form of its own, its totality describable in terms of the expression of both consciousness and unconsciousness. To Jung, "psychic existence is the only category of existence of which [one] can have immediate knowledge, since nothing can be known unless it first appears as a psychic image." The world exists as psychic images and the psychic process is one of imagining. Psychic truths are as valid as physical truths, the only difference being that the former are not explainable or measurable in physical terms; rather the "inner unconscious drama of the psyche" becomes conscious and consequently visible in the expression of mythological processes of nature, inherently religious, that emanate from an individual's assimilation of the culture. In his research, geared to the observation of the spontaneous manifestations of the unconscious, e.g., dreams and the fantasies characteristic of the waking state, Jung found that the psyche could be best understood in terms of its own symbolic language.

Jung determined that the psychic forces which affect us in our original prerational psyche are the cause of neuroses and psychotic disorders. He described these as "eternally inherited forms and ideas which have at first no specific content," and that appear later "in the course of an individual's life, when personal experience is taken up precisely in these forms." These forms, or *archetypes,* are "irrepresentable," "unconscious," and "pre-existent" forms that allude to our instinctual drive or striving toward a common spiritual goal, that of wholeness. These archetypes and instincts compose what Jung calls the "collective unconscious," the non-personal, universal, inherited unconscious which dominates the psyche. The religious and cultural symbolic manifestations of the search for wholeness (e.g., mandala, Christ) become an essential part of psychic existence. They are the products of the process of *transformation* and embody man's basic urge to become conscious of himself and develop human awareness. These symbols are *archetypal representations* which are mediated by the unconscious before reaching consciousness as images and ideas; the latter always refer back to the original archetype which is "the unconscious precondition of every human life."

According to Jung, consciousness develops out of

an innate unconscious condition, which is a strong influence throughout life. The conscious mind is accessible and can be conditioned. The unconscious mind cannot be trained, but is a source of religious experience and an autonomous, natural psychic entity "beyond the reach of subjective arbitrary control, a realm where nature and her secrets can be neither improved upon or perverted. . . ." At the center of consciousness is the *ego*, which is subordinate to the *self* and constitutes the total personality. The main characteristic of the ego is individuality. The ego is affected by certain archetypes, images from the collective unconscious, which Jung defines as the *shadow*, the *anima*, and the *animus*.

The *anima* and *animus* represent the feminine side of a man's unconscious, and the masculine side of a woman's unconscious, respectively. The animus is the masculine imprint on the unconscious, corresponding to the paternal *Logos*, or reason. It is the prime factor in the determination of opinions. The anima, in contrast, corresponds to the maternal *Eros*, and is the prime factor in shaping personal vanity. The ". . . anima gives relationship and relatedness to a man's consciousness, the animus gives woman's consciousness a capacity for reflection, deliberation, and self-knowledge." The *shadow* is made up of all those elements of personality which are unexpressed, hidden, or repressed, either because they are regarded as being inferior or because they are not consistent with the attitude of consciousness. The shadow can be assimilated into the conscious personality, but the process is often resisted through *projections*.

According to Jung, the human psyche obtains energy from sense experiences and instinct. This energy follows the principles of equivalence and entropy, striving for balance through the entire psychic system. The energy's motion can be 1) *progressive* in relation to the external world; 2) *regressive* in relation to the unconscious; 3) *canalized*, in which case instinctual energy redirects itself in a new situation in a manner corresponding to instinctual activity.

Jung viewed the development of the human psyche (personality) as a process of *individuation* and *integration*. Individuation requires that the aspects of the personality (as above) must not only differentiate themselves from each other, but also differentiate themselves within each other. Therefore, as the psyche develops, this internal process complexifies the structures within. Expression of the components of the psyche has to be conscious, otherwise individuation is hampered because of abnormal expression or retention of unconscious material (repression).

Integration of the personality includes individuation and *transcendence*. Transcendence is a process that directs individuated structures and, consequently, sometimes opposing ones (e.g., anima and animus) of the psyche into a unified whole. The *transcendent function* is the directive tool by which the self-archetype can be realized. Its operation is influenced by characteristics the personality inherits, and by childhood experiences with parents and the environment. The journey to selfhood moves from concern with adapting to the external world to concern with adapting to internal functions.

The task of education, as well as psychotherapy, according to Jung, should be to make the unconscious conscious for a realization of the whole person. Jung considered psychotherapy to be an encounter between therapist and patient. The patient is the object of the therapeutic process. However, the therapist must be just as aware of his or her own unconscious reactions as the patient's. The therapist should be flexible enough to question his/her skills and theories in order to help the patient discover "a new form for his finest aspirations."

According to Jung, dreams are products of the total psyche, and a realm in which we become whole again, as we were before ego consciousness. Dreams are evidence of "everything that has ever been of significance in the life of humanity." They are demonstrations of the impartiality and spontaneity of the unconscious psyche. Dreams manifest our contact with our basic human nature; their images are representative of a reality whose structure is formulated only on the materials of dreams. Dream images are the "utterance of the unconscious."

Jung believed the dream to have a nonfinal anticipatory form which is symbolic of the actual situation of the unconscious. The analysis of dreams becomes a process which first places the dream in context and then examines the dream content in terms of meaning. Jung believed that bringing assumptions and fixed meanings to dream analysis was "positively wrong."

There are two levels to the Jungian interpretation of dreams: the objective level in which dream images are analytically broken down into *memory complexes* that refer to external situations or real objects; and the *subjective level* in which memory complexes are separated from external causes and synthetically related back to the dreamer. In order to interpret a dream correctly, Jung felt that it was necessary to have a "thorough knowledge of the unconscious situation at that moment, because the dream contains its unconscious complement. . . ." Jung believed dreams to be natural occurrences to be viewed hypothetically. They are a means through which you can reflect on your life, your self, enrich your consciousness, and review those aspects of the unconscious which have been given consciousness.

One of the results of Jung's work in practical psychology was his theory of *psychological types*. Jung's intention was to abolish the generalizations that psychology hitherto imposed by describing basic psychological attitudes that would determine personality types. The terms *introversion* and *extraversion* refer to basic psychological attitudes. The introvert is concerned with the subjective, inner world of the psyche, and is introspective. The extravert is concerned with the objective external world, and is involved in extrapersonal interaction. Introversion and extraversion can exist in the same individual, manifesting their characteristics at different times and different levels of consciousness, i.e., introversion may operate on a conscious level while extraversion works on an unconscious level, and vice versa.

Jung's typology includes four *psychological functions*. "These four functional types correspond to the obvious means by which consciousness obtains its orientation to experience." *Thinking* and *feeling* are rational functions which deal with judgment. Thinking works on an intellectual basis and its goal is understanding. Feeling operates as an evaluator of ideas. *Sensation* and *intuition* are irrational functions, produced without thought. Sensation involves the functioning of sense organs and internal organs in response to conscious experience of the environment. Intuition is a perception or insight (a hunch) which is realized without thought processes. Psychological types are a result of a combination of introversion, extraversion, and the four psychological functions. The degree of conscious development of one aspect balanced with the degree of unconscious retention of another aspect allows for the differences among individuals.

Jung supplemented his psychological research with the study of parapsychology. Many of his theories are based on the work of J. B. Rhine at Duke University. Jung's *synchronicity principle* encompasses the core of his explanation of the chance aspect of events. He defines synchronicity as "coincidence in time of two or more causally unrelated events which have the same or similar meaning." His explanation of the working of the *I Ching* is largely based on this principle.

Jung's diversified research supported his original theories about the human psyche. His work embodied the union of opposing schools of thought, the occult and spiritual with science, or the Eastern ways of thought with Western ways of thought.

REFERENCES

Calvin S. Hall and Vernon J. Nordby, *A Primer of Jungian Psychology*. New York: Taplinger Publishing Co., 1973.

Aniela Jaffe, *From the Life Work of C. G. Jung*, trans. by R. F. C. Hull. New York: Harper & Row, 1971.

C. G. Jung, *The Undiscovered Self*, trans. by R. F. C. Hull. Boston: Little, Brown & Co., 1957.

————, *Psyche and Symbol: A Selection from the Writings of C. G. Jung*, ed. by Violet S. deLaszlo. New York: Doubleday & Co., 1958.

————, *Memories, Dreams, Reflections*, recorded and edited by Aniela Jaffe. New York: Random House/ Vintage, 1965.

————, *C. G. Jung: Psychological Reflections, A New Anthology of His Writings 1905–1961*, edited by Jolande Jacobi and R. F. C. Hull. Princeton, N.J.: Princeton University Press, 1970.

————, *Psychological Types: or the Psychology of Individuation*, trans. by H. G. Baynes. New York: Pantheon Books, 1962.

————, *Collected Works*, ed. by Herbert Read, Michael Fordham, and Gerhard Adler. New York: Pantheon Books, 1953.

STANLEY KELEMAN, poet, painter, metal sculptor, author, and group leader, was born in Brooklyn, New York. He studied with Karlfried Durckheim at the Center for Religious Studies in Todmos, Germany, and Alexander Lowen at the Institute for Bioenergetic Analysis in New York. He was trained by Nina Bull, the director of research for motor attitudes at the College of Physicians and Surgeons, Columbia University. Keleman is a senior trainer at the Bioenergetic Institute in New York and the Gestalt Institute in San Diego, California. He is a workshop leader for Esalen Institute in San Francisco, and has a private practice in Berkeley at the Center for Energetic Studies, of which he is the director. Keleman has lectured and conducted seminars throughout the world. He is the author of several books, the most recent, *Your Body*

Speaks Its Mind: The Bioenergetic Way to Greater Emotional and Sexual Satisfaction.

Keleman's work is closely related to and derived from the work of Alexander Lowen and Wilhelm Reich as well as Nina Bull and Kalfried Durckheim. Keleman considers "you, as *body,* are the life process." The life process builds your structure, physically and psychically. Keleman equates emotional conflict with distortion of body movement. Life is the expression of the unique processes of the development of the body. This development cannot occur in "fantasy worlds" which deny the body. Keleman is concerned with the bioenergetic approach to life, which treats body as an emotional process.

Bioenergy is cosmic energy, whose "specific application in the human sphere is biological functioning that is a state of unity." Interference with this unity leads to alienation from yourself and your environment. Keleman's theory is that many people have no choice other than to suppress their body movements and expressions in order to fit into the set boundaries of social structure. Keleman's goal is to re-eroticize the body through a process he calls *grounding.*

Grounding integrates your processes of excitation with the earth and is a means to become "connected" with the world. "Being bodied" structures your relationship with the world; your body experiences various excitatory levels through expansion or contraction. These levels generate the forms of your personality and are experienced as vibrations, pulsations, and streamings. The resulting excitement is self-regulating, and allows for the digestion of your experience and gives you an enhanced capacity for your growing self.

Boundary formations, characteristic of the development of a self-limiting system, become individual, personal acts of becoming aware of the self. Forming boundaries means intensifying excitement; letting them go means expressing excitement. The formation of boundaries occurs in three phases: the prepersonal phase, during which there are undifferentiated and expanding feelings; the personal phase, during which there is containment and embodiment and shaping of excitement; and the postpersonal phase, during which there is expression of excitement, resulting interaction, and the establishment of new social realities.

If excitement is accepted, it tends to extend your boundaries in the development of emotional attitudes. Self-formation is a process of activating fulfillment-oriented attitudes embodied as forward-going, upright, balanced, flexible body shape. In this process, it is natural to encounter obstacles. To overcome these obstacles successfully entails your forming new attitudes and experiencing the feelings and sensations of mental and muscular reorganization. Your identity is formed by the replacement of stereotypical images with living images created by your contact with your body and its experiences. Learning is experiencing and embodying new patterns of excitation. Growing is changing the shape of your living, of your enlarged excitement.

According to Keleman, energy flow exists in four forms of aliveness: a streaming state; a pulsatory state; a vibratory state; and a rhythmic state. These are qualitative states of tissue feeling and consciousness. They are the natural functions of protoplasm, cells, and organs, as well as basic to all human relationships, concepts of freedom, and social concerns. When you block these states, you experience feelings of guilt, shame, anxiety, etc. Persistent muscular contractions limit your body from expressing itself, from being alive and expanding. These contractions also prevent graceful maturation or aging.

Maturation is manifest in your ever-growing contact with life and your ability to sustain that contact. Sexuality and maturation working together comprise the organismic process. Your body is the basis, the *ground* of experiential reality. Having a sensual relationship with the world is determined by your ability to express emotional energy. The steps devised by Keleman to realize your aliveness concern getting in touch with your body feelings and establishing your sexuality. The joy of pleasure is only achieved in the movement toward contact, self-expression. "Grounding yourself, allowing yourself to be grounded, is the process of incarnation, is manifesting yourself in this world."

Keleman believes that a grounded person can experience dying in the same way as he or she experiences living. Approaching dying means living a life process. "Little dyings," the process of giving up old ways and adopting new ways, can prepare you for "big dying." Each turning point in self-formation is an indication of unforming, unbounding, dying, experiencing the unknown. Replacing social myths of dying with your own experiential myths gives you the ability to accept responsibility for your living and dying. Knowing about living is to know about dying. Understanding dying (little dyings) allows you to creatively live your bodily life. "Accepting dying is the willingness to be alive your way."

REFERENCES

Stanley Keleman, *The Human Ground*. Menlo Park, Ca.: Science and Behavior Books, 1975.

————, *Your Body Speaks Its Mind: The Bioenergetic Way to Greater Emotional and Sexual Satisfaction*. New York: Simon & Schuster, 1975.

————, *Living Your Dying*. New York: Random House/ Bookworks, 1974.

THE KELLY METHOD/SLEEP. Charles P. Kelly, A.B., B.D., has achieved recognition for the clinically proved method he has created for inducing natural sleep and preventing sleep disorders, commonly described as insomnias. Kelly's method is based on research done by Dr. Seymour Kety of the University of Pennsylvania in 1955. Kety's investigations revealed that during sleep there is an increase in the amount of carbon dioxide in the blood. This condition, called *respiratory acidosis,* is also produced by drugs that induce sleep. Using the evidence from Kety's work, Kelly determined that sleep can be induced naturally and effectively through conscious control of the body.

You spend an average one third of your life in a state of sleep, a relaxed and restful period during which you have a low responsiveness to external stimuli and experience no purposeful motor activity. Physiological processes such as respiration, heartbeat, body temperature, and blood pressure decrease. Sleep has different stages which occur in cyclical patterns of one and one-half to two hours long. During each cycle, you spend approximately three fourths of the time in what is called "S" sleep. During S sleep the electrical activity of the brain shows up as slow, large Delta brain waves on the EEG (electroencephalograph). The other stage of sleep is called "D" sleep. During D sleep your nervous system is active and rapid eye movements (REMs) occur. In experiments, people awakened during the occurrence of REMs usually reported that they had been dreaming.

There are differences in styles of sleep among individuals. Some people sleep longer than others; some people sleep differently within the length of time they are asleep. These differences establish a range within which sleep can be defined as normal. Outside this range, there are sleep disorders: *Primary disorders,* such as narcolepsy and hypersomnia, are those in which sleep interferes with the waking state; *parasomnias,* such as somnabulism, sleep-talking, and bed-wetting, are those in which waking characteristics interfere with your sleep state; there are also troubled states of sleep that are generally described as *insomnias.*

Insomnia can occur chronically or episodically. The symptoms can range from difficulty falling asleep, waking up in the middle of sleep and not being able to get back to sleep, awakening early. The disturbances are described as: *long latencies,* in which you take a long time to get to sleep; *early terminations,* in which you have a "gap" awakening that extends to the point where sleep is ended; *awakening* that occurs frequently in midsleep or as early awakening; and *"light" sleep,* in which you never reach the state of deep sleep. These symptoms of insomnia may occur in singular or multiple forms and vary in their chronicity and severity. Basically they are objective disturbances, which are probably the result of subjective complaints.

Another kind of insomnia is situational insomnia, which occurs as the result of your concerns with the external world and your attempt to respond to and deal with these concerns while you are asleep. Treatment of situational insomnia begins with understanding the naturalness of your problems so that they may be reduced. Arrhythmic insomnias are determined by choice and needs, i.e., you do not sleep according to the rising and setting of the sun, which means that the rhythmic "cues" for going to sleep and staying asleep might disappear altogether. Other insomnias can be drug related, i.e., a drug depended upon to induce sleep is abandoned and thus causes a disturbance in ability to sleep. Some insomnia can actually be the result of a malfunction in your sleeping/waking mechanism; in such cases, treatment with drugs has proved ineffective.

Kelly's method for relieving insomnias outlines four aids to bring on sleep: controlled breathing aimed at retaining carbon dioxide in the blood to create a state of respiratory acidosis (this method of breathing is restful and nerve quieting); positioning the eyes so that you feel drowsy; forming mental pictures in your mind; fatigue. The breathing exercises designed by Kelly are to be done in bed where the body can be completely relaxed, in a dark and quiet room. The goal of the exercises is to retain more carbon dioxide in your body while, at the same time, supplying it with oxygen. This is done by alternating periods of maximum breaths with holding the breath for forty seconds (or less). Maximum breathing involves an inhalation in which the abdomen and chest are fully expanded, and an exhalation in which as much air as possible is expelled, the abdomen being completely drawn in. Maximum breathing is done three times before the breath-holding begins. Kelly recommends that the entire cycle be carried out several times. Fatigue, a basic condition for sleep, is produced by the breathing exercises.

There are many theories which try to explain the necessity of sleep. It is known that sleep deprivation results in less effective mental and physical functioning, irritability, a decrease in perceptual accuracy, difficulty with conceptual thinking, and maladjustment to the environment. Kelly discovered his sleep method accidentally, while searching for a cure to his own insomnia.

Dr. Maurice E. Linden, director of the Division of Health in Philadelphia, has said of the Kelly method: "A mode of inducing sleep such as . . . Kelly's is not only quick, easy and safe, but may well prove to be a scientific breakthrough which will simultaneously help master the age-old problem of sleep and be a contribution to man's knowledge, carrying us to a new plateau."

REFERENCES

David Foulkes, *The Psychology of Sleep.* New York: Charles Scribner's Sons, 1966.

Charles P. Kelly, *The Natural Way to Healthful Sleep.* New York: Award Books, 1961.

Wilse B. Webb, *Sleep: The Gentle Tyrant.* Englewood Cliffs, N.J.: Prentice-Hall, 1975.

PIR VILAYAT INAYAT KHAN, master of meditation, is the leader of the Sufi Order of the West, having succeeded his father, Hazrat Inayat Khan, who founded the order in 1910 and formulated the goals of the religion as they exist now. In his early years, Pir Vilayat studied with Murshid Abu Hashin Madani. At that time, he displayed an interest in all religions and was thought to have been pursuing heretical ways. Yet, his efforts were aimed at synthesizing Eastern and Western religions in order to present them as ways of approaching the same concerns within different cultural contexts. As explained by James Tillinghast (author of the foreword to *Toward the One*), "this synthesis of esoteric schools may serve as a key to the coming evolutionary jump in consciousness toward which humanity seems to be moving . . ."

Sufism is a mystic religion of Islam. It is believed that it originally took hold in the Arab and Persian countries of the eighth century A.D., although Sufism essentially has no religious dogma to which it adheres, no specific place of worship or special city. Scholars have observed that traditions of monastic asceticism and mysticism set forth in Western Asia and Egypt were influential to its development.

The basic principle of Sufism focuses on the evolution of consciousness, as manifested in the development of intuition, feelings of the heart, group consciousness, and thinking in terms of the world. The point at which this evolution can be realized in the individual is in an identification with the self. According to Pir Vilayat, this is achieved through liberating the mind from the supposed necessity of objectivizing experience so that you transcend time and are "suspended in a state of 'ego loss' beyond the causal plane beyond the seeds of multiplicity." In this state, you realize the common ground upon which all beings rest. This is the state of "the one," the reality of the absolute for which man struggles and has discovered in God, Buddha, and Christ.

Achieving the state of the one is a process with several stages. The first is "experiencing the life of one's life." This means focusing on the causal level of your existence in order to see how you are a link in the chain of existence. The second stage in the process includes the extension of your consciousness from the cause of your own being to the cause of all beings. The third stage involves experiencing the laws that govern all occurrence. This is the state of *panna,* or transcendental knowledge, "the ability to see the causal law of conditioned genesis," and it is your goal. Integral to distinguishing between the single self and all selves as one is the ability to understand and discriminate between that which is subject to change on all levels (physical, psychological, and mental) and that which is not subject to change being insubstantial, formless, and without quality.

According to Pir Vilayat, meditation is the means through which you can gain the state of the one in the universe. It should be done daily, in the morning, at midday, and in the evening. Each meditation session should hold to a schedule of practices which you have decided upon. Any meditative session can extend into a "state of ecstasy" which ends when the energy supporting it is exhausted. After experiencing such a session, you should continue with your schedule. Each meditative session can be concluded through autosuggestion which you train yourself to do. Prior to meditation, physical relaxation exercises (yoga, for example) are recommended. Posture for meditation is important; you should sit cross-legged on a pillow, and when you feel that you have reached a balanced position, you should not move because movement "will draw consciousness back into body consciousness." Nonmotion of the body will create nonmotion of the mind and, thus, concentration.

The goal of Sufi meditation is to unfold and bring into your being the richness that is the universe through experiencing, rather than intuiting. Meditation becomes the key to growth—the introduction of higher dimensions of consciousness into your awareness. Pir Vilayat's method for meditating begins with the withdrawal of your attention from the "ambient world," releasing your mind from the outside impressions which are based on your emotional attachment to experience. This is achieved by increasing your imagination of the world as *maya* ("illusion"), distant and unreal. Upon attaining the consequential state of timelessness, you should realize that what is happening outside of you is not in the same space that you inhabit. "You have become emotionally detached by enjoying that wonderful feeling of freedom, detachment, indifference beyond the beyond, beyond all created things." You will support the flow of your thought, allow your consciousness to be lifted away from "the gravity of ego identity that coerces thoughts and emotions." You will "experience yourself in your reality, experience yourself being created . . . being formed, experience reality becoming yourself and then lose yourself becoming reality . . ." Achieving clarity and building centers of perception are the result of becoming one with a body of light, becoming "pure luminous consciousness."

The physical state required in meditation is attained by slowing down your rate of breathing, and consequently your heartbeat, so that your willpower yields to the automatic control of your body functions. There are various methods of breathing which serve to purify you with earth, air, fire, water. The state of pure vibration is achieved by making sounds using several specific techniques. The ultimate meditative practice is the *Dhikr*: the repeating of the phrase *La Illaha Illa Lla Hu,* which means "There is no God but God," in coordination with the circular motion of the head and the breathing rhythm.

As taught by Pir Vilayat, Sufism is the culmination of man's effort to reach the peak of experience that is mergence with the Absolute. Once you reach this vision of Oneness, you will be able to carry it with you through all life experience, for in One is the "perfection of love, harmony, and beauty, the only being united with all the illuminated souls who form the embodiment of the master, the spirit of guidance."

REFERENCES

Toward the One, ed. by the staff of the Sufi Order, U.S.A. New York: Harper & Row, 1974.

Idries Shah, *The Sufis.* New York: Doubleday/Anchor, 1971.

MELANIE KLEIN (1882–1960), a pioneer in the development of *child psychology,* was born in Vienna. Her interest in psychoanalysis began as a result of her association, both as a patient and later a colleague, with Sandor Ferenczi, a former student of Freud's. Klein presented her first paper on child development in 1919. After settling in Berlin, she became an associate of Karl Abraham, another student of Freud's. From

1921–34, Klein worked on techniques for the analysis of children. By 1926, her theories had been accepted by the psychoanalytic community and she began training child analysts. *The Psychoanalysis of Children,* her definitive work which has become a classic, was published in 1932. After 1934, she used her theories in relationship to adults. Among her other works are *Envy and Gratitude, Narrative of a Child Analysis,* and *Love, Hate and Reparation* (with Joan Riviere). The latter two books were published after Klein's death in 1960.

A key premise in Klein's theories concerning the psychoanalysis of children is that the process must be different than that employed with adults. By interpreting the development of children using Freudian concepts and terminology, Klein believed the psychoanalysis of children to be a method by which to mold healthy adults, rather than simply stabilize children at an early age. It was Klein's contention that the first year of the child's life is especially crucial in its sexual development.

According to Klein, child psychoanalysis resolves ". . . the sadistic fixations of the child, and thus decreases the severity of its superego, at the same time lessening its anxiety and the pressure of its instinctual trends; and as its sexual life and superego both reach a higher stage of development its ego expands and becomes able to reconcile the demands of its superego with those of reality as well, so that its new sublimations are more solidly founded and its old ones shed their erratic and obsessive character." Analysis is a means to control, within natural limits, the superego at each stage of development so that adjustments are made between the superego and the id which consequently make the ego stronger. This involves lessening of anxieties and guilt feelings which otherwise could lead to the development of fears and compulsions. It also involves controlling the related sexual activities typical to each stage of development to prevent adverse sexual growth. By controlling anxiety situations in the child, the potential for inhibitions, neuroses, or sexual maladjustment in the adult is decreased.

In the development of the child, libido (sexual function), superego, and object relationship (corresponding to fantasies versus real situations) interact. The anxieties related to this interaction manifest themselves in destructiveness. Analysis can be a means to lessen this destructiveness by supporting the positive aspects of the interaction of these forces in the child's growth. As Klein observed, anxiety situations created early can never be completely eliminated; psychoanalysis can never effect complete cure, only a reallocation of tendencies.

Klein used a play technique for observing children. Since they do not yet have control of language or a full grasp of reality, ". . . play is a child's most important medium of expression." In the analysis of children aged six months to five years, the play technique involves the use of toys. When a child plays with toys, what is observable are ". . . the general connections and dynamics of the mental processes . . . and of time-order of the child's various phantasies and experiences." In early analysis, children play make-believe games which vividly represent transference, i.e., the actual play situation approximates an original or fantasy experience. It is a manifestation of a child's inner world and embodies what Klein called *projective identification,* typical of the unintegrated nature of the ego and influential on the child's relation to other persons and objects. In this regard, toys take on many meanings. Understanding their significance requires seeing the true relation of a toy to a child's feelings of guilt. Analyzing a child's play is analogous to analyzing the dreams of an adult.

Klein believed that all play activity is a means of releasing masturbatory fantasies, and that inhibitions in play activity at an early age can develop into inhibitions in sexual activity in adulthood, as well as into inhibitions toward learning in general.

In the analysis of children from five to ten years of age, Klein believed it necessary to contact unconscious fantasies in order to deal with a child's anxieties or guilt. During this period, children tend to act out experiences in a fashion that is more related to reality. This is due to a dynamic interaction between an intense repression of fantasy and an "obsessional over-emphasis of reality." In the latency period of a child, it is important to see behind the ego.

Pubescent children are involved with fantasy in terms of an expression of the instinct and the unconscious. Fantasies become more closely related to reality because of a fuller development of the ego. Children also rely on verbal associations to demonstrate their interests and their relation to reality. Children's relationships to objects become less fantasy oriented. At this stage, anxiety situations find different expression because the child is learning how to master anxiety. The stabilization of the child in which the ego and superego merge should occur at this stage. The child adapts to a larger external world, is less dependent on objects, and begins to express his or her own personality.

Klein observed that disturbances in a child's eating habits as well as an inability to sleep are particular manifestations of anxiety situations. Neuroses in children become obsessional because they express the intensity of feelings. The destructive nature of a child's acted-out fantasy demonstrates extreme feelings of frustration. This leads to the buildup of sadistic tendencies. For example, at an early age a child may experience oral frustration because he/she cannot suck the mother's breast, and as a result a fantasy in which the child bites off the mother's nipple is created. On the other hand, the child will create another fantasy situation in which he/she will try to repair the damage that has been done because of guilt feelings resulting from injuring someone the child loves and needs.

The dynamic interaction between love, hate, and the act of reparation (which, as the child grows, is done unconsciously and not acted out) is integral to the formation of feelings of love in adulthood. The act of reparation is a way of increasing feelings of love toward all people and nature. Given a loving relationship between parents as a condition, a psychologically derived goal in adulthood becomes gaining satisfaction from experience by giving love and receiving love: this "ensures our own contentment, and contributes to pleasure, comfort or happiness of other people."

Klein believed strongly in the importance of the psychoanalysis of children: ". . . Analysis can do for children, whether normal or neurotic, all that it can do for adults, and much more. It can spare the child the many miseries and painful experiences which the adult goes through before he comes to be analyzed, and its therapeutic prospects go beyond those of adult analysis. The experience of the last few years has given me . . . good grounds for believing that psychoses and psychotic traits, malformations of character, asocial behavior, grave obsessional neuroses and inhibitions of development can be cured while the individual is still young. . . ."

REFERENCES

Melanie Klein, Paula Heimann, R. E. Money-Kryle, eds., *New Directions in Psychoanalysis: The Significance of Infant Conflict in the Pattern of Adult Behavior.* London: Tavistock, 1971.

Melanie Klein and Joan Riviere, *Love, Hate and Reparation.* New York: W. W. Norton & Co., 1964.

Melanie Klein, *The Psychoanalysis of Children,* trans. by Alix Strachey. New York: Delacorte Press/Seymour Lawrence, The Melanie Klein Trust, 1975.

————, *Narrative of A Child Analysis.* New York: Delta, 1976.

————, *Envy and Gratitude.* London: Tavistock, 1957.

ALFRED KORZYBSKI (1879–1950), a Polish-American scientist, linguist, and philosopher, was the founder of a "non-Aristotelian" system he called *General Semantics,* the purpose of which is to create a framework in which a distinction can be made between words and the objects they describe or symbolize.

During World War I, Korzybski served as a Russian intelligence agent. He arrived in the United States in 1915 on a military mission, and remained there after the overthrow of the Tsarist regime. In 1933, after twelve years of research, Korzybski published his major work, *Science and Sanity,* which became the primary text for the study of General Semantics. In 1935, he began conducting seminars in General Semantics in schools, colleges, and universities, attracting a wide audience of educators, scientists, physicians, and psychiatrists. In 1938, Korzybski established the Institute of General Semantics the purpose of which was to research and teach neurolinguistics, neuroepistemology, and science. As director of the institute, he worked to research and collect empirical data necessary for the application of his system in the analysis and evaluation of personal experience. He conducted seminars and wrote papers throughout this residency at the institute, which continued until his death. Korzybski also wrote *Manhood of Humanity* and "Time Binding: The General Theory," a series of papers presented at the International Mathematical Congress, the Washington Society for Nervous and Mental Disease, and the Washington Psychopathological Society, in the 1920s.

Korzybski stated that General Semantics is not a system of philosophy, psychology, or logic; rather "it is a new discipline which explains and trains us how to use our nervous systems most efficiently." According to M. Kendig, director of the institute in 1950, General Semantics as a natural empirical science is in the form of "a body of coordinated assumptions, doctrines, principles, etc., and methodological procedures and techniques for changing the structure of . . . neurosymbolic reactions to fit an assumptive world of dynamic processes."

Korzybski's theory of *time binding* was instrumental in his formulation of General Semantics. Man's timebinding capacity is found in his ability to transmit ideas from generation to generation as a result of the study and refinement of the use of language. This time-binding ability of humans, according to Korzybski, leads to the development of "feelings of responsibility and duty toward others and the future, and therefore to some type of ethics, morals, and similar social and/or sociocultural reactions." If man has a time-binding consciousness, he is interested in the growth of human potentialities, as is demonstrated in the operation of the whole of man.

This theory was the foundation for Korzybski's analysis of humankind as an "organism-as-a-whole-in-an-environment." He believed that environment shaped human personality and behavior patterns. These environments were not only geographic, ecological, and sociocultural, but neurolinguistic and neurosemantic as well. Therefore, the constitution of a "normal" person is judged from his/her tendency to certain *psychological* reactions.

In order to study these psychological manifestations, it is necessary to develop a terminology that can analyze both verbal and nonverbal experiences. According to Korzybski, consciousness exists between these levels of abstraction. The terminology is one of *evaluation.* The result is the implementation of "an empirical general theory of values . . . with its roots in the methods of exact sciences . . . ," the study of which reveals the "factors of sanity." When these factors are further analyzed in terms of the relation between nonverbal and verbal expression, the "factors of structure" are revealed, which is the sole content of all human knowledge.

One of the primary processes of General Semantics is extensionalization. It occurs on the neurological level, with the individual orienting his neurological mechanisms to *fact,* thus integrating the corticothalamic functions through the use of *extension devices.* Described by Korzybski, "orientation by extension induces an automatic delay of reactions, which automatically stimulates the cortical region and regulates and protects the reactions of the usually over-stimulated thalamic region." This is the biological transition from Aristotelian to non-Aristotelian systems of thought, ". . . from macroscopic to sub-microscopic . . . from 'objective' to process orientations, from subject-predicate to relational evaluations . . ."

According to Korzybski, the process is laborious and can take months to achieve. Integral to the optimum functioning of the nervous system is normal blood pressure, which, in the practice of General Semantics, is achieved through *neurosemantic relaxation*. It will either lower abnormally high blood pressure or raise abnormally low blood pressure regulating blood supply and circulation. It implies a reduction in tension, which is often emotional, and is exhibited in blood pressure.

On a larger scale, along with a reorientation on a physiological basis, the practice of General Semantics also results in a reorientation in the command of the structure of language. The world can no longer be conceptualized with "intensional" or "elementalistic" means. Instead, a language is used that implies no *splits* in the context of a total realm of *formulations* (vs. mere concepts). The problems involved in this process of reorientation are inherent in the functioning of the neurosemantic and neurolinguistic mechanisms which control reactions and language. Therefore, averting anxiety, fear, etc. can only happen by being conscious of the functional capacity and actual operation of these mechanisms.

In his introduction to the second edition of *Science and Sanity,* Korzybski states: "The prevalent and constantly increasing general deterioration of human values is an unavoidable consequence of the crippling misuse of *neuro*-linguistic and *neuro*-semantic mechanisms. In general semantics, we are concerned with the *sanity* of the race." The sanity of the race can only be established through the use of a workable (non-Aristotelian) system of perception, contacting consciousness, etc., so that man no longer faces personal and social problems without the resources of a healthy nervous system.

As of 1949, Korzybski's theory of time binding as well as the extensional methods of General Semantics had been applied in educational, scientific, and managerial fields. Methods of General Semantics were also being studied in universities and schools throughout the world. The Institute of General Semantics in Lakeville, Connecticut, publishes a semiannual bulletin.

REFERENCES

Alfred Korzybski, *Manhood of Humanity.* Lakeville, Conn.: The International Non-Aristotelian Library Publishing Co., Institute of General Semantics, 1921.

————, *Science and Sanity: An Introduction to Non-Aristotelian Systems and General Semantics.* Lakeville, Conn.: The International Non-Aristotelian Library Publishing Co., 1933.

J. KRISHNAMURTI (1895–), born in southern India and educated in England, has been active as a spiritual teacher since his early years. His lifework entails speaking and counseling on tours throughout the world, and he has acquired a large following. He often structures his teaching in the form of a dialogue so that a clearer understanding of truth is attainable by his audience as well as himself.

The pursuit of wisdom lies at the core of Krishnamurti's teaching, wisdom that can be attained through achieving self-awareness, acquiring the ability to acknowledge, and discovering the truth. Truth is what *is,* apart from interpretation, criticism, justification, or identification, and cannot be translated into another form to correlate with your past education. Truth is a product of your state of mind and direct perceptual activity. In discovering truth, you activate your capacities to look, observe, listen, and be aware of actuality. Any preconceptions you have will alter your perception. Actuality is always changing and you acknowledge this by remaining flexible. Confusion about actuality stems from a preoccupation with the process of the mind, with beliefs in propagandistic treatises on politics, religions, or in "isms," and with the sensual value of things.

The attempt to escape confusion through religion, economy, society, ambition, power, or searching for reality avoids the presentness of truth, and creates a path for destruction. According to Krishnamurti, the only feasible way to end confusion is to reach a state in which you can perceive truth instantaneously: "to bring about this transformation . . . is the only true revolution." Truth is not idea, dogma, or words; it is moment-to-moment experience and silent thought.

In order to know yourself, you must rid yourself of impatience and allow yourself time to observe. Self-knowledge includes understanding how you think, how you are conditioned, why you believe in aspects of your culture (i.e., art, literature, etc.). You must be alert and sensitive to all the intricacies of your thought patterns, feelings, responses. If you are able to understand yourself, you can be meaningfully active and give yourself creative happiness.

The invention of a method for attaining self-knowledge is unnecessary. The method itself would impose a pattern on you and you would find yourself knowing the pattern rather than yourself. When you follow a method, you are seeking results that will ensure your security, your certainty, and make you subject to the authority of the method.

The transformation of yourself into a state of knowing, which exists apart from time and the accumulation of ideas, results in tranquility and brings about creativeness. Being aware of process and feeling only leads you to see an existing battle, and to struggle to alter actuality and contradictions that stem from the conflict beween past and present. When you can see the complete working of the self, you can know selfless love: "In the state of tranquility of mind that is really still there is love. And it is love alone that can solve all our human problems."

Your mind functions in a process of isolation, fragmentation, and partiality. Eliminating the separateness of thought, which is present in belief, knowledge, discipline, experience, and the whole process of achieving an end result, comes only in loving cooperation. Love comes when there is no mind to compartmentalize and intellectualize. The mind must understand the desires which lead to self-deception, before it can become tranquil. If the mind utilizes consciousness as self-activity, then time, with its accompanying miseries, conflicts, and deceptions, is exposed. When the mind understands this process it can stop, and "love can be." Your goal should be to render mind still, tranquil, not seeking any answers, but intent on being silent in the activity of looking and listening and immediately understanding.

Through constant awareness of the internal and the external, you can develop a discipline which is not conformist, imitative, or obedient. With this discipline, you can meditate in a way that does not isolate you from your relationships and becomes part of your everyday existence. Meditation should not be practiced without understanding the self, or it becomes a sensuous activity without significance. A meditative mind leads you to a space which cannot be imagined or speculated about; there is no center in the space of meditation. Meditation must occur deliberately, apart from thoughts that lead to self-deception. A meditative mind sees, watches, listens. It does not form opinions or comments, and it is attentive and sensitive in all relationships. You do not meditate by "repeating words, experiencing visions, or cultivating silence." You meditate to comprehend the world. Meditation frees the mind of the entire structure of thought which breeds dishonesty. Time is transcended through meditation. In this sense, truth is no longer abstract: seeing, listening, and watching become processes of doing, of complete engagement.

According to Krishnamurti, happiness and joy of relationship are a means to a state of everlasting bliss, unhampered by the sensuous indulgence which is a distinctive characteristic of thought, and without continuity which is a distinctive characteristic of time. Meditation is the nonfragmentary essence of life, and of daily activity, and comes in the silence of being attentive to awareness. Human confusion will be alleviated only when people attain the highest intelligence, the highest form of sensitivity where love in relationship can create a dynamic balance.

Krishnamurti foundations have been established in England and in the United States and are, in part, responsible for the publication of his lectures. Among Krishnamurti's books are *The First and Last Freedom, Freedom from the Known,* and *Commentaries on Living.*

REFERENCES

J. Krishnamurti, *The First and Last Freedom.* London: Theosophical Publishing House, 1954.

————, *The Only Revolution,* ed. by M. Lutyens. London: Victor Gollancz, Ltd., 1970.

————, *Freedom from the Known.* New York: Harper & Row, 1969.

————, *Talk and Dialogues.* New York: Avon Books, 1968.

ELISABETH KÜBLER-ROSS, a psychiatrist at the University of Chicago, has been investigating the subject of death for the last decade and is largely responsible for opening up the subject to widespread scientific investigation. Kübler-Ross was the medical director of the Family Service and Mental Health Center of South Cook County, Illinois. When she first arrived in the United States from Switzerland, she taught psychiatry under Dr. Sidney Margolin in Denver, Colorado. Her interest in death was the result of discussions of the topic with students. Her work has become well-known throughout the United States, Canada, and Europe.

Kübler-Ross recognized that the trend of Western society has been largely one of dreading death, denying death, and building psychological defenses against it: death is taboo. In her studies, she discovered that a leading factor in the reluctance of most people to accept death is that the act or process of dying has become a depersonalized and desperately lonely experience, resulting from the sophisticated technology of hospital machinery used to keep people "alive." Her philosophy calls for the renewal of faith in interpersonal relationships rather than in technology so that we will be able to face our own personal death without fear. Then we may be able to influence many other aspects of our culture, from the care of dying patients to the attitudes of the nation: "If science and technology are not to be misused to increase destructiveness, prolonging life rather than making it more human, if they could go hand in hand with freeing more rather than less for individual person to person contacts, then we could really speak of a great society."

Kübler-Ross's analysis of the characteristic attitudes in an individual's encounter with death divides it into five stages. The first stage is shock, followed by recollection of self, and an initial denial of death's imminence. Denial can bring feelings of isolation and extreme loneliness, depending upon the way the dying person is treated by family or hospital staff. The second stage sees the replacement of denial with feelings of anger, rage, envy, and resentment. Expression of these feelings is found in every aspect of daily activity, especially when the dying person realizes that he or she no longer has control over life. Family or outside help is not accepted. If the dying person is treated with respect and understanding rather than resistance, and if the person's anger is accepted and not taken personally, this rage will subside. The third stage is the bargaining stage through which the dying person routes feelings of guilt into hopes of delaying death. Death is seen as a punishment. The fourth stage is one of depression; the fact of the illness can no longer be denied. At this point, the person usually exhibits more pronounced symptoms of illness. The depression is embodied in feelings of loss connected with the body, as well as related to finances, career, and the inability to function normally in a social context. The depression can also be connected with the impending loss of love objects. This is a time when the dying person begins to look ahead rather than behind; too much interference from "cheery" visitors can upset the person's emotional stance. The fifth stage is one of ultimate acceptance. It comes when the dying person has had sufficient time to work out the previous stages (alone or with a therapist) and he or she no longer faces death with anger or depression. The acceptance of death comes almost entirely without conscious thought. The dying person has found inner peace.

At this point, Kübler-Ross feels that more harm than good is done by imposing any life-prolonging methods. "If members of the helping professions can help the patient and his family to get 'in tune' to each other's needs and come to an acceptance of an unavoidable reality together, they can help avoid much unnecessary agony and suffering on the part of the dying patient and even more so on the part of the family that is left behind."

Those with enough inner strength to express their love by being with a dying person will begin to recognize that the peaceful cessation of the body's functioning is neither frightening nor painful. There is much to be learned from the dying person about finiteness and the uniqueness of each individual.

According to Kübler-Ross, death should be considered the culmination of all that you are and have been throughout life. The intellectualization of the concept of death and dying should be surpassed in order to experience the meaning of death as it affects you, personally, the people you know, and the way you live on an emotional level. By creatively and productively accepting changes experienced in the face of the unknown, you will be able to achieve the "ultimate goal of growth," which is knowledge of the self. This demands that you commit yourself to transcending your purely individual existence and interact with others. Knowing that death is the final stage of growth will allow you to adopt an enduring spiritual self-consciousness.

REFERENCES
Elisabeth Kübler-Ross, *Death: The Final Stage of Growth.* Englewood Cliffs, N.J.: Prentice-Hall, 1975.

———, *On Death and Dying.* New York: Macmillan, 1969.

R. D. LAING (1931–), a Scottish psychiatrist, is renowned worldwide for his work in the field of schizophrenia. Born in Glasgow, Laing was educated at the University of Glasgow. He received his Doctor of Medicine degree there in 1951. He then served for two years in the British Army as a psychiatrist. From 1953–56, he taught at the University of Glasgow in the Department of Psychological Medicine. From 1956–62, he conducted clinical research at the Tavistock Institute of Human Relations in London. Laing was the director of the Langham Clinic in London from 1962–65, when he cofounded the Kingsley Hall Clinic. Since 1970, he has lectured at various colleges in the United States. He is the author of several books, among them, *The Divided Self, The Self and Others, The Politics of Experience, Reason and Violence, Knots,* and *The Facts of Life: An Essay in Existential Biology.*

Laing's concept of the schizophrenic describes an individual whose total life experience is divided in terms of its unsatisfactory relation to the world and its disruptive nature of the relation with the self. Despair, aloneness, isolation, and incomplete being characterize the schizoid's life experience. He describes the psychological disturbances suffered by schizophrenics as *ontological* insecurity, i.e., feeling more unreal than real and differentiated from the rest of the world so that their identity and autonomy are always in question. The schizophrenic's fear of losing him/herself results in a preoccupation with self-preservation rather than self-satisfaction. Three forms of anxiety are experienced: *engulfment,* in which identity is threatened to the degree that being burned, buried, drowned, or smothered is imagined; *implosion,* in which the schizophrenic feels empty and threatened by reality; and *depersonalization* and *petrification,* in which the fear is of being depersonalized by others and turned into a dead thing without subjectivity.

Schizoids tend to divorce the self from the body; the self wants to become imbedded in the body but such an occurrence is prevented by the fear that once the self is in the body it would be in danger and unable to escape. Schizoids experience primitive oral orientation and a terror of taking anything in; hatred of that which is outside; feelings of self-destruction; the split of the inner self; unrelatedness to the external world; an unbearable quality of the self; losing identity in another person, etc. The schizophrenic wants to be understood, but at the same time being understood poses a threat to the defense systems that have been built up.

Laing feels that in the treatment of the schizophrenic, it is of primary importance to maintain a view of the whole, and a concept of the human being in relation to other human beings: the idea that we cannot exist without our world and the world cannot exist without us. Treatment should occur on a level that avoids an accounting of the human being as a machine or as an "organismic system of it-processes." A science of persons is founded objectively but practiced apart from depersonalization which, according to Laing, yields false knowledge. The patient can use psychotherapy as a means to find freedom and the comfort of self-responsibility toward securing a definition of the total self.

Laing observes that psychiatrists do not pay proper attention to the experience of schizophrenics. They tend to assume that their experiences are unreal and can be understood only through interpretation. Laing believes that "schizophrenics have more to teach the psychiatrists about the inner world than psychiatrists their patients." Recent studies of the nature of schizophrenia in the wide social context show that schizophrenics are part of a network of disturbed and disturbing patterns of communication. Schizophrenics are diagnosed as such because their behavior and experience are judged to be "a special strategy invented so that life can be lived in an unliveable situation." According to Laing, schizophrenia is *not* a condition, but rather is a label denoting a political event. A person labeled "schizophrenic" becomes invalidated as a human being; his or her experiences are distorted through various methods of therapy and not allowed to occur naturally. The natural "healing" processes which apply to those people labeled schizophrenics have been lost sight of. Laing believes that along with the redefinition of psychiatric terms, there should be places provided for people where they can, under guidance, further their understanding of their inner selves, rather than be put in a situation where the "ceremony" of psychiatric examination, diagnosis, and prognostication occurs. In this way, schizophrenia can be viewed existentially rather than clinically.

Laing believes that society, in general, is founded on the denial of the self and experience, whereas the purpose of life should be to experience and conceive reality in its fullness and wholeness. Dealing with inner and outer reality is a way to distinguish between behavior and experience, yet the functions of inner and outer realities are modalities of experience. Behavior is a function of experience, and experience indicates actions: "If our experience is destroyed, our behavior will be destructive."

Psychotherapeutic relationships should be a means of "researching" whereby the present sharing experience between therapist and patient is important. According to Laing's theory of centering modes of psychotherapy within a total vision of the ontological structure of human beings, it is necessary to formulate concepts which address the interaction and interexperience between two persons in which "the relation between each person's own experience and behavior within the context of the relationship between them" can be understood. This includes the dismissal of the idea of fantasy that psychoanalysts have observed as disturbing and latent in their patients, and an admittance of the idea of fantasy into real experience. Laing contends that the fantasy aspect of experience, which is sometimes described as unconscious, is meaningful. Acceptance of it will allow for the communication necessary, both within the self and with others, which will promote relational understanding.

REFERENCES

R. D. Laing, *The Politics of Experience*. New York: Pantheon Books, 1967.

———, *The Divided Self*. New York: Pantheon Books, 1960.

———, *The Self and Others*. New York: Pantheon Books, 1961.

———, *The Facts of Life: An Essay in Existential Biology*. New York: Pantheon Books, 1976.

———, *Knots*. New York: Pantheon Books, 1971.

JOHN C. LILLY (1915–   ), scientist and psychoanalyst, was born in Minnesota and is a graduate of the California Institute of Technology and the University of Pennsylvania Medical School, where he received his M.D. in 1942. By 1949, Lilly was involved in medical research on the brain. He pursued his studies at the National Institute of Mental Health as a public health officer. From 1954–68, he pioneered research work in interspecies communication, founding the Communication Research Institute for the biomedical studies of communication between man and dolphins in 1959. From 1968–70, Lilly was a group leader resident and associate at Esalen Institute in California. Lilly has conducted research in a variety of scientific fields, including biophysics, neurophysiology, electronics, and neuroanatomy; he is a qualified psychoanalyst. He spent eight months in Chile investigating and participating in an esoteric group. Lilly is the author of *The Mind of the Dolphin; Programming and Metaprogramming in the Human Biocomputer; The Center of the Cyclone; Simulations of God: The Science of Belief; The Deep Self;* and coauthor of *The Dyadic Cyclone.*

In his work with dolphins, Lilly set up an experimental situation in which humans interacted with dolphins in a special flooded room for a specific length of time (seven days to two and one-half months). His goal was to verify certain assumptions about the viable relationship between man and dolphin, which included: 1) Given the proper environmental situation, a human and dolphin can develop mutual trust, mutual understanding, and shared methods of communication; 2) a human can communicate emotional reactions to a dolphin and a dolphin can respond properly, and vice versa; 3) a dolphin can plan ahead using strategies for developing interactional situations; 4) a dolphin can understand "metalanguage" via instructions about how to pronounce, raising and lowering volume, mimicking, etc.; 5) a dolphin is capable of knowing what is expected and purposely doing the "wrong" thing in order to elicit a response from a human, with the intention of maintaining a reactional and interactional relationship.

After a two-and-one-half-month "living-in" situation with Margaret Howe and a dolphin called Peter, the following conclusions were drawn: Dolphins can learn and enjoy learning, as well as learn things humans cannot know about; dolphins can play with a human being; dolphins are cognizant of human limitations and can teach humans; dolphins can intentionally please as well as annoy humans. With regard to the advancement of the vocal capabilities of the dolphin, this experiment proved that dolphins can imitate the inflections in the human voice, can remain silent when "taking a lesson," and will engage in speaking and listening interaction with humans at all times (not only at feeding time).

Lilly projected the long-range goal of interspecies communication as a means of creating mutual teaching exchange situations in which information of a descriptive, predictive, and cognitive nature could be exchanged. He believed interspecies communication could take place between man and medium-sized whales, and the great sperm whale, as well as dolphins. Lilly believed this kind of communication would open up new ways of thought, new experiences, and new philosophies for mankind, and it was his contention that we should stop exploiting these sea animals and realize that despite the fact that they have a different anatomical structure and live in a different environment, dolphins and whales have the capability of becoming "cognitively" equal to humans.

Lilly stopped his research with dolphins as a result of his experience with them and their teaching him "a new ethic." He concluded that the experiments he had been conducting had not taken the proper form; he had essentially imposed a "concentration camp" situation on the dolphins, and therefore was not allowing for the function of the "new ethic" of the world and universe he had discovered, which would have been implemented had he permitted the dolphins to move freely, in and out of the experimental situation as they pleased. Lilly was convinced that the theories about the brain (or *biocomputer*) needed to be adjusted to include information about higher states of consciousness.

Lilly spent ten years working with isolation tanks and LSD. He began his tank experiments with the belief that the body would continue to function despite its condition, allowing the mind to move on to other "spaces." This belief was confirmed in his first undertakings and he continued to experiment with the knowledge that if his body was in danger, his mind would return to it, ensuring his survival. As a result of this group of experiments, Lilly concluded that all and everything that can be imagined, including all possible forms of life in the universe, exist in "spaces" that cannot be known in lower states of consciousness unless they have been experienced before. Lilly explored the discovery of these spaces using other methods (e.g., working with William Schutz, Fritz Perls, Oscar Ichazo). At this stage, Lilly believed that our inner realities allow us to create a general principle of living and being; in order to design this principle, we take certain "metaprogrammatic" steps: 1) Examine whatever one can of where the new spaces are, what the basic beliefs are to go there; 2) take on the basic beliefs as if true; 3) go into the area fully aware and store everything, no matter what the experiences become; 4) come back to the best of consensus realities, shed the basic beliefs of the new area, and become the investigator, examining recorded experiences and data objectively; 5) test current models of this consensus reality; 6) construct a model that includes this reality and the new one; 7) do not worship, revere, or be afraid of any person, group, space, or reality.

Lilly approached his research with the theory that we are programmed biocomputers. When we learn, we make models and analogues of the real situation, using and inventing the languages of our culture. Our capacity to *metaprogram* prevents us from relearning: "Metaprogramming is an operation in which a central control system controls hundreds of thousands of programs operating in parallel simultaneously." We are *self-metaprogrammers,* consisting of all that is built-in, all that has been acquired, and our conclusions about both. By reducing our minds to levels of consciousness (via Gurdjieff's vibration levels of states of consciousness, for example) and corresponding our findings to the reality of the universe, we can see the programmatic nature of our biocomputers in our individual models of the universe. The quality of the model is measured in "how well it matches the real universe."

Lilly approaches the study of the human brain with nearly forty basic assumptions about its construct and its complete functional nature with regard to programs and metaprograms, in an effort to correlate it with the language and mechanism of the man-made computer system. He defines the *brain* as the palpable, visible, living set of structures included in the human biocomputer, the boundaries of which are known; the *mind* is the sum total of all the programs and metaprograms of a given human biocomputer, its software, the boundaries of which are unknown.

Through his experiments with LSD, forms of mentation, utilization of mental exercises, and by studying the graphable vibrations of the levels of consciousness, Lilly determined that there are ten structural levels of the human brain, which define in what capacity the mind can operate. The levels range from that which is now unknown to the level where the brain and body operate with external reality. Lilly considers the level of *essence metaprogramming* as the means to the highest possible state of consciousness; it is achieved through operating on each preceding level of consciousness and being aware of the operation. The essence level allows us to identify with our ability to metaprogram completely and come in contact with the Essence, no matter what its shape. Connecting with the Essence becomes being connected with something greater than we are individually, greater than all humanity, greater than the universe. According to Lilly, the study of yet unknown extensions of our minds, incorporated with our belief systems, is a science that goes beyond that of natural sciences, falling within the bounds of mathematics, theoretical physics, and the sciences of states of consciousness.

Lilly feels that our *belief systems* correlate with our *simulations of God;* belief systems are the means developed by our biocomputers to "construct certainty and determinacy in the face of the essential indeterminacy of the macro- and micro-structure of the universe." In this way, God (Essence) has been equated with certain ideas such as power, love, eternity. When we can reach the experience of knowing the process of metaprograms that lead to a simulation of God and can allay the "authorities" that would have us do otherwise, we can create our own simulation of God. We will then realize that we only "inhabit the structure" of our bodies. By becoming fully aware of the actuality of our bodies and their processes, we have the freedom to use our brains and mind without emotion to project the complete, natural structure of the physical universe, for which we, as individuals and as nations, no longer need substitute simulations of God.

REFERENCES

John C. Lilly, *Lilly on Dolphins, Humans of the Sea.* New York: Anchor Books, 1975.

————, *The Center of the Cyclone: An Autobiography of Inner Space.* New York: Bantam Books, 1973.

————, *Programming and Metaprogramming in the Human Biocomputer.* New York: Bantam Books, 1974.

———, *Simulations of God: The Science of Belief*. New York: Bantam Books, 1976.

———, *The Deep Self*. New York: Simon & Schuster, 1977.

——— and Antoinette Lilly, *The Dyadic Cyclone*. New York: Simon & Schuster, 1976.

ALEXANDER LOWEN (1910–) is a practicing psychoanalyst who has made a significant contribution to the exploration of the function of the body in relationship to the psyche in his Bioenergetic Therapy. Lowen was born in New York City. A former student of Wilhelm Reich and a Reichian therapist from 1945–53, he was influenced greatly by his teacher. In 1953, in association with Dr. John C. Pierrakos, Lowen developed a series of clinical seminars which resulted in the founding of the Institute of Bioenergetic Analysis, of which he is executive director. Lowen is a seminar leader at the Esalen Institute in California, and lectures and conducts workshops throughout the United States and Europe. He is the author of several books, the most recent being *Bioenergetics.*

Lowen noted that within the last decade, psychoanalytic therapy has proved ineffective for a large portion of those who have undertaken it; it adheres to Freudian principles and is structured on an exclusively verbal exchange between patient and analyst, an approach which Lowen felt to be procedurally antiquated and insufficient. Most psychiatrists, he found, are confounded by the relationship between body sensations and the verbal expression of body feelings, the relationship between somatic processes and psychological phenomena, and the relationship between body structure and temperament. The questions that must be asked are: 1) Can the character of a patient be changed without causing a change in body structure and improvement in motility? 2) Is it not possible to effectuate these changes in temperament which the patient demands?

Lowen believes personality and character are physically structured, and that neuroses manifest themselves in the body, its structure and movement. Bioenergetic analysis and therapy function on the premise that how your body feels as shown in the way you move is a key to your emotional status; they deal with movement in terms of basic physical laws, i.e., movement demands a discharge of energy in which action is equal to reaction; and all energy is interchangeable and can be reduced to a common denominator. Therefore, one basic energy in the body can manifest itself either as psychic phenomena or somatic motion; this energy is *bioenergy*. Theoretically, bioenergetic therapy is structured according to somatic parallels to the ego, superego, and id principles of consciousness: Its goal is to reunite the mind and body by getting rid of obstacles which inhibit or prevent the body from releasing tension spontaneously.

Bioenergetic therapy emphasizes the fulfillment of the pleasure principle, a functioning mechanism of the id, and the reality principle, a functioning mechanism of the ego, and, by nature, instrumental in the furthering of pleasure. According to bioenergetic theory, healthy instinctual motion evolves when your fundamental energy spreads evenly, producing either spatial movement, essentially superficially ego oriented and aggressive, or sensations that are erotic, loving, or tender. In principle, instincts involving the ego are equivalent to sexual instincts. The quality of sexual function is related to the condition of your ego function; this idea is the basis of the reality principle and the crux of bioenergetic principles and therapy.

Lowen describes society's trends toward depersonalization and alienation of the individual as a process in which love is romanticized, sex is compulsive, work is mechanical, and achievement, egotistical; images have been substituted for personal meaning. This results in your diverting your body from its natural role and exaggerating the role of your ego, thus putting ego and body in conflict and diffusing your central energy. "Betraying" your body renders you 1) neurotic, when the ego dominates the body and your guilt and anxiety-ridden fear of the body cause a panic and subsequent denial of the body in order to survive; 2) schizoid, when you deny your body and your struggle becomes one of life and death; 3) schizophrenic, when the ego dissociates itself from the body, splitting the personality.

Healthy people represent the image of the body successfully, verbally and graphically. Any disparity between your social or ego image and your physical or body image reflects your schizoid tendencies, which Lowen feels manifest themselves in a negation of life and lack of identity. In order to have an adequate body image, you must necessarily be free to mobilize your body feelings. The repression of these feelings or an inadequate sense of body image results in a breakdown in performance, an inability to recognize and locate body sensations, and general physical and mental confusion about the body's capacity to express itself and respond. In their extreme form, schizoid disturbances place you in a limbo between fear of abandonment and the loneliness and isolation which is the result of your inability to have satisfactory relationships. The result can be a tendency to self-destruction. Lowen labels the study of this form of character disposition the *psychology of desperation.*

In order to retrieve your "lost" body, you must understand that physical tension limits the function of your personality; the *release* of tension *liberates* your personality. Lowen has found that most patients of bioenergetic therapy are unable to trust the feelings that can guide behavior. Headaches, backaches, and bad posture are regarded as normal or natural to being alive. Bioenergetic therapy will cause you to recognize your tensions through the execution of a variety of physical stress positions; the disintegration and uncoordination of your body, the division between the upper and lower portions of your body, will be revealed. The resolution of this psychological-physical delineation involves concentration on the analysis of unconscious resistances and the development of physical capacities.

Lowen determined that the capacity for expressing

emotions is "proportionate" to muscular coordination, and that an emotional-physical adjustment will occur with a certain amount of pain, which, in this context, is a positive factor. Rediscovering your "lost" identity involves regaining an awareness of desires, recognizing needs, and perceiving body sensations. In the bioenergetic therapy situation, you and the therapist confront each other; the therapist represents the reality of the world and the reality of the body, and guides you to 1) the truth of your body as revealed in its expression, attitude, state; 2) the function of your ego which in an identification with both body (feeling) and mind (knowledge) is to test reality.

Sexual instincts and their functioning reflect personality. Lowen places the expression of sexual feeling on two levels: 1) Sexual sophistication; this denotes ego orientation. For a sexual sophisticate, the sex act is a compulsively realized performance, a way to obtain freedom from sexual guilt, a way to build the ego. It involves no strong feeling and becomes a defense against the body, an activity of showing off adequacy, a performance. A sexual sophisticate is a "perfect lover," an advocate of the pleasure principle. 2) Sexual maturity; the sex act is an expression of feeling and essentially an embodiment of satisfaction in and commitment to living. Sexual involvement relates to love when the reality principle is operating. Lowen finds one of the main functions of love to lie in discrimination in the search for a sexual object. The pursuit of loving is carried on by the integrated personality. When the sexual act relates to loving, it increases in quality and intensity, expressing tenderness, sensitivity, and respect. Satisfaction in sexual activity is a measure of commitment to the activity, to your sexual partner: "Sexual response touches and actively involves the heart," and "the deepest and most satisfying expression of love in the sex act is the response of the orgasm." According to Lowen, orgasm, a function of body movement, cannot happen unless you are secure in your body. The voluntary phase of the sex act is based on your body's dynamics (i.e., its mobility, stability, tonicity, and ego direction); the involuntary phase occurs apart from the ego and is attained through an experience of intense, unfrightened feelings. In Lowen's view, sexuality is a way of being in which the dual nature of the mind and body is not in conflict.

Bioenergetics, the study of the energetic processes of the body as they determine the activity of mind and body, is based on the principle that *you are your body.* The body is not viewed as a machine; it possesses a spirit and contains a soul. Mind and spirit are connected to the body in terms of the vibrancy and energy you demonstrate in your activity. Soul is an aspect of the mind-body union which allows you to sense a relationship with the energy of the world and universe. You acquire an ability to move "in harmony with the universe." The language of the body is the language of your *first nature,* free of structured physical and psychological attitudes, characteristic of your unnatural *second nature.*

REFERENCES

Alexander Lowen, M. D., *The Language of the Body.* New York: Collier Books, 1971.

———, *The Betrayal of the Body.* New York: Collier Books, 1974.

———, *Love and Orgasm.* New York: New American Library, 1965.

———, *Bioenergetics.* New York: Coward, McCann & Geoghegan, 1975.

———, *Pleasure.* New York: Lancer, 1970.

LSD THERAPY. LSD, or lysergic acid diethylamide, an alkaloid, one of the most powerful drugs known, was accidently discovered by Albert Hofman, a Swiss chemist, in 1943. Since then, the use of LSD has been a subject of controversy. One of the first controversies resulted from LSD being used to induce psychoses-simulating circumstances in patients, so-called model schizophrenics. Later, LSD was investigated for its psychotherapeutic value, especially as it affected chronic alcoholics, narcotic-drug addicts, and severe character neurotics; this research was supported in a paper by Sidney Cohen of UCLA in 1960. LSD seemed to be much safer than other methods used in psychiatric therapy, i.e., shock treatment, insulin coma treatment, and psychosurgery. In the early 1960s, LSD was considered useful for research into psychiatry, psychiatric training, and therapeutic experimentation, as well as an agent for inducing heightened aesthetic, religious, and mystical experiences. Research into LSD's use as a therapeutic drug revealed that this substance magnifies and brings into the open mental processes embedded in the unconscious which embody conflicts inherent in human nature. LSD experiments provide information for a better understanding of the human mind and personality changes and, in a larger context, the nature of man and society.

The therapeutic use of LSD depends upon the skill and knowledge with which the drug is used. It is effective on patients of two types: those who are neurotic due to repression and those who require the satisfaction of subjective needs in a socially unacceptable manner, e.g., alcoholics, drug addicts, kleptomaniacs, etc. The effect of LSD is to increase tolerance and acceptance of subjective needs, as well as expose and change those needs which create a conflict between personality and reality. This can occur through the elicitation of fantasies and images which reflect the inner emotional state of a patient as well as the patient's subjective attitudes toward external situations.

LSD encourges the release and dissipation of repressed emotions in the patient which allow him/her to live out experiences as a child or an animal. The influence of these repressed emotions is instrumental in shaping personality; once they are revealed, they can be changed and provide a key to changing the whole personality. LSD increases a patient's capacity for transference, and thus the realignment of past relationships with father, mother, and siblings, and eventually the realignment of ongoing relationships.

LSD exposes memories in a way that every aspect of a memory, smells, emotions, attitudes, etc., is re-experienced. This total recall is beneficial in relieving trauma, the memory and emotions of which have been suppressed in the subconscious, only appearing as forms of fear and guilt. Relief of trauma alleviates the burden of repression, anxiety, and sublimation.

It has been found that those who benefit from LSD therapy tend to suffer from common neuroses and personality disorders such as anxiety, depression, phobias, obsessions, compulsions, sexual neuroses, etc. The therapy concentrates on an examination and discussion of those elements that are revealed while the patient is under the influence of LSD, after the drug's effects have worn off. This allows for the integration of the patient's personality.

The therapist administering the drug must be aware that he/she is often the only person on whom the patient can depend. Therefore, the therapist must simultaneously perform the roles of confidant, objective observer and analyst, guide for the patient in foreign territory, an object of the act of transference, and a storehouse of conceptual tools.

LSD can be taken orally, or it can be injected intramuscularly, intravenously, intraperitoneally, or directly into the cerebrospinal fluid in the vertebral canal. The drug does not begin to take effect immediately; there is a latency period of anywhere from ten minutes to three hours, depending upon the method of administration, the amount administered, and psychological resistance. An LSD therapy session can last from four to twelve hours. The physical symptoms of LSD reaction are measurable in terms of the stimulation of the autonomic, motor, and sensitive nerves. When the parasympathetic nerves are affected, the pulse rate slows down, blood pressure drops; hypersalivation, secretion of tears, diarrhea, nausea, and vomiting can occur. Stimulation of the sympathetic nerves results in an increase in pulse rate and rise in blood pressure, the pupils dilate, vision becomes blurred with difficulty in focusing, thick saliva is secreted, sweating is profuse, the arteries in the appendages are constricted, and body hairs stand up. Effects on motor nerves are muscular tension, tremors, twitches, jerks, complex twisting motions, or complete relaxation of the muscles. When the sensitive nerves are affected by LSD, headaches may occur, along with pains in other parts of the body, feelings of heaviness in the extremities, sexual feelings, and a variety of strange sensations. Perceptual changes, with respect to vision, and sensitivity to sound, taste, smell occur. Experience of time and space is altered; in an extreme form, there is an awareness of infinity or eternity. The psychological symptoms of LSD can occur in feelings of euphoria, despair, inferiority, apathy, aggression, etc. A change in psychomotor response may occur either as inhibition of activity or excitement in the form of unmotivated laughter, theatrical performance, acting out impulses, etc. The effects of LSD can elicit a unique perception of art or music, and occasionally an increase in creativity.

Currently, LSD therapy is being used in a variety of therapeutic frameworks. In Europe, the *psycholytic* method of LSD therapy predominates. Developed in England by Dr. Ronald Sandison, it involves administering low dosages of LSD or psilocybin and the activation and deepening of the psychoanalytic process through discussion of relevant information in numerous individual and group sessions. Its goal is to cure through a reconstruction of the personality in a maturing process. In the United States, the therapy implemented is *psychedelic*. This involves giving large doses of LSD to cause cosmic-mystic and ecstatic experiences. This therapy concentrates on one single overwhelming experience, the information from which is not specifically related to classical psychology, but rather focuses on religio-psychological and mystical interpretations.

There are indications, as yet inconclusive, that LSD can alter chromosomes, induce birth defects, increase the possibility of cancer, etc. Other psychotomimetic drugs such as psilocybin, mescaline, etc. are also being explored for their therapeutic use, as a possible replacement for LSD.

REFERENCES

W. V. Caldwell, *LSD Psychotherapy: An Exploration of Psychedelic and Psycholytic Theory*. New York: Grove Press, 1968.

Stanislav Grof, *Realms of the Human Unconscious*. New York: Viking Press, 1975.

THE LUSCHER COLOR TEST is the result of work done by Dr. Max Luscher who became interested in color psychology early in his education. Luscher first presented his color test at an international medical conference in Lausanne in 1947. Since then, he has continued research and experimentation to revise and refine the test.

The Luscher Color Test is a method of determining physical and psychological information about an individual through the selection and/or rejection of colors. Extended, the information gathered from a test of this kind can be referred to by manufacturers, the success of whose products often depends upon color, and by those in businesses who need information concerning the kinds of employees best suited to work in a given situation.

The first indication of the influence of color on our activity began with primitive man and the environments to which he was originally subject: day and night. It is considered that day elicits a work-oriented response, and night a more peaceful, nonworking response. For primitive man, the kind of activity that occurred during the day was either aggressive, i.e., hunting or attacking, or passive, i.e., those actions directed toward self-preservation against being hunted or attacked.

Studies of primitive man institute universal interpretations of the colors associated with his environments. For example, day is associated with bright yellow, a color that is conducive to activity. Night is generally associated with dark blue, a color which causes the ceasing of activity. Red is associated with aggressive self-regulated activity; green with passive activity. These four colors are the psychological primaries and are basic to the design of the Luscher Color Test.

In keeping with the analyses and interpretation regarding primitive man, it can be determined that variations of colors can cause physiological responses. Judging from physical responses (e.g., increase or decrease in heart rate, change in breathing, etc.), the psychological status of an individual can be ascertained. The patterns of the physical response to color, discovered through a vast amount of experimentation, allowed for the development of a standard method of interpretation toward the understanding of the psyche.

The test should be administered by a physician or psychiatrist, professionally trained to use the test and apply insightful interpretations to the results. The test is structured so that no color is to be considered in terms of its aesthetic value. The colors are selected and rejected without attaching a function to any color, e.g., the color of a dress, the color of a room, etc. In a selective process, colors are chosen according to preference. Once all the colors have been selected, they are laid out again and selected a second time, as if this has never been done before. When the test is concluded, the monitoring therapist can extract from the compiled data large amounts of information which pertain to both your physical and psychological state.

Information about your physical state often acts as a warning signal for ailments in the early stages of growth (e.g., cardiac malfunction, disorders of the gastrointestinal tract, etc.). This kind of information can be extremely valuable to your physician's ability to diagnose certain illnesses as well as to generally deepen his understanding of you. Information about your psychological state can indicate psychic stress, emotional dissatisfaction, fear, humiliation, frustration, etc.

There are two types of Luscher Color Test: the full Luscher test and the "quick" test. The quick test involves the use of eight colors, the primaries (yellow, blue, green, and red) and the auxiliaries (violet, brown, gray, and black). The primaries represent fundamental psychological needs such as the need for contentment, the need for affection, the need to assert yourself, the need to look forward and aspire. When a well-adjusted individual, free of conflicts and tension, takes the test, it has been found that the primaries are the first colors that are selected. The auxiliaries, or achromatic colors, are essentially colorless. They indicate negative attitudes toward life. If you select any of the auxiliaries among the first four or five colors you choose, it indicates a state of frustration or anxiety.

The quick test is used when physicians need aid in diagnosis, but cannot spend the time required to implement the test on a full scale. The full Luscher test involves using seventy-three color patches, including the primaries, the auxiliaries, and all their variations. The test takes from five to eight minutes to administer, but the results require lengthy interpretation so that every facet of your psychological state may be exposed.

The use of the Luscher Color Test has been worldwide, most notedly in education, ethnology, religio-psychological studies, gerontological studies, and marriage counseling. It has also been used to determine the necessary requirements for guidance in vocational and personnel selection in industry and commerce (Luscher Personnel Service, London, England).

REFERENCE

Ian Scott, trans. and ed., *The Luscher Color Test*. New York: Pocket Books, 1971.

MACROBIOTICS (shokuyo) became known in the United States with the publication in 1960 of *Zen Macrobiotics* by George Ohsawa, who began teaching macrobiotics on a wide scale in 1953 in India. Ohsawa toured Europe in 1956, teaching his macrobiotic philosophy; a macrobiotic factory was established in Belgium, and macrobiotic stores and restaurants began opening throughout the continent. In 1960, *Macro-*

biotic News, a magazine, now called *The Macrobiotic,* was started in New York City. It is published by the George Ohsawa Macrobiotic Foundation in San Francisco. In 1962, a camp of thirteen families in Chico, California, began the first American macrobiotic food manufacturing and distributing company. At one point Ohsawa counseled Mao Tse-tung on his health and the policy of China. Ohsawa claims to have cured his own tropical ulcers with a macrobiotic diet.

Macrobiotics is a way of life, based on the ancient principles of yin and yang, central to the philosophy of *In'yology,* which integrates science and philosophy. According to Ohsawa, the theory of yin and yang, or the theory of polarized monism, "has an organic mechanism invisible to mechanical researchers. It is like the 'flying arrow,' out of reach of those who want to possess it through analysis; once one has grasped it, it no longer is the 'flying arrow.'" The theory of polarized monism is a theory of the universe and creation which holds that there is a fundamental life force that speaks of one life; this is the *unique principle* which lies at the core of Ohsawa's teachings. The unique principle states that the universe is the oscillation of the two activities of yin and yang, and their interchange. If, in fact, this interaction is operative, "it can produce itself at all levels, be it in the depths of the sea or on a high plateau —of necessity assuming different forms according to the milieu and the time—because any being is *its transformed environment,* no being existing independently of its surroundings."

The universe, or *Taikyoku,* is polarized into the opposite activities of yin and yang, in a continual occurrence. The activity of yin is dilating and produces cold and an upward, centrifugal direction. The activity of yang is constrictive and produces heat, creates weight, and centripetal power. Each being and phenomenon in the universe are vested with these two activities in varying proportions so that there is dynamic universal balance, "endless movement" as Ohsawa describes it. No being or phenomenon is completely yin or yang, but rather comprised of aggregates of the two. Yin and yang attract each other and produce each other. Yin resides on the exterior; yang resides in the center of all beings.

Within the context of macrobiotic philosophy is a new method for studying the philosophy and sciences of ancient China. The method directs you to deal with the five ancient *Ching:* the *I-Ching,* which plots the dynamic order of the universe; the *Che-Ching,* an anthology that teaches morality, manners, conduct; the *Chou-Ching,* a collection of ancient imperial dictates of national codes and rulings; the *Tch'ouen-ts'ieou,* a critique of moral practices written by Confucius; and the *Li-Ki,* outlining the administration of the government. Supportive of this method of study is the use of the Sticks of Logos which symbolize the forces of yin and yang.

Macrobiotic philosophy poses questions about being, knowledge, self and free will, consciousness, language, and reality. The unique principle is applied to systems of chemistry and biology to determine the forms in which yin and yang exist in the chemical elements and vegetation. In the analysis of vegetation, yin is equated with acidity (K) and yang with alkalinity (Na). The fundamental principle of the macrobiotic diet is one which calls for a balance of these two elements in the body. Man, like plant life, cannot exist properly, given the conditions of cell metabolism, environment, species, etc., when either element exceeds the amount dictated by the unique principle.

According to macrobiotic philosophy, health care is based on the only law of Chinese medicine: *Shin do fu ji,* which means man is the result of his environment. This law implies that you can maintain natural and perfect health provided you nourish yourself with the foods that are in your environment "in the very same proportions as they are naturally produced."

Imbalance is created in your system when there is an excess of either yin or yang elements, and the result is illness. Treatment of illness is based on the unique principle. Yin diseases are treated with yang elements and vice versa. In macrobiotics, it is therefore assumed that every illness can be eliminated through an adjustment in diet.

REFERENCES

Jean Hewitt, *New York Times Natural Foods Cookbook.* New York: Quadrangle, 1971.

George Ohsawa, *The Unique Principle: The Philosophy of Macrobiotics.* San Francisco: The George Ohsawa Macrobiotic Foundation, 1973.

————, *Macrobiotics: Invitation to Health and Happiness.* Tokyo: Japan Publications, 1971.

ABRAHAM H. MASLOW (1908–70), a psychologist, sought to establish an alternative to objectivist, behavioristic psychology and Freudianism with *humanistic psychology,* or the *psychology of being.* Maslow was born in Brooklyn, New York. He taught at Brooklyn College from 1935–51. He was appointed chairman of the Department of Psychology at Brandeis University in 1951. From 1961–62, he was the Andrew Kay Visiting Fellow at Western Behavioral Sciences Institute at La Jolla, California, and from 1967–68, president of the American Psychological Association. Maslow was the author of several books, *Motivation and Personality, Toward a Psychology of Being, Religion, Values and Peak Experiences, Eupsychian Management: A Journal, The Psychology of Science, The Farthest Reaches of Human Nature,* as well as numerous articles for a variety of journals and books on psychology. He was awarded a grant from the Ford Foundation's Fund for the Advancement of Education. Maslow's psychological theories were the result of over thirty years of research and psychotherapeutic work with psychologically healthy individuals. He felt that the study of "healthy" individuals would permit the creation of a firm foundation for the theories and values of therapy. He discovered that healthy individuals are moti-

ABRAHAM H. MASLOW / 309

vated toward *self-actualization,* defined as the "ongoing
actualization of potentials, capacities, talents, as fulfillment of a mission (or call, fate, destiny, or vocation),
as a fuller knowledge of, and acceptance of, the person's own intrinsic nature, as an increasing trend
toward unity, integration, or synergy within the person."
They have satisfactorily gratified their basic needs for
safety, belongingness, love, respect, and self-esteem.
Self-actualization lies at the core of the psychology of
being.

The main theme of the psychology of being is that
each of us possesses an inner nature that is biologically
unchanging and unique to us as individuals, and which
can be explored scientifically. This inner nature shelters
our basic human emotions and capacities; it is basically
good, although weak and delicate, and should not be
suppressed. The more we introspect and examine our
inner natures, the more we are able to get in contact
with the "hows" of satisfying our needs.

Maslow observed that healthy people possess the following qualities: a superior perception of reality; an
increased acceptance of self, others, and nature; increased spontaneity; increased detachment and desire
for privacy; increased autonomy of self; resistance to
conformity and identification with humanity; an increased sense of problem centering; a greater sense of
appreciation and emotion. The healthy person is more
creative and more conscious of having interpersonal relations and peak experiences and creating a satisfactory
set of values.

In experiencing something, the cognitive process
works on many levels. Average cognitive experiences are
partial, incomplete, and often lack perceptive richness
and clarity. On the other hand, *peak experiences,* which
is the label Maslow gives to those cognitive experiences
undergone by self-actualizing individuals, have an entirely different character. In a peak experience, the
experience is dealt with as a whole of "being"; the
object or experience is perceived with complete atten-

tion, independent of classification, relations, usefulness, expediency, or purpose. This perception can be egoless and felt as a self-validating span of time which has its own intrinsic value. A characteristic of a peak experience is the participant's disorientation from both time and space. (In contrast, average cognitive experiences are hampered by history, culture, the definitions of time and space, and connected with a greater whole.)

A peak experience is, to a degree, absolute. The cognition related to such an experience is usually more passive and receptive than active. Emotional reactions in a peak experience have a quality that can be characterized as awe, reverence, and humility. In a mystical/philosophical peak experience, the world is seen united into a total entity; in the love or aesthetic peak experience, the experience itself is given the quality of the complete world. Fears, anxieties, and inhibitions are momentarily replaced by fulfillment, individuation, and great maturity. In a peak experience, we are closer to the "being" of the world, as well as the "being" of ourselves. Peak experiences are our healthiest moments.

Self-actualizing creativeness has a quality of being radiated and free of the inhibitions of problems and product orientation. Self-actualizing creativity concentrates on the revelation of personality through boldness, freedom, spontaneity, and self-acceptance. It is characteristic of essential humanness and will lead the way to the fullest humanness.

There are several reasons why self-actualization and growth may be prevented: Our instinctual tendencies toward self-fulfillment are weak and can get lost in the realm of habit; history has determined that our "instinctoid" needs are evil; we are subject to the pressures of sickness and weakness. Maslow found that the process of self-improvement is very difficult for most people, and that the aid of a skilled, professional therapist who can understand and respect the forces which hinder our growth can be crucial. Self-knowledge is a means to overcome the problems encountered in self-improvement.

In order to become fully human and approach "being," we must understand that in the effort to "realize" ourselves, we are often afraid, unwilling, and unable to carry through with the process. Once we have overcome the fear of knowing, seeing, and dealing autonomously with ourselves, we have the potential to receptively integrate ourselves with the environment and its elements with a set of values that is discoverable and intrinsic to our nature. Maslow was ultimately interested in the creation of "One Good World," the foundation of which is the advancement of knowledge and "being."

REFERENCES

Abraham H. Maslow, *Eupsychian Management: A Journal.* New York: Irwin-Dorsey, 1965.

———, *The Farthest Reaches of Human Nature.* New York: Viking Press, 1970.

———, *Motivation and Personality.* New York: Harper & Row, 1954, rev. 1971.

———, *The Psychology of Science, A Reconnaissance.* New York: Harper & Row, 1966.

———, *Toward a Psychology of Being.* Princeton, N.J.: Van Nostrand Reinhold, 1968.

MASTERS (1915–) AND JOHNSON (1925–)

are a team of researchers whose clinical findings have contributed significantly to the understanding of human sexuality. The results of their work have been published in medical journals as well as their popularly accepted books, *Human Sexual Response, Human Sexual Inadequacy,* and *The Pleasure Bond.*

William Masters was born in Cleveland, Ohio. He attended Hamilton College in New York and the University of Rochester School of Medicine and Dentistry, receiving his M.D. in 1943. Originally intending to go into laboratory research, Masters changed his mind while working with George Washington Corner, M.D., an anatomist and pioneer in sex research and education. On Corner's advice, Masters trained in obstetrics and gynecology (1943–47), which he later taught at Washington University. In 1945, he began his association with Virginia Johnson in researching human sexual physiology. Johnson, born in Springfield, Missouri, had a diverse education in music and sociology, later pursuing activities in advertising research, administrative work, and business writing. She received an academic appointment to Washington University School of Medicine in 1960, and in 1962 became a research instructor there; in 1964, she was a doctoral candidate in psychology. Masters and Johnson now run the Reproductive Biology Research Foundation in St. Louis, which was established to provide a center where therapy for sexual distress could be provided.

Masters and Johnson conducted the major part of their initial research with a group of volunteers who had a history of successful sexual response and stability, including unmarried persons and young divorcees with children. The aim of the research was to observe and record volunteer subjects enacting "manual and mechanical manipulation, natural coition with the female partner in supine, superior, or knee-chest positions, and, for many female study subjects, artificial coition in supine and knee-chest positions." This often required the use of mechanical equipment that could be ". . . adjusted for physical variations in size, weight, and vaginal development" with "rate and depth of penile thrust . . . initiated and controlled completely by the responding individual" to observe and photograph the sexual response in the vagina and evaluate intravaginal contraceptive devices. Their research also included sexual intercourse between unmarried couples in the laboratory.

The results of their research center around the four phases of sexual response: excitement, plateau, orgasm, and resolution, which constitute the *human cycle of sexual response*. The first phase "develops from any source of somatogenic or psychogenic stimulation," the strength of which is an important factor in establishing a sufficient amount of sexual tension to continue the cycle. The plateau phase occurs as a result of sufficient stimulation. During this phase, the intensity of sexual tension increases to the point where orgasm may occur. The orgasmic phase lasts for a period of seconds; the concentration of blood (vasoconcentration) and muscle tension (myotonia), which is the result of stimulation, are released. The response is involuntary. In the female, it is concentrated in the clitoral area, the vagina, and the uterus; in the male, in the penis, prostate, and seminal vesicles. The resolution phase, also involuntary, marks the loss of tension, and the pattern of the cycle is reversed, resulting in an unstimulated state.

Masters and Johnson discovered that if this cycle of sexual response does not complete itself or does not occur successfully, there are certain side effects. Females go through periods of irritability, emotional instability, restlessness, pelvic discomfort, insomnia. Males may experience pain due to congestion in the increased size of the testicles in the plateau phase (this congestion is released through nocturnal emissions or masturbation).

Masters and Johnson clarified the myths concerning vaginal versus clitoral orgasm in women: The vaginal orgasm does not exist per se; the clitoris is the necessary key to the female orgasm; both the clitoris and the vagina are stimulated in intercourse. Despite this, intercourse is not a particularly effective way for a woman to achieve orgasm. They also resolved the controversy surrounding the circumcised versus noncircumcised male, concluding that there is no difference between reaction time, sensate focus, etc., in the two cases.

They determined that sexual tension ("the physiological concomitant to, and reflection of, elevation in an individual's psychic sex interest, expressed in increased blood concentration and muscle tension") can be denied and expressed in a nonsexual manner through nocturnal emission, vaginal lubrication, etc., and that birth control devices (even the pill) can affect the sexual response in women.

As the result of their clinical findings, Masters and Johnson concluded that in the majority of cases, sexual dysfunction is the product of fear that is aroused when either male or female has difficulty in collaborating mental signals with corresponsing physical functions. The aim of the therapy given at the Reproductive Biology Research Foundation is to restore sexual performance to its natural rhythm, dispensing with the fears which can cause a variety of sexual dysfunctions.

The therapy is structured around the premise that the emotional and sexual barriers between men and women can be eliminated more easily through the help of a trained male and female team of therapists. The function of the therapy team is to 1) bring about an understanding between partners of their sexual distress and its causes; 2) restore the natural pattern of sexual activity; 3) eliminate fear, embarrassment, misunderstanding, anger, defenses that are inhibiting communication between the two.

The therapy process involves a combination of interviews and private physical therapy sessions over a two-week period. The interviews focus on the couple's sexual history initially, and later on the changes in the couple's sexual value system. The physical therapy sessions are designed to initiate a process of relearning pleasurable sensate reactions with the emphasis, at first, on touch. Later, the concentration shifts to the particular sexual dysfunction that is problematic. It has been found that dysfunctions are primarily the result of a blockage of sensate feedback.

The therapy of the foundation proved successful in a large percentage of cases, with very few people returning for a second session. Follow-up sessions a year after the initial therapy, and again four to five years later, confirmed this. According to Masters and Johnson, failures in the therapy are generally rooted in a marriage situation in which divorce is imminent, in situations where the couple is cynical about or hostile toward the therapy, or if an outside therapist is involved with either member of the couple.

REFERENCES

William H. Masters, M.D., and Virginia E. Johnson, *Human Sexual Response*. Boston: Little, Brown & Co., 1966.

———, *Human Sexual Inadequacy*. Boston: Little, Brown & Co., 1970.

———, *The Pleasure Bond*. Boston: Little, Brown & Co., 1975.

ROLLO MAY (1909–), an American psychoanalyst and existential therapist, was born in Ado, Ohio. He was educated in Vienna and was a student of Alfred Adler. He attended Oberlin College, and the Union Theological Seminary in New York City, receiving his Bachelor of Divinity degree in 1938. He received his Ph.D. in psychology from Columbia University in 1949. From 1948–55, May was on the faculty of the William Alanson White Institute of Psychiatry, Psychology and Psychoanalysis. He lectured at the New School for Social Research in New York City. In 1958, he was appointed training fellow and supervisory analyst at the White Institute. May has taught at Harvard, Princeton, and Yale, and was Regent's Professor at the University of California, Santa Cruz, in 1973. He has been a trustee of the American Foundation of Mental Health and on the board of directors of the Society of Arts, Religion and Culture. He has been the recipient of numerous awards, among them an award given by the New York Society for Clinical Psychology for distinguished contributions to the profession and science of psychology. May is the author of *The Meaning of Anxiety, Man's Search for Himself, Love and Will,* which won the Ralph Waldo Emerson Award, and *The Courage to Create.*

May contends that modern man is plagued by feelings of emptiness and loneliness, which are a part of the greater experience of anxiety. The feeling of emptiness stems from a sense that man is powerless; it evolves as despair, futility, and eventually apathy. Loneliness is the result of this feeling of emptiness, as well as the loss of the experience of the self which, until modern times, was substantiated through relationships with others. May asserts that man is a bisocial mammal, dependent upon others for security, especially in childhood, during which time a consciousness of self is acquired which can be relied upon for a lifetime. Fear of loneliness is further increased by the emphasis society places on acceptance; when relatedness is threatened, the individual's strength must come from an internal source, a source which, in May's opinion, has not yet been fully developed. Anxiety becomes a "confusion and bewilderment about where we are going," both in an individual and social context. May defines anxiety as a "human being's basic reaction to a danger to his existence, or to some value which he identifies with his existence." Its intensity is geared to the quality of an experience that triggers inner conflict. Anxiety can be neurotic or it can be normal, the latter being the form with which May is primarily concerned. The source of normal anxiety is the social struggle with all the radical changes that are occurring regarding sexual mores, marriage styles, family structure, education, religion, technology, etc. May interprets our response to these changes as a loss of sense of self, of relationship to nature, of a language that effectively conveys personal feelings, and of the tragic significance of human life. What is needed, therefore, are individuals who are rediscovering their sources of inner strength and integrity. This implies that we should work to reestablish self-awareness through rediscovering our feelings about what we want, our relationship with our bodies, and with our subconscious, and confirm our aliveness in creative activity.

According to May, creativity necessitates a courage of the kind that indicates a centeredness within our being. Having courage becomes a means to be or to become. Subsidiary to this courage are other forms of courage: physical courage, based on the use of the body for the cultivation of sensitivity; moral courage, rooted in sensitivity to the suffering of others (perceptive courage) and eliciting the righting of wrongs; social courage, to relate openly and intimately with others; and the courage to commit ourselves, with full knowledge that we might be wrong at some point. Creative courage, "the most important kind of courage of all," takes into account the discovery of new forms, new symbols, and new patterns that establish the groundwork for building a new society.

May defines creativity as the process of bringing something into being. Creativity is an act of encounter, the intensity of which elicits awareness and heightened consciousness. This encounter embodies the interrelation between an individual and the world which, of itself, is a pattern of meaningful relationships involving inner self and outer reality. Creativity can interact with the unconscious in terms of insights that occur according to our commitment and in a manner that works against that to which we consciously adhere. According to May, creative people engage in an act which creates anxiety, but they live with that anxiety that threatens their being by encountering it and forcing it to produce something that is meaningful and therefore substantiates their being.

May believes it necessary for people to *form* their lives through a creative process that is the expression of "passion for form . . . against disintegration . . . to bring into existence new kinds of being that give harmony and integration." Communication is integral to form. Thus, relating to the world becomes a process of *willing* it, or creating it through choice, and *loving* it by supplying the energy, power, and love with which to affect it so that we may properly interact with it.

Innate sexuality can be transformed into a personal expression of love for the individual we choose, and eventually develop into a consciousness that allows for "the more sensitive understanding of bodies as body . . . and of the meaning of love in human life . . ."

Through the imagination, sexuality can be further embodied in art, passion, and eros, which is the heart of a culture. The union of love and will is a part of conscious development. Will builds the foundation for mature love, beyond what May calls the first bliss of physical union, in such a way that new psychologically derived relationships are founded, and autonomy, mature freedom, and resultant responsibility are achieved.

REFERENCES

Rollo May, *Man's Search for Himself.* New York: W. W. Norton & Co., 1953.

——, *The Courage to Create.* New York: W. W. Norton & Co., 1975.

——, *Love and Will.* New York: Dell Books, 1969.

——, *The Meaning of Anxiety.* New York: Ronald Press, 1950.

MARSHALL McLUHAN (1911–   ), a Canadian by birth, was educated in Canada and England. He received a Ph.D. in English literature from Cambridge University and has taught at several universities in the United States including the University of Wisconsin and St. Louis University. He was director of the Center for Culture and Technology at the University of Toronto. Since the early 1960s, the overview of McLuhan has been used as a tool in the formation of attitudes toward the ever-expanding technological society of the world.

McLuhan sees the onslaught of the new technologies as an instrument of change in the cultural environment which results in the alteration of perception of the society constituting the culture. In McLuhan's words, "the medium is the message," and the message conveyed by a new technology indicates the need for appropriate change in the patterns of daily life in the society in which the technology is activated. This statement means, furthermore, that how we assimilate technologies is a means of letting us know how we are, or are not, operating in society. McLuhan has said, in effect, that what the media communicate is how we are changing socially, in scale, pace, or pattern. ". . . It is the medium that shapes and controls the scale and form of human association and action," not the content of the messages that is communicated. Thus, the true pattern of our social existence is not abstract, nor does it have to be guessed. Rather, it is communicated through our use of technologies. According to McLuhan, it is necessary to pay attention to find both the positive *and* negative aspects of our use of technologies so that we may discover our wide-scale inadequacies in the global framework in which we now exist.

Media increase the society's ability to move into a consciousness it has never known before. Present society can see itself for the first time instantaneously in a global framework. Moreover, society is no longer capable of fragmenting itself and remaining isolationist, for it is too involved in a relationship with every other society on earth. The same theory applies to individual members of the present society. We can no longer escape from the whole, or dissociate ourselves; we are compelled to participate. Privacy has yielded to continual involvement. The technological age has the reverse effects of the industrial age: The technological age tends toward the integration and the decentralization of the cultures of the world.

Media are "hot" and "cool." A hot medium, radio, for example, extends one single sense into a state of being filled with information. The participation required by a hot medium is on a low level, according to McLuhan; there is not much room for the audience to complete it. Hot media create an environment of specialism, fragmentation, and disintegration.

A cool medium, television or the telephone, for example, by nature conveys very little information and therefore requires participation by the audience on high levels for completion. Cool media increase the intensity of involvement and thus tend to centralize the culture within which they are operative.

Expanding the use of hot and cool terminology, McLuhan sees our present society as moving out of the hot age of mechanics into the cool age of television.

McLuhan has explored the effects of the new technologies (media) on society. This kind of investigation is useful in defining self-perception and heightening self-awareness. The development of technologies is a means by which society extends itself, and these extensions support what is inherent in the nature of the human being. For example, clothes are extensions of the skin, wheels are extensions of the foot, books, extensions of the eye, shelters, extensions of systems of self-regulated heat control, the telephone is the extension of the voice, and electronic circuitry is the extension of the central nervous system. These various technological extensions have become integral parts of the structure of society.

McLuhan finds the present society, because it has not yet adjusted to the new technologies, using the methods available to it in the electronic age to reflect the mechanized environment of the industrial age. The industrial age has become the "content" of the electronic age: new technologies have begun to function as "art forms" supposedly providing a means by which society can separate itself from its environment in order to understand itself in relationship to its environment. This is the wrong way to use the media. Television has become an environment which requires little or no participation. The level of the TV image should be raised to accommodate the energies within the culture.

McLuhan feels that education subjects students to methodologies of learning which, in fact, decrease involvement in the learning process, methodologies which serve to instruct and classify information rather than integrate it. The amount of information offered by the media is overwhelming, and this information overload cannot in the present educational system be assimilated by the students. The result: a wave of school dropouts, an indicator of the frustration experienced in handling an educational system which depends solely on methods of teaching from the past. McLuhan often expresses the view that it is the function of education to instigate the necessary changes in the attitudes and practices of a society which is experiencing the advent of new technologies.

One of the most important thinkers of the present era, McLuhan has contributed articles to many periodicals, and is the author of several books, the most noted being *Understanding Media: The Extensions of Man,* and *The Medium Is the Message.*

REFERENCES

Marshall McLuhan, *Understanding Media: The Extensions of Man.* New York: McGraw-Hill, 1964.

Marshall McLuhan and Quentin Fiore, *The Medium Is the Message.* New York: Bantam Books, 1967.

MEDITATION. The development of meditation and its techniques has been generally attributed to the mystics. In the past, the word "mystic" implied someone who lives in a world that is incomprehensible to most people; recent attraction of Western culture to meditation has clarified the essence of mysticism. A mystic, characteristically, has a higher efficiency in his normal daily activities, and will possess attitudes of serenity, peace, joy, zest, and be able to have good relationships with others. A mystic has acquired certain knowledge that is the result of searching for and experiencing an individual relationship with the total universe. A mystic considers this search to be a means to retrieve the natural way of being. The search shuts out all the artificialities which obstruct the attainment of oneness. The *via ascetica,* a process of assault on ego and body through self-flagellation and fasting, and the *via illuminata,* a sudden total change in personality, integration, and understanding, are examples of rare methods of meditation.

In recently designed studies of the general effects of meditation, it has been shown that meditation produces a physiological state of deep relaxation and wakeful, mental alertness. This state is not similar to the sleep state or the hypnotic state, and it is opposite to a state of anger and anxiety. Your body responds to the meditative state in several ways: 1) Your metabolic rate slows down; 2) you use less oxygen and produce less carbon dioxide; 3) your heartbeat slows down; 4) the rate and volume of your respiration decrease; 5) your blood lactate level, which indicates a state of tension when high, is lowered; 6) your brain wave patterns change; 7) your skin is more resistant to mild shock. There is an indication that, because in meditation you are dealing with one thing at a time, the sensory and mental signals your body produces and experiences are more coherent and simple than at other times. It remains to be seen, however, exactly why the body reacts to the meditative state in the above manner.

The psychological effects of meditation are the result of consistent practice. In general, the work involved in meditation has been found to strengthen the organization of the personality, which is a prerequisite for the assimilation of a new view of reality. Meditation will divert you from the self-created distractions of your normal activities. By concentrating on one thing at a time, you will gain a capacity for serenity in an environment of diversity. Your will, purpose, goal-oriented behavior (confidence), and capability to involve yourself in your activity completely (competence) will increase. The new view of reality which will be achieved through meditation should be integrated into your daily life; it will permit you to treat yourself and others with equal intensity and calmness.

There are several structured methods of meditation which have specific tenets of application and discipline. 1) *One-pointing:* This method entails looking at an object with total attention and experiencing it nonverbally, tactilely. Your expectations about the object should be different each time you encounter it. 2) *Breath counting:* This method of meditation is characteristic of Zen training. It involves counting the exhalations of your breath; the key is to have your entire body at one with the activity of counting, without being conscious of the number of times you have counted. Once you have established a way of counting, you must be consistent, doing it the same way each time you meditate. 3) *The bubble:* The meditation of the bubble is focused on your stream of consciousness, i.e., you watch each of your thoughts, feelings, and perceptions as if they were bubbles, rising into and passing through and out of the space you are observing. You contemplate through the bubbles for approximately the same length of time, let each one go without connecting them. 4) *The mantra:* Meditating with a mantra is a method used in most mystical schools, with the exception of the Hasidic school. The value of the mantra, which is a word or phrase repeated over and over again, depends upon its *content,* and according to the Yoga or Sufi mystical schools, the *vibrational qualities* of certain sounds and their effect on the mind and body. (There are those who believe that any phrase or word will have the same effect.)

Other methods of structured meditation are "Who am I," a meditation which concentrates on verbally defining yourself through a pattern of questions and answers; the Theraveda meditation which entails the contemplation of a certain body rhythm; the Thousand Petaled Lotus meditation which is the examination of one thing in associational patterns; Sufi movement meditation, which focuses on the establishment of a unified awareness of body motions and chants among as many as fifteen people; sensory awareness meditation, developed by Elsa Gindler, which concentrates on breathing and the three-dimensional nature of every part of your body; the meditation called the "Safe Harbor" which allows you to guide your consciousness to an imaginary cove that is comfortable, safe, and secure.

Unstructured meditation simply involves your choosing a meaningful subject on which to meditate, e.g., how you see yourself, how you respond to others, how you can fulfill your potential. No matter what form your meditation takes, it is important to pursue it with persistence and consistency, and remain open to the unexpected discoveries you will make about yourself.

Learning to meditate can require a teacher, and it is important to evaluate teachers of meditation with regard to their interest in you, their ability to guide you and answer questions about your needs and goals. You should be aware of teachers who are on a "guru trip"; those who demand trust and obedience without any justification. If you can find a teacher with whom you can have a good relationship, he/she can help you surmount certain problems which might obstruct you from certain goals. Pursuing meditation without a teacher can be a difficult process, as the results tend not to be immediate.

The practice of meditation has therapeutic value. Essentially meditation and psychotherapy have similar objectives: to teach you how to invest your life with real value, to make your being a totality, to enable you to function in daily life without inhibition and anxiety. Meditation can aid you in breaking down defenses, and through a process called *centering,* allow you to become comfortable with yourself and your environment, to strengthen your ego, and to achieve a more coherent personality organization.

REFERENCE

Lawrence LeShan, *How to Meditate: A Guide to Self-Discovery.* New York: Bantam Books, 1975.

MEGAVITAMIN THERAPY, also known as *orthomolecular psychiatry,* evolved partially as the result of the discovery that many mental hospital patients diagnosed as chronic schizophrenics were found to be suffering from pellagra, a disease caused by a deficiency of Vitamin B_3, or niacin, which in the advanced stages manifests itself in neurological disorders and dementia.

Two psychiatrists, Abraham Hoffer, president of the Huxley Institute for Biosocial Research in Canada, and Humphrey Osmond, associated with the New Jersey Psychiatric Institute in Princeton, who had both used niacin in the treatment of schziophrenia in the 1950s, formally proposed the theory in the early 1970s that psychoses could be treated successfully with certain nutritional measures.

In general, vitamins are organic substances which are necessary to the proper regulation and maintenance of the body processes. The discovery that a vitamin deficiency can cause disease was made in 1912 by Sir F. G. Hopkins, an English biochemist, and Casimir Funk, an American biochemist. For example, Vitamin A deficiency can cause eye disorders (e.g., night blindness), and if chronic will result in total blindness.

Megavitamin therapy uses massive doses of specific vitamins, as well as minerals, and in some cases a high-protein, low-carbohydrate diet. The amount of vitamins used in this therapy is determined by the measure of the optimum concentration of elements normally found in the nervous system. Megavitamin therapy is used in the treatment of schizophrenia, depression, anxiety, alcoholism, and drug addiction. It is used to treat hyperactivity, learning disabilities, and autism in children. Megavitamin therapy has often replaced the need for hospitalization, shock treatment, and other alternative therapies.

In the treatment of schizophrenics, who occupy one fourth of the hospital beds in the United States, the therapy used may include doses of several forms of niacin, psyridoxine (Vitamin B_6), Vitamin E, thyroid medication, Vitamin B_{12}, lithium, tranquilizers, possibly accompanied by a special diet to correct blood sugar levels. When the treatment is successful, the schizophrenic patient responds in the following ways: Sleep patterns improve, anxiety is reduced, manic depression is reduced, problem-solving ability increases, etc. In 1971, a study by the American Schizophrenic

Association reported that megavitamin therapy not only reduces patient costs, but also the amount of time the patient must spend with a doctor or therapist.

According to orthomolecular psychiatry, alcoholism is an illness caused by a quirk in body chemistry, probably because of abnormal carbohydrate metabolism. The result is a chemical imbalance. The treatment for alcoholism is megadoses of Vitamin B_3 (niacin), Vitamin C, and a high-protein, low-carbohydrate diet. A similar chemical imbalance because of low blood sugar, and resulting in mental disturbances, depression, etc., a condition known as *hypoglycemia,* is treated also with a high-protein, low-carbohydrate diet which is structured to slowly release the caloric energy that maintains the blood sugar level by putting high amounts of protein into the system. The diet calls for fruits and vegetables that have a low natural sweetness, and high-protein snacks. (Elizabeth Roth leClair, a psychiatric social worker and dietitian for an orthomolecular clinic in California, has created an antihypoglycemic diet.)

Patients in drug-withdrawal clinics are being treated with megavitamin therapy. The director of the Do It Now Foundation, founded by former drug users, has reported that this therapy, specifically the use of niacin, has aided chronic users of amphetamines, barbiturates, heroin, alcohol, and methadone. Dr. W. D. Hitchings of the Fryer Research Center, New York City, believes that drug withdrawal for hard-drug users is more successful when megavitamin therapy treatment is applied in a controlled situation, rather than on an outpatient basis. Dr. David Hawkins, who runs a mental health clinic on Long Island, has therapeutically treated hundreds of drug users. According to Hawkins, an important factor in his method of treatment is assuring that his patients get the boost of blood sugar levels: ". . . in a schizophrenic—or an LSD tripper in a similar perceptual state—a lowered blood sugar can produce an agonizing experience."

Megavitamin therapy is also being used as a treatment for schizophrenic children. Dr. Hoffer has treated successfully thirty-three cases of disturbed children with megavitamin therapy which included doses of niacinamide (a form of Vitamin B_3), Vitamin C, and programs for proper nutrition, and in some cases, small doses of tranquilizers and antidepressants. Dr. Hoffer determined that these children, diagnosed as "ill, very disturbed, and . . . hyperactive," suffered from a Vitamin B_3-dependent disease that is inherited. Other doctors who have treated children this way have found that some side effects of vitamin megadoses such as flushing can be eased through the introduction of other elements into the therapy; that diet is sometimes the most important factor in treating children; but that other therapy (besides vitamins, diet, medication) is usually required to return the child to normal behavior.

Megavitamin therapy has been used to curb senility and malnutrition in the elderly. Dr. Hoffer prescribes a diet which includes high-quality protein, moderate high-quality fat, little sugar, whole grains, and megadoses of vitamins, depending upon the individual patient's needs. Dental care, acid and fibrous content in foods, and injections of vitamins, in cases where food is not supplying enough of the patient's nutritional needs, are also recommended.

The controversy over megavitamin therapy stems from the claim of several scientists that some forms of mental illness are caused by a chemical imbalance in the body that can be restored by natural substances, i.e., vitamins. In general, the federal Food and Drug Administration has taken a stand which states that vitamins and minerals are beneficial but not in large doses. The FDA has imposed regulations on Vitamins A and D, which have been found to be harmful if taken in large quantities. Vitamins and minerals containing no more than 50 per cent of the RDA (recommended daily allowance) can be sold as food; those containing 50–150 per cent more than the RDA can be sold as food supplements and for special dietary purposes; those containing more than 150 per cent of the RDA must be sold as drugs, by prescription or over the counter.

REFERENCES

Ruth Adams and Frank Murray, *Megavitamin Therapy.* New York: Pinnacle Books, 1975.

Lynn Lilliston, *Megavitamins: A New Key to Health.* Greenwich, Conn.: Fawcett Publications, 1975.

MEMORY is the power of reproducing or recalling what has been learned and retained, especially through associative mechanisms. Psychological research into memory and what causes you to remember something has resulted in an hypothesis that defines three stages in the memory process: the perception and registration of the stimulus; the retention of the perception, which, if temporarily maintained, results in short-term memory; and a period of maturation of the information which causes long-term memory.

Memory, its importance and application, can be traced back to the orators of ancient Greece and Rome. Circa 500 B.C., Simonides devised a method of memory training. In *De Oratore,* Cicero wrote that he used memory systems which he felt to be essential for the training of orators. Aristotle qualified memory systems as a way to increase the powers of thinking and reasoning. *The Phoenix* by Peter Ravenna, 1491, was one of the first memory-training books for the public. King Francis I of France and Henry III of England used memory systems. William Stoke, in 1888, published a book on memory systems.

Currently, Harry Lorayne has brought the subject of memory to the attention of the public in *How to Develop a Super-Power Memory* and *The Memory Book* (coauthored by Jerry Lucas). Lorayne's interest in developing a technique of building memory capacity is practical, based on the usefulness of memory in daily life. The goal of his method is to show you how you can train your memory as a useful tool.

Observation and *association* are the first principles of the Lorayne method; when you observe something by seeing it or hearing it, you will remember it by associating it with something you already know. According to Lorayne, association, as it is related to memory, is the subconscious process of "connecting or tying up . . . two (or more) things to each other." What Lorayne's method aims to do is teach you how to make this process conscious and habitual. Memory training therefore becomes a process of conjuring up mental images or pictures that *link* together words, objects, etc. The *link method* calls for the successive association of one item to the next in a group, making your association "as ridiculous and/or illogical as possible," and then visualizing the items in a mental picture. There are several tricks to help you do this: picturing things out of proportion; imagining the items to be memorized in action; exaggerating the number of items you are trying to remember; substituting one item for another in order to remember how the items occur in a group.

The *peg system* is another Lorayne memory-training method. The basis of this system originated in 1648 with the work of Stanislaus Mink von Wennshein and was later modified by Richard Grey, an Englishman, in 1730. Its goal is the easy memorization of numbers and letters by associating numbers with letters (and vice versa) in mental pictures of objects, rather than as disconnected abstractions. Lorayne's version calls for learning ten phonetic consonant sounds in connection with ten digits. Once you have memorized how the sounds are connected with the digits, you then memorize words that refer to objects but which can be associated with a specific number; these words are *pegs*. There are one hundred peg words. According to Lorayne, each peg word must create a different picture in your mind if it is to work successfully. After you have learned to use the peg words Lorayne supplies, you can invent your own.

The link and peg methods have numerous practical uses: remembering errands, shopping lists, speeches, many digit numbers, dates, playing cards, etc. In connection with these methods, it is also important to train your observation skills: practice by memorizing the details of a room in your house, a showcase window, etc. until you are able to totally recall the items.

By using *substitute words,* names, or the vocabulary of another language, or other items which are not meaningful can be remembered: "Substitute words or thoughts are used whenever you want to remember anything that is abstract, intangible, or unintelligible; something that makes no sense to you, can't be pictured, yet must be remembered."

Lorayne's theory as to why you may remember faces easily, but forget names, is that you are "eye-minded," registering images that you see more readily than names you hear. His formula for remembering names is: 1) Be sure that you hear the name; 2) if you are not sure of the pronunciation, ask that the name be spelled out; 3) associate the new name with that of a friend or relative, or register its peculiarities in your mind; 4) use the name many times in conversation with the person you have just met, and in saying good-bye.

Furthermore, names can be separated into categories that have some meaning to you, no meaning at all, or a made-up meaning. If the latter method is used, it is important to remember the main part of the association; after that, the rest will fall into place. Remembering names and faces is naturally influenced by your intention to further a relationship and what the person might mean to you in the future.

Lorayne stresses the fact that his memory systems are only successful through constant use. He claims that using his methods will give you further incentive to learn because you will be better able to control information.

REFERENCES

Harry Lorayne, *How to Develop a Super-Power Memory.* New York: New American Library, 1972.

Harry Lorayne and Jerry Lucas, *The Memory Book.* New York: Ballantine Books, 1974.

MEN'S LIBERATION. Since the Masculine Mystique Force of the National Organization for Women was established in the 1960s, men have been exposed to a revision of the definition of masculinity in an attempt to alter their social and sexual roles. Men are hindered by similar problems as women with regard to changing the traditional routines and formulas of their lives. They have found it necessary to overcome the myths associated with masculinity and the barriers society has erected by establishing new ways to function in society with the help of unified consciousness-raised attitudes.

In general, the male stereotype assigns a man to a role that puts him in a superior position to that of a woman. There are several clichés which clothe the mythological male image that has predominated in American society. For example, men talk rather than listen; men are logical whereas women are emotional; men are adventurous and aggressive rather than introspective and passive; men make decisions quickly; men are charismatic and dynamic but often lack credibility; men crave power rather than achievement not necessarily concerned with power; men prefer business and politics over human concerns; men are tough and show their strength visibly rather than through inner growth; men are more concerned with their sexuality than their sensuality, etc. All these cliché qualities of manhood are considered to be a part of the real world. In contrast, characteristics considered typical of a feminine nature are regarded as nonfunctional or useless in society. The promotion of male dominance in general runs through all facets of the media.

The goal of men's liberation is a redefinition of all the areas in which men can play a vital part, but until now have not been allowed to, psychologically and socially, e.g., child care, housework, etc. This would eventually mean that the standard job schedule which requires a man to be at his job five days a week from nine to five would have to be reorganized. This way, the abilities of women to assume traditionally male positions in the business and political worlds can also be realized. Men's liberation therefore would become a way of re-balancing society; men would become less elevated in their importance, and women less subjugated. Some changes have already been adopted within this context with "management awareness programs" in large business organizations such as IBM. Further action is required, however. For example, employment agencies and labor unions still operate according to unwritten rules, e.g., women can work for lower salaries than men require, often for the same kind of job; child-care centers don't hire men; men cannot become involved in elementary school teaching; men cannot be nurses; men cannot be guidance counselors, etc.

In order to change behaviorally, men should recognize that the roles played by both men and women aggrandize their sexual differences, not their intellectual, emotional, or capability differences. It is important for men to know that they can be freed from the stereotype; women's liberation can help in this psychological adjustment. This implies that men can let go of their "security objectness"; men can free themselves of the pressure of being the breadwinner; men can give more time to their children and alleviate the tensions that build up between mothers and children; men can feel less competitive about the entrance of women into men's jobs; men can accept lower paying jobs; men can share in the responsibilities of the home, etc. Consciousness raising for men becomes a matter of dealing with the problems men have in common, of focusing on the self, both intellectual and emotional, and of asking questions about masculinity in order to redefine it.

To get free of anxiety about sexuality, much of which is instilled at an early age through the familiar stereotype of the "stud," men must give up all ideas about performance and dominance in sexual relationships, and learn about passivity, sensuality, and receptivity in themselves. A new definition of sexuality for the man should imply cooperation, trust, openness, sensitivity, and freedom.

Men's liberation can be a way to revitalize men and free them as human beings. It is a process of educating men about themselves beyond the mythologies of male appearances, prestige, specialty, expertise, and objecthood. Men's liberation can ease the tension that exists between men and women on all levels, and help them to function in their human, rather than sexual, roles.

Men's liberation, it has been observed, has been misconstrued as an effort to simply respond to the changes set in motion by the women's liberation movement. It has been dismissed by some critics as "silly" and without a perceivable purpose. Others, however, contend that the movement is directed toward introspection on the part of men to contact their sensitivities and understand that they do not have to force themselves into the roles that Western tradition has structured for them. Jack Nichols, author of *Men's Liberation,* has observed that the idea of men's liberation in America is new only in its manifestation. Nichols describes Walt Whitman as "a prophet of men's liberation." Whitman proclaimed that he embodied the universal qualities that are potential in every man.

Although men's liberation and women's liberation are separate movements, they are both striving toward the same goal of unification. According to Warren Farrell, author of *The Liberated Man,* the movements have to undergo the separate preliminary processes of realigning human interests before they can ever come together and be called a liberation movement of all humanity.

REFERENCES

Warren Farrell, *The Liberated Man—Beyond Masculinity: Freeing Men and Their Relationships with Women.* New York: Bantam Books, 1975.

Jack Nichols, *Men's Liberation: A New Definition of Masculinity.* New York: Penguin Books, 1975.

METATALK is a word coined by Gerard I. Nierenberg and Henry H. Calero to represent the unspoken meaning that frequently underlies ordinary conversation. Nierenberg is president of the Negotiations Institute and author of *The Art of Negotiating* and *Creative Business Negotiating*. Calero is a business executive and consultant in the field of negotiating techniques. The authors have substantiated their theory of metatalk through observation of thousands of participants in their seminars in nonverbal communication.

According to Nierenberg and Calero, talk has at least three distinguishable levels of meaning: what the speaker is saying, what the speaker thinks he is saying, and what the listener thinks the speaker is saying. The first level applies to words spoken out of habit, regardless of their meaning, e.g., "how do you do," etc. The second and third levels of talk apply to those conversational situations in which words are spoken offhandedly or carelessly, and interpreted on a deeper level than was intended. The speaker using metatalk can convey inexplicit meanings that can be misconstrued by the listener.

The "content" of metatalk varies with regard to the differences in cultural orientation, personal connotation, emotion, and intellect between the speaker and the listener. Metatalk frequently contains clichés, truisms, aphorisms, vacuous and overused words and phrases (e.g., "incidentally," "by the way," "that's just the way things are," "a stitch in time saves nine," "well, you can't have everything," etc.). Clichés have no logical meaning and are often self-contradictory; they can transform a conversation into silence by putting distance between the actual situation and what is being said.

Metatalk can indicate likes and dislikes by the order and choice of words, as well as by grammatical usage. The order of words used to discuss a chain of events or a certain subject matter will reveal what the speaker would like to experience first. The choice of personal pronouns demonstrates prejudices and detachment. The way verbs are used (e.g., active or passive voice, etc.) can reveal emotional distance between the speaker and what is being discussed, as well as the immediacy of concerns.

One objective of metatalk can be to put the listener into a frame of mind so that you may negotiate your way into a situation. Using phrases like "in my humble opinion," or "I'm not boasting, but . . . ," or "as you are aware," etc. in a particular situation can give you, the speaker, an attitude of arrogance and false humility, setting you apart from the listener. Phrases like "you are right, but . . . ," "would you be kind enough to . . . ," etc. can be used to influence your listener in a positive manner or "soften" him. Phrases like "nothing is wrong" are often used to indicate that something *is* wrong, putting the listener into a negative and anxious frame of mind. By using what Nierenberg and Calero call "continuers" (e.g., "what else is new"), you may try to get a person to say what you want to hear.

Metatalk can be used for a variety of reasons: to keep your listeners interested, to make them feel guilty or arrogant, to convince them that their opinion is correct, to express frustration, hostility, anger, or to urge the continuation of gossip. Through metatalk, you can convey your own anxieties and motivation to others.

You can untangle the mental activity of someone else through understanding the uses of metatalk and studying the consistent use of certain phrases. When recognized, the various forms of metatalk will reveal your hidden assumptions, how you feel in relationships, e.g., with your husband or wife, lover, children, parents. Hidden assumptions about your relationships often become clichés about them, and in this way, can be damaging. For example, in the parent-teenager relationship, teenagers resent their parents' insensitivity to their adolescent nature. The generation gap, which exists anyway, can become greater the more parents schematize and stereotype their children's growing-up process.

Metatalk can be used to manipulate negotiations in

business dealings and create advantageous relationships. In a potential buyer-seller relationship, you, as buyer, must be aware of all the "deals" the seller might want to push on you, and you must be conscious of how the seller is trying to manipulate in order to urge your buying something you do not want. In other business situations, the use of clichés can break down the communication process, for example, when used to invite a suggestion if the suggestion is to be rejected, no matter what it is (as in a boss-secretary relationship). Metatalk can reprimand the secretary and please the boss.

In general social situations, metatalk can increase distance in a relationship. The overuse of "I" as a preface to statements can separate two people who might have had an interesting relationship. Enduring relationships are not built on ego orientation. Clichés often become the conversational tools for starting a relationship with a stranger.

The better able you are to recognize forms of metatalk and understand the reasons for its use, the more enlightening and dynamic conversations can become. Talk, in general, is a means to involvement with others and a means of enriching relationships.

Nierenberg and Calero have combined their efforts to write two books on verbal and nonverbal communication. *Metatalk* deals with its techniques, its psychology, and a list of metatalk phraseology. *How to Read a Person Like a Book* examines the quality and meaning behind the silent body language of gestures.

REFERENCES

Gerard I. Nierenberg, *The Art of Negotiating*. New York: Hawthorn Books, 1968.

————, *Creative Business Negotiating*. New York: Hawthorn Books, 1975.

Gerard I. Nierenberg and Henry H. Calero, *Metatalk*. New York: Pocket Books, 1974.

————, *How to Read a Person Like a Book*. New York: Hawthorn Books, 1971.

J. L. MORENO (1892–1974), the founder of *psychodrama,* a method of group psychotherapy, was born in Rumania and educated at the University of Vienna, where he received his medical degree. He practiced psychiatry in Austria from 1919–27, and formulated his principles of group psychotherapy, which were based on sociometry, the study of interpersonal relations in a group of people. In this science, knowledge about the abnormal organization of groups and how to control deviate group behavior is gained through *sociatry* (analogous to *psychiatry*). Moreno went to the United States in 1927, where he worked as a psychiatrist and psychodramatist. From 1936 until his death, he was the physician in charge at the Moreno Sanatarium in Beacon, New York. Between 1929 and 1936, he founded the Spontaneity Theatre in Vienna and the Impromptu Theatre and Therapeutic Theatre in New York City. In 1964, he was made honorary president of the First International Congress of Psychodrama. He lectured at the New School for Social Research in New York City, Columbia University, and other establishments throughout the United States and Europe, the U.S.S.R., Czechoslovakia, and Hungary. He was founder of the American Society of Group Psychotherapy and Psychodrama, the journal *Sociometry and Group Psychotherapy,* and *The International Journal of Sociometry and Sociatry.* The *International Handbook of Group Psychotherapy* was published in 1966. The definitive work on psychodrama, *Psychodrama,* was first published in three volumes in 1946.

Moreno created psychodrama after rejecting Freudian psychoanalysis, which he felt had "replaced the mystery of existence by a scheme of unreal transactions, promising self-realization to the patient, but actually depriving him of finding his essence in life itself." Psychodrama is based on *encounter,* the essential principle of which is "antimimesis" (anti-imitation). However, psychodrama becomes an enriched dynamic process because of its two opposing tendencies, one toward encounter, the antimimetic aspect, and one toward theatre, a mimetic aspect. The object of the encounter, the psychodrama, is the self which Moreno calls the "Thou." The goal is to discover truth through "drama," or the acting out of feelings.

According to Moreno, psychodrama "enables the protagonist to build a bridge beyond the roles he plays in his daily existence, to surpass and transcend the reality of life as he lives it, to get into a deeper relationship with existence, to come as close as possible to the highest form of encounter of which he is capable . . . to reach the highest level of existence . . . the deepest essence of life . . ."

The practice of psychodrama consists of five necessary elements: the stage, the subject/patient, the director, the staff of therapeutic aides or auxiliary egos, and the audience.

The stage designed by Moreno is circular and consists of different levels, "levels of aspiration, pointing out to the vertical dimension," which create the groundwork for relief of tension and an increase in flexibility. The stage offers the subject a living space that is both multidimensional and flexible, allowing for freedom of self-expression and experience.

The *subject/patient* plays him/herself on the stage, and is asked to act out roles which are applicable to past events or current problems. This is done spontaneously, the intention of this activity being to trigger the subjects "to be on the stage what they *are,* more deeply and explicitly than they appear to be in life reality."

The *director* functions as producer, therapist, and analyst, maintaining the consistency of the subject's performance, interjecting when necessary, and interpreting the drama either in his/her terms or in the terms of the audience.

The staff of *auxiliary egos,* or therapeutic actors, perform three functions: They play various roles in the subject's life; they guide the subject; and they act as "social investigators."

The *audience* consists of the subject's relatives or neighbors, and has a double purpose: to help the subject or to become the subject in the sense of role reversal.

The performance structure of psychodrama has prompted research into action, action therapy, role tests, role training, situation tests, and situational interviews (all of which apply to the individual subject/patient), as well as creating forms of group psychotherapy utilizing methods that involve lectures, drama, and film.

According to Moreno, the intention of psychodrama is to try to reach "that level of existentiality and depth which Plato described as being only for the elite, only within the reach of the gods, the supermen, and which he denied the average man, whom he disposed of and rejected as vulgar and mere imitators of life." Moreno addresses the average man, whom he believed able to encounter the self, the Thou, and to understand that he and others are capable of restructuring and bettering a hitherto problematical integration.

REFERENCES

Jacob L. Moreno, *Psychodrama.* Beacon, N.Y.: Beacon House, 3 vols., 1959, 1969, 1972.

————, *Who Shall Survive? A New Approach to the Problems of Interrelation.* Washington, D.C.: Nervous and Mental Disease Publishing Co., 1934.

SWAMI MUKTANANDA Paramhansa was born in southern India. As a youth, after taking a vow of renunciation and studying Yoga and Vedanta, Muktananda persevered through a life of poverty in his search for a guru. In 1947, he came to Ganeshpuri where he was initiated by Swami Nityananda, receiving divine grace, and underwent *sadhana* (spiritual discipline) for nine years, finally achieving self-realization. Muktananda remained with Nityananda as his disciple until Nityananda's death in 1961. During this time, he acquired the name "Baba" by which he has been known ever since. After the death of his master, Baba inherited the leadership of Shree Gurudev Ashram in Ganeshpuri.

Baba is a Siddha Guru. He teaches and practices Siddha Yoga (or perfect yoga) which he has received from a Siddha Guru (a perfected being). The reception of the yoga is a process of inner awakening of Kundalini, which is described as energy lying dormant at the base of the spine. According to Siddha Yoga, Kundalini is the essence of all living things. Once it has been experienced, the individual has reached the internal being that is the realization of God, or Shakti. According to Baba, you can awaken to Kundalini Shakti because you have it in your essence. This awakening is achieved through meditation only because: "Neither the entertainment experienced in the waking state nor the void experienced in sleep can provide the mind with true repose."

Baba believes that meditation is the source of an unforgettable knowledge. It is also the source of cleverness, logic, intelligence, poetry, courage, compassion, steadfastness, and wisdom. The acquisition of these qualities allows you to see your way in any situation because you have inner peace and quiet. To meditate and receive Siddha Yoga, you must find "the teacher who will awaken your Kundalini"; you must yearn for a spiritual life; you must be devoted to your guru; you must practice your own mantra. Siddha Yoga is not solely dependent upon your effort; it is the "grace" of the guru which allows you to dispel your mental confusion and find peace.

Kundalini is the directive of your discovery of equation with God. It is the enlightening and liberation of all that is already within you. Nothing from the external world will awaken the spirit within you.

Siddha Yoga is natural, spontaneous, and results from your inner concentration, which is instigated by your guru. Siddha Yoga transcends daily life activities.

You may do what you do normally to live in the world: Siddha Yoga, as taught by Baba, is not intended to divide your life between the spiritual and the temporal life. Rather, you will do everything within your spiritual existence; you will live *sadhana*. According to Baba: "In this very world, in this very body, in the midst of your life, while living with your family in your home, without retiring to a forest or a mountain, without involving yourself in complicated techniques, meditate and find the center of rest within you."

Siddha Yoga is the "perfect yoga" because it includes all other yogas in its principles. After you have awakened the Kundalini, you are said to be able to automatically assume yogic postures without previous training. These postures are Hatha Yoga, and through their practice you become strong and healthy. You are filled with a selfless love that takes everything into account. You are instilled with a feeling of beauty never before experienced. This is the aim of Bhakti Yoga, the yoga of devotion. As in Raja Yoga, your mind becomes centered; you can concentrate. As in Juana Yoga, the yoga of knowledge, you intellectually understand what you have never understood before and achieve spiritual enlightenment without effort. As in Karma Yoga, the yoga of selfless action, greed, lust, anger, and delusion are replaced by an energy that directs you to be selfless in your actions. Your sense responses are keener; your psychic ability to foresee events might be activated. You become how your inner being dictates you to become.

Baba's home is the Shree Gurudev Ashram, a thirty-acre property in California, that houses a temple, meditation rooms, quarters for men and women, and a dining hall. The ashram grows its own food and has its own well. There are strict rules pertaining to inhabitants and visitors to the ashram. For those staying at the ashram for extended periods of time, there is a daily schedule directed to obtaining maximum benefit from the stay. The overall goal is meditation and inner searching. In his autobiography, *Chitshaki Vilas,* Baba says: ". . . our aim is to live in a perfect state. All our actions bear full fruit, for the grace of a Siddha never fails. . . . Do not lose your patience, steadfastness and strength through anxiety. Always remember that a disciple of a Siddha cannot remain in Bondage."

There are nine centers, or ashrams, in the United States (California, Texas, New York) and others around the world, as well as books by and about Swami Muktananda available through the ashrams of Siddha Yoga.

REFERENCES

Uma Berliner, *Introducing Swami Muktananda* (monograph). Oakland, Ca.: S.Y.D.A. Foundation.

Swami Muktananda, *Chitshaki Vilas.* New York: Harper & Row, 1971.

CLAUDIO NARANJO, a Chilean psychiatrist, is recognized in the fields of psychiatry and psychology for his exploration of alternatives to psychoanalysis through the use of drugs.

Naranjo studied at Harvard University, at the University of Illinois on a Fulbright scholarship, and at the University of California, Berkeley, on a Guggenheim fellowship. From 1965–66, he was a research psychiatrist at the Centro de Estudios de Antropología Medica, the medical school of the University of Chile. During this time, Naranjo, with the support of Franz Hoffman, director of the center, decided to investigate the "vitalizing" properties of drugs. Naranjo has been associated with Esalen Institute where he has conducted seminars and experiential workshops. He is an advocate of Gestalt therapy, contributing to its present formulation, and has used it in connection with his own therapeutic techniques. Naranjo has lectured and conducted seminars throughout the United States. He has written a book on meditation with Robert Ornstein, *On the Psychology of Meditation,* and a documentation of his studies in Chile, *The One Quest.*

Naranjo believes in the potential power of certain

drugs to induce specific states of consciousness (rather than the "peak experiences" typical of psychedelics) that would be advantageous in psychotherapy because the processes at work would bring about ". . . the breaking of vicious circles in the psyche, bringing into focus unknown domains of feelings or thought, or facilitating corrective experiences, in which underdeveloped functions are temporarily stimulated or overdeveloped ones inhibited."

In his investigations, Naranjo used two different types of drugs to test his hypothesis: "feeling enhancers" and "fantasy enhancers." Feeling enhancers are phenylisoprophylamines (including what are known as MDA and MMDA). According to Naranjo, these drugs elicit sharpening of attention, enhancement of feelings, and an increase in the fluency of associations and communications. Fantasy enhancers are polycyclic indoles, including harmaline and ibogaine, which induce dreamlike states without actual sleep. Both types of drugs allow the experience of unconscious processes in a way that is different from the experiences induced by perception-altering hallucinogens (e.g., LSD). The experience is one in which awareness is the primary constituent.

Naranjo considers psychotherapy to be one of the stages of "the continuous process of consciousness expansion, integration, and self-realization." The journey to this end contains both "agony" and "ecstasy." The agony is the result of encountering reality and resolving conflicts; the ecstasy is the freedom achieved from the hindrance of psychological obstructions. These two seemingly opposite aspects are coordinated in the drug-related psychotherapy Naranjo has created.

MDA (methylenedioxyamphetamine) is a chemical product of safrole, an essential oil of nutmeg. The substance is psychoactive and toxic. Naranjo found that because of its toxicity, dosages of MDA must be regulated carefully according to the chemistry of the person taking it, i.e., a dosage that would not affect one person could be fatal to another.

Naranjo found the effects of MDA to be enhancement of feelings, increased communication, and a heightened reflectiveness resulting in attention to both individual and social problems. Neurotic subjects taking the drug within a psychotherapeutic program experienced physical symptoms as well as visual occurrences. The most predominant effect of the drug was age regression: Past feelings from childhood, and sometimes physical pain or pleasure, were experienced. Naranjo calls MDA the "drug of analysis," and considers its therapeutic value to be its capacity to cause personality change.

MMDA is a synthetic derivative of one of the essential oils of nutmeg. The possible effects of the drug, according to Naranjo, are: peak experiences, involving feeling enhancement; magnification and intensification of habitual feelings and conflicts; visual (or eidetic) imagery and physical symptoms; lethargic states, in which mental activity is similar to dreaming. In contrast to MDA, MMDA encourages attention to the present. Naranjo theorizes that the psychotherapeutic value of MMDA is its capacity to intensify what normal experience obstructs. It creates circumstances in which imagination takes over from verbalization or conceptualization, and by the shrinking of habitual feelings the person experiences the *now,* "a present free from transferential bondage to past conditions and stereotyped mechanisms."

Naranjo has also explored the drug *harmaline,* an alkaloid contained in the seeds of a plant native to Central Asia and Syria, which grows along the Mediterranean coasts of Africa, Europe, the Near East, and in Persia, Afghanistan, and Tibet. Harmaline is most effective when taken in a dark environment. The person taking the drug should be physically comfortable. The effects have been found to be physical relaxation, desire for withdrawal from the environment, numbness in the limbs, and feelings of nausea or even actual vomiting. The most predominant effect is the experiencing of visual images which are similar to meaningful dreams.

The images frequently have a mythical quality comparable to Jungian archetypes. Naranjo found the general psychotherapeutic value of harmaline to be a person's spontaneous ability to accept his or her feelings, impulses, and the self, which all occur nonverbally.

Ibogaine, an alkaloid obtained from the root of a plant native to West Africa, is another drug Naranjo explored. Ibogaine is similar to harmaline in its effects on the body. It is also similar in its tendency to induce visual images, particularly archetypal or in the form of animals. The content of dream sequences can resemble each other as far as destruction and sexuality are concerned, although there is often a difference in thematic substance. Ibogaine is especially effective in calling up the past. Naranjo describes the experience as one in which elements of the past are nonprejudicially seen and, therefore, confronted freely. The effects of both ibogaine and harmaline are subjective in nature, eliciting the "instinctual side of the psyche."

In his investigations, it was Naranjo's intention to reveal that these nonpsychotomimetic psychedelics exist in a class of their own. They "acted as psychological catalysts or lubricants, removing the obstacles, facilitating an attitude of openness to experience." Used by qualified persons, the drugs could become psychotherapeutically significant tools, eliciting responses different from those ordinarily produced by psychedelics. The drugs could become agents in prompting "contagious" self-awareness.

REFERENCES
Claudio Naranjo, *The Healing Journey: New Approaches to Consciousness.* New York: Ballantine Books, 1973.

———, *The One Quest.* New York: Viking Press (Esalen Book), 1972.

——— and Robert E. Ornstein, *On the Psychology of Meditation.* New York: Viking Press, 1971.

NATURAL CHILDBIRTH.
In 1933, Grantly Dick-Read, an American obstetrician, published a book called *Natural Childbirth.* His theories, although not

well-enough supported on the physiological side to give them wide appeal, marked the beginning of the effort to establish a psychotherapeutic method of childbearing. Since that time, other physicians have worked to design methods of bearing children, specifically Fernand Lamaze and Frederick Leboyer, both French gynecologists and obstetricians.

Lamaze researched his method, known technically as the *psychoprophylactic* method of childbirth, for four years with a team of doctors at the Maternité du Metallurgiste in Paris. The practice of this method originated in the U.S.S.R., deriving from the Pavlovian school of thought, and was developed through the work of Bykov, Velvosky, and Nicholaiev. Velvosky had explored the idea of the psychoprophylaxis of pain in childbirth as early as 1920, and came to the conclusion that there should be an attempt "not to cure the pain of childbirth by the use of drugs (since childbirth is not a disease), or inhibit it by means of hypnosis or suggestion, but to make every effort to destroy the concepts that breed this pain." According to Lamaze, Velvosky inspired the development of a precise, rational, safe method of childbirth, which enabled 86 to 92 per cent of Soviet women to bear children painlessly.

After visiting Russia in 1951 and 1955, and China in 1953, where painless childbirth methods were practiced nationally, Lamaze returned to France and introduced his method of childbirth to the West.

The Lamaze method entails the psychological and physical education of women during pregnancy. The training period begins in the third month of pregnancy with a lecture that covers the anatomical nature of pregnancy and the physiological processes that take place in the body of a pregnant woman. Proper diet, body cleanliness, and attitudinal health are stressed. Lamaze considers it important that the pregnancy is welcome and wanted by both the wife and husband: "A husband versed in the principles of childbirth without pain will offer his wife active support which can but increase her chances of success."

The second stage of the training period involves the clarification of the anatomical and physiological relationship between breathing, pregnancy, and delivery. According to Lamaze, breathing exercises "allow the conscious appraisal of the physical existence of anatomical relations between organs directly or indirectly concerned with labor." The exercises build good muscular tone and control, and improve the pulmonary ventilation in the mother, which will ensure adequate oxygenation of the child during gestation and labor. The mechanics of breathing that are taught emphasize the diaphragm as the essential muscle of respiration, especially because of its indirect relationship to the fundus of the uterus. The exercises increase the tone of the diaphragmatic muscles and the capacity of the chest to expand, as well as tone up abdominal muscles and improve the ability of these muscles to work with precision. Other exercises are also taught in preparation for labor. They concentrate on neuromuscular action, and involve learning how to maintain muscles, which will contract in labor, in a state of relaxation, and how to control the contractions of these muscles in coordination with breathing.

The practice of the Lamaze exercises is aimed at establishing the conditions for uterine contractions: 1) *good oxygenation,* through controlled neuromuscular relaxation and respiratory rhythm coordinated with uterine contractions; 2) *satisfactory elimination of waste products,* which could cause cramping, etc., and eventually induce pain in labor and delivery; 3) *good cortical control,* which ensures that the above conditions are not lacking. The Lamaze method places emphasis on the function of the mind during childbirth, for without its proper rational functioning, the mother will experience everything she is trying to avoid in bearing a child. The Lamaze method stresses that in delivery the mother must realize the exact position of the child in order to know when to push, the right way to push, and when to stop pushing.

The success of the psychoprophylactic method is

shown in the results of the practice over a three and a half-year period at the Maternité du Metallurgiste: 65 per cent of nearly 4,500 women treated experienced childbirth with no pain, and little or no discomfort. Classes in the Lamaze method are taught throughout the United States.

In contrast to Lamaze, who was mainly concerned with the feelings of the mother during childbirth, Leboyer's method of childbirth is aimed at securing a nontraumatic birth experience for the child. His "birth without violence" method is the result of his intense reexperiencing of the unpleasantness of his own birth during a period of psychoanalysis. Leboyer believes that the newborn child's transition should happen as comfortably and nonviolently as possible. A child is born with a wide-open, unprotected consciousness and therefore should be introduced into the environment "as progressively as possible with the lowest intensity."

During a Leboyer birth, the room is quiet and dimly lit. No surgical gloves are used in the delivery. Immediately after its birth, the child is placed on the mother's stomach, still attached to the umbilical cord, and massaged gently. After a certain period, the cord is cut and the child is bathed in lukewarm water. When the child is fully relaxed, light is gradually introduced into the room. Leboyer contends that since the normal healthy child is breathing at birth, it is not necessary to spank it. Furthermore, inducing the child to cry does not strengthen its lungs.

Birth without violence was implemented several years ago for the first time. More than a thousand children have been born this way since then. Follow-up studies on these children by two psychologists from the Sorbonne found that they are happy, positive minded, have strong personalities, and have avid, nonpassive interest in whatever they do. According to Leboyer, "in birth . . . the emotional aspect is just as important" as the requirements of the body. He feels that the emotional state of the child at birth determines its emotional state throughout the rest of its life.

Leboyer's method is being practiced in various parts of the United States, although many obstetricians have raised objections to it primarily because Leboyer doesn't wear surgical gloves. In San Francisco, the newly formed Institute for Wholistic Childbirth (IWC) not only promotes Leboyer's ideas, but has instituted whole programs involving exercises for pregnant women in mind-body control, breathing, classes in the physiology of pregnancy, infant psychology, the education of midwives, etc.

REFERENCES

Grantly Dick-Read, *The Practice of Natural Childbirth*, rev. and ed. by Helen Wessel and Harlan F. Ellis, M.D. New York: Harper & Row, 1944, 1953.
Fernand Lamaze, *Painless Childbirth: The Lamaze Method*. New York: Pocket Books, 1972.
Frederick Leboyer, *Birth Without Violence*. New York: Alfred A. Knopf, 1975.

NUMEROLOGY, the study and interpretation of numbers as they relate to a person's life and personality, is an ancient science of divination practiced by the Hebrew cabalists and the Greek Pythagoreans.

Wilhelm Fliess, a Viennese nose and throat specialist and mentor to Freud, practiced numerology and postulated a numerical relationship between human physiology and the stars. Arnold Schoenberg, the Austrian–American composer, born in Vienna, who developed the twelve-tone row which greatly influenced the design of modern music, practiced numerology. One of the most infamous numerologists was Dr. Irving J. Matrix, a fictitious character created by Martin Gardner. Dr. Matrix numerologically predicted the election of John F. Kennedy and compared numerologically the correspondence of Kennedy and Lincoln. In modern times, Hollywood numerologists create names for hopeful film stars with the "proper vibrations."

Numerology focuses on the cyclically recurring patterns in your life, the frequency and duration of those patterns, and the reasons for the instigation of the patterns. It pursues the same ends as astrology, palmistry, the *I Ching,* Tarot, and psychology. It can reveal the strengths, weaknesses, and potential problems connected with your personality, as well as give you an opportunity to become aware of choices available with regard to certain decisions to be made. Predictability in numerology is circumstantial to what it can reveal about your personality potential. Having self-awareness and the ability to observe the patterns of your life will allow you to acquire self-responsibility through knowing that the solutions to your problems, in a numerological sense, are inherent.

Numerology is based on frequency of vibrations or pulsations, and its structure is not complex. The most important information required for accurate application are your date of birth and your full name, including maiden name, married name, pseudonyms, etc. Numerology uses the single digits 1–9, and the *master numbers,* 10, 11, 12, 13, 22, and 33, which are not reducible to single-digit numbers; they are "higher octaves" of the single digits they would represent when added together. Their meaning pertains to a higher quality of the person (e.g., 33 means sainthood). The application of numerology will determine your path-of-life number, the number of your basic overall vibrations, the number of the year you are in, and the composition of the various numbers which are either *predominant* or *lacking* numbers. All the numbers concerning you are related to one another and indicate harmonious or discordant relationships, and with what and whom you have coincidental or divergent vibrations.

Your date of birth represents three aspects of your life: The month represents your family, childhood, environment, and rules your first life cycle (each life cycle has a duration of approximately twenty-seven years); the day represents your self, your personality and potentials, and rules your second life cycle, which is the most important one as it is during this cycle that you determine the means by which you can fulfill your potentials; the year represents your social environment, your "era," and the conditions of the world around you, and rules your third life cycle. Your month, day, and year, added together into a single digit (e.g., 21 = 3) is your *path-of-life* number. To determine your *year* number, add the numbers of your current birthday year down to a single digit form. There are numerological numbers assigned to each letter of the alphabet, which will determine the numbers of your name. The vowels and consonants in your name have meaning in relationship to your basic temperament, your approach to life, etc.

Odd numbers in numerology are *male* and signify personality, characteristics of impetus, incentive, intuition, etc., implying potential progress. Even numbers are *female* and signify intellect, logic, analytical capacity, etc., implying potential stability. Each number from one to nine has a certain significance that reveals qualities of personality, and can be interpreted in either a positive or negative aspect of the same idea, e.g., light and dark. Each number is specifically interpreted as to your path of life, your life cycle, your name, and compatibility capacity. For example, the number 3 means fulfillment. It is the result of the union of 1 and 2, and represents the child and family. Three is active, and "light in full manifestation." It means motion, implying restlessness and instability. Three also represents a kind of love that eliminates a subjective or passive approach to the divine idea; its antithesis is fear. The symbol of three is the triangle. The path of life of three is characteristically full of self-expression, competitiveness, ambition, and on the negative side, inconsideration, self-indulgence, restlessness, distrust, arrogance, hatred, etc. Threes are tied to the family and work at their best when they are involved with self-expression (i.e., music, painting, writing). Because of their ambition, threes can often make connections with the wrong people in a social context. Threes are preoccupied with light, either in the physical or spiritual sense. The year of three is fulfilling and successful, especially with regard to beauty and harmony.

Numerology can be used as an aid to self-awareness. It can help you steer your life in a direction that will be most beneficial to you. For example, you can use it to look for the kind of person with whom you will be able to form a strong relationship, and you will be able to avoid situations that irritate you because you know the shape of your personality. According to numerologist Ursule Molinaro, "the 'awareness-hygiene' for the mind is no different from a sensible diet. . . . It is a 'thought-diet' . . . which puts the accent on inner truth. On facing oneself, in order to be able to face up to life."

REFERENCES

Martin Gardner, *The Numerology of Dr. Matrix.* New York: Simon & Schuster, 1967.

Sybil Leek, *Numerology: The Magic of Numbers.* New York: Collier Books, 1969.

Ursule Molinaro, *Life by the Numbers: A Basic Guide to Learning Your Life Through Numerology.* New York: William Morrow & Co., 1971.

ROBERT E. ORNSTEIN (1942–) has achieved recognition in the field of psychology for his theories regarding the structure and function of the human brain.

Currently an associate professor of psychology at the University of California, Berkeley, and research assistant at the Langley-Porter Neuropsychiatric Institute, Ornstein is a graduate of Queens College in New York City and Stanford University, where he received his doctorate. His dissertation, published as *On the Experience of Time,* was awarded the American Institute of Research Creative Talent Award. In 1969, Ornstein received a postdoctoral fellowship to continue his interest in biofeedback at the University of California, Berkeley. There he became associated with David Galin with whom he pursued experiments in split-brain research begun by Roger Sperry at California Institute of Technology in the 1950s. A result of this work was Ornstein's book *The Psychology of Consciousness,* which has become a college textbook used throughout the country. Ornstein has also published *Common Knowledge,* which is concerned with exposing the existence of often unrecognized paranormal experiences, and coauthored *On the Psychology of Meditation* with Claudio Naranjo.

The primary source of Ornstein's theories lies in the research of Roger Sperry, which resulted in the conclusion that the two hemispheres of the brain are specialized in both internal function and the way in which they relate to the external world. According to Ornstein, the thrust of this fact is that the two "sides" of the brain have characteristically different modes of consciousness: The left side operates rationally; the right side, intuitively. Furthermore, these two modes operate complementarily: In normal activities, the appropriate side functions, while the other side is inhibited. The operation of one side of the brain is never substituted for the operation of the other side: "Within each person the two polarities seem to exist simultaneously as two semi-independent information-processing units with different specialties."

Illustrations of this can be seen in scientifically controlled experiments, using subjects with normal brains. It was found that the right hemisphere of the brain has superior function to the left side in depth perception (spatial information processing). Verbal response to information is controlled by the left hemisphere. Eye movements are clues as to which side of the brain is operating: A person will look to one side more frequently than the other if a question is asked that involves logical functioning. Different brain wave patterns occur in each hemisphere depending upon the task being performed, for example, dealing with verbal rather than spatial information.

Ornstein notes the predominance of the idea of the duality of consciousness in different cultures. For example, the *I Ching* polarizes the creative and the receptive, light and dark, time and space, male and female, etc. He considers the symbol of yin and yang illustrative of the complementarity of two existing poles of consciousness. He observes a similar polarity in the forms of inquiry posed in philosophy, religion, and psychology. Because of the scientific information that has been accumulated to attest to such duality as existing physically in the brain, Ornstein believes that ". . . we may be able to redress the balance in science and psychology, a balance which in recent years swung a bit too far to the right, into a strict insistence on verbal logic that has left context and perspective undeveloped."

The need for the latter process is exemplified by the exclusively rational and logical sciences which accept the gaining of legitimate knowledge as coming only via rational and logical thought. Ornstein views past psychologies as focusing on "one *special* case of man" which can be analyzed. Scientific information has become so "refined" that its importance to the general public has been overlooked and, therefore, lost. Our goal should be, according to Ornstein, a "complete psychology." Such a formulation would be the result of the recognition that there exists more than one way to think, and a means for us to come together in our investigations, without opposition. The questions then become: How is a complete psychology to be approached, and how is the creative, intuitive, and more mystically oriented functioning of the brain to be integrated into the realm of psychology?

According to Ornstein, the first step would be the recognition of the temporal dimensions of consciousness. His investigations into this aspect of consciousness support his conclusion that "the contents of normal consciousness are a personal construction." The normal way in which we experience time is "only one particular personal construction of reality" and there are other ways to experience time.

Normal experience of time seems to be linear during the day and nonlinear at night. The left hemisphere of the brain tends to process information sequentially, or in linear fashion; the right, more spontaneously, as in the necessarily quick integration of motor, visual, and kinesthetic information. In linear experience, time is directional, durational, and our considerations of it include ideas of simultaneity and causality. "Linear construction of temporal experience constitutes the essence of the active mode of consciousness." Linear experience inherently implies logic, analysis, and words. In contrast, nonlinear, "timeless," experience occurs in our dream states, in states of altered consciousness (e.g., with the use of drugs), in meditation, etc. To analyze this kind of experience linearly is paradoxical.

Given such differences in temporal experience, Ornstein believes that the gradual shift of interest in Western culture from the development of technologies and science to the desire for increasing self-knowledge, self-awareness, and inner peace through meditation, for example, is evidence of our need to explore the nonlinear mode of consciousness in order to culturally survive, as well as to support the way in which the brain functions. This calls for a synthesis of what Ornstein calls "the esoteric traditions" (Zen Buddhism, Sufism, Yoga, etc.). The basic elements of this synthesis are: 1) the recognition of two modes of consciousness, with the cultivation of the intuitive mode that has not, until now, been prevalent in our previous activities; 2) the shift of interest to consciousness itself as a subject of scientific inquiry; 3) the recognition of our capacity to be influenced by "subtle sources of energy from geophysical and human forces . . ."; 4) the change in the concepts of normal and paranormal.

Ornstein is not interested in seeing a complete shift in culture to an involvement with "the other mode," but rather in culture becoming an integration of the two modes. Such an occurrence would open the doors to important psychological research in which the brain would be as significant as behavior in the measuring of mental functions.

REFERENCES

Edwin Kiester, Jr., "Robert Ornstein: A Mind for Metaphor," *Human Behavior,* Vol. 5, No. 6, June 1976.

Claudio Naranjo, and Robert E. Ornstein, *On the Psychology of Meditation.* New York: Viking Press, 1971.

Robert E. Ornstein, *The Psychology of Consciousness.* New York: Penguin Books, 1975.

Wayne Sage, "The Split Brain Lab," *Human Behavior,* Vol. 5, No. 6, June 1976.

P. D. OUSPENSKY (1878–1947) is known for his interpretations and extensions of the teachings of G. I. Gurdjieff. Ouspensky was born in Russia and raised in cultural surroundings. Both parents were painters and his father was also interested in music and mathematics. At eighteen, Ouspensky began to travel and write. During that time, he studied biology, psychology, and mathematics, especially the idea of the fourth dimension. At the turn of the century, Ouspensky was working as a journalist, touring Russia, the East, and Europe. In 1905, during a time of political unrest in Moscow, he wrote a novel dealing with the idea of "eternal recurrence": *The Strange Life of Ivan Osokin.* This book was published ten years later. After 1907, Ouspensky's interests turned to theosophy, religion, mysticism, and occult literature. He experimented with the psychology of yogic and mystic ways. He published several books, one of which was *Tertium Organum.* In 1915, he began lecturing on his travels and his spiritual ideas in St. Petersburg and Moscow. He met Gurdjieff the same year and began nine years of study with him, before finally breaking away.

Later, Ouspensky went to London to organize groups for the purpose of studying, developing, and practicing the teachings of Gurdjieff, as well as to continue his own work that was to become research into "a psychological system based on the study of 'self-consciousness' and 'objective consciousness.' " Ouspensky's best-known works are *Tertium Organum* and *In Search of the Miraculous,* an autobiographical report of Gurdjieff's teachings. Other works include *A New Model of the Universe, The Fourth Way,* and *The Psychology of Man's Possible Evolution.* The latter is composed of five lectures to be read aloud at sessions of groups interested in learning the Ouspensky-Gurdjieff philosophy of being.

Ouspensky's life work was aimed at creating a specific condition for solving the problems of man and the universe. The basis for it lay in the teachings of Gurdjieff, the central theme of which was the *change of being.* Ouspenksy believed that "live" conditions (or a "school" as he called it) were essential for the assimilation of Gurdjieff's ideas. A school would provide a place where the search and struggle for the change of being could be experienced.

According to Ouspensky, this change of being necessitates your commitment to do the work of becoming conscious and developing the connection with higher centers: "This work admits of no compromise and it requires a great amount of self-discipline and readiness to obey all rules and particularly direct instructions." It requires a realization of "your mechanicalness and your helplessness," a release of prejudices, fixed opinions, personal identifications and animosities, and the development of an attitude toward suffering which entails a conscious effort to destroy your mechanicalness, self-will, and deficient *self-remembering.*

Consciousness itself depends upon four different functions of the human being, each of which is controlled by a center in the mind: 1) The *intellectual* function accounts for all mental processes, including the "realization of an impression, formation of representations and concepts, reasoning, comparison, affirmation, negation, imagination, formation of words, speech . . . etc." 2) The *emotional* function can only be understood when it is shown how it differs from the intellectual function. 3) The *instinctive* and 4) *moving* functions are more difficult to understand because they are basically un-psychological in nature. Ouspensky described the *instinctive* function as being comprised of physiological and sensory functioning, pleasurable and unpleasurable physical sensations, and reflexive functioning, including outwardly expressed reflexes and the inner reflexes of physical memory. The *moving* function includes all external movements and memories of them, and the so-called instinctive movements. Instinctive functions are inherent; moving functions must be learned. Each of the four functions can appear in each of the three states of consciousness: sleep, the waking state, and self-consciousness. Ouspensky felt, however, that the observations made in a waking state are often deceptive without your realizing it; these deceptions block the way of the functions to the state of self-consciousness.

Ouspensky states that you only live in the sleep and waking states of consciousness, although there are two higher states of consciousness that can be attained "only after hard and prolonged struggle": *self-consciousness* and *objective consciousness*. Objective consciousness cannot be realized until you have understood sleep and waking consciousness and are "awakened." Self-consciousness is attained when you know the full truth about yourself; objective consciousness when you know the full truth about everything. Self-consciousness cannot be the product of relative consciousness characteristic of the waking state. Rather, it can only be realized through the recognition of the need to be self-conscious, in a "school" in which you can enter into the next phase of evolution. This means learning how to observe yourself, recognizing your functions and their centers, and seeing how they differ from one another, recognizing different states of consciousness, and the many "I's" within you.

Harmful characteristics are those that are proof of your mechanicalness. They are the products of lying, imagination, negative emotions, and unnecessary talking. They are also evidence of "sleeping," which comes about in two ways: through the act of *identifying,* in which you are unable to look impartially on that which you identify, and the act of *considering,* in which you worry about what others think of you. Before identifying and considering can be eliminated, you first must recognize that they exist in you. You must also see how you evolve, apart from others, aim for that state in which you are "immortal within the limits of the solar system," and develop the language necessary for talking about yourself in the patterns of your evolution.

Ouspensky characterized man according to seven categories. Physical man, emotional man, and intellectual man are born as such. The fourth category of man is "a product of school culture"; he has gained self-knowledge through the methodology of schooling and can move toward being a man of *unity* and *self-consciousness* (category five). A man of even higher center and function is one who has acquired *objective consciousness* (category six). A man who has found a *permanent I* and *free will* "can control all the states of consciousness in himself and . . . not lose anything he has acquired." This is the highest state of man. To understand it requires the use of a universal language that is precise and beyond any existing "terminologies and nomenclature." The work that you must undertake to change your being is "connected with self-remembering and . . . cannot proceed successfully without this . . . partial awakening . . . no work can be done in sleep." Your struggle is a search for the miraculous, a "penetration into . . . unknown reality" that exists beyond "the thin film of false reality," the "labyrinth of contradictions in which we live . . ."

REFERENCES

P. D. Ouspensky, *The Fourth Way.* New York: Alfred A. Knopf, 1959.

————, *In Search of the Miraculous*. New York: Harcourt, Brace & World, 1949.

————, *The Psychology of Man's Possible Evolution*. New York: Alfred A. Knopf, 1950.

————, *Tertium Organum: A Key to the Enigmas of The World*. New York: Vintage, 1970.

PARENTING. The concepts surrounding child rearing within the last decade have taken a turn away from traditional sources of authority, e.g., Arnold Gesell in the 1940s, Benjamin Spock in the 1950s, Haim Ginott in the 1960s. Three important contributors to the change in the approach to child rearing are Lee Salk, M.D., the director of the Division of Pediatric Psychology at New York Hospital, and professor of psychology and pediatrics at Cornell University; Fitzhugh Dodson, Ph.D., from the University of Southern California; and Thomas Gordon, M.D., a clinical psychologist, founder and president of Parent Effectiveness Training Associates, a nationwide program for parents, teachers, and others who work with children. In general, new ideas about "parenting" focus on the development of a psychologically balanced parent-child relationship in which feelings of love and respect, and facts about the circumstances of life are shared openly, honestly, and purposefully.

Salk believes it is necessary for parents to understand how to prevent the causes of emotional disturbances which can be potentially debilitating to a child. From the beginning, parents should know how to cope with the emotional confrontations a child experiences on a daily basis. Mothers have an inherent desire to touch, hold, and talk to their newborn infant. The fulfillment of this desire affects the child by creating an environment for him; the child learns that as he acts, the environment reacts. It is important that the mother does not deny her biological tendencies; otherwise, the child will lose the opportunity to learn what he should be learning.

According to Salk, the newborn infant needs the right kind of attention in order to learn about the environment sensorially and develop feelings of trust for the people around him. Any prolonged separation between mother and child in infancy can be damaging to the child's emotional development. When a mother spends full time with her child, the child will have "increased capacity to withstand stress and will know how to establish warm and close relationships with other people." The father is instrumental in the child's development through his demonstration of affection for both the child and the mother and the amount of time he spends with them. This demonstration is a tool by which the child may be taught values. Toilet training is a way the child learns to master his body and control his behavior; toilet training should not start until the child is two or three years old. At this stage the child can communicate and make the connection between speech and internal feelings; he will also learn the purpose of toilet training more easily because of a tendency to want to imitate his parents.

Salk believes that discipline is an integral part of a child's healthy growth and development and, if applied consistently, will aid the child in adjusting to the world and learning to behave in a socially acceptable manner. Discipline provides the means for the child to gain respect for the rights of others, to steer interest away from himself, to understand structure and organization. Salk stresses, however, the vast difference between discipline and punishment: Punishment is effective only when used in support of discipline and should not occur unwarranted simply in order to satisfy the parent. Rewarding a child with interest in and feelings about his behavior is more instructive than acts of punishment. This way, the child is given the opportunity to participate in the discipline rather than being isolated from a sense of family relatedness.

Salk believes that education begins at birth with sensorial stimulation. As the child grows older, it is important not to force learning upon him. Toys and the activity of play are the tools of education. At the age of three to five, when the child is ready to attend school, the parents should prepare him so that he knows generally what to expect; this will help to avoid the negative feelings children often attach to the school situation. Sex education should be an honest undertaking; otherwise, the child will develop the notion that sex is bad or dirty, which could lead to sexual problems in maturity.

Essentially, Salk contends that what a child wants from his parents is a relationship in which he feels wanted, even with regard to the restraints put upon him as discipline, and a relationship in which he feels supported as an individual in his independent activity. The child's needs will be fulfilled by his parents in a relationship which contains reciprocal love and respect.

Dodson's concept of child rearing focuses on the interaction of love and discipline, an approach he believes to be distinctly different from what he contends are the misconceived notions of modern child psychology (i.e., concerning permissiveness, inactive attention of parents during the child's developmental years, spanking, etc.). Dodson stresses the first five years of a child's life as being most important to both his intellectual and emotional development. It is during this period of time that the child's basic personality and *self-concept* are developed. Each stage in a child's growth is a precondition for the next stage; parents cannot push the stages. The first stages of infancy establish the child's basic outlook on life. In order for a child to develop the necessary trust both in himself and the environment, which will lay the groundwork for a strong and healthy self-concept, certain basic needs must be satisfied: being fed when hungry, being warm, sleeping, getting rid of waste products, being physically cuddled and "spoiled" with affection. A child fulfills his intellectual needs by playing with household objects and other things that he can be involved with on every sensory level. If these needs are satisfied, the child will move into "toddlerhood" with the best preparation.

Toddlerhood begins at approximately one year when the child begins to walk and continues for a year or so. In this stage, the child engages in solitary play with toys (a toy can be anything the child likes to play with) and will develop his muscles through physical activity (running, crawling, jumping, pulling, etc.). Playing and having the freedom to explore gives the child an education about the world, how to manipulate it and how to manipulate within it. Sound stimulation is important in toddlerhood; language development begins in this phase on a listening level.

Dodson calls the second year of childhood the *first adolescence* and it is essentially a year of transition. This stage involves the dynamic quality of personality, which is a very important psychological resource and should not be ignored. The child will gradually become active in cooperative play; he will be toilet trained, he will begin to internalize the limits and controls his parents teach him, he will ask numerous questions as he develops language skills. From three to five years of age, the child will pass from a state of equilibrium to one of disequilibrium and then back again. At three, the child will be in equilibrium with himself and others; temper tantrums will subside; the child will enjoy conforming to activities and applying patience to activities; language capabilities will improve; the child may have an imaginary friend, and will enjoy companionship.

At the age of four, the child moves into a period of disequilibrium, insecurity, and uncoordination. At this age, the child will be very social; possession will mean owning; the drive to talk and move and the need for variety are extraordinary. Parents must handle a four-year-old firmly. At the age of five, the child again experiences equilibrium and tends to be stable, reliable, and well-adjusted. The child enjoys present situations, is poised and skillful muscularly; he becomes more independent of his mother, conscious of his peers, responsive to intellectual stimuation, and will express or repress feelings. Discipline is effective for the child as an aid to his becoming self-regulating and developing a stronger self-concept through individualization and having learned as the result of natural consequences. Dodson feels that discipline should be based on "environmental control" where the structure of environments will tend to minimize other methods of discipline. An act of discipline can take the form of deprivation, spanking, or isolation. Dodson advises against certain disciplinary measures which he feels are inappropriate and will hinder the child's development of his self-concept, which is the essence of healthy growth.

Parent Effectiveness Training (P.E.T.), which originated in California, has become popular on a wide scale; it is taught in communities in the fifty states and in several foreign countries. Thomas Gordon, its founder, bases the training program on a theory of human relationships. Gordon believes that the parent-child relationship can be improved if parents learn the proper skills to be utilized in raising their children. In P.E.T., parents are exposed to everything known about parent-child relationships, with the emphasis on the expression of the true feelings of both parents in terms of their *acceptance* or *unacceptance* of their children's behavior. In this regard, acceptance must be demonstrated. This can be done through passive or active listening, or through verbalization.

The way parents communicate with their children is crucial. It can be designed so that children feel invited to talk or listen. Active listening by the parent is "a method of influencing children to find their own solutions to their own problems." When a child presents problems that will directly affect the parents, they can confront the child in terms of "you-messages" and "I-messages," which will allow parents to convey their feelings honestly and to become transparent to the degree that the child will be able to recognize their feelings. Effective disciplining taught by P.E.T. takes place through changing an environment in order to change a child's unacceptable behavior. When a child behaves in such a way that changing the environment or confronting the child does not alter behavior, conflicts can develop; in Dodson's terms, "the relationship owns the problem."

Dodson considers the resolution of conflict a critical factor in determining the kind of relationship which will exist between parent and child. P.E.T. focuses on the "no-lose" method for resolving conflicts; it involves the use of the *principle of participation* according to which children are motivated to carry out a decision that has been made with the entire family. This principle allows for acceptable and, therefore, stronger solutions to problems. It allows the child to use his thinking skills and to be treated as an adult. It creates an atmosphere of love rather than hostility, and of working together rather than an implementation of power. When it works, this method proves that parents and children care for each other and care that family problems get solved. P.E.T. generally mobilizes self-awareness and the desire to change in parents; it reveals ways in which they can aid their child to become more responsible and creates a means to achieve a parent-child relationship built on friendship, love, and respect.

REFERENCES

Fitzhugh Dodson, *How to Parent*. New York: New American Library, 1970.

Arnold Gesell, Frances Ilg, *Infant and Child in Culture Today*. New York: Harper & Row, 1943.

Haim G. Ginott, *Between Parent and Child*. New York: Macmillan, 1965.

————, *Between Parent and Teenager*. New York: Macmillan, 1969.

Thomas Gordon, *P.E.T., Parent Effectiveness Training*. New York: New American Library, 1970.

Lee Salk, *What Every Child Would Like His Parents to*

Know. New York: Warner Paperback Library, 1973.
Benjamin Spock, *The Common Sense Book of Baby and Child Care.* New York: Duell, Sloan and Pearce, 1957.

FRITZ (FREDERICK S.) PERLS (1893–1970), the founder of Gestalt therapy, was born in Germany, near Berlin, of Jewish parents. Rebellious as a child, especially against his father, Perls renounced his Jewish heritage before the age of fourteen and became a staunch atheist. As a youth, Perls was interested in theatre. He studied and worked with Max Reinhardt, director of the Deutsches Theater, who first introduced Perls to the importance of body language in the communication of ideas. Perls graduated from the Askanische Gymnasium at sixteen and enrolled in the University of Berlin to study medicine. World War I interrupted his studies. However, Perls qualified for his M.D. in 1920 and applied to begin practice as a neuropsychiatrist. At this point, he began to associate with the bohemian crowd in Berlin, and he remained associated with people of the counterculture for the rest of his life.

After a period spent in New York City in which language difficulties prevented him from continuing his work, Perls returned to Europe. In 1926, he entered psychoanalysis with Karen Horney. This led him to begin to conceptualize his own therapeutic technique, as well as to study other schools of thought, including existentialism and Gestalt psychology. From 1926–32, Perls practiced Freudian psychoanalysis in Berlin, Frankfurt, and Vienna. He met with Wilhelm Reich for the purpose of enlarging upon ideas that had been sparked in Perls by Reinhardt.

The Nazi infiltration in 1933 brought a halt to his practice. After living in poverty in Holland, Perls went to South Africa where he established the South African Institute of Psychoanalysis in Johannesburg. He remained in South Africa for twelve years, developing his therapeutic theories to the stage where he challenged

Freudian principles and wrote his first book, *Ego, Hunger and Aggression*.

Due to marital problems, Perls, once again, halted his practice and decided to return to New York, in 1946, where he remained until 1956. During this time, he became friends with Paul Goodman and Ralph Hefferline, who later coauthored the definitive text, *Gestalt Therapy* (1951). In 1952, Perls opened the Institute for Gestalt Therapy in New York. He began traveling for the purpose of spreading information about his therapy, and in 1954, opened the Cleveland Institute.

In 1964 Perls began residency at the Esalen Institute at Big Sur. He left after five years, moving to Canada to establish the Gestalt Institute of Canada with a group of followers from Esalen. Cowichan, as it was called, became Perls's base of operations. In the winter of 1969, Perls began his European travels, which were scheduled to end with stops in New England and New York. When he arrived in the United States, he contracted a flu-type illness, and died.

Gestalt therapy evolved out of an assimilation of the various disciplines, philosophical and psychological, Perls had studied. In addition to Freud and Reich, Perls studied dianetics, psychodrama, the work of Charlotte Selver and F. M. Alexander in body awareness and body language, bioenergetics, Taoism, and Zen, as well as the work of Julian Beck and the Living Theatre. He also experimented with drugs.

Gestalt therapy is a technique of personal integration which is based on the idea that all of nature is a unified and coherent whole (gestalt). This is a *holistic* frame of reference. Within the unified and coherent whole, all organic and inorganic elements flow continually in an ever-changing pattern of coordinated activity. These elements, on all aggregate levels, from the simplest to the most complex, function as integrated processes. In this respect, we are considered wholly in terms of our physical being, our thoughts, emotions, and sociocultural surroundings.

In practice, Gestalt therapy emphasizes the uniting of elements in the world. We have an inherent tendency to want to integrate all the elements of the world, including ourselves, into a whole. Gestalt therapy works to support this tendency. Furthermore, the discovery of the regularities of our behavior, as well as our physical characteristics, unveils our potential. The realization of this potential within the present universal construct is the aim of Gestalt therapy.

Organismic self-regulation is one of the general principles of Gestalt therapy. Biologically, an organism is considered in terms of its natural ability to satisfy its own needs, i.e., when an organism lacks something, it will supply itself with what is lacking; similarly, when an organism has too much of something, it will rid itself of the excess. On the human level, this principle indicates that we possess the natural capacity to cope with the environment and realize a harmony in the self. We are aware of what is required within the boundaries of availability in order to maintain this balance. Gestalt therapy considers awareness to be a binding factor in the universe. Organismic self-regulation occurs within a context where the organism is conscious of its operation in its environment. In this way, we control our relationship with the environment, and when the environment does not meet the necessities for optimal functioning, we can modify ourselves without undue hardship.

Each element in the environment has a goal to actualize itself within the environment as it is. This applies to larger, more complex organizations such as societies. Yet, a basic conflict exists between the individual element and society. The demands of society are not as immediate as those of the individual. The result is that an individual's existence is falsified by parents, teachers, etc. The individual is unable to extend himself into the situation, and thus is unable to realize a full potential and develop in relationship to the entire structure of the whole. The interruption of this growth process causes the individual to shrink back and squelch his or her feelings.

Gestalt therapy is implemented through a patient-therapist relationship. The therapist is taught the principles of Gestalt therapy, but is not trained in any therapeutic technique and thus is free to create his own style of treatment. This is consistent with the experimental and existential nature of the therapy.

The Gestalt therapist attempts to embody what is lacking in you, and you deal with the therapist in terms of your missing potentials. The therapist's job is to route your consciousness to see that whatever you think the therapist can do, you can do equally as well. You cast away expectations of being manipulated, i.e., by parents, and can discover the ability to retrieve all aspects of personality which led you to integrate yourself with the whole environment.

The therapist will channel your activity to deal with present situations and problems. If you are concerned with a dream or past event, you will be encouraged to bring it to the present by acting it out. This will increase your ability to concentrate on the development of awareness. You should be able to recognize your emotions and be free to express them, answer questions on your own, and not be afraid to behave spontaneously. As Perls put it: "Be here now and be truly yourself." Once in touch with your own reality, you will have realized your full potential through interacting with a universe which is everything, including, most importantly, yourself.

Today, there are Gestalt institutes throughout the United States and in Canada where therapists are trained and therapeutic activities provided for other individuals. Gestalt therapy has recently come to be considered a more viable therapy than those which profess instant cures. Perls put together an accounting of his thoughts, periods in his life, and theories, in an autobiography which takes its title from one of his poems: *In and Out of the Garbage Pail.* Other books by Perls are *Gestalt Therapy Verbatim* and *The Gestalt Approach and Eyewitness to Therapy,* published posthumously in 1973.

REFERENCES

Joel Latner, *The Gestalt Therapy Book*. New York: Bantam Books, 1973.

Frederick S. Perls, *Ego, Hunger and Aggression*. New York: Random House, 1947.

————, *Gestalt Therapy Verbatim*. New York: Bantam Books, 1971.

————, *In and Out of the Garbage Pail*. New York: Bantam Books, 1972.

Martin Shepard, *Fritz*. New York: Bantam Books, 1976.

PRIMAL THERAPY is the result of the work of Arthur Janov, Ph.D., who trained for seventeen years in insight therapy as a psychiatric social worker and a psychologist in a Freudian clinic. From 1952–55, Janov was on the staff of the psychiatric department of the Los Angeles Children's Hospital. He is a member of the American Psychological Association and the Los Angeles Society of Clinical Psychologists. In the late 1960s, Janov had clinical experiences which led to his development of Primal therapy, now implemented in the Primal Institute in Los Angeles.

At the core of Primal therapy is Janov's theory that mental discomforts suffered in childhood, when suppressed in growth, evolve as neuroses. Primal pains are occurrences in the past that were not acted upon but instead were stored up as tensions or shaped into defenses. Primal pains prevent you from being "real." These tensions and neuroses can cause physiological responses which manifest themselves as headaches, ulcers, constipation, etc.

The primal experience is "being" the pain, feeling the experience which has created the pain, and getting rid of it through the act of screaming. When primal experience has been achieved, you are considered "real."

Primal therapy seeks to dispel the "unreal" system

which drives you to drink, smoke, take drugs, or make hasty unwarranted decisions simply in order to tolerate the steady internal growth of tensions. The "unreal" system is a breeding ground for living in the past and never changing the way you view the world, i.e, living at the age of forty the way you lived as a teenager because you continually speak and act neurotically, unable to release the feelings which a certain situation created.

Primal patients range in age from late teens to middle age. The therapist treats you with the idea that it is your responsibility to get in touch with the feelings which manifest themselves as primal pains. In therapy, you follow a stringent set of instructions. You are to give up all habits acquired because of pent-up tension, i.e., drinking, smoking, taking drugs. The first phase of the therapy lasts approximately three weeks, during which time you are not allowed to work or attend school. After the third week, you join a Primal therapy group which meets two or three times a week for several months.

The carefully planned process of Primal therapy begins with a discussion of your problems with a trained primal therapist who watches attentively for signs of tension, defenses, neuroses, etc. The discussions are aimed at gradually releasing your defenses so that you become essentially defenseless. Once you have joined the primal group, the therapeutic discussions continue but are automatically subject to more inter-action; this may induce the group members to ex-perience more primal emotions than experienced in individual therapy. Interwoven with the general therapy sessions are lessons in deep breathing in order to get you away from short, shallow, neurotic breathing, and get you closer to feelings of deep pain. Your speech patterns, which are also regarded as defense mecha-nisms, are also adjusted. The therapist will ask you to "take pains" with talking; this may mean slowing down rapid speech, imagining that you have someone else's voice, etc. These various techniques are aimed at getting you in touch with pain and, thus, increasing your awareness as to how you feel as well as your ability to express those feelings without inhibition.

Postprimal patients are said to confront problems without pretense or recourse to the past. They no longer require the recognition or acceptance they once needed. What a postprimal patient does has significance, and does not have a quality of "unreality," both in terms of personal comfort and on social levels. The relief of tension results in better coordination, heightened sensation, and easy articulation of thought. A new feeling about the self permits a postprimal patient to know exactly how he/she feels emotionally and physically in any instance.

To be "real," according to Janov, is to be free of anxiety, depression, phobias, nervous habits, and to be able to act in the present, without compulsion to satisfy needs.

Primal therapy was one of the first methods of psychotherapy which took a radical departure from pure analysis, concentrating on the focusing of feelings and wholeness of the self. Janov's initial book on the subject, *The Primal Scream,* traces the history of its evolution.

REFERENCE

Arthur Janov, Ph.D., *The Primal Scream, Primal Therapy: The Cure for Neuroses.* New York: Dell, 1970.

IRA PROGOFF, a psychotherapist, is credited with the modern formulation of *depth psychology.* He is the director of the Institute for Research in Depth Psychology at the Graduate School of Drew University. Progoff founded and is director of Dialogue House, a center for the application of his techniques. Progoff has produced three major works: *The Death and Rebirth of Psychology* outlines the important contributions of psychologists in history (Freud, Jung, Rank, etc.), which laid the foundations for a psychology of personal growth; *Depth Psychology and Modern Man* describes the principles, according to Progoff, upon which man's creative personality can evolve; *The Symbolic and the Real* examines how depth psychology can be applied practically and in a religious context. Progoff is a member of the American Psychological Association.

The term "depth psychology" was used originally by Eugen Bleuler, a Swiss psychiatrist, in the early twentieth century. At that time it referred to Freud's theory of the unconscious and the study of psychological occurrences on the nonconscious level of personality, opening the field for the development of post-Freudian conceptions of man. Depth psychology, according to Progoff, has evolved, going "full circle from the psychoanalytic diagnosis of man in his illness and incompletedness to a view of *wholeness in depth* as the most adequate way to understand the magnitude of human nature." Thus, the idea of depth now implies growth toward wholeness. Depth psychology is a means to perceive how such growth can take place.

Depth psychology is an holistic psychology, operating on the assumption that each individual possesses the capacity for growth: "the seed of growth, the seed of creativity, the seed of divinity in man are one and the same." This "seed" is activated and reaches fulfillment through processes that are characteristic of man's animal condition, but are also psychological. Depth psychology focuses on these processes in order to uncover them, to interpret them, and to develop them: "The processes of growth . . . are the processes by which what is potential in man progressively becomes more real, more actual, so that the meaning of man's life as a spiritual being in the natural world and in history is fulfilled in the individual's existence."

These processes are active in the unconscious and control your ultimate existential experiences. They are organic resources which, when factually understood, provide the springboard for your identification with a spiritual existence and your self-transformation. These processes define the functions of the *psyche,* a concept which Progoff uses in place of the concept of the unconcious: "Psyche is the directing principle in the individual that sets the pattern of growth and works to sustain it throughout the life of the organism."

The psyche unifies the conscious and the unconscious. Its composition, although difficult to determine, can be envisioned as consisting of internal events, dreams, images, tensions, fears, desires, intuitions. The manifestations of the psyche govern the pattern of development of the personality by establishing a goal toward which the personality strives. The pattern will reveal itself as it acts itself out, and it is "in the course of this enactment that the person discovers the nature of the goal he is truly seeking."

The manifestations of the psyche take shape in symbolic images that can be visual, auditory, and/or olfactory; these images essentially describe intuitive feelings. Their symbolic nature contains the expression of a pattern of growth characteristic of your life as a whole, as well as a pattern of images "required by the formative symbols in the psyche." The symbols can be *representational* of a cultural belief system, or *elemental* reflections of the processes of the universe, its phases and aspects. Through identification with the latter symbols, the meaning of existence is disclosed; an aware being, you become a participant in the process of reality.

One technique of depth psychology, called *evoking,* aims to elicit the flow of the psyche in imagery expressing the "principle of the psyche itself moving at its elemental, unguided depths beyond the influence of . . . special environmental situations, beyond . . . habits and . . . thoughts." By transcending conscious control, you are able to contact the real self that is beyond the limits of your finitude and enables you to become aware of *transpersonal love.* Transpersonal love calls forth the seed of growth and determines the conditions for working in the depths of yourself; this work is the function of creative love.

Progoff believes that a new symbol must be created that will redirect man to the energies of the personality in order for transformation to occur in modern man. This symbol must be operative and define the process "by which inward reality unfolds in the dimension of depth of the psyche." Although the symbolic process can only be determined individually, its experience can eventually pervade a community so that an atmosphere is created in which the depth dimension is the context of reality. According to Progoff, the creation of such an atmosphere will occur as the result of a program of personal discipline that entails: 1) regular face-to-face consultations in a dialogue relationship to explore and evoke the individuality of the psyche; 2) the maintenance of a psychological *workbook,* or *journal,* in which all the varied contents and encounters on the depth level of experience are kept as a continual record; 3) participation in group workshops in which experiences are shared with others who have embarked on a path of personal growth, and in which group techniques can be used by a competent leader to develop greater sensitivity to the symbolic dimension.

Progoff calls the psychological workbook aspect of the therapeutic process *journal feedback.* It focuses on a systematic exploration of your conscious life through intensive journal keeping. The therapy is a means of attaining a steady personal growth and coping with aspects and problems of this growth that might have warranted psychoanalysis as simply steps in your normal pattern of psychological development. The material of journal feedback is called *twilight imagery,* and consists of those thoughts that come to the surface of your consciousness when you are in a semisleeping or semiwaking state; this includes descriptions of dreams, imaginary dialogues, etc. Journal feedback can help to induce what Progoff describes as "deeper contact with spiritual and creative sources." Progoff calls his therapy *psyche-evoking* rather than psychoanalytic because it is up to you to trust your psyche enough to allow telling mental images to flow into the pages of a journal.

Progoff is the director of Dialogue House in New

York City, which is the main headquarters of journal-keeping workshops. His book, *At a Journal Workshop,* outlines the goals of this therapeutic method.

REFERENCES

Ira Progoff, *Depth Psychology and Modern Man: A New View of the Magnitude of Human Personality, Its Dimensions and Resources.* New York: Julian Press, 1959.

————, *The Symbolic and the Real: A New Psychological Approach to the Fuller Experience of Personal Existence.* New York: McGraw-Hill, 1963.

————, *At a Journal Workshop.* New York: Dialogue House, 1975.

PSYCHO-CYBERNETICS was founded by Maxwell Maltz, M.D., F.I.C.S., a plastic surgeon. Maltz received his baccalaureate in science from Columbia University and his doctorate in medicine from Columbia's College of Physicians and Surgeons. He was a professor of plastic surgery at the University of Nicaragua and the University of El Salvador.

Psycho-cybernetics is a method by which you can change and/or improve the course of your life by changing the way you think and feel about yourself. The key is self-image, the mental blueprint or picture that you carry around with you whether or not you are aware of it.

In 1940, Maltz published a book of case histories describing how plastic surgery, especially of the face, had caused radical personality changes. According to Maltz, in most cases, a person who had an apparently ugly face, or a freakish feature which was corrected by plastic surgery, experienceed a noticeable rise in self-esteem and self-confidence, usually within a period of twenty-one days. However, in several cases, the patients continued to feel inadequate and inferior even after successful plastic surgery. These failures aroused Maltz's curiosity and led him into an investigation of personality and behavior changes. He coined the term "psycho-cybernetics" as he recognized that the field of cybernetics, concerned with analyzing control systems in machines and living organisms, provided psychology with a new and viable model by which to understand the human personality and how it operates.

In Maltz's view of cybernetics, mechanical and organic systems are seen as being goal-striving and goal-oriented, i.e., teleological or purposeful. Psycho-cybernetics applies these principles to the brain and interprets them psychologically. According to Maltz, the science of cybernetics has proven that the subconscious mind is a mechanism, "a goal-striving 'servo-mechanism' consisting of the brain and nervous system, which is *used by* and *directed by* mind." Maltz calls this mechanism the creative mechanism. It works automatically and impersonally like a machine in order to achieve certain goals. These goals are mental images created by your imagination. You feed your creative mechanism with information and data which it processes, and acts upon. The resulting answer is an objective experience. The most important goal image is your self-image: if your self-image is negative, you feed your creative mechanism negative data and it will work for failure. If you have a positive self-image, and feed your creative mechanism positive data, it will strive for success.

Maltz believes that the key to changing human behavior is changing your self-image. In order to find life a reasonably satisfying experience, you must possess or develop an adequate and realistic self-image that you can live with happily and that you find acceptable.

Psycho-cybernetics is a program of learning, experiencing, and practicing new habits of thinking, imagining, remembering, and acting in order to develop an adequate and realistic self-image and use your creative mechanism in a positive way to achieve particular goals which are success-oriented rather than bent on failure.

The principles of psycho-cybernetics are implemented by means of practice exercises. The exercises range from spending thirty minutes a day alone and undisturbed, concentrating on building a new self-image through the use of your imagination, and storing new "memories" and information in your mid-brain upon which to act, to "acquiring the habit of happiness" which is achieved by changing your thinking habits, and beginning each day with the thought: "I am beginning the day in a new and better way."

Maltz's book, *Psycho-Cybernetics,* is arranged so that you have the opportunity to participate and creatively respond to the contents of the chapters and the exercises by providing your own case history in writing.

The main condition or "contract" which you are enjoined to agree upon when embarking on a course in psycho-cybernetics is to give the program twenty-one days to work. Maltz believes that this period of time is the minimum amount it takes to successfully change, or begin to change, your self-image, and to consequently change the direction and quality of your life.

REFERENCE

Maxwell Maltz, M.D., F.I.C.S., *Psycho-Cybernetics.* New York: Simon & Schuster, 1960.

PSYCHOPHARMACOLOGICAL PSYCHOLOGY, the use of drugs in the treatment of mental illness, originated in the late 1950s with the change in the treatment of emotionally ill patients in psychiatric hospitals. The use of potent antipsychotic phenothiazine tranquilizers and the drug reserpine began to replace the former physical treatment methods, i.e., utilizing physical restraint, electroshock therapy, hydrotherapy, insulin coma, and others. The introduction of this new chemical means of treatment into psychiatry prompted the funding by both government and private means of research projects for the development of other psychoactive drugs. In 1958, clinical research into the effects of lithium carbonate began; it was originally discovered in Australia in 1949. The American Psychiatric Association recommended the use of lithium for the treatment of manic depression to the Food and Drug Administration in 1969. Since 1955, statistics show that with the use of psychoactive drugs in the treatment of psychiatric patients, there has been a decline in the number of patients in mental hospitals; in 1973, a low point of three hundred thousand was reached. By 1969, approximately five hundred million patients throughout the world had been treated with psychotropic drugs, including tricyclic antidepressants and monoamine oxidase inhibitors.

The predominate goal of psychopharmacological psychology is the relief of mental depression. In 1974, the National Institute of Mental Health statistics revealed that nearly 1,500,000 people were being treated for depression. According to Dr. Nathan Kline, a physician recognized for his contribution to the study of antidepressant medication, mental depression is the "most common of all psychologic ills." Depression has both psychological and physical symptoms, all of which usually do not manifest themselves at the same time. Some of the psychological signs of depression are: lack of enjoyment and pleasure in normal activities; inability to concentrate or absorb what you see, read, hear; fatigue, lack of initiative and energy; insomnia; feelings of remorse or guilt about past developments which prevent your functioning as you think you should; inability to make decisions; decrease in sexual activity; a general loss of interest in people, ideas, etc.; irritability or hypersensitivity; thoughts about suicide or dying. Some of the physical signs of depression are: changes in bowel habits; dryness of the mouth; loss of appetite or insatiable hunger; aches and pains; numbness; tingling in the hands and feet; headaches. You may demonstrate your depression to others in the untidy way you dress, in the manner in which you respond in conversation, or by your awkwardness.

Depression is a psychobiological response to stress, and rarely results in severe mental illness requiring hospitalization. Depression can be acute or chronic. Acute depression can last for a few weeks or a few months, fluctuating in intensity because of stress factors. Acute depression can be considered an outlet for strong feelings with regard to major changes in life, especially with regard to loss. Chronic depression is not as obviously the result of a specific set of factors as is acute depression; its cause is not apparent. In chronic depression, a change in mood can become immobilizing, and life can become extremely complicated. Symptomatic of chronic depression is low self-esteem, sensitivity, withdrawal, etc. Depression, in general, can be considered a healthy response to stress, and can be remedied much more easily than the psychosomatic illnesses that are another way to respond to stress. Treatment of depression can give you the opportunity to gain insight into your character so that your ability to deal with future problems is strengthened.

The most obvious treatment of depression is to prevent it. This requires avoiding those situations which make you depressed, as well as experiencing depression rather than internalizing it, and resolving environmental and personal conflicts. A second method of treatment is drug therapy, of which there are four kinds that have been proved highly effective: 1) *monoamine oxidase inhibitors,* or MAO inhibitors, lower the rate of metabolism of amines which act as neural transmitters to the brain, by inhibiting the enzymes which catalyze the metabolic process. The result is that amines to the brain increase and thus heighten mental and emotional response. MAO inhibitors have been used in the treatment of schizophrenics and severely depressed patients. 2) *Tricyclics,* in the form of imipramine, also mobilize more amines to the brain in a different process from that of MAO inhibitors. 3) *Lithium salts*: Lithium is a metal substance that when combined with carbonates, phosphates, citrates, and chlorides can relieve a variety of depressions, especially manic depression. 4) *Sympathomimetic amines* affect the autonomic nervous system. They are often called "uppers" or "speed" and include dexedrine, methadrine, and ritalin.

REFERENCES
Ronald R. Fieve, M.D., *Moodswing: The Third Revolution in Psychiatry.* New York: William Morrow & Co., 1975.
Frederich F. Flach, M.D., *The Secret Strength of Depression.* New York: Bantam Books, 1974.

Nathan S. Kline, M.D., *From Sad to Glad: Kline on Depression*. New York: Ballantine Books, 1974.

RAM DASS (born Richard Alpert in 1931) is a contemporary spiritual leader who began his search as a psychologist and psychotherapist. He received his Ph.D. in psychology from Stanford University in 1957 and taught at Stanford, the University of California at Berkeley, and at Harvard University. Alpert served on the faculty of the Social Relations Department at Harvard, was associate director of the Laboratory of Human Development, and psychotherapist with the Harvard Health Service. In 1961, he took psilocybin, a consciousness-altering drug. Subsequently, he became associated with Timothy Leary who was doing research into altered states of consciousness through the use of psychedelics (i.e., LSD). Over a six-year period, he took hallucinogenic drugs more than three hundred times, lost his job at Harvard, and began to realize that the changes he was experiencing psychologically through his drug experiences were, in effect, limiting his consciousness rather than expanding it.

In 1967, Alpert went to India seeking enlightenment and wisdom. He studied under the guidance of Bhagwan Dass, and then met Neem Karoli Baba, known as Maharaji, with whom he studied the meditation techniques and yogic exercises of Raja Yoga for five months. Maharaji gave him the name Ram Dass. From 1968–70, he traveled between the United States and India. In 1973, Maharaji died, and Ram Dass decided to return to India. On his way there, he was persuaded by a friend, and a woman named Joya, who became his guru, to return to the United States and carry on his spiritual teaching. Since that time, Ram Dass has lectured widely about his experiences and what he has learned to be.

Ram Dass focuses on the evolution of consciousness, which he believes can be discovered only in an environment that supports the being of consciousness. An ashram is such an environment. It provides a community to live in, a spiritual leader to teach the relevance of consciousness, and is dependent upon the determination of its participants to keep it operative, financially as well as spiritually. Ram Dass believes that "the only thing [you] have to offer another human being is [your] own state of being." The "doing of [your] own being" and the state to which your consciousness has evolved are manifest in everything you do. In having consciousness, you can allow yourself to be free from attachment. This freedom will be demonstrated in your ability to serve others, to help them unleash themselves from their problems. Consciousness, and the way it effects a totality, is a means to maintain unity among people. Ram Dass believes in knowing about the various ways to achieve consciousness, and the search for other ways is integral to his concept of the ashram.

The use of the *mantra* is one way of achieving consciousness. The most widely used mantra is Tibetan in origin. It is *Om Mani Padme Hum,* which means "God's unmanifest form is like a jewel in the middle of a lotus, manifest in my heart." Mantras are repeated over and over again and generally are a means to empty your mind. You can become involved with mantras on different levels. The lowest level is hearing the mantra and thinking about its meaning; this involves you with one set of thoughts and dismisses irrelevant ones from your mind. As you begin to feel the mantra and its vibrations, you move toward a level of consciousness which puts you in "harmony with the universe, in the eternal present."

Another means for achieving consciousness is through the use of *mandalas.* Mandalas, or *tonkas,* are symbols of the universe, based on the idea that "mind manifests in matter." By concentrating on the image of the mandala, you become centered in your being.

Levels of consciousness operate on many planes. Depending upon how finely each level is analyzed, there can be as many as nine. The planes, interrelated with levels of energy, or *chakras,* determine your spiritual occupations. Increased consciousness will allow you to understand your nature more fully and manifest it in everything you do. The more conscious you are, the more creative your solutions will be to problems. Being enlightened, "in love with the universe in the sense that everything in the universe turns [you] on to that place in [yourself] where [you are] love and consciousness," begins in the present and involves everything in your life, both physical and spiritual.

Your body, according to Ram Dass, is the "temple in which [you] reside." How you treat your body is an essential part of working on your consciousness. You will change your ways of eating, breathing, etc., in order to meet the needs in keeping with the level of consciousness you are working on, or the level of consciousness you have achieved.

Higher states of consciousness allow you to live on fewer and fewer material goods as your energy becomes channeled in other directions. When you achieve a level of consciousness, you will affect others by transmuting your energies, and you can move together with others spiritually, unifying your relationships on higher and higher plateaus of experience. Your attachment to the physical plane, illustrated by your desires, will be transformed to a level of being where you no longer "collect," but issue out and become "pure instrumentality," beyond dualism. Ram Dass believes that your worldly business is the self: to integrate it with the fundamental laws of liberation, to become one with God, to become a perfect being.

In *Be Here Now,* Ram Dass describes the experiences of his first journey to India. After his second trip, he produced a six-record set called *Love, Serve, Remember. The Only Dance There Is* is a compilation of lectures Ram Dass delivered in 1970 and 1972.

REFERENCES

Ram Dass, *The Only Dance There Is.* New York: Anchor Books, 1974.

————, *Be Here Now.* New York: Crown Publishers, 1971.

Bill Simons, "Ram Dass: Going to God," *New Age Journal*, No. 9.

OTTO RANK (1884–1937), the founder of will therapy, was an Austrian psychoanalyst, called the most brilliant of Freud's pupils. His work advanced theories relating myths, legends, art, and the creative process to psychoanalytic theory. At the age of twenty-one, Rank showed Freud his first psychoanalytic study, *Der Kunstler* (*The Artist*), and was immediately taken into the psychoanalytic group. He became their secretary and began a relationship with Freud that would last for twenty years. In 1912, Rank became editor of two of the first psychoanalytic journals, *Imago* and *The International Journal of Psychoanalysis*. In 1919, he founded a publishing house for psychoanalytic works. With the publication of *The Trauma of Birth* in 1924, Rank separated himself ideologically from Freud. After suffering from the disapprobation of the Freudian entourage, Rank left Vienna to teach and practice psychoanalysis in Paris and New York. Among his works are *Art and Artist* (1923), *The Myth of the Birth of the Hero* (1914), *Will Therapy* (3 vols.), published from 1926–31. When he died, Rank was in the process of writing another major work, *Beyond Psychology,* which, although incomplete, was published posthumously by his friends in 1941.

When Rank departed from Freud and Vienna, his aim was to establish a method of psychoanalysis that did not approach human problems with the "philosophy of despair" that he felt Freudian analysis propounded. Rank's interpretation of the term "psychotherapy" describes an analytic technique that focuses on conscious will and creative impulse as a means to render the patient active and self-assertive, the primary creator of solutions to problems raised in the therapeutic process.

In contrast to Freud's theory that the source of neuroses is mainly sexual (Oedipus complex, etc.), Rank held that the key to neuroses lies in the *birth trauma:* The violent expulsion from the safety of the womb causes a shock that results in an underlying anxiety which will result in neuroses if not dealt with properly. His theory of the birth trauma encompasses the idea that at birth, you are faced with a fundamental noninstinctual dualism: fear of life and fear of death. Fear of life is indicative of the fear of living "as an isolated individual," that is, separate. This fear can develop into a fear of loss of individuality or fear of death. These fears are contended with throughout life. The neurotic ". . . gives the impression of a negative instinctual being who continuously strives to delay dying and to ward off death, but . . . only hastens and strengthens the process of destruction because he is not able to overcome it creatively." The neurotic expresses according to a destructive life principle. The sexual act is seen as resembling death; in aggressive acts, the neurotic is defending the ego against death. A conscious *will* that has developed since childhood "to a power equal to the outer environmental influences and the inner instinctual claims . . ." drives the neurotic to such behavior. Rank described this will as tending toward a "supra-individual self-maintenance." It is instinct playing against inhibition, and will against counterwill that is symbolic of one's self-limitation in the striving for an inner ideal which, when established as a moral norm, is the first step to freedom beyond compulsion.

Rank's method of therapy focuses on the will as the positive force that must be freed to develop the self-assertiveness of the individual. Rank describes the ultimate stage of his therapeutic development as ". . . a unified working together of three fully developed powers, the will, the counterwill, and the ideal formation born from the conflict between them, which itself has become a goal-setting, goal-seeking force. Here the human being, the genius, is again at one with himself; what he does, he does fully and completely in harmony with all his powers and his ideals. He knows no hesitation. . . . He is a man of will and deed in accord with himself, although . . . he is not in accord with the world, because he is too different from others."

The basis for the development of Rank's psychotherapy lies in his observation that art is both a social and personal phenomenon. As stated in the preface to *Art and Artist*, ". . . artistic creativity, and indeed the human creative impulse generally, originate solely in the constructive harmonizing of the fundamental dualism of all life." This dualism is revealed in the tendencies of the individual (artist) versus the tendencies of the collective contemporary cultural ideology (art). Furthermore, this dualism affects artistic creation as well as the development of personality in general. Rank saw parallels between the growth of the individual artist type out of the collective creative effort in Western culture (myths) and the development of individuality and personality throughout history. He saw this analogy as "the development and change in meaning of art forms from similar changes in the idea of the soul," a process that determined the development of the *productive* personality in individuals.

Rank saw the possessor of such a personality originally as a specific neurotic type, the *artist manqué*, who strives to express, although nothing may be actually produced. Artistic creation becomes "a compulsory dynamic" to monumentalize the individual as a genius, apart from the community. The drive for immortality is the main motivation for the artist's creativity. Therefore, the first work of the productive individual is his/her creative artistic personality, ". . . and it remains fundamentally his chief work, since all . . . other works are partly the repeated expression of this primal creation, partly a justification by dynamism."

According to Rank, artistic creation is the result of a creative urge (rather than a sexual instinct as Freud theorized). The expression of the individual is guided by the conscious or unconscious *will*. The will can also direct the alteration of any idealized plane of thought that grows out of collective-religious, social-artistic, and individual-erotic ideologies. What the artist, and the individual, tries to express is self-knowledge. Conflict occurs when there is no contemporary collective or social ideological means by which to phrase the expression. Rank believed that a solution to this conflict could be found in the restructuring of individual personality into a new kind of humanity in which traditions are obliterated and there is no necessity felt for ". . . any compulsion to justify . . . personal impulse to create by starting from the ideology of long-surmounted art forms."

REFERENCES

Otta Rank, *The Myth of the Birth of the Hero and Other Writings,* ed. by Philip Freund. New York: Vintage Books, 1959.

————, *Will Therapy and Truth and Reality.* New York: Alfred A. Knopf, 1945.

Jessie Taft, *Otto Rank: A Biographical Study Based on Notebooks, Letters, Collected Writings, Therapeutic Achievements and Personal Associations.* New York: Julian Press, 1958.

REALITY THERAPY was conceived by William Glasser, M.D. (1925–   ), a practicing psychiatrist in Los Angeles. Glasser was born in Cleveland, Ohio. He studied chemical engineering, clinical psychiatry, general medicine, and, in the early 1950s, trained as a psychiatrist at the Veterans Administration Center and the University of California at Los Angeles. He is the author of several books, *Mental Health or Mental Illness?, The Identity Society,* and *Reality Therapy,* which deals with the actual process of the therapy, using case histories.

Glasser developed Reality therapy toward the end of his psychiatric training, after judging classical psychiatric treatments to be generally futile. At the core of Reality therapy lies the formula of the three R's: reality, responsibility, and right-and-wrong. "Reality" is

defined as the world which surrounds you; "responsibility" is the ability to satisfy your needs without
depriving others of the ability to do the same; "right-
and-wrong" are the ramifications of your implementation of your standard of behavior. It is important that
this standard of behavior be at a certain level so that
your need to be worthwhile fulfills itself.

According to Glasser, the basic human needs are
relatedness and respect, and the way to fulfill these
needs is to live realistically, responsibly, and rightly,
not only in the present but in the future as well.

Crucial to this therapy is the creation of a patient-
therapist relationship in which you understand, possibly for the first time, that you are being accepted as
you are and guided so that you may satisfy your needs
in the real world, that your honesty is being appreciated,
and your conscience is being freed to become stronger
and fully active. A Reality therapist must be strong, responsible, and a practitioner of the principles of Reality
therapy. The therapist must be willing to discuss his
own problems with you and be subject to your scrutiny.
Most importantly, the therapist must permit the possibility of becoming emotionally involved with you. This
involvement is the essence of the therapy.

Initially, the therapist will take the first step by revealing a truth which you have continually tried to ignore, i.e., that you, alone, are responsible for your
behavior, and that excuses for irresponsible behavior are
not permissible. The focus is on behavior rather than
attitude, as this has been found to facilitate the success
of the therapy. Attempting to change your attitude stalls
the therapeutic process whereas a change in actual behavior will result consequently in a change in attitude.
The length of therapy depends largely upon the skill of
the therapist and how well you respond.

Reality therapy can be applied to groups of patients,
as well as individuals. It has been found that patients in
a group situation become more involved with each other
than directly with the therapist, and that the therapist's

function becomes that of a director or conductor, who intervenes when he ascertains that members of the group are straying away from reality or getting bogged down in their concentrated efforts to stay with reality.

Reality therapy has been used in schools and hospitals for the mentally ill, as well as in correctional institutions. An Institute for Reality Therapy has been established in Los Angeles where intensive training is given by professionals to those interested in learning the therapy as an aid in a professional career or in family life. Parents, probation officers, teachers, school administrators, ministers, drug rehabilitation counselors, and psychiatric technicians are some of the kinds of people who train at the institute.

Reality therapists are not numerous, especially in private practice. Glasser recognizes the problem and is trying to satisfy the need to reach more people. Nevertheless, it is possible to find social workers and marriage and family counselors who are familiar with the principles of Reality therapy despite the fact that they have not been trained at the institute as therapists.

REFERENCE

William Glasser, M.D. *Reality Therapy: A New Approach to Psychiatry*. New York: Harper & Row, 1965.

WILHELM REICH (1897–1957), Austrian psychiatrist and psychoanalyst, is probably most famous, or infamous, for his orgone energy theory which states that a cosmic energy (orgone energy) pervades the atmosphere and all living organisms, and that this energy can be collected and concentrated using a box called an "orgone accumulator." Reich also developed a system of psychoanalysis originally called *character analysis,* and later, *character-analytic vegeotherapy,* which was important in the psychoanalytic movement in its departure from Freudian analysis whereby it concentrated on curing neurotic symptoms and neuroses from a physiological basis. Bioenergetics and the work of

Alexander Lowen, among others, are derived from the work of Reich.

Reich's early education, influenced by his life on his family's farm, concentrated on the natural sciences. After a tour of duty in the Austrian Army (1915–18), Reich entered the University of Vienna Medical School, receiving his M.D. in 1922. In 1920, Reich became a member of the Vienna Psychoanalytic Society, then under the direction of Freud. During his last year in medical school, Reich began postgraduate work in internal medicine at the University of Vienna Hospital. From 1922–24, he studied neuropsychiatry at the Neurological and Psychiatric Clinic. He also did clinic work in hypnosis and suggestive therapy. From 1924–30, Reich conducted the Vienna Seminar for Psychoanalytic Therapy; its purpose was to try to organize a systematic and successful technique of analysis. By 1930, Reich had come into conflict with Freud and decided to move to Berlin to lecture and carry on his clinical work. Reich was a member of the Communist Party but his attempts to correlate his work with the Communist revolutionary movement were not approved of, and Hitler's rise to power forced him to flee to Denmark. (Reich was later officially expelled from the Party after his publication of an article about fascism.)

By 1934, even the International Psychoanalytic Association thought Reich's ideas were too radical, and he was officially dropped from its roster at the Lucerne Conference that year. The general reaction to his unorthodox ideas and practices forced Reich from Denmark to Sweden and finally to Oslo, Norway, where he lectured and taught at the university. Increasing negative publicity in Norway finally prompted Reich to move to New York City where he opened a private practice, trained therapists in his methods, and lectured at the New School for Social Research (1939–41). In 1941, Reich was arrested in New York and held at Ellis Island for several weeks without explanation. In 1942, the Orgone Institute was founded in New York, and later moved to a two hundred-acre estate in Maine called Organon. In 1954, the Food and Drug Administration filed an injunction against Reich and his institute, and ordered that all orgone energy accumulators, Reich's journals, and books be confiscated or destroyed. Rather than appear in court, Reich wrote to the judge informing him that in his opinion scientific matters had no place in a law court. Several months later, Reich reopened the institute and resumed selling books. He was tried in 1956 and sentenced to two years in Lewisburg Penitentiary, where he died eight months later. The government burned all of Reich's journals that were confiscated.

Reich's dissatisfaction with the methods of analysis implemented in the 1920s, as well as his unique perspective on neuroses and neurotic symptoms, led to his development of *character analysis,* and *vegeotherapy,* which later became *orgone therapy.* His approach was a radical departure from Freudian psychoanalysis, which was symptom-oriented, involving the patient in verbal therapy (i.e., free association). Reich observed that while many patients were incapable of verbalizing their feelings and thoughts, others had developed what he called *character armor,* which was a defensive mechanism that allowed them to verbalize and free associate quite easily without being affected by it. He compared this defensive system to layers of rock which were impenetrable, locking in the patient's history, i.e., the experiences that caused the defenses to build up originally. In his personal experiences with patients, Reich noticed that an observable physical change could be noticed after the release of a strong emotion, for example, a fit or violent physical action. From this, he hypothesized that neuroses had a physiological basis. He concluded that a neurosis is, in fact, "a physical disturbance caused by . . . unsatisfied sexual excitation," and related the severity of psychic illness to the severity of genital disturbance. The source of energy for the symptoms of a neurosis was contained within the genital disturbance. According to Reich, a neurotic person is orgiastically impotent, lacking the ability to permit biological energy to flow. Thus, the goal of his therapeutic techniques was to transform the patient from a neurotic character to a genital character, i.e., capable of releasing energy through complete sexual discharge.

Reich's theory of orgone energy was prompted specifically by his observations about the biological function of tension and charge. In his clinical research, he saw that sexual stasis and neurosis were destroyed by an orgiastic discharge of biological excitation. He concluded that the orgasm functioned in terms of a *four-beat rhythm,* beginning as a buildup of *mechanical tension* producing a *bioenergetic charge* that was released in the form of a *bioenergetic discharge,* which left the organism in a state of *mechanical relaxation.* Reich called this process the *TC function,* or *orgasm formula,* which he considered a life formula in support of his idea that "the sexual process is the productive biological process" applicable not only to procreation but to life, in general.

Furthermore, he determined that there exists in the living organism a specific biological energy called *orgone energy,* which has certain properties that 1) define its fundamental difference from and relations to electro-magnetic energy; 2) define its capacity to "permeate and govern an entire organism"; 3) define its function as basically pulsatory; 4) define its role as a determinant for sexual activity and form development; and 5) define its contributions toward the understanding of why living matter is distinctive of the earth.

Orgone therapy was developed to restore the biological functioning of an individual. Reich defined it as "neither a psychic nor physiological-chemical therapy but rather a bioloigcal therapy dealing with disturbances of the autonomic system." These disturbances appeared as hypertension, cardiac neuroses, phobias, etc. and "exist on the superficial layer of the psychosomatic apparatus." The treatment of both physical and psychological disturbances was a process of allowing the individual to tap the sources of the disturbance on a level that was much deeper and beyond language, in physical movement. The individual must surrender the muscular armor which prevents the flow of orgone energy, in successive segments, from the head, the mouth, the neck, the chest, and the diaphragm. Once the diaphragm begins to function freely, and "the trunk strives with each exhalation, to fold up in the region of the upper abdomen," the neck should tend toward the pelvis, the orgasm reflex is attained, and orgone energy permitted to flow.

In later life, Reich applied his theory to a philosophical realm. He believed that the creators of thought systems throughout history tried to define cosmic orgone energy but were inhibited by "the same human character trait that created religious prohibitions" and mechanistic overviews. His concept of orgonomic functionalism addresses the functional laws which govern nature. Body functions, ranging from growth to locomotion, to genital excitations, are rooted in the relationship between "mass-free orgone energy and orgone energy that has become matter." The basic principle of orgonomic functionalism clarifies the various means by which man operates within the structure of functional laws; this is the concept of psychosomatic identity that creates a correspondence between mental and physical functioning.

REFERENCES

W. Edward Mann, *Orgone, Reich and Eros: Wilhelm Reich's Theory of Life Eenergy*. New York: Simon & Schuster, 1973.

Wilhelm Reich, *Selected Writings: An Introduction to Orgonomy*. New York: Farrar, Straus & Giroux, 1973.

————, *Character Analysis*. New York: Noonday, 1949.

————, *The Function of the Orgasm*. New York: Noonday, 1942, 1961.

THEODOR REIK (1888–1969), an Austrian-American psychoanalyst and writer, was born in Vienna, and

received his Ph.D. in psychology from the University of Vienna in 1911. It was as a student that he first met Freud, beginning a relationship with his teacher that was to last for thirty years. In 1914, Freud awarded Reik a first prize for a paper on applied psychoanalysis. Freud encouraged Reik to continue his work and research in psychoanalysis rather than to enter the medical field, which Reik had intended to do. During the years from 1915–38, Reik lectured at the psychoanalytic institutes in Vienna, Berlin, and at The Hague. He came to New York in 1938, where he practiced psychoanalysis until his death. Once he had established a practice in America, his methods of psychoanalysis departed from those of orthodox Freudian analysis. In 1948, Reik founded the National Psychological Association for Psychoanalysis, of which he was appointed honorary president in 1952. He was the author of numerous books, many published originally in German. Among them are: *From Thirty Years With Freud* (tr. 1940), *Psychology of Sex Relations* (in which he rejects Freud's idea that neuroses are sexually based), *Psychoanalytic Experiences in Life and Music, Listening with the Third Ear* (1948) (an outline of the psychoanalytic process), and *The Search Within* (an autobiographical account of the important stages in his development). Reik was also the chief editor of *Psychoanalysis,* a journal, and contributor to other journals in both the United States and Europe.

Reik's primary psychoanalytic concern was the unconscious. It has been observed that his writings were the conscious means which revealed the depths of his own unconscious thoughts and feelings. Reik not only posed questions about the limits of psychoanalysis but, drawing from himself as a source, attempted to expose what he considered to be the existing paradox in the psychoanalytic process: Within the unconscious mind there are realms of often contradictory thoughts that can remain unknown, but which can also be brought into consciousness. These thoughts are the foundation of the most basic facts about humankind.

The development of Reik's psychoanalytic method was strongly influenced by an early obsession with Goethe. Reik states that at the age of eighteen he was on the verge of becoming a Goethe philologist. His infatuation with Goethe plus his own investigations led him to the process of self-analysis that was to become the basis for the remainder of his life's work.

Reik regarded psychology as the study of a world ultimately created through self-observation in which the individual views his/her mental and emotional processes as separate entities. According to Reik, this kind of observation is possible because of the split ego: "If the ego were undivided, it could not observe itself." The initial observation of the self occurs from the outside, from other people in the environment. Thus, "self-observation . . . originates in the awareness of being observed." Reik contended, therefore, that psychological observation, whose organ is the unconscious, can only occur within oneself; it is the unconscious mind that allows the individual to ascertain what happens internally.

Reik strongly believed that a psychoanalyst must understand his/her own inner workings before expecting to recognize and understand the psychological processes that occur in others, and he concluded that the psychological interest for a psychoanalyst can only arise out of the recognition of a disturbance within him/herself: "Without it no possibility of psychological recognition exists." The focal point for the psychoanalyst is the unconscious mind of the patient which the analyst meets with "his own unconscious mind as the instrument of perception." The psychoanalytic process becomes a constant internal conversation about how he/she is perceiving the expression of the unconscious mind of the patient in gestures, body movement, vocal delivery, facial expressions, and the sense impressions not necessarily attributable to conscious observation. The latter sets up channels of communication between the unconscious minds of two individuals, each of whom is crucial to the process.

396 / THEODOR REIK

The goal of the analyst is to apply a mixture of unconscious and conscious perceptions toward recognizing the "secret meaning" behind the psychical language of the patient. Thus, the analyst must train to be aware of the slightest indications of a patient's behavior that might otherwise pass unrecognized: The analyst must "trust his impressions as soon as he becomes aware of them." These impressions are the basis of further investigation and research into the psychological nature of all individuals. Reik describes how the analyst must learn: "The analyst's most significant knowledge must be experienced by himself . . . these psychological experiences are of such a nature that they must be suffered." Suffering teaches the analyst wisdom that can be drawn upon toward gaining insight into others.

Reik believed psychoanalytic experiences to be not only the result of one's direct life experiences, but also one's experiences with literature and music, which contain sources of identification with the imagery of the unconscious mind. He documented cases in which he paralleled characters in literature with the personalities of his patients. He considered music to be a means of evoking emotions that can be recalled in the midst of free association, which are significant indicators of the unconscious mind. The patient's biography also contains material relevant to psychoanalysis as an indicator of the development of character. This entails bringing aspects of the unconscious mind (via dreams, screen memories, etc.) into consciousness.

In order to understand human civilization, according to Reik, it is necessary to examine history in order to discover myths, customs, legends, and rituals that are antecedents contributing to the structure of contemporary culture. These remnants of past civilization contain psychological truths: "Scratch a superstition, a religious ritual, a myth or a legend, and you find unconscious facts." Reik termed this study *archaeological psychoanalysis*. For him, it was a means to better understand the present world that both surrounds and is within humankind.

REFERENCE

Theodor Reik, *The Search Within: The Inner Experiences of a Psychoanalyst*. New York: Jason Aranson, 1974.

CARL R. ROGERS (1902–   ), a psychotherapist, is responsible for the development of *client-centered therapy*, which has influenced the behavioral sciences in the development of processes and techniques of group therapy. Rogers was born in Oak Park, Illinois. He received his M.A. and Ph.D. from Columbia University in 1931. From 1924–26, he also studied at Union Theological Seminary. He was a fellow in psychology at the Institute for Child Guidance in New York in 1927, and from 1928–30 he acted as psychologist for the Society for the Prevention of Cruelty to Children in Rochester, New York. From 1940–45, Rogers was a professor of psychology at Ohio State; from 1945–57, he was at the University of Chicago, and from 1957–63, at the University of Wisconsin in Madison. Rogers also served as visiting professor at Columbia, UCLA, Harvard, and other colleges and universities. He was president of the National Research Council of the American Psychiatric Association and of the American Academy of Psychotherapists. Since 1964, Rogers has been resident fellow at the Western Behavioral Sciences Institute in La Jolla, California.

Client-centered therapy, which is non-Freudian in its approach, deals with the client as a person capable of the growth necessary to realize certain potentials inherent in the human being. The goal of client-centered therapy is self-actualization.

The attitude of the therapist is crucial. According to Rogers, it is important that the therapist have an attitude of "positive regard" toward you, one that confirms your *worth* and *significance*. Consequently, the therapist must ask certain relevant questions of himself: "How do we look upon others? Is our philosophy one in which respect for the individual is uppermost? Are we willing for the individual to select and choose his own values, or are our actions guided by the conviction (usually unspoken) that he would be happiest if he permitted us to select for him his values and standards and goals?" In general, the patient-therapist relationship should mark the beginning of the creation of viable interpersonal relationships. It should be a helping relationship which promotes growth, development, maturity, improved functioning, and improved ability to cope with others. This patient-therapist relationship can be enlarged to include the possibility of relationships developing within a group and, in a larger context, a community.

Rogers was prompted by his study of interpersonal relationships to ask further questions about the validity of helping relationships. These questions address the hows of the communication of your trustworthiness and dependability, and your capacity to have positive attitudes toward others, to be able to act separately from others and expect the same from them, to see another's feelings and understand them without judgment and evaluation, to be sensitive and nonthreatening in your behavior, and to "meet this other individual as a person who is in the process of *becoming*" without being fixed to your past.

Rogers' examination of the therapeutic process of client-centered therapy determined seven successive stages of growth. Stage one is a static phase in which you, the client, are unwilling to communicate, and block any communication of the self. In stage two, you let go enough to express yourself, but only in terms that address topics unrelated to the self. Problems are perceived as being external to the self, involving no personal responsibility. Your feelings, though occasionally expressed, are objects of the past, "unowned." At this stage, you are in fact ruled by the past, and unable to focus on the problems of the self, or your feelings, and will unknowingly describe the self and experiences in contradictory terms. In stage three, you begin to express the self and self-related experiences as objects, occasionally seeing the self as existing in others. You will begin to talk about past feelings and personal feelings, although still unable to accept present ones. You will begin to recognize contradictions and differentiate feelings and meanings from the whole. In stage four, the intensity of past feelings are expressed as if present, while present feelings remain unacceptable and therefore unexperienced. Problems begin to take form in growing feelings of self-responsibility. Feelings and meanings are increasingly differentiated, and contradictions between experience and self are beginning to be realized. In stage five, your feelings are expressed as they exist in the present. It is less painful to face problems and contradictions, and you have the desire to be the "real [you]." In stage six, you begin to live subjectively in experience. The self is no longer an object. Experiencing is a process. Your *loosening* becomes physiological as well. Stage seven occurs predominantly outside the patient-therapist relationship. This stage encompasses your conscious awareness of desires, personality, attitudes, and continuously growing sense of trust in yourself, and the acceptance of changing feelings. At this stage, experiencing is the basis for newness and presentness. The self, no longer object, "becomes increasingly simply the subjective and reflexive awareness of experiencing . . . and much more frequently something confidently felt in process." The boundaries you place on experience are tentatively imposed and validated through further experience. Communication with the self is clearly defined through a full recognition of feelings as consistent with meaning. Problems are your responsibility; new ways of being are chosen.

As a result of the success of single client-centered therapy, Rogers outlined a methodology and process of group therapy. Since then, he has examined and researched the effectiveness of the method. The result is a *philosophy of persons* and a hypothetical *Law of Inteerpersonal Relationships:* "Assuming a) a minimal willingness on the part of two people to be in contact;

b) an ability and minimal willingness on the part of each to receive communication from the other; and c) assuming the contact to continue over a period of time: then . . . the greater the *congruence* of experience, awareness and communication on the part of one individual, the more the ensuing relationship will involve: a tendency toward reciprocal communication with a quality of increasing congruence; a tendency toward more mutually accurate understanding of the communication; improved psychological adjustment and functioning in both parties; mutual satisfaction in the relationship." This law also states that a greater communicated *incongruence* of experience and awareness will have the converse effect upon the relationship.

Rogers describes his purpose as one of resolving the conflict between his role as "experimentalist" and "scientist." The problems that evolve out of this conflict are the result of a confusion between subjective and objective attitudes. Rogers concludes that a subjective, existential person and the values he/she adopts are the basis for both the therapeutic and scientific relationship.

REFERENCES

Carl R. Rogers, *Client-Centered Therapy: Its Current Practice, Implications and Theory.* Boston: Houghton Mifflin Co., 1951.

———, *On Becoming a Person: A Therapist's View of Psychotherapy.* Boston: Houghton Mifflin Co., 1961.

THE ROYAL CANADIAN AIR FORCE EXERCISE PLANS were originally conceived in the years following World War II. Subsequently, a team of doctors, scientists, and physical-fitness experts, after two years of research, devised exercise plans that would be available to a greater number of people. The purpose of the plans is to provide men and women of all ages with a viable means of achieving and maintaining physical fitness.

The exercise plans are built upon the basic idea that two kinds of power can be developed through exercising: muscular power and organic power. Muscular power is measurable in terms of strength, the ability to endure physical activity, speed, and flexibility. Organic power is measurable in terms of rate of blood flow, rate of air flow, and the chemical composition of the blood. The level to which these powers can be developed depends upon body type, diet, rest, and general health status. The capacity and efficiency with which your body works will increase as these two kinds of power are developed.

The research done by the RCAF teams revealed that if you are physically fit, you can withstand fatigue for a longer period of time; you can tolerate more physical stress; your heart is stronger and works more efficiently; and you are usually more alert and less tense.

The RCAF plans—5BX and XBX—are designed specifically for men and women. The 5BX plan for men focuses attention on the development of commonly used muscles, the development of muscles that require efficient use for long periods of time, the development of the speed response, flexibility and suppleness of the most important muscles such as the back and abdominal muscles, the development of the heart, lungs, and other organs, and the development of a capacity for physical exertion. The 5BX plan includes a specific group of exercises to follow, as well as exercises that can be done in connection with daily activity such as walking, climbing stairs, lifting, etc. The exercising done in accordance with this plan takes eleven minutes a day to complete.

The XBX plan for women takes into consideration the different aims involved in the achievement of physical fitness for women and girls. The plan concentrates on the same areas as the 5BX plan, but is designed so that the muscles developed are firm but not bulky. There are ten exercises to be done on a daily basis, for approximately twelve minutes. In both plans, it is emphasized that diet is an important factor in any physical-fitness program.

In following the RCAF exercise plans, you will set a goal for achieving physical fitness in accordance with specific recommendations made for your sex and age. You are advised to consult your physician if you are at all dubious about your capacity for exercise. Once you have reached your goal, it is up to you to maintain it.

According to the RCAF, it is very important to pay attention to the levels of exercise. The body cannot tolerate highly vigorous activity without the proper preparation. An example of the different levels of an exercise which you can follow illustrates how the exercises change. Level One: Stand with feet astride and your arms uplifted. Bend forward and touch the floor, then stretch upward and bend backward. Don't strain to keep your knees straight. At Level Two, when you touch the floor, bounce once, stretch upward and bend backward. Do this movement for two minutes. At Level Three, touch the floor six inches outside the left foot, between the feet, and six inches outside the right foot, move upward and bend as far back as possible. Then repeat the exercise in reverse. Do this for two minutes. At Level Four, after you return to a standing position, make a full circle from the waist, bending backward each time, your arms uplifted.

REFERENCE

The Royal Canadian Air Force Exercise Plans for Men and Women. New York: Pocket Books, 1972.

WILL SCHUTZ (1925–) is a behavioral psychologist whose concepts of bodymind encounter-group confrontations have become well-known. He was born in Chicago, Illinois. Schutz received his doctorate from the University of California, Los Angeles, in 1951, and taught and conducted research in group psychology at the University of Chicago. From 1954–58, he was lecturer and research associate in the Department of Social

Relations at Harvard University. He was lecturer and research psychologist at the University of California, Berkeley, and taught at the Albert Einstein College of Medicine, New York City. Schutz has acted as consultant for several business corporations, advising on group behavioral problems, and he has conducted small training groups for both public and private institutions (e.g., the Rand Corporation). In 1967, he was associate in residence and director of the residential program at Esalen Institute in Big Sur, California. Since 1973, he has continued consultations and has written several books.

The contemporary idea of the encounter group as a valid approach to the development of awareness, the encouragement of nonverbal communication, the exploration of interpersonal relationships, the reintegration of mind and body began in the late 1960s with Schutz's first book, *Joy*. Presently, existing forms of encounter groups have also been influenced by group psychotherapy techniques, T-groups, psychodrama, Gestalt therapy, T'ai Chi Ch'uan, theatre, dance, etc.

According to Schutz, the general principles of encounter are based on your unity as an organism, whose physical, psychological, and emotional being functions at an optimum level when it is integrated and ruled by self-awareness. Being honest, open, and aware permits you to discover and use your spiritual energies. The development of self-awareness in the encounter allows you to transcend self-deception and get to know and like yourself, to feel your importance as an individual and respect yourself and your capabilities, and to take responsibility for yourself. Self-awareness is developed through achieving contact with your body, feelings, motives, needs, and the consequences of your actions.

Concepts of normality, rightness, or what should be, which tend to obscure what actually exists, are not present in the encounter situation. You join an encounter group after having made a necessary choice about how you want to be. The participants in an encounter group are not considered "sick." Theoretically, the experiences in an encounter group encourage natural growth and promote a means by which you can enjoy your life more fully, relating to others and the world more honestly and openly and naturally through the union (or reunion) of your body, mind, and spirit.

Encounter has an important psychological basis: it assumes that the body is the center of human affairs; the body is the location of your history as well as the source of your pleasure. (In this respect, encounter differs from other group methods in its emphasis on the body, nonverbal techniques, guided daydream fantasies, etc.) Your body develops according to the way you use it and how you complete energy cycles. Full development of your body is prevented by blockages caused by physical and emotional traumas, which slow down your energy flow and prohibit physiological functioning, e.g., reduction in blood and oxygen supply, impeded nervous impulses, reduced organ functioning, and diminished intellectual capacity. These blockages can be seen in the actual structure of your body and its functional capabilities.

According to Schutz, the central psychological premise of encounter is *self-concept,* which originates in your relations to others. There are three basic interpersonal needs founded in self-concept: inclusion, control, and affection. 1) *Inclusion* deals with associational attitudes. In Schutz's terms, "the problem of inclusion is *in* or *out,* the interaction centers on *encounter,* and the physical aspect is that of *energy.*" Feelings of insignificance may lead you to be *undersocial,* introverted, withdrawn. These same unconscious feelings may also cause you to be *oversocial* and exhibit extroverted behavior. Problems of inclusion are physically expressed in a constriction of the facial muscles, breathing, and in sexual impotence. When these problems are ·resolved, your behavior is social, i.e., you feel comfortable with others, unpressured by anxiety, and are able to commit yourself to a group situation and feel significant. 2) *Control* pertains to decision-making processes between people and pertains to power, influence, authority. In Schutz's terms, "the problem of control is *top* or *bottom,* the primary interaction is *confrontation,* and the physical aspect is that of *integration.*" The need for control arises from a desire for authority over others, or the need to be controlled by others, lifting the responsibility from the self. If you are an *abdicrat,* you will submit, give up your power, and fall into a subordinate position. If you are an *autocrat,* you will want to dominate and compete, fearing that you cannot influence others and will wind up being dominated. Muscular tensions can be indicative of defense patterns which are the result of problems with control behavior. If you are a *democrat,* you will have solved your problems of control behavior, i.e., you are not overcome with fears of helplessness, stupidity, incompetence. Your body is well controlled and well integrated. You move easily and function properly. 3) *Affection* pertains to the personal, emotional feelings between two people and is based on building emotional ties. It is the last stage of development that occurs in a human relationship. According to Schutz, the problem of affection lies in *closeness* and *distance,* the essential affectionate interaction is the *embrace,* and the physical manifestation is *acceptance.* An *underpersonal* nature will cause you to both express and receive little affection, avoiding close relationships because of a fear of rejection. *Overpersonal* behavior will show up in your becoming extremely close to others in order to bring them close to you; this behavior expresses your anxieties concerning loveability. In *personal* behavior, you have resolved the possible problems which stem from feelings of affection and are capable of having and expressing genuine feelings.

In an encounter-group situation, these characteristics appear in phases in the order inclusion, control, and affection in terms of how the group relates to its leader as well as among themselves. An encounter-group session is held in a workshop and is usually scheduled as a five-day session (although it can be designed to last a weekend, two weeks, four weeks, four months, or nine months). Schutz's experience revealed to him that a single intensive week of encounter can be equivalent to two or three years of periodic, individual therapy sessions. During the workshop, the participants live at the same location. Workshops can involve a group of forty to sixty people, which is normally split up into smaller groups of ten to fifteen people. The encounter process will begin without preliminary testing or interviewing; the premise is that your own sense of responsibility indicates your willingness to participate. At the start of the first session, the rules are stated; they stress honesty, working in the present, being totally responsible for yourself, avoiding expressing yourself in generalities, taking action to correct things you don't like, etc.

In the emergence of an "encounter culture," encounter has become a life-style. The principle of encounter can also be applied to psychotherapy, industry (with regard to the workers), business meetings, theatre, education, raising children, religion. According to Schutz, becoming aware of feelings and body states should be an everyday occupation and will bring you closer to feelings of "joy."

REFERENCES

William C. Schutz, *The Interpersonal Underworld (FIRO).* Palo Alto, Ca.: Science and Behavior Books, 1966.

————, *Joy: Expanding Human Awareness.* New York: Grove Press, 1967.

————, *Elements of Encounter.* New York: Bantam Books, 1975.

———— and Evelyn Turner, *Evy: An Odyssey into Bodymind.* New York: Harper & Row, 1976.

HANS SELYE (1907–), an endocrinologist and biochemist, is an expert on the subject of stress. Selye was born in Vienna, and studied in Prague, Paris, and

Rome, receiving his M.D. and a Ph.D. in philosophy and science at the German University, Prague. It was during this time that Selye observed that the symptoms of diseases are not specifically characteristic, but rather are common to many diseases. He became interested in the subject of stress, although his theories were not formulated for twenty-five years. Selye has received nineteen honorary degrees from universities throughout the world as well as numerous other awards, medals, honorary citizenships. He is a Companion of the Order of Canada, the highest honor of the country, and a Fellow of the Royal Society of Canada. In 1936, he was assistant professor at McGill University in Montreal. Since 1945, he has been professor and director of the Institute of Experimental Medicine and Surgery at the University of Montreal. Selye is the author of thirty-two books and more than fifteen hundred technical articles. His most recent book is a revised edition of *The Stress of Life,* which was originally published in 1956.

Selye is primarily interested in clarifying the chemistry of stress, especially through the investigation of induced states of stress in rats, a procedure called *bioassay.* Selye defines stress as the common denominator of all adaptive reactions of the body; the stress state is "a state manifested by the specific syndrome which consists of all the non-specifically induced changes within a biological system." He concludes that stress is essentially the rate of wear and tear of the body. It can occur as *eustress,* which is pleasant and curative stress, or *distress,* which is unpleasant and disease-producing stress. Selye calls the totality of changes in the body which occur from stress, the *general adaptation syndrome.* These changes, which involve the nervous and endocrine systems that characteristically are the defense mechanisms against stress, affect both the structure and chemical composition of the body in terms of adaptive reactions and signs of damage.

Selye proved through his experiments with lower

animals and plants without nervous systems that stress is not simply a product of nervous tension. Biologically, stress is neither a discharge of hormones from the *adrenal medulla,* nor does it cause the secretion of *corticoids* from the adrenal cortex, hormones which can be secreted without producing evidence of stress. Stress can be elicited by normal activities and "is not the same as a deviation from the steady state of the body." Stress is not synonymous with alarm reaction or the general adaptation syndrome. The pattern of stress reaction is very specific and selective, affecting certain parts of the body (e.g., the adrenal glands, the thymus, the gastrointestinal tract).

Stress can be created by any agent or stressor (e.g., physical exertion, infections, etc.). A stress reaction as the nonspecific response of the body to any demand made upon it can have good or bad causes, and create good or bad effects. Stress should not and cannot be avoided; nonexcessive stress is a natural occurrence in the body, just as is body temperature. Stress has meaning only when applied in the description of a *precisely defined biologic system.*

The general adaptation syndrome is fully produced in the development of three stages: the alarm reaction, the resistance stage, and the exhaustive stage. Selye observed that normal active people undergo the first two stages frequently, in order to adapt to the rest of their activities and the demands made upon them. When the entire body is affected, however, exhaustion has reached its culmination. Most of the time, the effects of exhaustion are reversible because of the activation of the body's finite reserves of *adaptive energy.* When these stores are spent, general exhaustion occurs, followed by death (e.g., senility at the end of a normal life span, aging accelerated by an onslaught of stress, etc.). When adaptation to stress through biologic reactions is unsuccessful, the body can develop what Selye labels *diseases of adaptation.*

There are two ways in which to observe the danger

signs of possible maladaptation characteristic of a person's limits of stress endurance. Medically, there are certain symptoms which can be detected through the measurement of blood levels of adrenalines, corticoids, ACTH (a hormone affecting the growth of the entire body), blood eosinophils (which result from increased secretion of glucorticoids, anti-inflammatory hormones affecting both glucose metabolism and connective tissues), the electrical activity of the brain, blood pressure, galvanic skin resistance (the electrical conductivity of the skin manifested in perspiration).

You can determine the danger signals of stress by becoming aware of certain symptoms: irritability, hyperexcitation, depression, a pounding heart, dryness of throat or mouth, impulsive behavior or emotional instability, the urge to run, hide, cry, an inability to concentrate, feelings of unreality, weakness, dizziness, loss of energy, nonspecific anxiety, insomnia, trembling or nervous tics, high-pitched nervous laughter, stuttering, grinding your teeth, hypermotility, sweating, migraine headaches, etc. Selye has found that some diseases are often related to the production of substances by certain glands (cardiovascular disease, kidney disease, blood vessel disease). Inflammatory diseases such as rheumatism occur as the result of maladaptation to local stress situations. Their extent is "dependent upon insufficient mobilization of the body's alarm systems." Maladaptation is also influential in nervous and mental diseases, sexual disorders, gastric and duodenal ulcers, hypoglycemia, hyperthyroidism, etc. Selye has also investigated the relationship between stress and cancer.

As a result of his research into the biology of stress, Selye has determined that it should be your goal to create a code to live by "which reconciles the timeless natural drives that, as long as they are in conflict, cause most of man's mental distress." This code should include "earning your neighbor's love." This way will enable you to invent a purpose for yourself through which you can gain security and personal satisfaction by demonstrating your good will in usefulness. The guide lines by which you live should be compatible with biological laws, yet socially and morally acceptable. The structure of these guide lines should be shaped by your ability to 1) discover the cause of your stress, whether specific or nonspecific; 2) eliminate egocentricity and practice "altruistic egoism"; 3) determine how *you* can get the most satisfaction out of a minimal expenditure of adaptive energy; 4) keep your body active, taking care to choose between submissive and aggressive behavior in your daily life; 5) recognize that "to avoid the stress of conflict, frustrations, and hate, to achieve peace and happiness, [you] should devote more attention to a better understanding of the natural basis of motivation and behavior."

REFERENCES

Hans Selye, *The Stress of Life* (rev.). New York: McGraw-Hill, 1976.

————, *Stress Without Distress*. New York and Philadelphia: J. P. Lippincott, 1974.

————, *Stress in Health and Disease*. Reading. Mass.: Butterworth's, 1976.

SENSE RELAXATION. Bernard Gunther has been exploring and developing theories and techniques of sense relaxation at Esalen Institute in California. He has studied with Ida Rolf, Richard Hittleman, Charlotte Selver, and Fritz Perls.

According to Gunther, in childhood sensitivity awareness is often thwarted because of the emphasis placed upon cognitive and motor functions in formal educational circumstances. This *desensitization* results in an imbalance of your total being, a loss of feeling, the development of inhibitions, and alienation. In childhood, you also may have been conditioned to refrain from direct contact with others, and even with certain parts of your own body. This creates a separation between you and your environment. Gunther has observed that "excessive tension is a nonverbal message from your body asking you to become more receptive, permissive, to let go, and relax." The practice of sense relaxation, which is a process of sensory awakening, is one which allows you to contact your senses and permit your whole self to realize internal and external potentials.

Gunther calls the exercises he has devised to revive sensory awareness *experiences.* These experiences emphasize feeling, allowing, and being in your body. The general instructions for engaging in them call for comfortable clothes and silence. The initial activities are called "preludes" because they are often done before engaging in other experiences. They involve you in certain physical activities, e.g., tapping, slapping, touching, breathing, shaking, lifting, stretching. Tapping and slapping stimulate the nerves, increase the blood flow, and enliven your body as a whole.

Some experiences are designed to energize your body. Other experiences are gauged to tranquilize your body. When these experiences involve you and another person, their purpose is to get you feeling comfortable while physically relating to and feeling the presence of another person. These exercises can be extended to group activities: a group of people extend their arms to a central point where hands meet and touch; many people lift one person up; many people touch one person, etc.

Gunther devised *micro-meditations,* designed to put you in the present through the performance of a simple activity; for instance, peeling an orange using all your senses, washing your hands with your eyes closed, trying to feel what is going on around you with your eyes closed, stretching your body in order to feel every part of it, taking a walk in a familiar area in order to sense-experience the sounds, smells, sights.

When your body is in a state in which it automatically adjusts to the amount of muscle tension necessary to perform any act, it is in a state of *optimal tonus.* Optimal tonus requires your complete involvement in activity or inactivity, without needless expenditure of energy, as well as the muscular resiliency necessary to permit coordination, sensitivity, and integrity of body motion. Respiration, circulation, digestion, and elimination function smoothly. You are in an ideal state.

Gunther, in his investigation of optimal tonus, points out that the elimination of excessive tension is a crucial prerequisite. This implies your realization of responsibility for creating that tension, concentration on the places where tension exists, experience of the tension, and, finally, the letting go of it. Gunther observes that certain areas of the body tend to be tension centers, for example, the neck, the shoulders, the hips, and the eyes. Extreme tension solidifies muscles. It decreases their resiliency, shortening some and lengthening others, thus making the body imbalanced and misaligned.

Gunther believes that words contribute to the buildup of tensions: "Words are hypnotic conditioning." They divert you from the reality of your body's activity and close you off from exciting possibilities. You respond to situations with automatic behavior that is formulated on rules, laws, concepts, e.g., how you *should* be, rather than how you are. Thus, sensory awakening becomes a process of "de-hypnosis," away from rules, restrictions, constrictions, to *active meditation* that turns your consciousness to the "sensory experience of the here and now." It is a way of "de-conditioning" your mind, diverting it from its analyses, rationalizations, and apologies toward the "dynamic ease" that the body needs. The body is "re-sensitized," direct experience is of primary importance. Using your body, rather than words, to communicate with others begins to affect your relationships. You discover that you are in life, being life, aware of yourself and your body.

REFERENCE
Bernard Gunther, *Sense Relaxation: Below Your Mind.* New York: Pocket Books, 1973.

SENTICS (from the Latin verb *sentire,* meaning to "feel or perceive with the senses") is the science of "genetically programmed dynamic forms of emotional expression," founded by Manfred Clynes, M.D., who is currently active in conducting further research into the field, as well as lecturing on the subject.

Clynes, noted for his interdisciplinary approach to science because of a diverse education, received degrees in neuroscience and engineering from the University of Melbourne in Australia, and an M.S. in music from the Juilliard School in New York City. Clynes was chief research scientist and director of the biocybernetics lab at the Rockland State Hospital in New York for seventeen years, during which time he developed the science of sentics.

At Rockland, Clynes formulated the *Biologic Law of Unidirectional Sensitivity* which is concerned with the processing of information in living systems toward communication and control of functions. The law states that 1) the perception of information, from both the external environment and internal sources, is more acute when conditions for its perception are changing, and 2) the channeling of this information occurs in one direction. Using this law, Clynes explored the relationship between experience and the "standards" of perception. His experiments involved determining the specificity of brain waves in relation to visual perception (i.e., a particular brain wave can be measured against the quality of a visual perception). As a result of this inquiry, Clynes hypothesized that there could also be a similar correspondence between brain waves and inner experience. He applied this idea to the perception of music with positive results, and took his theory a step further: There could exist a correspondence between brain waves and human emotions. The latter is the central theory of sentics.

Sentics studies the natural form of the communication of emotion. There are characteristic forms for each kind of emotion, called *essentic forms*. The instrument developed to measure these forms is a *sentograph.* Essentic forms represent the natural "words" of emotion that are nonverbal biological configurations specific to the expression of a particular emotion. Their study in the context of neurophysiology affords their application in a therapeutic sense and, speculatively, in an educational sense.

The science of sentics considers the nature of the quality of experience, which entails looking for a "one-to-one correspondence between the elements of experience, which the central nervous system's physiologic code provides, and the words we devise to correspond with them." Clynes researched to see what brain processes were associated with experience, and discovered that the quality of experience is based on how an organism is genetically programmed. This implies that the quality of an experience is an *identity* and requires recognition. An example of this in physics would be the relationship that exists between elementary particles by which they can come together to form molecules "by chance but fall into place according to predetermined slots or 'holes' in the universal design." With human beings, it can be said that we experience qualities basic to our constitution, which are communicated to ourselves individually and to others "through the production and recognition of their precise forms." Clynes discovered that these qualities are confined, but exist in relationship to other functions of the brain. An example of this is the set of qualities that can be communicated because of its relationship to the motor system. This set of qualities can be defined as emotions.

The sentics theory holds that emotion and its expression can be measured precisely because the two are never considered divorced from one another. This measurement has revealed: 1) that there are specific emotional or sentic states; 2) that their expression is definable; 3) that they are generated in specific ways; 4) that they are influenced by the environment. Furthermore, sentic states are based partially in reality and partially in fantasy.

There are seven principles of sentics which have been tested in different cultures to prove their validity: 1) *Exclusivity Principle:* A sentic state is a single-channel system in which only one sentic state can be expressed at any one time. 2) *Equivalence Principle:* A sentic state may be expressed by any number of different output modalities. 3) *Coherence Principle:* Regardless of the particular motor output chosen to express a sentic state, its dynamic expression is governed by a brain program, or algorithm, specific for that state, which is called *essentic form.* 4) *Complementarity Principle*: The production and recognition of essentic forms are governed by inherent data processing programs of the central nervous system, and biologically coordinated so that a precisely produced form is correspondingly recognized; the recognized form in turn generates a sentic state in the perceiver. 5) *Arrhythmic Generation*: The intensity of the sentic state is increased within limits by the repeated arrhythmic generation of essentic form through E-actons. 6) *Experience of Generalized Emotion*: Sentic states may be experienced as pure qualities or identities, without reference to specific auxiliary relationships to generate or receive these qualities. 7) *Communicative Power as a Form Function:* The power of essentic form in communicating and generating a sentic state is greater the closer the form approaches the pure or ideal for that state.

Sentic cycles are a programmed sequence of sentic states that are voluntarily produced for therapeutic purposes. The idea behind sentic cycles is based on evidence that sentic states exist in a biological framework of time. According to Clynes, "Sentic cycles is a simple method by which a person, in his own home, can generate in himself substantially the entire spectrum of emotions in a period of approximately thirty minutes. This method allows one to experience emotions from different points of view, meditatively and with active expression. . . ."

Producing sentic cycles requires a "sentic cycle cassette tape," a tape recorder, and a finger rest. The process involves generating a cycle of emotions (i.e., no emotion, anger, hate, grief, love, sex, joy, and reverence). Each state can last for several minutes, according to the instructions on the tape. Each emotion is expressed through the action of pressing a finger on the finger rest. At the conclusion of one cycle or several cycles, you remain sitting quietly in a specified position for several minutes before resuming other activities.

The purpose of sentic cycles is to get in touch with your self and your emotions. When regularly practiced, they can induce a general sense of well-being or contentment, increased self-assurance, and an expansion of your sensitivity to emotional feelings, relationships with others, and the "nature of being." One of the most important effects is the way sentic cycles alter the dynamics of a drive, e.g., anxiety over a long-range goal is replaced by a creative drive. Clynes speculates that with supervision sentic cycles could be used to relieve anxieties, stress, phobias, and psychosomatically derived symptoms. The frequency with which the cycles are used is a matter of individual need. Overuse can "over tranquilize" you.

Clynes proposes that sentics can be applied for the purpose of making dreams more creative and as an aid in solving problems of sexual dysfunction, etc. In a socioethical context, sentic training in education could result in an increased sense of brotherhood among the members of society. Sentics could also be used in space travel as a method for assuring emotional well-being.

REFERENCE

Dr. Manfred Clynes, *Sentics: The Touch of Emotions.* New York: Doubleday & Co., 1976.

SETH is a personality who has made himself known through the medium of Jane Roberts, a poet and writer. Since his first manifestation in 1963, Seth has spoken through Roberts in hundreds of sessions. The material, which is recorded by Roberts' husband, has been published as *The Seth Material,* and *Seth Speaks: The Eternal Validity of the Soul.*

When Roberts first experienced the personality of Seth, consciousness left her body and she was overwhelmed with a flood of ideas which she proceeded to write down. Later, using a Ouija board with her husband, she confirmed Seth's existence. When Seth enters Roberts, she takes on a completely different personality. She speaks in a deep, masculine voice that varies in tone, volume, and pace. The accent in which Seth speaks has been described at various times as German, Russian, Dutch, Italian, Irish, and French. According to Roberts' husband, Jane Roberts also manifests an angular quality in her mannerisms, her facial muscles become rearranged, and her eyes darken. She smokes and drinks wine during her trance states.

Since Seth has spoken through her, Roberts has changed her own attitudes toward reality and reassessed her identity: "No longer do I feel as I did before, that man is a slave of time, illness, decay, and at the mercy of built-in destructive tendencies over which he has no control. I feel in control of my own destiny as never before, and no longer ruled by patterns subconsciously set during my childhood." Roberts has come to believe in the multidimensionality of human beings who are part of a mass of consciousness that should be explored. She believes that the insights and information concerning the nature of reality conveyed by Seth are vitally needed.

Seth describes his own being as "an energy personality essence, no longer in physical matter." The range of subjects about which he speaks is vast. He claims to be aware of truths that people have either forgotten or that have become so distorted throughout history that they must be clearly restated once again. In general, the message at the core of the Seth material is that people create the world that they know, including their own physical reality and all the various experiences that are a part of existence on earth.

According to Seth, nothing exists that does not have a consciousness of its own kind, a consciousness that "rejoices in sensation and creativity." If a human being can identify with such characteristics, then communication will transpire that will reveal knowledge of other dimensions which our physical senses obstruct. Such communication occurred when Seth spoke through Roberts. Within Roberts' psyche, according to Seth, there is a "transparent dimensional warp that serves almost like an open window through which other realities can be perceived, a multidimensional opening that has, to some extent, escaped being clouded over by the shade of physical focus."

Seth inhabits the universe, physical and non-physical, a plane that can be entered only after you have died many times. His environment is constantly changing, taking the form of many different kinds of consciousness, and of a variety of personality structures which are sometimes without gender. Each time Seth takes a form, he communicates within the context and principles on which the system he enters is based, which is the only way Seth's teachings can be understood.

Seth's philosophy is concerned with reincarnation, health, the nature of physical reality, the concept of God, dreams, time, identity, and perception. The groundwork of Seth's thought is based on his theory than an idea *is* an event, and has great influence on the lives of human beings: "All ideas, thoughts, and areas of concentration help create a dynamic and continually interrelating universe with the idea playing as important and as tangible a role as any physical event." Thus, an idea can become reality and control the process of history.

Roberts believes that Seth is her channel to revelational knowledge: "the psychological personification of the supraconscious extension of my normal self." As the result of her psychic experiences, Roberts has researched mediumship, ESP, and paranormal occurrences. She has conducted classes in ESP, during which Seth frequently speaks through her, and is the author of a book on the subject, *How to Develop Your ESP Power*.

REFERENCES
Jane Roberts, *The Seth Material.* New York: Bantam Books, 1976.
————, *Seth Speaks: The Eternal Validity of the Soul.* Englewood Cliffs, N.J.: Prentice-Hall, 1972.

SHIATSU, a therapeutic massage technique, originated in Japan in the eighteenth century as a combination of acupuncture and the *amma* form of Oriental masage, the pressing and rubbing of painful areas of the body with the fingers and palms. Beginning in 1940, shiatsu massage therapy was officially taught in Japan at the Namikoshi Institute of Shiatsu Therapy, named after one of Japan's shiatsu experts. Since then, the Nippon School and several Namikoshi Shiatsu Clinic centers have been established. Today there are more than twenty thousand licensed shiatsu therapists in Japan. For the most part, shiatsu did not attract any interest outside Japan until the investigation of acupuncture began in the West. In 1973, Toru Namikoshi and a group of his students toured Europe for the purpose of introducing shiatsu techniques to the West.

Shiatsu is a combination of the Japanese word *shi,* meaning "finger," and *atsu,* meaning "pressure." The technique of shiatsu is the application of carefully gauged pressure which is concentrated on specific points on the body surface. Shiatsu focuses on the areas of the body where the blood and lymph vessels, the nerves and ductless endocrine glands either are concentrated or dispersed. These areas are called *tsubo;* there are 660 such zones as designated by the ancient systems of analysis of the body.

Shiatsu is specifically geared to diffuse the lactic acid and carbon dioxide that accumulate in tissues, causing stiffness or fatigue because of improper blood circulation, abnormal pressure on the nerves, blood vessels, or lymph vessels. A professionally trained shiatsu therapist can detect these disorders by touch.

There are seven particular areas of the body which

can be therapeutically treated with shiatsu massage. The skin can be invigorated by stimulating the activity of the capillaries, encouraging the flow of nourishment to the skin, increasing the resistance of the skin, and aiding the complexion. Shiatsu can stimulate the blood vessels and lymph glands and thus prevent the congestion of these systems. By promoting blood and lymph circulation in the muscles, and stimulating the action of the capillaries to nourish muscle cells and remove waste, the muscle tone is improved. In young people shiatsu can be helpful in correcting bone structure by releasing fatigue-causing agents and permitting nourishment to reach the bones. When applied to the areas of the head, shoulders, and back, shiatsu aids the functioning of the nervous system. Shiatsu can restore the chemical balance in the body which is regulated by the endocrine glands. Shiatsu pressure applied to the shoulder blades, back, and abdomen, corrects and stimulates internal organ functioning to nourish the body, oxygenate the blood, and remove wastes.

The amount and type of pressure applied vary according to the area of the body being treated, as well as the condition of the patient being treated. The most common pressure is applied with the thumb or finger in a vertical direction for three to five seconds, or repeatedly. Sustained pressure is applied with the palm. Suction pressure employs the palm and/or fingers and is used in the treatment of abdominal areas. Flowing pressure is applied by moving the thumb in a horizontal line across the area of treatment; it is used especially on the shoulder blades. Concentrated pressure, for areas where muscles are very tense, is applied in a circular motion several times in a specific spot.

The advantages of shiatsu are that it can be performed under many different circumstances; it is a pleasant experience and, unless the recipient has an internal disorder or broken bones, etc., there are no adverse effects; it is beneficial to people of all ages; it can lessen the patient's vulnerability to sickness; and it deals with the entire body as one, concentrating on those areas that exhibit discomfort. The only necessary equipment is a blanket for the recipient to lie on and a towel or pillow for his/her head to rest on. The floor is a preferable surface, because it allows the person giving the shiatsu massage greater freedom of movement. Shiatsu can also be self-administered.

REFERENCES

Yukiko Irwin and James Wagenvoord, *Shiatsu: Japanese Finger Pressure for Energy, Sexual Vitality, and Relief from Tension and Pain.* New York and Philadelphia: J. B. Lippincott, 1976.

Tokujiro Namikoshi, *Shiatsu: Japanese Finger Pressure Therapy.* Tokyo: Japan Publications, 1972.

————, *Shiatsu: Health and Vitality at Your Fingertips.* Tokyo: Japan Publications, 1969.

Toru Namikoshi, *Shiatsu Therapy: Theory and Practice.* Tokyo: Japan Publications, 1974.

Watoru Ohashi, *Shiatsu Made Easy: How to Perform the Ancient Japanese Art of "Acupuncture Without Needles,"* ed. by Vicky Linder. New York: E. P. Dutton & Co., 1976.

William Schutz, *Shiatsu.* New York: Drake Publishers, 1975.

SILVA MIND CONTROL (or psychorientology) was created by José Silva for the purpose of teaching individuals how to voluntarily enter and control certain states of consciousness, or levels of brain function, hitherto untapped or unexperienced, to fulfill a variety of needs. Essentially, it is a method for increasing the powers of the mind.

Silva's research into mind control began over thirty years ago. Then, its purpose was to determine how the consciously realized lower brain wave frequencies could be used to increase an individual's capacity for retention and recall of information for the improvement of I.Q. A large portion of this research involved finding the frequency between Beta waves (indicative of normal consciousness) and Delta waves (indicative of deep sleep), i.e., the frequency at which subjects could control heartbeat, blood pressure, blood circulation, etc. Once a subject attained this state of wave frequency, it was discovered that the brain could also be influenced, and that the subject could sense information beyond him/herself and solve problems that had not yet been posed. Silva called this "The Guessing Phenomenon." The goals of the research were then reoriented to that of training individuals to sense information when their awareness was functioning at lower brain wave frequencies (inner conscious levels) for the purpose of increasing their capacity for *subjective communication*.

Using the electroencephalograph, it was discovered that the Alpha-Theta range of brain wave frequency could establish the inner conscious levels to be controlled (in contrast to the Beta wave lengths associated with the functioning of the senses [touch, taste, smell, hearing, and seeing]; in Silva Mind Control terminology, Beta frequencies are called outer conscious levels).

Alpha-Theta waves operate below the Beta wave frequency, i.e., they are slower. Alpha waves indicate a realm of consciousness where, according to Emilio Guzman (writer and lecturer on telepathy and subjective powers, and supporter of Silva's mind control methods), "the mind is freed from the rigid conditions of matter, and the imagination may spread its wings and fly unfettered by limitations of time and space, free to explore the visions of inner worlds, free to expand, free to create." This state of mind is often equated with spiritual consciousness achieved in meditation. The waves in the Theta spectrum can be applied to problem solving.

Once a subject has reached the Alpha level, the most important aspect of mind control can be achieved, according to Silva: ". . . Mind (Master Sense) can be projected to function from the Alpha perspective and can be oriented to develop controls by establishing points of reference within the Alpha dimension. The

Mind can learn to sense information impressed not only on its own Alpha neurons but can sense information impressed on the Alpha neurons of other brains, regardless of distance." Silva speculates that the willful control of the Alpha dimension in addition to the willful control of the Beta dimension, which happens naturally, will extend human abilities beyond what is currently known. A superior mental perspective will be attained, which will result in a richer educational experience, better problem solving, better health, improvement in the practice of religion. Education, in general, will become subjective education, for the development of both effective sensory perception as well as normal perception.

Formal classes in mind control began in Mexico in 1966 under the supervision of Silva's brother. That same year, Silva began teaching the mind-control method in the United States. Since that time, over 300,000 people have learned the method. Today, Silva Mind Control Lecture Series are available throughout the United States and in Canada, Mexico, Europe, and South America.

The lecture series consists of four basic lectures, each involving ten to twelve hours of study, dealing with the development of two forms of communication, *objective* and *subjective*. Lessons in objective communication focus on controlled relaxation and general improvement. You can learn how to control the relaxation of muscles, your ability to sleep and to awaken, your dreams, your headaches. You learn the basis for conducting subjective communication by improving your memory, your capacity to solve problems, and to control undesirable habits such as smoking or overeating.

Lessons in subjective communication consist of learning how to increase your effective sensory perception and then how to apply it. You can learn how to project your mind into inanimate objects, animate objects (e.g., plants), and animals. In these lessons, you begin to establish the personal reference points in your Alpha dimension. Through the application of effective sensory perception, you learn to project your mind into aspects of other humans, and solve problems characteristic of all kinds of matter. The latter is the culmination of Silva Mind Control.

There are also lectures designed specifically for those with special interests, e.g., elementary, high school, and college students. For the graduates of the four basic lectures, there are other lectures intended to extend what has been learned. The PSI (Psychorientology Studies International) graduate groups work on continued research into Silva Mind Control, and develop educational programs needed for the application of the theories and the practice of the method.

It has been claimed that Silva Mind Control is nothing more than hypnosis. Of this, Silva has said that there are certain crucial differences between the end results of Silva Mind Control and hypnosis, namely that 1) the deeper a subject is in the Alpha-Theta dimension, the more the subject can remember; 2) the subject can ask questions as well as answer them; 3) the subject is in control of the processes of visualization, which are not hallucinations.

Silva Mind Control International, Inc., located in Laredo, Texas, is the information center for all activity concerned with SMC.

REFERENCES

Emilio Guzman, *Mind Control: New Dimension of Human Thought.* Laredo, Tex.: Institute of Psychorientology, Inc., 1976.

Harry McKnight, *Silva Mind Control Through Psychorientology.* Laredo, Tex.: Institute of Psychorientology, Inc., 1976.

Research Studies of Silva Mind Control, Silva Mind Control International, Inc., Laredo, Tex., 1976 (monograph).

Silva Mind Control: Alpha-Theta Brain Wave Function, Silva Mind Control International, Inc., Laredo, Tex., 1976 (monograph).

B. F. SKINNER (1904–), a leading American behaviorist, is considered one of the most influential

and controversial figures in modern psychology. Skinner received his Ph.D. from Harvard University in 1931. He was research fellow for the National Research Council at Harvard from 1931–32, and from 1933–36 a junior fellow in the Harvard Society for Fellows. He taught psychology at the University of Minnesota from 1936–45; later, he served as chairman of the Department of Psychology at Indiana University. In 1947, Skinner was appointed William James Lecturer at Harvard and later became professor of psychology, a post he held for nine years, becoming in 1958 the Edgar Pierce Professor of Psychology. Skinner is a member of the American Association for the Advancement of Science, the National Academy of Sciences, the American Psychological Association, and the Society of Experimental Psychologists. Skinner was awarded a Guggenheim fellowship. In 1958, he received a grant from the National Institutes of Health for his distinguished scientific contributions to the field of psychology, and in 1968, he was awarded the National Medal of Science. Skinner is the author of *Walden Two,* among other works, a fictional description of a modern Utopia, which has been the subject of controversy since its publication in 1948.

According to Skinner, human behavior, although an extremely complex and ever-changing process, can be understood in scientific terms. The analysis of human behavior proceeds in two steps: the accounting of specific behavioral events, and the discovery of the uniformity in a series of behavioral events. Science can clearly define and make explicit these uniformities as exemplified in the procedures of anthropologists, social psychologists, psychological clinics, controlled laboratory experimentation, *and* mathematics and logic. Although Skinner notes that analyzing behavior scientifically raises certain objections, he contends that the lawfulness of the behavior of an organism as a whole cannot be known until that assumption is tested, using statistics and the controlled methods of the system of analysis.

Skinner totally rejects that which cannot be observed, stating that "the practice of looking inside the organism for an explanation of behavior has tended to obscure the variables which are immediately available for scientific analysis." The adequate analysis of behavior depends upon these variables which have a physical status in the immediate environment and environmental history of the organism. In *functional analysis,* predicting or controlling the behavior of an organism is structuring a *dependent variable.* The *independent variables,* those which cause behavior, structure the environment of which behavior is a function. The interaction between dependent and independent variables is evidence of natural scientific laws which, when expressed in quantitative terms, present a "comprehensive picture of the organism as a behaving system."

According to Skinner, there are six sources from which data analyzable in the science of behavior can be obtained: *casual observation,* which reveals the basis for hunches about a behavioral pattern; *controlled field observation,* in which data are sampled with more care and conclusions stated more explicity than in casual observation; *clinical observation,* which utilizes standard practices of interviewing and testing to elicit behavioral responses; *wide-scale observation* within controlled industrial, military, and other institutional research conditions; *laboratory studies of human behavior,* in which manipulation of the above-cited variables is deliberate so that response can be recorded over long periods of time; and *laboratory studies of the behavior of animals.*

Skinner's proposal for the analysis of behavior operates on several different levels of complexity. It examines how behavior changes when variables are changed; how an individual in one behavioral context alters some of the variables that affect other aspects of its behavior; how individuals interact socially; how government, religion, psychotherapy, education, economics, control individual behavior; how a total culture/social environment controls human behavior.

Skinner concludes that a culture in which the science of behavior reveals the consequences of cultural practices, and in which scientific methodology is practically and effectively applied to problems of human behavior, will survive. Thus, control within a culture can become a product of the scientific estimation of the survival value of these observed cultural practices.

Skinner's novel, *Walden Two,* describes a utopia which is behaviorally conceived and structured. Each member of the society is accepted as he or she is; no one is regarded as being superior to another, and each contributes to the whole process of the society in terms of money, tasks, etc. Intellectual pursuits and physical work are of equal importance and regarded with equal esteem. The utopia operates on the Thoreauian principle of avoiding unnecessary possessions; a very high standard of living is designed around a low consumption of goods. The family is considered an economic, social, and psychological unit. Children are raised in an atmosphere of genuine affection and are not tied to their parents. Their psychological makeup develops in response to the interests they have in common with others, or as the result of personality or character similarities they find in others. Each child is allowed to develop intellectually at his/her own rate and no child is required to develop the same skills or capabilities as another. The basis of education in the utopia, which begins when the children are babies, is "to uncover the worth-while and truly productive motives—the motives which inspire creative work in science and art outside the academies." Teachers supply the children with an array of techniques from logic to psychology and mathematics enabling them to learn how to think. The sciences are taught in active situations, i.e., anatomy is taught in the slaughterhouse, chemistry in a medical laboratory. Government is all participatory: "no one . . . ever acts for the benefit of anyone else except as an agent of the community." Leaders and laws do not exist. Personal triumphs are not stressed. Grievances can be taken directly to the managers and planners of the community. Everything operates in the present and is dealt with in a scientific manner; history cannot provide a model for the community of Walden Two. *Positive reinforcement* is the key to the success of the community whose members, as they follow a code, do exactly what they want to do. Inclination to behave, rather than final behavior, is controlled. Freedom is never questioned because there is neither a psychological nor a physical restraint on any working situation.

In contemporary society, Skinner believes that behavior cannot be changed until a *technology of behavior* is invented which reaches beyond the technologies of physics and biology and allows the precise definition and adjustment of behavioral problems. According to Skinner, we have been unable to recognize the feasibility of such a technology because behavioral science has always internalized behavioral problems. It is only recently that the interactional relationship between individual organisms and their environments has begun to be examined and understood. The application of such a technology of behavior would raise various controversial issues, e.g., the traditional value system in which the individual can achieve and gain recognition for his/her achievements would have to be given up: the apotheosis of freedom and dignity. Skinner contends that implementation of a technology of behavior would lead us to base our behavior on how it will affect our environment, rather than ourselves as "autonomous individuals."

REFERENCES

B. F. Skinner, *Walden Two*. New York: Macmillan, 1948.
————, *Science and Human Behavior*. New York: The Free Press; London: Collier-Macmillan, Ltd., 1953.
————, *Beyond Freedom and Dignity*. New York: Bantam Books, 1971.

PHILIP SLATER (1927–), a sociologist, is concerned with the sociological and psychological framework of America, and he uses many sources, i.e., Gregory Bateson, Freud, Norman O. Brown, Alvin Toffler, Erich Fromm, R. D. Laing, Herbert Marcuse, as well as his own study of Greek mythology and the character of the ancient Greek family, drawing parallels with contemporary life.

Slater was born in Riverton, New Jersey, and educated at Harvard University, receiving his A.B. in 1950, and his Ph.D. in 1955. From 1958–61, he was a lecturer in sociology at Harvard. He became assistant professor of sociology at Brandeis in 1961, and full professor in 1968. Slater's writings include *Microcosm, The Temporary Society,* with Warren Bennis, *The Pursuit of Loneliness, The Glory of Hera,* and *Earthwalk.*

It is Slater's contention that American society is in a schizoid state; it is a society which has been frustrated trying to fulfill desires for community, engagement, and dependence in a social situation which cannot tolerate such aims. We live with the illusion of progress based on the fallacious idea that it is possible to optimize everything simultaneously. In Slater's view, our culture can be compared to personality in that it is patterned in terms of differing and dissonant elements that form a perceptual whole. "Social change" becomes simply a restructuring of these elements.

Our desire for community is based on our need to live in trust and fraternal cooperation with the rest of society and be part of a viable social context. Our desire for engagement lies in our need to come to grips with social and interpersonal problems and come face to face with the environment on equal terms. Our desire for dependence lies in our need to share responsibility for controlling our impulses and the direction of our lives. In reality, however, these desires conflict with the prevailing social situation: We are trained in the pursuit of independence, we strive to be individuals, uninvolved except with our own egos and the extensions thereof. We have been forced into maintaining an emotional detachment from our social and physical environments by the idea that we should pursue our own destiny, competitively and despite others. We avoid dealing with reality and refute the importance of interdependence.

Technology keeps competitiveness alive: It emphasizes the idea of being "free" from the necessity of relating to or depending on others. The result for us emotionally is feeling disconnected, lonely, and unsafe. The individual should not be considered a "monolithic totality." Individualism diverts us from recognizing the significance of the group and the needs of humanity. Technological change indicates social change on a vast scale. Change in terms of our needs rather than the needs of technology tends to disrupt the status quo, and results in fear of any group or anyone who advocates change on a human level. We use technology, which oppresses us, to oppress others.

Technology provides a means of "overstimulating" us. We are confronted with needs and desires that cannot be immediately satisfied, but which we are conditioned to strive for in an effort to gratify them. According to Slater, most overstimulation occurs commercially and emphasizes sexuality. New products become a means of filling the gap between maximum sexual stimulation which occurs in the media and minimum sexual availability which is a fact of our lives. One of the ramifications of overstimulation is the attempt by different generations to deny the sexuality of each other. Parents perpetuate this process by hiding their own sexuality from their children in an attempt to control the sexual impulses of their children. The characteristics of radical youth, the process of parental desexualization, and the intense concentration on bringing up children to be successful are rooted in the importance that middle-class America places on the regulation of emotions and, more specifically, the control of sexual gratification.

In order to adjust the old culture to the new technological age, we must concentrate on altering our motivations and redirecting the premises of the old culture as they are found in existing institutions. Altering motivations can occur superficially by eliminating our assumptions about scarcity and supply-and-demand which have given incentive to our product makers. More significantly, it can be done through reform of the ways in which we raise our children. This can be achieved by creating communities in which children are not socialized by their parents, where parents do not live vicariously through their children, where the middle-aged and elderly are as important as anyone else, and where life occurs in the present rather than the future.

We can see how change occurs in the university which shelters both the new and old attitudinal forces. Universities cannot ignore the new culture, but they are threatened because they are supported by the old culture. Slater feels that if universities survive change, then the entire society might be able to do the same.

We must become aware of the condition which has been caused by the frustration between the old and new cultures, not only on the cognitive-ideological level, but also the emotional-visceral one. We observe change in the ways in which we are connected: organically, mechanically, symbolically, consciously, unconsciously, bodily, verbally, etc. The presently divided culture tends to substitute bureaucratic connections for emotional ones, to vitalize the individual rather than society, and to stress control, mastery, self-discipline, and technique. We must "attune" ourselves to be responsive to our needs; this involves taking risks in order to fulfill a commitment; it means testing our ability to be in harmony with nature, which can heal itself ecologically.

The latter is in contrast to our tendency to destroy as well as disconnect ourselves from the environment, while thinking that we are controlling and getting closer to it. As Slater sees it, "pollution is an inescapable part of humanity's relationship with the environment." Pollution is created not only by organic wastes but also by psychic wastes that take material form (e.g., cars) and are a product of our feelings of loneliness and alienation from the enviroment, which we seek to control technologically. Thus, committing ourselves to finding our responsiveness entails a reassessment of our place as participating members of a total ecology, rather than as individuals, separate and self-sufficient. As we look at our individual capabilities and seeming integrities, we set up standards which violate natural tendencies that "ultimately have higher survival value . . . since they serve to reconnect the individual with his or her environment." These natural tendencies reflect our connectedness with our bodies and nature and normal emotions despite the problems posed by technology. In effect, we are trying to reject the mechanical environmental schema which Western society had propagated.

According to Slater, we should steer in the direction of 1) *decentralization*: reroute our energies away from bureaucratic authoritarian channels of communication; 2) *deceleration*: become less transitory and return to our roots; 3) *depolarization*: shrink back from prescribed specialized roles; 4) *reconnection*: shed the idea of narcissism and, by collectively sharing our lives and experiences, become aware of our emotions.

In the epilogue to *Earthwalk,* Slater summarizes what we must do in order to return to ourselves and our environment: "We need . . . to listen, sense, and be here; to retrieve what we have cast off, to repossess what we have projected onto others, to make whole what we have truncated; to move together in a reciprocal dance of integrity and grace."

REFERENCES

Philip Slater, *The Glory of Hera.* Boston: Beacon Press, 1968.

―――, *The Pursuit of Loneliness, American Culture at the Breaking Point.* Boston: Beacon Press, 1970.

―――, *Earthwalk.* New York: Doubleday & Co., 1974.

Philip Slater and W. G. Bennis, *The Temporary Society.* New York: Harper & Row, 1968.

PAOLO SOLERI (1919–), an Italian-American architect, is the founder of *arcology,* a philosophy which, like the word itself, calls for the combination of architecture and ecology toward realizing the creation of organic and functional communities called *arcologies*.

Born in Italy, Soleri went with his family to Grenoble, France, at a young age, to join his father who had fled there to escape fascism. He studied at the Ecole d'Art Industriel. In 1935, Soleri returned to Italy to study at the Torino Accademia Albertine in the Liceo Artistico. In 1941, he entered the Turin Polytechnical Institute and after time spent in the engineering corps of the Italian Army, received his doctorate in architecture in 1946. Soleri worked in association with Frank Lloyd Wright from 1947–48, before leaving to begin work on his own ideas. His "House in the Desert," which has a glass dome roof that opens and closes as well as rotates according to weather and the position of the sun, is one of the best-known realizations of Soleri's architectural style.

In 1952, Solemne Artistic Ceramics commissioned Soleri to design a factory. The result is an example of Soleri's principle of maximum utilization of minimal space: The upper floors of the factory are cantilevered from the side of a cliff where the building is situated among other constructions, thereby facilitating the factory's production capacity. In 1955, Soleri moved to Scottsdale, Arizona, where he built a studio and house, the interior of which is excavated underneath the earthen cast roof. Soleri established the Cosanti Foundation in 1961 for the purpose of developing and applying his architectural ideas. "Arcosanti" is an experimental project, begun in 1970, and is an implementation of Soleri's arcology. Located on a site near Phoenix, this miniarcology is a vertical structure which will eventually be twenty-five stories in height, and house three thousand people. The University of Arizona sponsors summer sessions for students who wish to help Soleri realize his "organism of a thousand minds."

In 1970, Soleri achieved national and international acclaim as the result of an exhibition of his drawings and models at the Corcoran Gallery of Art, Washington, D.C., and the Whitney Museum of American Art, New York City. Since then Soleri has written *The Bridge Between Matter and Spirit Is Matter Becoming Spirit,* a description of arcological philosophy.

Soleri bases his work on the importance of the interaction that exists between people and the environment: ". . . we are what we make of our environment." He criticizes the oversights of technologists, energy experts, environmentalists, social engineers, politicians, of the "ineffable relationship" between what he calls "the quality of life" and its complex structure. Humanness has been ignored or avoided in the consideration of the structuring of livable situations in this stage of man's evolution. Soleri contends that the process of "urbanizing civilization" must be handled in terms of the coordination and synthesis of man and environment, allowing architecture to assume a positive ecologically based role in the "shaping of man's sociological identity." Instrumental to the creation of such a condition is a process of *vectoralization,* which Soleri sees as 1) a means to redirect priorities, 2) a means to restore the interrelationships between matter and mind, 3) a means to introduce the concept and experience of evolution, 4) a means to achieve a balance between the phenomena of esthetics and performance.

Soleri defines an arcology as an architectural organism identifiable with three-dimensional landscape "of such character and dimensions to be ecologically relevant." When realized, an arcology would embody the advantages of both urban and rural life, minimizing the problems inherent in relating the two living conditions (e.g., commuting, energy, waste, etc.). Leaving the concept of the one-layered city behind, arcologies would be high-density vertical structures, incorporating all aspects of life into one (work, education, recreation, etc.). They would embody the idea of *miniaturization* (spatial arrangements that organize social stresses) which Soleri feels is necessary for the assimilation of the increasing complexity of man. Miniaturization would occur as an increasing number of integrated functions taking place in appropriately shrinking spaces. According to Soleri, this would determine the explosion of creativity, ". . . the powerful thrust of the mental processes beyond the physical barriers of the mineral world."

Arcologies would be a means of assimilating the growing population as they can accommodate thousands to millions of people: ". . . It has become an immediate necessity that the modular nature of civilization, represented by the 'city,' moves towards the hyper-density possible by a truly three-dimensional evolution: upward for the living, downward for the automated services and production. . . ." The services in arcologies, according to Soleri, would by necessity equal 25 per cent of the bulk of services found in the present-day city due to its self-containment. Their operation would deflate the "service-administration-bureaucracy machinery" and therefore decrease the number of people necessary to maintain the "in-human" services, thus freeing others to contemplate the needs of humanity toward achieving a "metaphysical harmony."

Soleri envisions technology becoming an instrument to synthesize events, rather than a ruler of future activities. Technology is a means to create a transtechnological universe; it becomes the skill, the "how" necessary to build the structure that is the "skeleton of the spirit." Technology offers the methodology for realizing complexity, miniaturization, and the "durational deployment." If a civilization is to evolve, it can no longer use technology to focus on local problems, but rather must use technology to envelop the total problem: how to transfigure survival into esthetic experience.

Soleri believes that ". . . for real man, the city is the Civitate Dei." This City of God would operate on the basis of the transfiguration of man into spirit, as the means to survive. It would trigger man's compassion, intensity, and commitment in a life where economy, politics, and morals take second place to "the trans-biological creation of reality resultant from the combined thrust of genetic etherealization . . . and cultural metamorphosis . . ." The Civitate Dei would be the home of the Mutant Man.

REFERENCES

Catalogue for the 1970 exhibition of Soleri's work at the Corcoran Gallery of Art in Washington, D.C.

Paolo Soleri, *The Bridge Between Matter and Spirit Is Matter Becoming Spirit: The Arcology of Paolo Soleri.* New York: Anchor Books, 1973.

————, *Arcology: The City in the Image of Man.* Cambridge, Mass.: M.I.T. Press, 1969.

SPORTS PSYCHOLOGY. In the decade of the sixties, through the work of Thomas Tutko and his assistants, it was discovered that many of the problems encountered in coaching team sports were psychologically based. This revelation led to the founding of the Institute of Athletic Motivation at San Jose State University, where coaches were trained in "team behavioral science" to improve their relationships with athletes. The practice of sports psychology became instrumental in reshaping the attitudes of team sports players in order to better realize their sports potential. This method of coaching has been used in the Soviet Union, Japan, Czechoslovakia, and East Germany, as well as the United States. Today, sports psychology is well known to the general public and can be used in improving participation in team sports as well as individual sports such as tennis, jogging, golf, swimming, etc. Since the 1960s, the literature on sports psychology has increased, several books resulting from the training conducted at the Institute of Athletic Motivation.

The physical aspect of sports is commonly emphasized to the point where the psychological aspect is ignored and undeveloped. Thomas Tutko, a professor of psychology at San Jose, observed that the emotional content of sports is derived from three sources: the *intrinsic pressure* that evolves from the physical challenge; the *cultural pressure* that is a result of social criteria for good athletic performance; and *personal pressure* that is a result of your own feelings about and reactions to the sport in which you are engaged. Tutko believes that every athlete has to handle a combination of these three pressures which are in constant interaction.

Your emotional state crucially affects your physical performance. The stimulus posed by a game sets off a series of responses in your body. The adrenal glands release the hormones adrenalin, cortisone, epinephrine, and nonepinephrine. Muscle tension increases, rate of heartbeat and breathing increases, the bronchial tubes constrict, digestion processes are halted, the esophagus contracts, and blood begins to flow to larger muscles, leaving the small subcutaneous blood vessels and the vessels in the extremities almost incapacitated. If this syndrome of physical change occurs at the wrong time, tension and anxiety result in the form of physical disruptions such as shortness of breath, blurred vision, extreme tightness of muscles, muscle fatigue, and disrupted coordination; the possibility of injury is increased. Your anxieties can detract from your alertness, concentration, strategy, and exercise of good judgment in a game. According to Tutko, this anxiety will hypnotize you in the sense that you will do exactly what you have the most fear of doing, even causing injury to yourself.

In general, this physical debilitation is the result of an exaggeration of the pressures that affect you in a game. The key to preventing unsatisfactory sports performance lies in the development of your ability to make your emotions control your game rather than hinder it. For this Tutko has designed a program, originally conceived for use by professional athletes, that consists of three stages. The first is learning generally about the psychological dimensions of games. The second stage involves seeing how these psychological elements affect your performance. To help you heighten your awareness, Tutko has designed the "Sports Emotional-Reaction Profile" (SERP). The third stage involves learning specific techniques for handling what you have perceived as the problems that hinder your game. "Sports psyching" techniques initially take six weeks to develop, according to Tutko's plan. They prepare you to meet the emotional, mental, and physical challenges of the sport; the techniques will become increasingly effective the longer they are practiced on a regular basis. They can be used in warm-ups, between plays to increase consistency, and to relieve tension preliminary to the experience of new strategies, new sports equipment, or an altogether new sport.

Tutko emphasizes the disadvantages of so-called "psyching-out" techniques which are intended to instill fear in another player, but do not develop or improve your own performance; in essence, they simply demonstrate your weaknesses and vulnerability. The best defense against being psyched-out is your awareness of what feelings another player could evoke in you to divert your attention from a game.

The intention of sports psychology is to create a physical and mental attitude in you which will improve your game, as well as enable you to enjoy a sport more fully. In its broadest applications, sports psychology can be applied to your general behavior patterns, increasing your ability to concentrate and relax, lessening your anxieties, and allowing you to assume responsibility for your enjoyment of life.

REFERENCES

W. Timothy Gallwey, *The Inner Game of Tennis*. New York: Random House, 1974.

George Leonard, *The Ultimate Athlete*. New York: Viking Press, 1975.

Thomas Tutko, Ph.D., and Umberto Tosi, *Sports Psyching: Playing Your Best Game All of the Time*. Los Angeles: J. P. Tarcher, 1976.

THE STILLMAN DIET, designed by Irwin Maxwell Stillman, M.D., is a high-protein diet designed for quick weight loss. Stillman was attending physician in medicine at Coney Island Hospital and Harbor Hospital. He was a clinical instructor in medicine at Long Island College Hospital, and a fellow of the American Geriatric Society. He also worked as a consultant in internal medicine at Coney Island Hospital in Brooklyn, New York. Stillman died in 1975, at the age of seventy-nine.

Stillman successfully treated over ten thousand patients, most of whom had not been able to cope with a balanced low-calorie diet to lose weight. He developed his Quick Weight Loss diet as a result of his concern with the overall detrimental effects of obesity or overweight, i.e., high blood pressure, hardening of the arteries, diabetes, arthritis, heart attack, etc.

The Quick Weight Loss diet follows Stillman's theory that "quick action dieting which alters radically and suddenly your ways of eating is the best way to reduce," and that regular balanced dieting, which entails counting calories, fails because it is such a slow and tedious process. The reason the diet is successful is because of several factors: 1) You lose weight quickly, which encourages you to stay on the diet, even when eating out; 2) you can go back on the diet any time in order to lose any weight gained after going off the diet; 3) the foods allowed on the diet satisfy hunger because of the filling nature of high-protein foods, so food consumption becomes "self-limiting."

The food allowed on the Stillman diet is highly restricted to mainly lean meats, fish, eggs, cottage cheese. Fats, oils, and carbohydrates are strictly forbidden. By essentially eating only high-protein foods, the metabolism and chemistry of the body change, causing the body to begin to burn up its own fat for energy because it is receiving no readily available carbohydrates or sugars. Stored body fat is broken down into a small amount of carbohydrate and sugar, as well as fatty acids which provide the necessary energy and heat. Approximately 60 per cent of the fat is oxidized completely into carbon dioxide and water. The residue (fatty acids) is eliminated through the kidneys. Because fatty acids are irritating to the kidneys, it is essential to drink large amounts to water every day.

Stillman contends that you are better off eating six small meals a day rather than three large meals, but it is necessary that you eat only from the food list he specifies for the diet: for example, lean meats trimmed of fat, chicken and turkey without the skin, lean fish such as haddock, flounder; eggs poached or boiled or fried without using grease; nonfat cottage cheese or farmer cheese; black coffee or tea, club soda, noncaloric beverages.

The Quick Weight Loss diet is for those overweight adults who are otherwise healthy. However, Stillman recommends that you consult with your doctor before starting the diet, and have a checkup while you are on the diet. He recommends that a daily vitamin and mineral tablet supplement be taken while on the diet. If the diet is adhered to, weight loss is rapid, i.e., six to seven pounds average in extreme overweight cases in the first three days.

Stillman also designed a Quick Inches-Off diet, to follow the Quick Weight Loss diet, which is geared to pull fat out of the muscles and reduce the size of the muscle cell by pulling out some of the protein. The foods allowed on this diet contain minimal amounts of protein. A moderate amount of exercise twice a day for three to five minutes should accompany this diet, to firm the body and tone the muscles. The kinds of exercising Stillman recommends are swimming, bicycling, walking, as well as some specific exercises designed for firming the neck and chin, the bosom, the chest area, the upper and lower back, the upper arms, the abdomen, hips, buttocks, thighs.

The Stillman diets have been widely criticized for their lack of nutritional balance. They contain little or no carbohydrates, which doctors and nutritionists claim is harmful to the body because it causes metabolic changes, inducing fatigue and other complications. Dr. Harold Yacowitz of Fairleigh Dickinson University has speculated that Stillman-type diets could create a breakdown in body protein and bone. The Harvard Medical School in a study of the diets found that they could create a significant rise in blood cholesterol levels. Pregnant women have been cautioned against this type of diet because the metabolic changes that occur could injure the unborn child. Dieters with kidney and liver disease are also cautioned against this kind of dieting.

Despite these criticisms, the Stillman diets can work successfully for weight loss. Precautionary measures (e.g., a checkup) are advisable to determine if you are physically fit before beginning such a diet.

REFERENCES

Irwin Maxwell Stillman, M.D., and Samm Sinclair Baker, *The Doctor's Quick Weight Loss Diet.* New York: Dell Books, 1974.

————, *The Doctor's Inches Off Diet.* New York: Dell Books, 1974.

Theodore Berland and the editors of *Consumer Guide, Rating the Diets.* Publications International, Ltd., 1976.

STRUCTURAL INTEGRATION, popularly known as *rolfing,* was conceived by Ida Rolf as a method for improving the physical structure of the body. Rolf (1896–) was born in New York City. She received her Ph.D. in biochemistry and physiology from Columbia University in 1920. For twelve years, she worked with the Rockefeller Institute as an organic chemist. Rolf researched structural integration for forty years, using knowledge gained from her education, her interest in yoga, and the necessity of treating her own arthritic condition. She is currently director of the Rolf Institute in Boulder, Colorado, where "rolfers" are trained and research is conducted.

Rolfing is concerned with the relationship between the human body and gravity. Since we are bipeds, we have a tendency to put our bodies in unstable, although potentially flexible, positions. Because of this fact, we should keep our weight distributed about a central vertical axis, thereby maintaining good posture. It is this vertical axis upon which gravity acts. However, as Rolf has determined, most of us move away from this axis. Rolf analyzes the body in terms of a group of stacked, partially independent weight segments (head, shoulders, thorax, pelvis, legs). The result of moving away from the axis is the displacement of these segments. This causes an imbalance of the body and the tendency of the body to remain imbalanced, gravity working as a negative force to reinforce the imbalance. As a result, the segments of your body weight become comfortable in their shifted positions and both your skeleton and muscles support weight improperly. The consequences are increasing tension, tightness, and shortening of the fascia tissue. Fascia tissue surrounds the muscles and organs, and controls the positioning of the weight segments. Overall, the result is a decrease in the body's ability to move; the restriction of the joints; the constriction of circulation; chronic muscle tension; bad posture; and certain somatically derived psychological disturbances. "Stresses, aches, and pains" become "the body's language to express the strained imbalance between the field of gravity and the body integrals." The purpose of rolfing is to relieve this condition, restoring the proper fascial structure of the body, realigning the body's weight segments, and restoring normal economic body movement through the integration of body parts so that the forces acting upon the whole body act positively.

Rolfing is a process of deep massage or manipulation. The technique involves the exertion of force on parts of the whole body to reshape them and put them back where they belong. The fascial tissue is moved "in the specific direction demanded by its original design." The rolfer applies pressure with fingers, knuckles, or elbows to the places where there is tension, usually in a variety of muscles and tendons; once the body is restricted in any area, the restriction tends to spread. According to Rolf, the deeper layers of the fascia are relieved of their tension only after the superficial fascial layers have been relaxed. The movement of the fascial tissue can cause a great deal of pain, which eases when the rolfer removes the pressure. This pain has been equated with emotional release.

The immediate residual effect of rolfing is a feeling of trembling or lightheadedness, and soreness for a few days. More long-range effects are visible in the body's structural readjustment to its axial placements. The body lengthens and centers along the central vertical axis; body flexors and extensors work cooperatively again; the deep muscles begin to work with the superficial muscles; the body feels light and uses the effect of gravity positively. The body adjusts along its horizontal axis, where the shoulders and arms move, and along what Rolf calls the "Z axis," the line of motion of the leg. The joints are freed to move, creating greater rotational and hinging capacity of the body's weight segments. Less energy is required for movement, patterns of movement change, and the body is balanced and more self-contained.

The psychological effects of rolfing can be described as a kind of consciousness raising. Studies have shown that attitudinal changes occur in people who have experienced rolfing; they feel lighter and can do more, physically and mentally, with ease. The emotional tension that has been released aids in the process of body integration.

Research into the electrical activity of muscles in motion and neurological control of muscles was done by Valerie Hunt, director of the Movement Behavior Laboratory at UCLA, and Julian Silverman of the California Department of Mental Hygiene. Their conclusion is that "rolfing creates a more spontaneous, open, rhythmic reaction to the environment and to one's own kinesthetic and proprioceptive sensations." Rolfing encourages not only the efficient use of muscles, but also a decrease in energy used, more adequate response of the body in motion, and a shifting of movement control to the reflexive centers of the spine.

A rolfing program is conducted in ten one-hour sessions. In the first seven sessions, the rolfer will concentrate on various parts of the patient's body: in the first hour, on the chest and abdomen and the muscles around the hips; in the second hour, on the feet and legs, etc. Manipulation of the neck and other areas of tension is usually done in each session for the relief of superficial tension. The final three sessions concentrate on the reintegration of the entire body along its axial lines.

Judith Aston, using Rolf's theories, has created a program called "structural patterning," which is designed to be used in conjunction with rolfing sessions. It is a method of reeducating your basic pattern of movement so you may become more efficient in the motions of daily life (e.g., walking, bending, lifting, etc.), or in more specialized movements; rolfing has proved to be especially effective for athletes.

REFERENCES

Kalen Hammann, Ph.D., "What Structural Integration (Rolfing) Is and Why It Works," *The Osteopathic Physician,* March 1972, reprint.

Roger Pierce, Ph.D., *An Introduction to Rolfing (Structural Integration),* monograph, Rolf Institute, 1976.

Ida P. Rolf, "Structural Integration: A Contribution to the Understanding of Stress," reprint from *Confinia Psychiatrica.*

———, *Structural Integration: Gravity, An Unexplored Factor in a More Human Use of Human Beings,* monograph, Rolf Institute, 1972.

Sue Turner, "Structural Integration and Stress," *Aquatic World,* March 1976, reprint.

Gene Vier, "Rolfing: How It Works," *Let's Live: The Natural Way to Vibrant Health,* November 1974.

———, "Sing the Body Electric," *Psychology Today,* October 1970, reprint.

HARRY STACK SULLIVAN (1892–1949),

a psychiatrist known for his revision of psychiatry in relationship to the social sciences, studied schizophrenia with William Alanson White, superintendent of St. Elizabeth's Hospital in Washington, D.C. From 1923–30, he was

assistant physician and then director of clinical research
at Sheppard and Enoch Pratt Hospital in Towson,
Maryland. During this time, he was also associate professor of psychiatry at the University of Maryland. In
1930, he began a private practice in New York City
with the aim of studying the obsessional processes of
his patients. He had formal analytic training with
Clara Thompson, M.D. Sullivan worked with Harold
D. Lasswell, Lawrence F. Frank, and others to synthesize the findings of psychiatry with social sciences in a
meaningful way. In the late thirties, Sullivan operated
the Washington School of Psychiatry and worked with
the William Alanson White Foundation, whose purpose
was to cooperate with the government in planning
methods for preventive psychiatry. He delivered the
first lectures sponsored by the White Foundation at the
U.S. Department of the Interior in 1939. Sullivan also
served as editor and political commentator for the
journal *Psychiatry* for twelve years.

The foundation of Sullivan's theories and techniques
is rooted in his studies with White, whose work centered in psychiatry as a treatment applicable to the
whole of humanity in all its endeavors as well as to
the mentally ill. Sullivan's definition of psychiatry is "the
study of processes that involve or go on between people." Thus, psychiatry becomes a field of observation
of interpersonal relations in any circumstance. Crucial
to interpersonal relations is personality, defined by
Sullivan as "the relatively enduring patterns of re-
current interpersonal relations which characterize a
human life." Personality is not a factor which can be
isolated from the network of interpersonal relations in
which we exist. Sullivan's methodology focuses on improving the techniques of human performance through
the integration of persons on an interpersonal level.

Our "performance" is based on our acts and speech.
Our acts, which are interpersonal, can be grouped into
two categories: those that are satisfactions, and those
that are security. Satisfactions are acts performed to

achieve an end state and are connected with bodily organization, e.g., desires for food, drink, sleep, sex, etc. Acts of security reflect the culture which has influenced our movements, actions, speech, thought, and, on a larger scale, our social institutions, traditions, and customs. Satisfactions and securities are closely related in terms of conditioning which, in turn, is connected with our feelings of power, essentially inborn. We gain satisfaction and security through the use of power in interpersonal relations.

Sullivan's concept of infancy is an important factor in his interpersonal relations. Infancy is designed around *empathy* and *symbol activities*. Empathy is defined as the unique emotional link between child and mother (or nurse). The symbol activities of the child occur on three levels: the *prototaxic* level pertains to the symbolization occurring without formal distinctions, without references to the ego, without connections in time and space; the *parataxic* level pertains to the discrimination between the child and the rest of the world when the original wholeness of the world is destroyed; and the third level is the *artistic* level which manifests itself in the verbalization of the distinctions which have been made in the parataxic level.

As children, we begin to create our personalities and *self-dynamism,* which Sullivan defines as "a relatively enduring configuration of energy which manifests itself in characterizable processes in interpersonal relations." Empathy and symbol activities are fundamental in the development of self-dynamism. *Anxiety* is equally fundamental. Anxiety occurs as feelings of discomfort which are the result of the child's "empathized" disapproval of the mother (or nurse) who has shown disapproval of the child's performance. Anxiety, according to Sullivan, is a tool which we use as children to restrict our activities in order to avoid experiencing disapproval which may create a new anxiety. The development of our self is geared to what we learn from adults. Self-dynamism, through anxiety, selects and organizes the determinants for the growth of the self in terms of direction, characteristics, and interpersonal relations (or "me-you" patterns). The limit to self-dynamism is the personality.

Personality manifests itself only in interpersonal relations. It includes the self, all its me-you patterns, as well as what exists outside of awareness as a result of "selective inattention" and "dissociation." Personality is the seat of creativity and innovative thought. Through it, self-dynamism, or the self-system, can become richer through greater self-awareness. The personality directs us toward mental health.

Personality development occurs in several stages: In infancy, we begin to delimit our experiences empathetically with the vague identification to the one that mothers us, and we begin to establish our realm of power. In childhood, the self-system created in infancy becomes acculturated with the learning of language, eating habits, toilet habits, etc. In childhood, the organization of anxiety is a quality of the instrumentality of the self. The juvenile period marks the beginning of cooperation with others (play). In preadolescence (eight and a half to twelve years), the capacity to love is developed. Love exists when another person becomes as important as ourself. In adolescence, we mature physically (puberty) and experience sexual impulses. Reaching mature adulthood requires our development of self-respect and an equally intense respect for others "with the dignity that befits high achievement of the competent personality and with the freedom of personal initiative that represents a comfortable adaptation of one's personal situation to the circumstances that characterize the social order of which one is a part."

The interpersonal situation, the process of interaction between two or more individuals, rather than the unobserved fixed drives, is the object of Sullivan's study. Drives are manifested in a tendency toward actions and coming together in dynamism. The behavior of the interaction is varied and always changing, and therefore susceptible to reorientation. Observation of action indicates the character of the interaction to the observer or psychiatrist, who, in order to interpret the observed behavior, must use theories and insights learned through experience as well as knowledge of his own self-system. According to Sullivan, interpretation should meet the requirements of adequacy with respect to the observations to which it is applied, and of its exclusiveness with respect to other conjectures which might pertain to the data of observation.

When interpersonal relations are inadequate for the situation in which we are involved, or are complex as a result of the memories of past interpersonal relations (i.e., with regard to parents), mental disorders occur. The mentally ill are unable to feel, sense, or understand the uniqueness and differences among interpersonal relations. When we understand what we are doing, when we expand ourselves to grasp the significance of uncomplicated interpersonal relations, when we are knowledgeable of ourselves and have greater insight into the social order as it exists and are able to enjoy richer experiences, we have mental health.

Sullivan delivered his lectures at the U.S. Department of the Interior and they were published in *Psychiatry*. In 1947, the William Alanson White Foundation authorized the reprinting of the lectures for students, and they were used as a textbook in several universities. *Conceptions of Modern Psychiatry* was the only book of Sullivan's writings to be published during his lifetime.

REFERENCES

Harry Stack Sullivan, *Conceptions of Modern Psychiatry.* New York: W. W. Norton & Co., 1940.

————, *The Interpersonal Theory of Psychiatry.* New York: W. W. Norton & Co., 1953.

————, *The Fusion of Psychiatry and Social Science.* New York: W. W. Norton & Co., 1964.

SYNECTICS (from the Greek, meaning the joining together of different and apparently irrelevant elements) is a management creativity technique developed by William J. J. Gordon to encourage success in the solving of problems and the invention of new ideas especially related to business. Gordon began his research into the technique in 1944, aided by people from Invention-Research Group in Cambridge, Massachusetts, Arthur D. Little, Inc., Harvard University, and the Rockefeller Foundation. This research intended to reveal "the psychological mechanisms basic to creative activity." To do this, Synectics groups were formed, consisting of people who differed in personality, educational background, and professional status. (The criteria for selection of persons were later expanded to include emotional constitution.) According to Gordon, the group situation was intended to force "each participant to verbalize his thoughts and feelings about the problem at hand," thereby bringing "elements of the process out into the open where they can be identified and analyzed." In this way, human creativity could be seen operationally through interaction.

According to Gordon, the initial assumptions of his theory were: 1) that the human creative process can be so described that the description can be integrated into a teaching methodology which would promote "the creative output of both individuals and groups"; 2) that the psychic processes involved in general creativity are also found in the "cultural phenomena of invention in the arts and sciences"; and 3) that the creative process of the individual is paralleled in the creative process of a group.

After testing these assumptions in group operations, the theory was expanded to include the following hypotheses: 1) that creative efficiency can be increased provided the individual understands the psychological process by which he or she operates; 2) that in the creative process, the emotional and irrational components are more important than the intellectual and rational ones; 3) that the emotional irrational components are the key to increasing the probability of success in problem solving and invention.

In practice, Synectics involves the establishment of a

group which occurs in three phases: selecting personnel; training them in Synectics; and reintegrating them into their "client environment." According to Synectic theory, the subconscious is considered a major force in the creative process. Therefore, Synectics entails the use of concrete mechanisms which trigger the activity of the subconscious. Concrete mechanisms are ". . . psychological factors which support and press forward creative process." However, they "do not pertain to the motivations for creative activity, nor are they intended to be used to judge the ultimate product of an esthetic or technical invention."

The process becomes twofold: making the strange familiar, and making the familiar strange. The former involves understanding the problem at hand through analysis, a basic move in any problem-solving situation. Synectics, however, doesn't stop here. Rather, it emphasizes the necessity to look at a problem from a unique viewpoint in order to elicit a new basic solution, i.e., making the familiar strange. As described by Gordon: "To make the familiar strange is to distort, invert or transpose the everyday ways of looking and responding which render the world a secure and familiar place." In Synectics groups, the means developed for making the familiar strange are characteristically metaphorical. They are personal analogy, direct analogy, symbolic analogy, and fantasy analogy. The latter are considered "specific and reproducible mental processes, tools to initiate the motion of creative process and to sustain and renew that motion." Through practice, these mechanisms can become "habitual as ways of seeing and acting," consciously or subconsciously.

Personal analogy allows you to identify with an element of a problem and, thus, view it apart from how it was recognized in previous analysis. According to Gordon, personal analogy "demands extensive loss of self" in order to avoid the hesitation to think differently. *Direct analogy* involves seeing an element of a problem in comparison with a parallel fact, knowledge, or technology. *Symbolic analogy* employs objective and impersonal images to approach and describe the problem. In a sense, this mechanism functions poetically; its advantage is its immediacy as compared to direct or personal analogy. *Fantasy analogy* is a way to express wish fulfillment in an artful rather than scientific way. This kind of analogy serves to lay the groundwork for the use of other mechanisms.

On the whole, the Synectics process involves the oscillation between the discoveries of new viewpoints in the analogy process and the comparing of analogies with actual elements of the problem. Of this, Gordon says: "Individuals who can learn (or who already know) how to entertain a great variety of variables without becoming confused are much more apt to be effective in a creative situation . . . the price they pay is exhaustion which is physical."

The most important aspect of a Synectics group is the implementation of what has been created as a solution to a problem, which takes the form of a working model for a new product or invention, for example. The successful testing of the discoveries made through the use of Synectics proves the operational effectiveness of the theory on which the mechanisms are based. Synectics has proved most successful in industry, especially with regard to product improvement. It can also be applied in government, education, and the arts. Gordon's book, *Synectics: The Development of Creative Capacity,* documents case studies of the use of the Synectics process.

REFERENCE

William J. J. Gordon, *Synectics: The Development of Creative Capacity.* London: Collier-Macmillan, Ltd., 1961.

T'AI CHI CH'UAN is a Chinese system of exercise dating back to A.D. 1000. Its development is credited to Chang San-Feng, a philosopher of the Sung dynasty, who combined Confucian and Taoist views with his own experiential philosophy for the purpose of expanding contemporary exercise systems in the creation of new forms and techniques. The goal of T'ai Chi Ch'uan is the development of your intrinsic and potential powers, a concern that differs from the concerns of ancient Chinese schools of philosophy. The mode of exercise of T'ai Chi Ch'uan involves the utilization of both mind and body in order to achieve two of its main goals: health and tranquility.

Ch'uan literally means "fist." Figuratively, it implies action, connoting power and control and culminating in the essence of organized movement and the ultimate protection of the self. In ancient Chinese thought, the fist is symbolic of concentration, isolation, and containment. Ch'uan is basically techniques of organized harmonious forms in which a continuity of action is maintained so that each movement becomes a part of the next movement, and all movements are one. Ch'uan indicates mental and physical coordination. This is based on the premise that if your body functions in a healthy way, your mind will function effectively; the mind, as spirit, is the driving force behind the body.

T'ai Chi represents the concept that the whole of life is composed of, and has been set in motion by, the continual complementary interaction between two vital energies: *yin,* as the passive principle, and *yang,* as the active principle. T'ai Chi is a circle divided into two curved shapes of equal size. The right side, which is dark, represents yin. The left side, which is light, represents yang. A dot of the opposite color is found in each curved shape of the circle; this represents the concept that yin and yang are part of each other. The line between yin and yang is in the form of a wave, and acts as a wave in the manner in which it rises and falls. Rising and falling are yin and yang.

All movement represents the continuity of life force. In T'ai Chi Ch'uan, the opposite elements are balanced, harmonious, and have a perfect relationship. In the practice of T'ai Chi Ch'uan, the benefits are both physical and psychological. You become aware of your intrinsic energy. Your mind, in concentration, directs your energies to exercise your body. You develop energy and strength without becoming fatigued. You experience vitality without nervousness. Most importantly, you become tranquil. According to the *I Ching,* you are tranquil when your "human faculties display all their resources, because they are enlightened by reason and sustained by knowledge."

In the practice of T'ai Chi Ch'uan, the structure of movement is based on *forms* from which all movement originates, evolving into patterns. All movement flows continuously in a *soft* style. Energy is not unnecessarily expended; energy is developed. No single part of the body is ever overexhilarated. As you move from form to form, it is essential to pay attention to every motion in order to achieve physical and emotional equilibrium. For this reason, it is necessary that your power of concentration be developed.

Movement of forms is patterned so that strong alternates with light, active with calm, expansion with contraction, in a constant and consistent slowly executed sequence of events. The yin and yang are integral to the configuration of forms. Each form is comprised of a totality in which one part of the body is quiet and another is active, or all body weight is on one side, while the other is weightless and flexible, or one hand is in a yin position and the other in a yang position. The principles of yin and yang also apply to the way you use your inner power to control external action. To the observer, your motion will seem effortless, easy, and without energy. This is the result of focusing your mind to create a continuous, soft, intrinsic line of motion with your body.

Since body action works as one with the mind, the techniques of T'ai Chi Ch'uan are not automatic. The flow of forms is logical. The mind must apply the logic of the flow in order not to upset the continuity of motion. The procedure of the forms is designed so that the mind and body work with alternating intensity; this way, there is time for both mental and physical rest, although the mind never strays from controlling the action of the body.

The intrinsic principles of T'ai Chi Ch'uan are softness and circular motion. Softness is seen in the unstrained nature of your motion. Moving slowly and continuously allows free circulation so that you may store up energy. The softness of nonforced motion results in flexibility and resilience. The breath is never quick and the heartbeat never accelerates. Movements are calm and light. Circular movement is the basic pattern of all T'ai Chi Ch'uan movements. The forms are motions in the shapes of circles, arcs, curves, parabolas, executed in a certain direction and at a certain tempo. Circular movement helps to limit the extent of your body action (there are no extraneous movements in T'ai Chi Ch'uan). The circular movement is evenly paced and centered in your center of gravity; it functions so that no single part of the body is ever in continual motion or rest. The yin and yang elements move in and out of circular movement.

The five essential qualities of T'ai Chi Ch'uan are slowness, lightness, clarity, balance, and calmness. Slowness provides a means for developing awareness, patience, and poise. Lightness allows endless and continuous motion. Clarity addresses the pure function of the mind as it controls the body, rendering its action purely and accurately. Balance allows the body to act without strain. In order to have balance, you must have physical ability, an understanding of the forms, the ability to move evenly and control how you are *not* moving at the same time, an ability to control the changes of motion from yin to yang, mental awareness, and a calm spirit. Calmness allows you to concentrate so that you can sustain the structural integrity of the movement in and out of the forms.

There are basic positions in T'ai Chi Ch'uan which are rudimentary to realizing the forms and to the continuous flow of motion. Each requires a certain posture and stance. The way you step is regulated, the way you raise a leg, hold your hands, your eyes, the way your weight is shifted, the way you breathe. Each position requires a space orientation which enables you to move in patterns so that when the exercise is completed, you finish in the same place as you began.

Today, there are four styles of T'ai Chi Ch'uan being practiced: Yang, Wu, Ho, and Sun. The Wu style, which has been described here, focuses on self-development, philosophically as well as psychologically. It has become very popular as a result of a book by Sophia Delza, the first master of the Wu style in the Western world. Delza studied in China for many years with the Master Ma Yueh Liang.

REFERENCES

Sophia Delza, *T'ai Chi Ch'uan: An Ancient Chinese Way of Exercise to Achieve Health and Tranquility.* New York: Cornerstone, 1961.

Al Huang, *Embrace Tiger, Return to Mountain.* New York: Bantam Books, 1977.

I Ching, trans. by James Legge. New York: Dover Publications, 1963.

TANTRIC SEX is a form of yoga that is concerned with the control or harnessing of sexual energy. It derives from Buddhist or Hindu scripture, the Tantra, which calls for the worship through certain rituals and ceremonies of the Shakti, or Mother-Goddess, a female diety.

One of the most common elements in Indian philosophy is the concept of the absolute underlying the phenomenal universe. The Tantric view emphasizes the identity of both the absolute and the phenomenal world through the experience of *sadhana*. Sadhana elicits the merging of conceptual and intuitive extremes in a realization of the noninteractional absolute oneness of the universe. Essentially, Tantra can be considered a philosophy that describes the nature of and the relationship between male and female. The principles of Tantric philosophy are founded in the idea that through love,

456 /   TANTRIC SEX

which is both physical and emotional, a higher spiritual plane of being can be achieved. The goal of the Tantric sadhana and Tantric life is freedom from the misery of attachment achieved in the psychic unity—the result of an *enstatic* state.

The realization of an enstatic state comes through the immobilization of the breath, seminal fluid, and the mind. Breathing is regarded as the most conscious somatic function; breath control leads to the control of less conscious somatic functions such as the heartbeat. Controlling seminal fluid implies the control of all passions toward achieving a state of desirelessness. The control of the mind means the cessation of the functions of the mind on cognitive, conative, and volitional levels. The three processes of the mind are represented by the mandala, a sacred diagram of an equilinear triangle whose apex points downward, symbolizing the female principle, the three sides of which represent cognition, volition, and conation. To be engaged in all three processes of control simultaneously is the ultimate Tantric goal.

A yogi is taught to perform this triple control by a guru. The techniques vary in accordance with the physical and psychological makeup of the training yogi and his Shakti. Breath control is achieved by holding the breath for increasing periods of time, using a mantra as a time unit. The effect produced is one of euphoria. Breath control is then practiced in intercourse with the Shakti. Enstatic postures take many forms; for example, the female will sit astride the yogi who assumes the traditional yogic position. All the functions of the mind are transcended at a point of suspension, achieved when breath control and seminal retention are practiced in intercourse with the Shakti. The suspension of all object thought and concentration on the internal object of meditation culminate in enstasy.

In Tantric sex, the partners are nearly motionless. Because this static pose might cause the loss of the male's erection, the female learns through yoga exercises to use her vaginal muscles to maintain her partner's erection as well as her own state of excitement. When the female leans over her partner's body, she stimulates her clitoris, at the same time minimizing the pressure on the penis, which continues to delay orgasm in the male. The cycle of the sexual act is called *maithuna* and focuses on the female's capacity for response. The goal of the cycle is to delay the male orgasm entirely and bring about the female orgasm sooner and more frequently. Meditation is incorporated into the sexual act with both partners concentrating on one object: the other individual.

In contrast to traditional Western sexual practices, sexual intercourse in the Tantric manner can elicit sensations of complete unity between partners, dissolving the polarity of male-female identities. The emphasis, rather than being on arousal and culmination of the sex act in orgasm through a state of physical tension, is on the flow of sexual energy between the partners. More than simply a physical act, Tantric sex is a process of the mind aimed at experiencing the universe.

Kinsey, Masters and Johnson, and other sex experts have recognized that many of the principles of Tantric sex offer useful techniques for coping with common Western sexual problems.

A controversial aspect of Tantric sex, particularly in the West, is the use of drugs. Tantrics use drugs in order to facilitate the dissolving of ego and encourage the activity of meditation prior to sexual activity. Sometimes alcohol is used, although cannabis and mescaline (peyote) are claimed to be less risky because you can consciously reject their effects if you use them prudently. This "risk" is not one of overdose, but rather possible loss of potency. The idea behind the use of drugs is to extend the Tantric experience in real time and not to precipitate sexual arousal, which should be a natural occurrence in the Tantric ritual.

REFERENCES

Agehananda Bharati, *The Tantric Tradition*. New York. Anchor Books, 1965.

Omar Garrison, *Tantra: The Yoga of Sex.* New York: Julian Press, 1964.

Robert K. Moffett, *Tantric Sex.* New York: Berkley Publishing Corp., 1974.

THE TAROT, originally called the Book of Thoth, is a unique deck of cards which can be used as a fortune-telling device, and has existed since antiquity. The earliest recorded date attributed to a Tarot deck is 1390, although Hermetic philosophy contends that the Tarot existed thirty-five thousand years ago.

The stories of the origin of Tarot cards are numerous. Generally, the Tarot has been linked to the Egyptians. The pictures in the Major Arcana supposedly derive from the pages of the oldest book in the world of Hermes Trismegistus, counselor of Osiris, King of Egypt. Another story relates the origin of the Tarot to the city of Fez, which became the intellectual center of the world after the fall of Alexandria: The people of Fez created a universal language of pictures composed of mystical symbols, today called the Major Arcana. The Tarot has been related to Egyptian mythology, ancient Hebrew Cabala, the Chinese, and gypsies of India. It has been explained in the context of Rosicrucian systems of thought, numerology, astrology, the Hebrew alphabet, etc.

There are several different Tarot decks. The Egyptian deck has symbols that are universal in nature rather than specifically associated with fortune-telling. A. E. Waite, a British scholar, designed the Rider deck which is known for its clear, well-delineated pictures. This is the standard Tarot deck available today.

The Tarot can be used in four different areas of universal symbolism: as a science of vibration; as a spiritual science (these two applications are considered positive and scientific, electric and masculine in nature; they are rooted in the esoteric principles of life); as a system of divination by cards; and as a system of divination by numbers (these two applications are considered negative, magnetic, and feminine in nature, and rooted in the exoteric principles of life). The Jod-He-Vau-He, or *magical quaternary,* is a means by which these four systems can be related to signs of the zodiac (Leo, Scorpio, Taurus, Aquarius) and the elements (fire, water, earth, air).

The Tarot deck is made up of seventy-eight cards. Originally the cards were made of metal or leather. Today they are paper. Fifty-six cards are called the *Minor Arcana;* the remaining twenty-two cards are called the *Major Arcana.*

The Minor Arcana is divided into four suits and is similar to an ordinary deck of playing cards. The suits correspond to the thirty-six decans and four quadrants of the zodiac. The *Wands* (clubs) have a divinatory meaning associated with animation, enterprise, energy, and growth. They always appear with leaves on them and are identified with fire. The *Cups* (hearts) suggest love, or happiness, and are indications of emotion rather than intellect. They are always accompanied by a glyph, which refers to water. The *Swords* (spades) relate to aggression, ambition, force, courage, etc., and when accompanied by certain specific cards can indicate transformation, hatred, or war. They are identified with air and indicative of both the constructive and destructive world of activities. The *Pentacles* (diamonds), symbolically represented by circles surrounding five-pointed stars constructed from intersecting triangles, indicate situations involving finances. They are identified with earth and represent man's five senses, five elements of nature, and the five extremities of the human body. Each suit contains fourteen cards. Ten are numbered from ace to ten, and have different meanings. The remaining four cards, called the Court Arcana, are the King (spirit), the Queen (soul), the Knight (ego), and the Page (body).

The twenty-two cards which make up the Major Arcana are numbered from zero to twenty-one and depict by title a specific principle, law, power, or element in nature. Each card bears an individual picture or symbol. For example, one is the Magician, two the High Priestess, three the Empress, etc. The Fool is the zero card. These archetypal symbols stem from images which arise from the unconscious or the imagination, and characterize the workings of the mind. Theoretically, the Tarot is a medium through which your subconscious is channeled for the purpose of acquiring information relevant to your life activities. The accuracy of this information depends upon the concentration of your electromagnetic energy, which will allow subconscious thoughts to rise into consciousness. Therefore, prior to a reading, the more you handle the cards by shuffling and cutting them, the more your magnetism will be invested in the cards, facilitating the emergence of your subconscious.

The cards should be read on a flat wooden surface, used exclusively for the Tarot, that can accommodate the largest spread of the cards. You, both as querist and reader, should have your mind clearly focused on the question at hand, which can be personal, spiritual, or mundane in nature. You then shuffle the cards, cut them into three packs, and gather them together. This is done three times, before handing the cards to the reader who proceeds to lay them out, one at a time, according to the spread that has been selected.

There are different spreads that are used specifically for answering certain kinds of questions; the more cards used, the larger the spread, and the more complex the question being asked. For example, the "yes-or-no" spread requires five, seven, or nine cards, depending upon how much detail is desired in answer to the question. The Pyramid spread employs twenty-one cards spread out face down from left to right in the shape of a pyramid. It is used to answer a question, solve a problem, or demonstrate certain tendencies in your life. The Sephiroth spread uses twenty-six cards. The three-seven spread is specifically used for reading the past, present, or future. The Magic Seven spread, which is in the form of a six-pointed star, emphasizes the importance of the center card in answer to questions about the past, present, or future. The Solar spread uses seven rows of cards which read vertically relate to the planets, and horizontally, to the past, present, and future.

Throughout history, the interpretations of the Tarot have been mystical and secret, in keeping with the veil of divination that accompanies the cards. Until recently the literature concerning the Tarot has been concerned with its philosophy. Today there are many books which deal with the applications of the Tarot.

REFERENCES

Doris Chase Doane and King Keyes, *How to Read Tarot Cards.* New York: Funk and Wagnalls, 1967.

Eden Gray, *A Complete Guide to the Tarot.* New York: Bantam Books, 1971.

————, *The Tarot Revealed.* New York: New American Library, 1960.

A. E. Waite, *A Pictorial Key to the Tarot.* New York: University, 1959.

CHARLES T. TART (1937–) is known in the United States for his investigations of states of consciousness. Tart was born in Morrisville, Pennsylvania. He studied electrical engineering at M.I.T. and psychology at the University of North Carolina, where he received his Ph.D. He was an instructor in psychiatry at the Medical School of the University of Virginia and lecturer in psychology at Stanford University. Recently he taught humanistic and experimental psychology at the University of California at Davis, where he was an associate professor of psychology. Tart has done experimental work in the fields of psychophysiology, sleep and dreaming, hypnosis, and parapsychology. He is the author of *States of Consciousness* and author-editor of *Altered States of Consciousness,* a collection of essays on the scientific study of altered states of consciousness as they influence behavior.

Tart's aim was to develop a systems approach to viewing states of consciousness which would serve as a means to coherently relate the data of psychological research to the mind. Consciousness as a whole complex system can be broken down into parts whose functions, which can be studied in isolation, can only be understood when considered integral to the total system of consciousness: ". . . understanding the complexity of consciousness requires seeing it as a system and understanding its parts."

Tart analyzes the components of consciousness on the basis of human experience. The first aspect of consciousness is an awareness he calls *attention/awareness,* which can be conceptualized and experienced voluntarily despite its content, e.g., the awareness of a table is analogous to the awareness of a chair. Attention/awareness depends upon your state of consciousness and your personality structure. What are important psychologically, according to Tart, are the varying degrees of self-awareness that occur in the separation of attention/awareness from the content of the experience. Attention/awareness can be seen as the major *energy* of the mind within the context of ordinary experience: that which affects consciousness through volitional activation; that which creates phobias, blindnesses, long-term desires and concerns; and that which prevents the functioning of particular psychological structures.

The mind is composed of many *structures* which refer to "a relatively stable organization of component parts that perform one or more related psychological functions." These structures can be observed in terms of output information responding to input information. The structures that relate to consciousness have to do with sexual needs, coping with societal pressures, language ability, etc. Structures have basic patterns that vary in intensity and quality; they can be permanently fixed to affect the nervous system, and they can be the products of conditioning, learning, and enculturation. On the whole, most structures can be explained on the basis of experiential, behavioral, and psychological data.

Structures are distinctly psychological when interacting with attention/awareness in such a way that 1) they are initially formed; 2) they operate, or are prevented from operating; 3) they are modified; 4) they are destroyed. The multiple, simultaneous interactions of psychological structures are rooted in the activation of attention/awareness energy, the success of which depends upon the properties that "limit and control their potential range of interaction with one another."

Tart proposes that the concept of state of consciousness be defined more precisely in order to describe what he labels the *discrete state of consciousness* (d-SoC), which is characteristic of the waking state, nondreaming sleep, hypnotic states, intoxication by alcohol or marijuana, and meditative states.

D-SoC's function basically as tools that interact with the external environment in a manner that is characteristically *dynamic*. There are four ways to stabilize the system of the d-SoC. Tart calls the first, the *loading* or *ballasting* stabilization. The sources of this process are your body, its movements, and your thinking processes, the activities of which load your consciousness so that "too little (attention/awareness) energy is left to allow disruption of the system's operation." The second kind of stabilization occurs as the result of *negative feedback,* a process which determines when a structure, or subsystem, is operating beyond its limits and corrects it. The third kind of stabilization process is called *positive feedback,* which rewards and strengthens a structure's operation. The fourth means of stabilization is *limiting* the range within which structures can function (e.g., tranquilizers). These four stabilization processes can occur simultaneously, at any time. They control the interaction patterns among the structures in order to maintain the integrity of the functioning of the d-SoC system as a whole.

When you determine that your d-SoC does not allow you to cope with the environment, you can move into

464 / CHARLES T. TART

a *discrete altered state of consciousness* (d-ASC). Tart considers the d-ASC to have properties which are distinct from the restructuring of consciousness. They are products of induction out of a *baseline,* or ordinary state of consciousness (b-SoC) by means of disruptions of the stabilization of the latter, and enforced *patterning* of that which has been disrupted.

According to Tart, the b-SoC is that patterning of psychological functions which is active, stable, overall, and maintains a distinct identity through the stabilization process, even though the environment might change. The three-step induction process from b-SoC to d-ASC is based on two psychological-physiological operations: that which you do to yourself, and that which is done to you. The former deals with the disruption of the stabilization of your b-SoC so that it cannot operate with integrity. Psychological functions are pushed beyond their limits through overstimulation, deprivation of stimuli, or the introduction of stimuli which cannot be assimilated. The latter psycho- and physio-logical operation requires the application of patterning forces that establish the level at which the d-ASC can function. The same stimuli that disrupt stabilization can act as patterning forces.

Sleep is the first step toward achieving a d-ASC, the process of eliminating the loading of your consciousness, e.g., lying down and closing your eyes and getting to the point where you realize that there is "nothing important to deal with."

There are three kinds of meditative states which can be achieved through specific meditative techniques: A state of voidness, blankness, or nothingness can be achieved through *concentrative* meditation in which you fix your attention on one thing; a state whereby you experience things more clearly and intensely can be achieved through *opening up* meditation in which you remain aware of what is happening without thinking about it; and *expressive meditation.*

Tart defines subsystems ("the assembly of multiple

structures into major experiential and experimental divisions of consciousness") which are affected in the d-ASC. The first is that of *exteroception*. In a d-ASC, the exteroceptive organs (eyes, ears, nose, taste buds, touch organs) are active but have limited responsiveness. You can voluntarily control input into them or change their function, as in a d-ASC induced by LSD. The second is that of *interioception,* in which you may determine the internal activity of your body. Other subsystems acted on by d-ASC's are memory, subconscious evaluation, decision making, emotions, space/time sense, sense of identity, and motor output.

From the evidence of his research, Tart concludes that in order to develop ourselves as human beings and be able to further understand d-ASC's, we must create *state-specific* sciences which would concentrate on coordinating information gathered from experimentation about both d-SoC's and d-ASC's. Tart speculates that through the acquisition of such knowledge, and specifically regarding the samsara or higher states of consciousness, we can come to the realization that so-called "normal" states of consciousness do not exist and that present modes of psychotherapy are limited in their aims to merely "readjust deviant persons to consensus realities of the culture."

REFERENCES

Charles T. Tart, *States of Consciousness.* New York: E. P. Dutton & Co., 1975.

Charles T. Tart (ed.), *Altered States of Consciousness.* New York: John Wiley and Sons, Inc., 1969.

TEILHARD DE CHARDIN (1881–1955), philosopher of man's evolutionary process, attended school at a Jesuit college in Auvergne, France, where he became interested in field geology and mineralogy. He entered a Jesuit order at eighteen, and at twenty-four was sent to teach physics and chemistry at a Jesuit school in Cairo, Egypt. He studied theology in England for four years, and was ordained a priest in 1912. By 1919, because of his intense interest in the facts and theories of evolution, he decided to pursue a professional career in geology and paleontology, as well as focus on developing a generalized theory and philosophy of the evolutionary process, which would cover the realms of human history, human personality, biology, and the relationship between facts of religious experience and those of natural science. In 1922, he received his doctorate from the Sorbonne, while professor of geology at the Catholic Institute of Paris. During his lifetime, he studied in China, Java, Burma, Abyssinia, and the United States, doing geological research and paleontological work on the evolution of mammalian groups. His controversial ideas on the evolution of man caused his writings to be banned in Europe. By 1951, he was established in the United States, and the period until 1954 saw his valuable contributions toward the framing of anthropological study, as well as the development of his ideas. All his written works were published after his death, the most significant being *The Phenomenon of Man.*

At the core of Teilhard's philosophy is his viewpoint that man operates collectively as a phenomenon which can be described and analyzed like any other phenomenon. All manifestations of the phenomenon, including its history and the values imposed on actions, can be studied scientifically. In pursuit of this knowledge, it is necessary to maintain an evolutionary viewpoint, for phenomena are never static; they are working processes or parts of processes. According to Teilhard, the universe is in a continuous process of becoming, of attaining new levels of existence and organization which can be called evolution, or *genesis.* Similarly, cosmology can be viewed as *cosmogenesis,* and the gradual evolution of the mind, *noogenesis.*

Teilhard believed specific terminology to be important to the design of his philosophy. He coined the term "noosphere," to denote the sphere of the mind (or "thinking layer") as distinct from the sphere of life. The noosphere participates in the creation of *hominiza-*

tion, the process whereby original organisms become and continue to become more human in the realization of all their capabilities. The term "convergence" specifies the process of differentiation which saw man separating into distinct races, migrating, and intermarrying. An all-pervasive tendency in the universe is *complexification,* which is defined as the genesis of increasingly elaborate systems of organization within the universe: from single cell to primitive man to civilized societies. Complexification also applies to the development of an increasingly conscious mind.

Working within the context of the definitions of such terms, Teilhard concluded that since evolutionary phenomena, including the phenomenon of man, are processes which cannot be described solely in terms of their origins, they must be defined in terms of their direction, their inherent capabilities and limitations, and their imminent future activities. Human convergence involves the process of complexification within the differentiation of culture. It aims toward the unification of the entire human species into a single interthinking group, based on a single self-developing framework of thought, or noosystem.

The increase in human population has created an atmosphere of highly refined organization because of the establishment of communication systems bringing the parts of the noosphere together. Thus mankind can achieve more intense, complicated, and integrated mental activity, and consequently higher levels of hominization. Teilhard believed that the mere fact that the environment is spherical could cause psychological interaction to be more intense. This way, idea encounters idea and creates a vast network of energetic thought.

According to Teilhard, personality is of great importance to an extremely personal mode of organization. We are more than simply highly individualized creatures. We think consciously in terms of ourselves and how we relate to the external world. We have converted our mere individuality into personality. Personality is a key to more valuable achievement in the future. The organization of thinking humanity is a kind of organism, the success of which depends upon the proper and fulfilling utilization of all its component parts toward the realization of one complete unit. Future success depends upon the recognition of all personalities within the world. That success can be secured by pursuing the knowledge which helps us understand ourselves and the world, and by controlling our relationship to it in a continuing process of growth.

Teilhard labels the final state of humanity, where the noosphere will be unified and have extreme personal organization, *Omega*. The forces leading us to this point are the increased knowledge about the universe, and the parallel increase of psychosocial pressure, coupled with a greater intensification of the noosphere, and an increased intensification and unification of the system of human thought.

REFERENCES

Teilhard de Chardin, *The Phenomenon of Man*. New York: Harper & Row, 1959.

———, *The Divine Milieu*. New York: Harper & Row, 1965.

TOTAL FITNESS was developed by Laurence Morehouse, Ph.D., a professor of exercise physiology and founding director of the Human Performance Laboratory at the University of California at Los Angeles. Since 1946, he has been working with physicians at UCLA, NASA, as well as on other medical research projects investigating the advantages and disadvantages of programs geared toward physical fitness. In the course of these efforts, the distinction between the physical activity required for a fitness event and the physical activity required for a sporting event was made. Morehouse realized that the exercise appropriate for an athlete is not necessarily good for the average person; in many cases, people who try to achieve a level of physical fitness like that of an athlete are doing themselves harm.

Morehouse believes that exercise does not have to be boring or harmful, but rather, should be a means to an alert, active long life, and should have priority in a daily schedule. You will acquire a reserve of fitness which will allow you to enjoy recreational activities, rid yourself of late-in-the-day "drag," be more self-aware, and be ready for the quick response needed in an emergency. Fitness, says Morehouse, is "a piece of cake." Overindulgence in exercise, formalized, rigid exercise programs, or expensive equipment are not necessary parts of the formula for the shaping and maintaining of a healthy, fit body.

Morehouse makes a point of examining the diverting myths which surround the exercise syndrome, e.g., don't eat certain foods before exercising, eat extra protein to maintain strength, take sugar for extra energy, etc. These myths prevent us from paying attention to the phenomena of our bodies which will enable us to correctly judge our individual capacity for exercise.

A main point in his theory is that the pulse rate is a measure of how much exercise we require and is also an important indicator of how well our bodies are functioning. The pulse rate is significant with regard to body temperature, the rate at which energy is being burned up and oxygen used, how well the blood is handling chemical wastes, how the muscles are working, rate of heartbeat, and even how emotions are affecting us.

Morehouse points out that age should not be an inhibitory factor in daily exercise. Although the capacity to exercise declines with age, it is important to realize that as your effort to be physically active declines, your performance capacity will also diminish. Age is often equated with a weak heart when, in fact, with proper exercise, your heart becomes stronger, richer in oxygen, more efficient, and beats at a slower rate when you are at rest than it would if not reconditioned.

The Total Fitness program structures three levels of satisfactory fitness. The first is the level at which your body requires a minimum amount of exercise. At the second level, you are able to go through a normal day without fatigue. The third level is the level at which preparation for exertion, either for a sport or job, is necessary. *Level one,* the minimum maintenance level, can be achieved by concentrating on certain motions such as twisting, lifting, standing, walking, during the course of normal daily activities. *Level two* has three stages of specific exercises to follow for a period of eight weeks, thirty minutes per week. Each stage concentrates on the development of a certain aspect of fitness, e.g., muscle bulk, endurance, and strength. *Level three* requires the practice of specific exercises for a specific kind of strenuousness. The intensity of these exercises should equal the intensity of the sport or job to be engaged in.

Morehouse's key to losing weight is to diminish the daily intake of food by two hundred calories, and to burn up three hundred calories in physical activity each day. The amount of physical activity is determined by your individual capacity.

Morehouse is a distinguished physiologist and the author of a standard textbook used in colleges and universities throughout the world. He has written articles on exercise and physical fitness for several encyclopedias including the Encyclopaedia Britannica. *Total Fitness,* published in 1975, describes a complete program of exercise and body maintenance.

REFERENCE

Laurence Morehouse and Leonard Gross, *Total Fitness: In 30 Minutes a Week.* New York: Simon & Schuster, 1975.

TRANSCENDENTAL MEDITATION (TM) originated in India, and its technique has been passed on for thousands of years. According to historical records, however, a thorough knowledge of the practice of transcendental meditation was achieved only at the time of Krishna, as told in the *Bhagavad-Gita,* and during the time of Buddha and Shankara. Shankara, 2,500 years ago, revived the ancient wisdom crucial to TM by instituting plans for its teaching; those plans maintained the integrity of TM until about 150 years ago when the teaching processes had become muddled and misunderstood.

In 1941, Guru Dev assumed the post of Shankarcharya of Jyotir Math in Badarinath in the Himalayas, the position of wisdom. He taught all those who came to him for guidance the ancient meditative technique. It is through Guru Dev that the present modes of TM have come to us. Until his death in 1953, Guru Dev taught Maharishi Mahesh Yogi. In 1955, after coming out of seclusion in the Himalayas, Maharishi began to lecture throughout India. Later, he traveled to Burma, Singapore, and Hong Kong, and in 1959, he arrived in Hawaii; from there he continued his teaching throughout the United States. In 1961, Maharishi conducted the first TM teacher-training course in India. From 1961–66, he set up training centers all over the world. The Students' International Meditation Society was created in 1965 in response to interest in TM at UCLA. Because of Maharishi's lectures at Berkeley, UCLA, and Harvard in 1967, college students in the United States requested courses in TM, and created chapters of SIMS on campuses in every state. By 1973, 350,000 Americans, predominantly college students and young adults, were practicing meditation. Since 1970, teacher-training courses have been conducted three times a year. By the middle of 1973, the Maharishi International University had granted over 6,000 students the qualifications necessary to teach TM. Statistics show that 10,000 people a month begin TM in the United States, and that by 1976, over a million people were practitioners of TM worldwide.

In the practice of TM, you allow your mind to reach a relaxed and enjoyable state in which it is both quiet and alert, and you are focused inward. It is a state of pure awareness, which Maharishi defines as "the essential basic nature of the mind." Practicing TM on a regular basis can improve the quality of your life, both physically and psychologically. Its aim is the realization of your full human potential. Achieving pure awareness leads you to the level of the mind where the source of your energy and intelligence lies. Furthermore, TM allows you to rest deeply and gradually dispense with the long-term accumulation and intensity of stress. The depth of rest achieved in TM permits the nervous system to normalize to the maximum extent. According to Maharishi, once your nervous system has adjusted to the regular practice of TM, your body will normalize to the maximum comfortable rate. TM can be useful in improving health, regaining emotional stability, and revitalizing performance capacity.

The process of TM occurs when your attention is diverted from the surface level of the mind to the deep levels of the mind where thoughts begin. TM minimizes mental activity as you progressively turn your attention to extremely quiet thought and its flowing nature. To arrive at this quiet state of mind, you must disengage it from superficial mental activity by thinking a single thought. The mind is allowed to remain active in this respect, but undirected. "Thought sounds" called mantras can be used to help disengage the mind from external activity. Mantras must be chosen specifically for each individual; the selection of the correct mantra is critically important, for each mantra has a specific influence on the meditator. Learning how to use the correct mantra necessitates the guidance of a qualified teacher, according to Maharishi, or ill effects can result.

The effects of TM have been the subject of recent research. It has been found that TM could be the most effective means to relieve stress and restore psychophysiological integration through achieving distinct states of consciousness. Scientists have noted that the interrelationship between states of awareness and physiology can be measured in terms of the changes in heart rate, rate of breathing, length of brain waves, etc. Researchers believe that TM produces a fourth state of consciousness, determined by brain waves, levels of oxygen consumption, and blood chemistry. It is distinct from the consciousness of waking, sleeping, and dreaming.

The way in which TM improves psychological health can be seen in the work done by psychologist Maynard Shelley. Shelley contends that there is a direct connection between happiness and autonomic arousal: i.e., happiness and psychological health depend upon your ability to maintain an optimum level of arousal. In this respect, Shelley hypothesizes that by lowering the brain's optimum level of arousal through TM, the enjoyment of daily activities can be increased. Through his study, Shelley determined that transcendental meditators, compared to nonmeditators, are happier, more relaxed, experience enjoyment more often, seem to develop deeper personal relationships, depend less on external surroundings for happiness, are more reflective of a deep sense of purpose.

Psychologists have found that TM, by heightening awareness, improves overall performance, especially with regard to perception. It is a valuable therapeutic technique, encouraging the resolution of emotional conflicts and permitting aspects of the personality considered unacceptable to become integrated. TM has been effective in the treatment of anxiety neurosis, obsessive-compulsive symptoms, chronic low-grade depression, and psychosomatic illness. According to Roberto Assagioli, "the course of therapy is shorter with meditation because one is not dependent upon the mood of dreams and comes more quickly, both diagnostically and therapeutically, to the psychic conflict. . . ."

Although Maharishi Mahesh Yogi states that the correct practice of TM can only be taught by a qualified teacher, the effects of TM can be achieved, according to Herbert Benson, M.D., through what he calls the "relaxation response" of the body. The same beneficial physiological changes characteristic of meditation can occur. Benson's theory outlines four basic requirements for elicitation of the relaxation response: a quiet environment; an object to focus your mind on, i.e., a word or phrase, a feeling, to eliminate confusing thoughts from your mind; a passive attitude; and a comfortable position, one in which you can remain for twenty minutes.

REFERENCES

Roberto Assagioli, *Psychosynthesis*. New York: Hobbes, Corman, 1965.

Herbert Benson, M.D., *The Relaxation Response*. New York: William Morrow & Co., 1975.

H. H. Blooomfield, M. P. Cain, and D. T. Jaffe, *TM, Discovering Inner Energy and Overcoming Stress*. New York: Delacorte, 1975.

M. W. Shelley, "A Theory of Happiness as It Relates to Transcendental Meditation" (Summarized by G. Landrith). Lawrence, Kansas: University of Kansas, 1972.

Maharishi Mahesh Yogi, *The Science of Belief and the Art of Living*. Stuttgart, Germany: Spiritual Regeneration Movement Publications, 1966.

CHOGYAM TRUNGPA, RINPOCHE (1939–), a spiritual leader, was born in Geji, Kham, Tibet, and raised to be superior of the Surmang monasteries in eastern Tibet, engaging in both meditative and intellectual studies in the traditions of Kagyi and Nyingma. Compelled to leave Tibet by the Chinese Communists in 1959, he spent three years in India and then went to England where he studied comparative religion and psychology at Oxford University. After four years at Oxford, Trungpa founded Same Ling in Scotland, the first Buddhist study and meditation center in the West. He arrived in the United States in 1970 where, because of the favorable response to his teachings, he decided to remain.

Trungpa has founded several Buddhist contemplative communities in the United States, the largest ones being Karma Dzong in Boulder, Colorado, and Tail of the Tiger in Barnet, Vermont. The Naropa Institute in Boulder grew out of a class in meditation given by

Trungpa in 1974. Here, people experience the interaction between Buddhist and Western intellectual disciplines in an academic framework. The publication *Loka*
is a result of the first meeting of the institute and includes
articles by Gregory Bateson, Ram Dass, and others.
Trungpa is director and principal teacher of these Buddhist centers. He has toured the United States and
Canada, lecturing and conducting seminars. Since 1973,
he has taught at the University of Colorado at Boulder.
Trungpa is the author of several books: *Born in Tibet,
Meditation in Action, Mudra,* a book of poetry, and
Cutting Through Spiritual Materialism, a collection of
lectures.

One of the keys to the teachings of Trungpa is the
process of "cutting through *spiritual materialism,*" which
he defines as a fundamental distortion leading you to
believe that you are following a spiritual path when, in
fact, you are only strengthening your egocentricity
through spiritual techniques. Merely acquiring knowledge and experience of various philosophies, Western or
Oriental, does not render you truly spiritual. True spirituality can only be realized once you have gone beyond
intellectual rationalizations about the pursuit of spirituality, beyond the desires of the ego to comfort and
justify itself, beyond evaluating consciousness about your
state of being. The interruption of the journey on the
spiritual path by the dualism of philosophical theories
and beliefs will confuse you in a self-destructive manner.
You are not guided by any external force on the spiritual
path; you are alone.

By supporting spiritual materialism, you defend and
improve yourself; you do not *surrender* your hopes,
expectations, fears, which is the way to open yourself
up to the world as it actually exists, unclassified, full of
inspiration. In this respect, a guru (master, lama, etc.)
should become a spiritual friend to whom you open
yourself and surrender completely. The relationship between guru and student is one of intensity: "the very
meaning of your life depends on him." The relationship
evolves to the point where you achieve complete open-

ness and see all of life as your guide. According to Trungpa, spirituality must be accompanied by a kind of intelligence that will allow you to pass through the emotion, romanticism, and charisma superficially attached to a guru, in order to see, hear, and understand the essence of spiritual teaching and wisdom as it has been assimilated throughout history, from one generation of meditators to another. This is the process of *initiation.*

The journey along the spiritual path often leads to self-deception, which can take the form of a search for a tangible substance to believe in, a desire to see miracles, an attempt to prove your own uniqueness. According to Trungpa, self-deception is difficult to deal with once it has been discovered; it is experienced as despair, hopelessness of ambition, paranoia, and self-criticism. At this stage, meditation can become a way to trust yourself, discipline yourself, and develop a sense of compassion and warmth, the expression of which is found in your relationship to the world. Arriving at a non-self-referential attitude is essentially an act of leaving your ego behind and establishing self-confidence. "To be completely open, to have that kind of absolute trust in yourself is the real meaning of compassion and love."

Spiritual development in the Buddhist tradition occurs in stages or *yanas* (meaning vehicle). The first yana is the *Hinayana,* which prepares you to begin the journey on the spiritual path. It includes the *Shravaka Yana,* or listening to the Four Noble Truths expose evidence of the problems of life, its suffering and pain, and the *Pratyebabuddha Yana,* the intellectualization of the confusion of your situation of self. Meditation becomes an agent for centralizing the simplicity of nowness, the experience of the *vipassana.* As this occurs, you move into the third yana, the *Bodhisattva Yana,* in which you lose self-consciousness and yield to the self-lessness of the Bodhisattva ideal toward the development of transcendental knowledge of egolessness. You no longer deal with nature dualistically or conceptually; you have found *sunyata,* nothingness, at this stage. At the disappearance of sunyata, comes *bodhi,* or birth into luminosity. From here you experience the death of luminosity, the vajra-like samadhi, and move into the *Vajrayana,* where you intensely perceive energies as reality, or *Tantra.* The Tantric attitude in Buddhism approaches universal energies in terms of the dakini principle, dakinis being the creative-destructive patterns of life. In the *Kriya Yana,* the purity of energies overtakes you. In the *Upa Yana,* Tantric knowledge is rooted in the *Mahamudra,* the awakened state of mind. The Upa Yana entails application to the yogic practices of the Kriya Yana in the manner of the meditation of the *Yoga Yana.* The Yoga Yana reveals a three-fold mandala symbolizing the external situation, the physical body, and the state of consciousness, the boundaries of which are destroyed through the discovery of the four mudras: seeing in terms of mirrorlike wisdom, hearing in terms of discriminating wisdom, feeling in terms of the wisdom of equanimity, and perceiving in terms of automatic fulfillment. The *Mahayaga Yana* celebrates the union of joy and openness; you perceive the mandala as valueless. At this stage, Mahamudra has transformed into *Maha Ati,* the highest Tantra; you merge with your own true nature and see the true quality of forms, images, and sounds. Thereafter, space and wisdom are united. Their union dissolves and through your consequential recognition and experience of all that is, you discover freedom in its most real form: "This is the end of the journey which need never have been made. This is the seamless web of what is."

The true spiritual path, envisioned by Trungpa, becomes the process of the metamorphosis of your mind in which its function is no longer determined by ego, and meditation is a means to express "basic sanity and enlightenment." The spiritual path reveals the end of the struggle to prove your existence; your mind is focused on the truth of life and the joy of living.

REFERENCES

Rick Fields, ed., *Loka: A Journal from Naropa Institute.* New York: Anchor Books, 1975.

Chogyam Trungpa, *Mudra.* Berkeley, Ca.: Shambala, 1975.

————, *Cutting Through Spiritual Materialism,* ed. by John Baker and Marvin Casper. Berkeley, Ca.: Shambala, 1973.

————, *The Myth of Freedom: And the Way of Meditation,* ed. by Baker and Caster. Berkeley, Ca.: Shambala, 1976.

JOHN B. WATSON (1878–1958) was the founder of the school of psychology known as *behaviorism.* He introduced his theories in 1913 in a presentation of his paper, "Psychology As the Behaviorist Sees It," at which time his theories were widely criticized in the United States. Over a period of years, however, they gradually gained favor.

Watson was born in Greenville, South Carolina. He received his Ph.D. from the University of Chicago in 1903. From 1908–20, he was professor of psychology at Johns Hopkins University. He published the definitive text of his work in a book entitled *Behaviorism* in 1924. He died in New York City in 1958.

Behaviorism offered an alternative to the so-called introspective psychologies practiced in Germany and the United States in 1912. Introspective psychologies were first advocated with the work of Wilhelm Wundt (1832–1920) who, in 1879, promoted the idea of a scientific psychology. Wundt took the dualistic nature of man, that of soul and body, and assigned the term "consciousness" to what was implied by soul. Consciousness is observable through introspection. For a behaviorist, this is an invisible process. This is the hinge of the difference between introspective psychology and behaviorism.

As defined by Watson, behaviorism is a physiological psychology, which considers what can be observed, the behavior of an organism measured according to what it does or says. Another term for behaviorism is objective psychology. The analytic units used in this measurement are stimulus-response activity. Behaviorism encompasses "the whole field of human adjustments," both in terms of physiology and in terms of what a human being does. Its aim is "to predict and control human activity" through the evidence offered by scientific data.

As Watson proposed, behaviorism is based on a principle that eliminates the difficulty in describing psychologically oriented phenomena. Its vocabulary does not include subjective terms, e.g., sensation, desire, perception, emotion. It is a "true natural science." Stimuli, in the behaviorist's language, are those conditions imposed upon or generated by the body that cause it to react. For example, a darkened room will cause the pupils of the eyes to expand; tension in a muscle will create a response in that muscle or in another muscle.

Response is the measurable reaction of the organism to stimuli. In its reaction, the organism usually moves in some way, internally or externally, so that the response to a particular stimulus is no longer necessary (e.g., satisfaction of hunger). A response can be very small (movement of the eye) or engage the entire organism. There are classes of responses, according to Watson, which include external and internal response manifestations as well as learned and unlearned (conditioned) responses. The latter are further classified according to the location of their occurrence: visual, visceral, kinesthetic.

Stimulus-response data constitute the essential material of behavioristic psychology. Knowledge of the human body's components, structure, and capabilities provides the foundation for it. It is on the basis of the kind of information gained from the observation of the above that behaviorism can be understood and further applied in a social context.

The physical body in behavioral psychology is viewed in terms of how behavior is possible. Watson described the body as an organic machine which is observed for how it works as a whole, not solely in terms of the functioning of its parts. The central nervous system is "no more mysterious than muscles and glands," and is a system that catalyzes the body's response to stimuli. Watson analyzed the organs of the body in terms of the specific cells of which they are composed, and divided them into three classes: the sense organs, the reacting organs, and the nervous system (or connecting organs). The organs are seen for the ways in which stimuli are exerted and response is manifested. The behaviorist believes that the human organism is built around "rapid—and when needed, complicated—reactions to simple and complex stimuli."

Watson studied the ideas behind instinct, and promoted the thesis that a person is born with a capacity for unlearned behavior, i.e., breathing, heartbeat, etc., that varies among individuals. People are also born with what are believed to be instincts but which, from the behaviorist's viewpoint, are actually learned behavior patterns. Therefore, we develop from our innate structure and as the result of what we learn. To account for the variations among people, Watson contended that people are "structurally shaped (within limits) by the kinds of lives they lead." Thus, how you are built physically and mentally, provides you with the capacity to act as you do until you have learned otherwise. Inheritance of traits is not supported by any evidence which a behaviorist can justly consider; the same is true for emotions.

Emotions are considered to be complex patterns of response to the environment. They are formed from birth as unconditioned responses to unconditioned stimuli. The same stimulus, through experience, can indicate a range of responses, which adds to the complexity of emotions. Emotions are simply a set of habits. These habits are considered able to be learned and also able to be reversed. This becomes the crux of the behaviorist's purpose: "to substitute natural science in . . . treatment of the emotionally sick in place of the doubtful and passing unscientific method . . . of psychoanalysis."

Watson believed that personality is the result of habits which have been formed. Viewing the personality behavioristically is a procedure of studying the individual's educational and achievement background, recreational activities, emotional manifestations during normal daily activity, and the evidence of certain psychological tests. Curing a "sick" personality is a process of unconditioning and conditioning, not analysis. Cures are produced by the same stimulus-response pattern which formed the sickness.

Watson believed that behavioral psychology allowed the principles of behavior to be understood. Applying that which was understood would allow us to shape our children's behavior in order to build a world "fit for human habitation."

REFERENCES

H. J. Eysenck, W. Arnold, R. Meili, eds., *Encyclopedia of Psychology*. New York: Herder and Herder, 1972.

John B. Watson, *Behaviorism*. New York: W. W. Norton & Co., 1930.

ALAN WATTS (1915–73), a philosopher, was an important contributor to the consciousness-expansion movement. He was born in England and attended the King's School at Canterbury. He came to the United States in 1938, and coedited the *Wisdom of the East* series until 1941. Watts received his S.T.M. degree from Seabury-Western Theological Seminary in Evanston, Illinois, in 1948, and his Doctorate of Divinity at the University of Vermont in 1958. From 1944–50, he was the Episcopalian chaplain at Northwestern University. He then was professor of comparative literature at the American Academy of Asian Studies at the University of the Pacific, San Francisco. From 1957 on, Watts lectured at many universities and psychiatric institutes, including the Carl Jung Institute in Switzerland. Watts was a research fellow of the Bollingen Foundation in 1951 and 1962, and from 1962–64, research fellow at Harvard University. In 1968, he was visiting scholar at San Jose State College in California. Watts was a member of the American Oriental Society and president of the Society for Comparative Philosophy. He wrote seventeen books dealing with Zen, religion, and the union of Eastern and Western thought.

Watts was particularly interested in fusing Western science with Eastern modes of intuition and exploration of totality as exemplified by the Vedanta philosophy of Hinduism. He believed in the valuable function of the construction of a "new experience." This experience would differ from the way of life we are accustomed to living, whose structure is founded on myth. Knowing the self eludes conceptual thinking and becomes a process of feeling and experiencing infinite energy. Our new experience should divert us from attentiveness to our separate egos in a context that is connected with neither Western science nor the "experimental-philosophy religions" of the East.

Watts saw that the basis of Western thought lies in the polarization of opposites which, in its extended form, emphasizes separateness and a narrowed perception of existence. According to Watts, we have no means to approach oneness, Existence, Being, God, or the Ultimate Ground of Being; nor do we have the means to perceive everything as moving together. Our socially based attitudes are especially notable in our views of death: We try to delay death continually by clinging to ourselves in chronic anxiety, expecting that death is a nightmare. Our views of death demonstrate our selfish nature. It seems that the science fiction "fantasies of the future" are coming upon us in the present, as seen in the technological conversion of everyday life into plastic and electronic equivalents. Technological progress functions to increase our rate of living, based on the idea that "man and nature, the organism and the environment, the controller and the controlled are quite different things." In this way, we contribute to the continuance of the conflict between opposites.

According to Watts, the basic realities of nature have traditionally been invented as *social fictions;* for example: the notion that the world is composed of separate bits or things; that things are differing forms of the same bits of stuff; that individual organisms are inhabited by and partially controlled by independent egos; that man, individually and collectively, should aspire to be the top species, in control of nature, etc. We often accept these fictions as facts and neglect to examine their contradictory nature; in this way, we confuse how we relate fundamentally to the world.

In order to avoid confusion, it is essential that we realize that things, individuals, nations, plants, etc. exist in relationship to one another and are the necessary parts of a unified process. We must extend ourselves beyond the Newtonian conception of the world where causal determination affects separate things. We can know the world through knowing ourselves. Knowing, according to Watts, is a "translation of external events into bodily processes, and especially into states of the nervous system and the brain . . . we know the world in *terms* of the body, and in accordance with its structure."

Our confusion about the relationship between the organism and the environment is psychological. It is demonstrated by a biblically oriented false humility and a conception of ourselves as separate egos, battling to control the physical world. We are incapable of realizing that we cannot exist without everything else. We should have enough self-respect to recognize that, as individual organisms, we demand knowledge of the whole universe.

In order to attain a new vision of oneness, traditions which have instilled in us the so-called integrity of the individual must be sacrificed. Watts felt that the methods which have evolved for overcoming the feeling of separateness (e.g., yoga, meditation, psychotherapy, Zen Buddhism, prayer, relaxation therapies, drugs, etc.) result in the formation of cults and groups which, paradoxically, emphasize separateness.

Becoming "perfect" in the spiritual sense means playing another (though loftier) version of an ego game.

The solutions to our problems can be found in our realization that 1) biologically, we will always have to eat at the expense of another living being, and that our organism is limited in its function, and 2) morally, we depend on other forms of life, including our enemies and competitors.

Watts diagnosed the political and personal morality of the West, especially the United States, as schizophrenic. We manifest "a monstrous combination of uncompromising idealism and unscrupulous gangsterism . . . devoid of the humor and humaneness which would enable [us] to sit down together and work out reasonable deals." We must realize that we define ourselves in accordance with our opposition. It is essential that we understand this (especially those involved with civil rights, international peace, nuclear disarmament). The "real goodness" of human nature is found in the unique balance between love and selfishness, reason and passion, etc., the positive pole always remaining one step ahead of the negative, which eliminates the possibility of a stalemate social condition. Our lives are a game, and we must live them conditionally, in the spirit of play rather than work, and with the knowledge that no species can survive without its natural enemy.

We need to move away from the social emphasis on practicality, results, progress, aggression, and focus our energies and skills on the contemplation of knowing and being rather than the action of seeking and becoming. This can be done by developing a *correlative vision,* in which we see that all explicit opposites are implicit allies, moving together, and unable to exist separately. In Vedanta philosophy this unity is called *"nonduality."* The essence of our activities should be in the practice of this vision and the realization that we are a part of the continual "central self" and the "it" which "appears as the self/other situations in its myriads of pulsating forms—always the same and always new, a here in the midst of a there, a now in the midst of a then, and a one in the midst of many."

REFERENCES

Alan Watts, *The Book: On the Taboo Against Knowing Who You Are.* New York: Collier Books, 1966.

————, *The Way of Zen.* New York: Pantheon Books, 1957.

————, *Nature, Man and Woman.* New York: Pantheon Books, 1958.

————, *Psychotherapy East and West.* New York: Pantheon Books, 1968.

————, *The Joyous Cosmology.* New York: Pantheon Books, 1962.

NORBERT WIENER (1894–1964), an American mathematician, developed the science of *cybernetics,* which is the application of mathematics to the communication of information and to the control of the system of such form of communication, with regard to both the nervous system-brain complex and mechanical-electrical communication systems.

Wiener was educated at Tufts University in Boston and at Harvard University, where he received his Ph.D. at the age of eighteen. He studied further at Cornell, Columbia, and Cambridge universities, and in Copenhagen, Denmark, and Göttingen, Germany. In 1919, he joined the faculty of the Masachusetts Institute of Technology. During World War II, Wiener worked as a mathematician designing antiaircraft defense systems and developing improvements in radar and navy projectiles. In 1947, he decided to dedicate his life to the study of the influence of automation on society. In 1959, he was appointed Institute Professor at MIT and gave advanced instruction despite limitations imposed on him by his department. He retired in 1960, and in 1964, he was awarded the National Medal of Science.

Wiener was influenced by the work of Ludwig Boltzmann in Germany, and Josiah Gibbs in the United States. These two men introduced statistics (the science of distribution) into physics, rejecting the belief that systems of the same total energy may be clearly and completely explained in terms of causal laws. This statistical approach could be applied to both simple and complex physical systems. The revolution that Gibbs, in particular, began, affected physics to the degree that its frame of reference was shifted from dealing with physical events that always happen, to those that will happen with an "overwhelming probability." In this probabilistic world, Wiener observed that "we no longer deal with quantities and statements which concern a specific, real universe, as a whole, but instead ask questions which may find their answers in a large number of similar universes. Thus, chance has been admitted, not merely as a mathematical tool for physics, but as a part of its warp and weft."

With the discoveries of Gibbs as a foundation, Wiener proposed a probabilistic theory of messages which took into account not only an electrical engineering theory concerning the actual transmission of messages, but also the larger field of modes of communication between human beings. Wiener coined the term "cybernetics" to describe the activity of his theory. (The word is derived from the Greek word *kubernetes,* meaning "steersman.") The discussion of the technical implications of cybernetics is found in *Cybernetics* (1948), in which Wiener mathematically analyzes biological and social problems and describes communication among individuals in terms of the controls imparted by the messages communicated. (Wiener later wrote *The Human Use of Human Beings,* in which he discusses his theories for comprehension by the layman.)

Crucial to Wiener's communication theory is the idea that society can be seen in terms of the messages it communicates and its mechanisms for communication. This means that the message interaction between man and machine, machine and man, and machine and machine will become increasingly important in the understanding of society's control of the environment.

According to Wiener, control of the environment is subject to the "kind of information we impart to it." Information constructs messages. When we receive and use information, we are participating in an exchange with the environment and, thus, adjusting to it in order to "live effectively." Just as the physical universe tends toward disorganization (*entropy*), so can sets of messages capable of being communicated in society. The information of these messages can also become a measure of their organization (*negative entropy*). For example, as a message becomes more predictable (e.g., a cliché), then the less information it contains (e.g., since you know the content of a cliché you learn nothing). Therefore, for effective communication to occur and instigate action or change, the messages communicated must contain a quantity of information "which can penetrate into a communication and storage apparatus sufficiently to serve as a trigger for action."

Wiener held that the functioning of the human body serves as an appropriate model for the operation of modern communication machines. This process is one in which entropy (tendency toward disorganization) is controlled through *feedback* (information that tells of actual performance rather than probable performance). The human body is analogous to a communication machine in terms of its sensory receptors. Sensory receptors are a regulatory apparatus that collects information from the environment, transforms it, and makes it available for use in further stages of performance (the activity of memory).

Similarly, communicative behavior is based on how established patterns of behavior are modified in relation to past experience: we can modify our behavior so that one aspect of it will deal more effectively with the environment (this is an *antientropic* situation). Feedback is instrumental in this behavioral change because the feedback process returns information to the organic system about its performance. Thus, feedback is a function of learning. Wiener believed that the process of feedback can occur in society and serve as a means to change ourselves to meet the standards of our technological advancement.

According to Wiener, we develop our communicative

capability on three levels. The first level is the ear and that part of the brain connected with the inner ear. The ear, which works in response to sound vibrations from the environment, is a machine concerned with the *phonetic* aspect of language; its process is innate. The second level of communication is the *semantic* aspect of language. Semantic reception requires utilization of memory and occurs in terms of ideas. The third level is the *behavior* aspect of language, the translation of conscious experiences into externally observable actions; these actions can be those characteristic of lower animals (e.g., chimpanzees) or can take the form of a coded, symbolic system of actions, either in spoken or written language, characteristic of human beings. The amount of information contained in each of the three levels decreases from level to level because of the increasing complexity of influences. Cybernetically, this loss of information contributes to a decrease in effective communication. When applied, cybernetics can allow for the transmission of messages that contain significant information. This would be a realization of a cybernetic goal.

Once the importance of making communication meaningful in the course of evolution is realized, we can better use the technology we have developed to widen our capabilities to communicate beyond face-to-face encounter (e.g., telephone, telegraph). Furthermore, we shall enable ourselves to broaden our participation in the environment and see the responsibilities we have in controlling both ourselves and the machines we have invented. Because we are becoming *information dependent,* to positively assimilate this dependence, we must establish new standards of privacy, secrecy, and rights to use the physical channels of communication such as radio and television in order to avoid a psychological downfall. Wiener believed that communication is essential to the welfare of society, and effective communication is ultimately based on how we handle the technology we have introduced into society.

Wiener's approach to science and society is considered of classical importance and fundamental to the development of contemporary sociological, psychological, and scientific attitudes.

REFERENCES

Isaac Asimov, *Biographical Encyclopedia of Science and Technology.* New York: Doubleday & Co., 1972.

Norbert Wiener, *Cybernetics: or Control and Communication in the Animal and the Machine.* Cambridge, Mass.: M.I.T. Press, 1961.

————, *I am a Mathematician.* Cambridge, Mass.: M.I.T. Press, 1970.

————, *The Human Use of Human Beings.* New York: Avon Books, 1967.

LUDWIG WITTGENSTEIN (1889–1951), a philosopher whose work after 1925 influenced the development of logical positivism, linguistic analysis and semantics, was born in Vienna. At seventeen, he went to Berlin to study engineering, leaving there in 1908 for England where he became a research student in aeronautics in Manchester, and designed a jet-reaction engine and a propeller. After reading Bertrand Russell's *Principles of Mathematics* he gave up engineering and was admitted to Trinity College where he studied with Russell from 1912–13. During World War I, Wittgenstein served in the Austrian Army. From 1918–19, he was held prisoner of war, after being captured in Italy. From 1920–26, he was an elementary schoolmaster in village schools throughout Austria. During this time his *Tractatus Logico-Philosophicus,* which he completed in 1918, was published in Germany in 1921 and in England in 1922. This would be the only work, besides an article, to be published during his lifetime. From 1926–28, Wittgenstein remained in Vienna, working as an architect with Paul Engelmann. During this period he came into contact with the Viennese circle of philosophers, including Moritz Schlick, Rudolf Carnap, and Frederich Waismann. In 1929, Wittgenstein made Cambridge his permanent residence. He received his Ph.D. the same year, having submitted *Tractatus* as his doctoral thesis.

From 1930–35, as well as lecturing to small audiences, he was a fellow of Trinity College. He is said to have rejected the privileges that accompanied this position. In 1938, he was declared a naturalized British subject. In 1939, he became professor of philosophy at Cambridge, later inheriting the chair of philosophy upon the retirement of G. E. Moore. During World War II, Wittgenstein worked in a London hospital as a porter and later in a medical laboratory in Newcastle. He resigned his position at Cambridge in 1947 and returned to a private existence. He died of cancer in Cambridge. His final words were: "Tell them I've had a wonderful life." In 1953, his other major work, *Philosophical Investigations,* was posthumously published. Also published after his death were: *Notebooks, 1914–1916,* the preparatory studies for *Tractatus; The Blue and Brown Books,* which were preparatory studies for *Investigations; Zettel,* compiled of fragments from work dating from 1929–48; *Philosophische Bemerkungen,* written in 1929 and 1930 and available only in German; and *Remarks on the Foundations of Mathematics.* There have also been numerous biographical studies of Wittgenstein, as well as interpretations of his philosophy.

Wittgenstein's main intent was the examination of the structure and limits of thought through the examination of the structure and limits of language. The difference between his two major works, *Tractatus* and *Investigations,* lies in the method and reshifting of focus: in the former, the focal point is the development of a scientific theory of language that occupies a place in reality; in the latter, the concern is a criticism of both the theories propounded in *Tractatus,* as well as the analytical means used to arrive at the theories. *Investigations* is essentially based on an intuitive measure of "the case" that required a new mode of expression in *remarks* that followed a certain progression, rather than in *propositions* that followed one another in a closed logical sequence.

In the preface to *Tractatus,* Wittgenstein states that his purpose is to examine philosophical problems posed because "the logic of . . . language is misunderstood." Examining the problems of philosophy meant examining the problems of the expression of thought in language. This process revealed another question to Wittgenstein: What are the limits of thought and, consequently, what are the limits of language? Working with the presumption that only in language can the limits of language be set and, thus, the limits of thought, Wittgenstein examined the foundations of logic, the sources of which are *factual propositions* and *elementary propositions* that are logically independent of one another and trace the reduction of language to its *necessary* limits. Wittgenstein also intended to develop a theory of factual propositions that would explain logical necessity so that when factual propositions are exhausted, so is the logical necessity of their progression. The limits of language would therefore be an absolute necessity. What remains is beyond the set-forth limits of language and logic and qualifiable as nonsense: "What can be said at all can be said clearly, and what we cannot talk about we must pass over in silence."

According to Wittgenstein, meaning is derived from the precise "sense" of factual propositions. This sense is a product of the words that *represent pictures in logical space;* the words or signs that compose the factual propositions are *names.* Names represent *objects;* objects compose reality. The existence of objects as presented in the propositions can be seen as such, but propositions cannot assert the existence of an object. This is an example of what can only be shown and not talked about. Similarly, two propositions (i.e., "p" and "not-p") can be seen to exist as independent entities in propositions; their relation is reducible to a tautology (i.e., "p" or "not-p"). According to Wittgenstein, a tautology is not a factual proposition. He concludes that reality's atomistic structure is inherent in the structure of language, given the basis for the structure of all languages in propositions. The limits of *factual* discourse are the limits of language. Metaphysical insight into reality can be gained through logic, not a description thereof.

In the preface to *Investigations,* Wittgenstein contends that he had made "grave mistakes" in the writing of *Tractatus.* In this new work, he did not want to spare people the trouble of thinking, but "stimulate someone to thoughts of his own." In *Investigations,* he largely rejects what he had proposed in *Tractatus,* namely that there is an essence of propositions that is "the essence of all description and thus the essence of the world." He intended to understand and communicate the "problems of life" which, if dealt with in the method set forth in *Tractatus,* would not be comprehensible or communicable. In this way, *Investigations* has no method.

In *Investigations,* he abandons the theory that all factual propositions can be analyzed in terms of a single, independent elementary proposition whose relationship could be reduced to tautology: the theory of *necessary truth.* Rather, elementary propositions are related to one another in systematically related groups. This indicates that the only theory that can exist is a theory of linguistic facts which, by themselves, could be described but could not be considered as alluding to objects in reality. According to David Pears, one of Wittgenstein's biographers, what he proposed is that "the sources of the necessities of logic and mathematics lie within . . . areas of discourse, in actual linguistic practices, and, when those necessities seem to point to some independent backing outside the practice, the pointing is deceptive and the idea that the backing is independent is an illusion." Language becomes a means for the expression of *sensations.* Then Wittgenstein raises the issue: If using a language is a learned ability, how can we be sure that the reactions we express are truthful? And how is a language of sensations justifiable?

Essentially, *Investigations* is the refutation of the scientific analysis of nonfactual systems of thought (e.g., religion, ethics) and the defense of the idea that the only philosophy possible is a philosophy of language. According to Wittgenstein, it is impossible to impose generalizations on areas of life that involve sense impressions (e.g., behavior and art) and are consequently too complex to approach.

REFERENCES

Allan Janik and Stephen Toulmin, *Wittgenstein's Vienna*. New York: Simon & Schuster, 1973.

David Pears, *Ludwig Wittgenstein*. New York: Viking Press, 1969.

Ludwig Wittgenstein, *Tractatus Logico-Philosophicus*, trans. by David Pears and B. F. McGuinness. London: Routledge & Kegan Paul; New York: The Humanities Press, 1961.

————, *Philosophical Investigations*, trans. by G. E. M. Anscombe. England: Basil Blackwell and Mott, Ltd., The Alden Press, 1958.

————, *Notebooks, 1914–1916*, trans. by G. E. M. Anscombe, ed. by G. H. Von Wright and G. E. M. Anscombe. New York: Harper & Row, 1969.

————, *The Blue and Brown Books, Preliminary Studies for the Philosophical Investigations*. New York: Harper & Row, 1965.

————, *Zettel*, trans. by G. E. M. Anscombe; ed. by G. E. M. Anscombe and G. H. Von Wright. Berkeley, Ca.: University of California Press, 1970.

YOGA is the general term applied to certain philosophical-spiritual disciplines of the Hindu and Buddhist religions aimed at the achievement of spiritual awareness and liberation. The word "yoga" stems from the Sanskrit root *yuj* which has several meanings: to attach and yoke, to bind, to direct and concentrate attention upon, to use and apply, and union or communion of man's will to the will of God. Although there are several branches of yogic practices, the general aim of the philosophy is to teach the means by which an individual human spirit, or *jivatma,* can be in communion with or united to the Supreme Universal Spirit, or *Paramatma*.

In India, over the centuries, many forms of yoga developed, the result of the diversification of Indian culture and the appropriation of religious beliefs and accompanying techniques of yogic practice in accordance with the rise of sects and orders in Indian society. All were based on the attainment of some kind of personal freedom. The assimilation of these various forms into an orthodox trend, Hinduism, was complex. The embodiment of this synthesis is contained in the *Bhagavad-Gita* (500 B.C.), which was added to the *Mahabhavata*, a spiritual poem. The basic theme running through the *Gita* is concerned with the importance of spiritual experience rather than scripture. The yogic techniques described in the *Gita* resemble classical yoga with regard to postures, etc., but the meditative aims are different.

In the fifth century B.C., with the development of Buddhism, the aims of yogic practices changed. According to Buddha, truth had to be understood and known experientially. The culmination of this experience is *nirvana*. Yogic techniques (e.g., *pranayama*) laid the foundations for meditation which consisted of assuming four psychic states, which preceded four more spiritual exercises that were to prepare one for the approach to nirvana. All were aimed at the transcendence of profane existence.

Tantrism, whose methodologies are geared to the ritualization of yogic procedures necessary for attaining supreme truth, arose outside the major part of India, and influenced Hinduism and Buddhism, popularly. Tantrism gave birth to *mantras* and *dharanis,* the language of meditation; the *mandala,* symbol of the universe on which to concentrate to find one's own center; Hatha yoga, for the development of the body; Kundalini, or spiritual awakening; and mystical eroticism and techniques of sexual experience. In general, Tantrism is concerned with the experience of death in life. The final process of *sadhana,* or realization, is one of cosmic reabsorption, metaphorical death followed by rebirth.

Yoga was systematically outlined for the first time in the *Yoga-Sutras* of Patanjali (200 B.C.), which set forth in a composite form the doctrinal and technical traditions of yogic practices which had long been in existence. Essentially, Patanjali combined the metaphysical Samkhya philosophy and the more practical Yoga system.

This "classic" yoga is theistic; its methodology is meditation for the purpose of finding a way to God and liberation. It is aimed at dissolving the psychological, personality aspects of living so that freedom from suffering and pain, caused in the first place by a nonmetaphysical ignorance of the true nature of the self, is achieved. Patanjali states that the yogin must experience the knowledge of different states of consciousness in order to do away with them. These different states of consciousness are considered to be sources of pain. To carry out this process, the yogin must detach himself from psychic life before he can change the states of consciousness that are the source of "psychomental" states.

All classical yoga requires the practice of physical and spiritual exercises, which lead to liberation. They include: *yama,* restraint or abstinence from sex, violence, possessions, etc.; *niyama,* discipline or observance of virtue, purity, contentment; *asana,* positions or postures of the body; *pranayama,* controlled respiration; *pratyahara,* detachment of the senses from the external world; *dharana,* concentration; *dhyana,* yogic meditation; and the highest form of *samadhi,* bliss, becoming all-Being. A necessary tool of yoga meditation is the ability to concentrate on a single object, or *ekagrata.* This requires the integration of mental processes through concentration on a thought, a lighted candle, the tip of the nose, or some other specific object. The mode of concentration differs according to the discipline being practiced, e.g., Tantric yoga, etc.

Today, the yoga system, although retaining its essential philosophical goal, is popularly applied in a psychotherapeutic context. A primary goal of its practice is the attainment of physical and mental well-being. The basic discipline employed is Hatha yoga. Hatha yoga aims for the attainment of good health and physical strength in order to be able to endure the more rigorous yoga training. Hatha yoga includes the third phase of asana and the fourth phase of pranayama, and is a step-by-step system of physical education which involves the entire body in stretching and holding postures. The stress is upon the integration of the body as a whole through correct body posture, the strengthening and realignment of the body so that it achieves a state of unified balance. The rhythm of the exercises is slow and precise; there is no call for exertion or strain as in other forms of physical exercise; the overall attitude is one of quietness or peacefulness in concentration.

The postures affect every major system of the body (skeletal, muscular, nervous, respiratory, glandular, etc.), and they can be used therapeutically for relief of nervous disorders, tensions, and functional and organic diseases such as anemia, arthritis, high blood pressure, obesity, ulcers, etc.

All asanas should be done on an empty stomach and with empty bowels. You will find that they are easier to do after taking a warm bath and in the evening or early morning. The more proficiency you acquire, the more asanas you will be able to do for a longer time each session. Initially, it is advised to do each posture once, and for the first week no more than three of the easiest postures. The simplest postures are the *halasana,* or plough pose, which is beneficial to the spine, the lumbar vertebrae, the abdominal muscles, and the neck; the *sarvangasana,* or whole body pose, which affects the thyroid and is rejuvenative to the entire body; the *pashimatasana,* or posterior stretching pose, which benefits the hamstring muscles, the nerves in the pelvic region, and the abdominal muscles. The more difficult postures will be added to your practice gradually. The corpse, or dead pose, in which the whole body is completely relaxed, should conclude any group of exercises. Special attention should be paid to your breathing rhythm in order to achieve maximum relaxation.

In yoga, the correct posture (positioning) of the body allows the greatest freedom and poise and is the key to the harmonious regulation of breathing. The four poses which are exclusively for breathing are the *sukasana,* or easy pose; the *siddhasana,* or perfect pose; the *vajrasana,* or adamant pose; and the *padamasana,* the lotus pose, which is the most difficult.

When incorporated with physical attunement and proper breathing control, the practice of meditation becomes one of the primary aspects of all yoga. Concentration precedes meditation. The mind is centered by focusing on an object or by chanting. Concentration should be achieved without effort or unwarranted expenditure of mental energy. Meditation furthers concentration by focusing on abstractions to render them real; meditation is a process of refining the mind. It approaches realizing a key energy that opens the mind and body to otherwise unknown spaces.

In addition, there are specific dietary principles which determine the kinds of foods to be eaten if you are practicing Hatha yoga. The main precept is to eat simple, light foods which are as close to their natural state as possible and therefore contain *prana,* or life force. A yoga diet will consist of fresh fruits, nuts, raw vegetables, rice, fresh milk, oil, and clarified butter. Certain foods such as garlic, onions, tea, coffee, meat, and alcoholic drinks are to be avoided entirely. Fasting one day a month, or more, is also recommended.

REFERENCES

B. K. S. Iyengar, *Light on Yoga.* New York: Schocken Books, 1965.

Yogi Vithaldas, *The Yoga System of Health and Relief from Tension.* New York: Simon & Schuster/Cornerstone Library, 1957.

ZONE THERAPY/REFLEXOLOGY (the terms are practically synonymous) is a method of treatment that involves the application of pressure to certain specific points or areas on the body to achieve relief of a specific physical problem, or for a more general and overall effect. The theory on which this method of therapy is based is similar to the theory that is the basis for the ancient Chinese practice of acupuncture.

The various methods of pressure therapy practiced in the United States today are largely the result of work done by William H. Fitzgerald, M.D., Edwin F. Bowers, M.D., and George S. White, M.D. In the early twentieth century, Fitzgerald was working with the application of pressure and discovered certain relationships between points or areas on the body and organs. He proceeded to divide the body into ten zones, five longitudinal zones on the right side, and five on the left, and attempted to systematize these relationships and the application of non-opiate anesthetics. Bowers, his assistant, coined the term "zone therapy" for this work.

Recently, there have been photographic studies done by the Kirlians which show that biological differences can be read graphically, especially in terms of the registration of colors emanating from the skin, confirming the concept of zones.

Zone therapy concentrates on the reflex areas in the hands and feet where the nerve endings are close to the skin and therefore more accessible for massage. A reflexology chart of the body correlates the right foot with the right side of the body, and the left foot with the left side. The big toes correspond with the head; the reflex of the pituitary gland is located in the center of the big toes. Neck and throat reflexes are in the base of the big toes. From the base of the big toes to the heels, along the inside of the foot, are the reflexes of the spine. The reflex area of the liver is on the right foot; the heart on the left foot; the colon on both feet; the appendix on the right foot, etc. Thus, each reflex area on the feet directly corresponds to the location of the organs of the body, whether right, left, or center.

The reflex points on the bottoms of the feet are also located in the palms of the hands. But, because the palms do not sustain the same kind of pressure and are not usually as tender as the feet, their reflex areas are not easily located.

It is often difficult to locate a reflex area because some of them are small. If you do not know what area in the foot corresponds to an area in the body, or vice versa, you would press gently, but firmly, using a rotating motion, to locate a point of tenderness or pain under the skin. This point is one through which your blood is not flowing normally to the disturbed area of your body. By massaging it for a few seconds, the pain will be relieved. Massaging the entire foot will make sure you do not miss any of these tender points.

Massaging both feet will stimulate the entire body. One effective method of massage is to walk barefoot over rough terrain, e.g., small stones or smooth gravel. The rough surface will come in contact with the reflex areas, break up the crystals in your feet that are inhibiting blood flow, and cause the blood to flow freely throughout the body.

There are a variety of tools that can be used for massage: your thumb, a rubber pencil eraser, a reflex massager, a hand massager, and rubber bands or clothespins for the application of stronger pressure.

It is advised that the length of treatment for the first week be limited to ten minutes every other day. At all times, it is important not to overdo massaging, especially in the reflex area of the kidneys.

Zone therapy/reflexology can be used to treat a variety of physical problems, e.g., back pain, colds, ulcers, arthritis, chronic fatigue, allergies, heart conditions, etc. Treatment might involve concentrating on massaging several different areas. A doctor should be consulted for any persistent problems, however. Zone therapy can be used for the purpose of anesthetizing by a doctor or dentist. For example, pressure applied to certain fingers or toes will relieve pain in certain teeth connected with the nerves being pressured; pressure applied to the big

500 / ZONE THERAPY/REFLEXOLOGY

toe will anesthetize the incisor region of the mouth, allowing for a painless extraction. The anesthetic effect can last from half a minute to over four minutes.

According to Mildred Carter, a practicing reflexologist for more than fourteen years, zone therapy can revitalize your whole body: "In massaging the whole foot, all the cells will be stimulated as the circulation is released to allow the natural life force to bring renewed vigor to every part of the body . . . the vibrations of the life force will bring harmony and health back to every part of the body."

REFERENCES

Anika Bergson and Vladimir Tuchak, *Zone Therapy*. New York: Pinnacle Books, 1974.

Mildred Carter, *Helping Yourself with Foot Reflexology*. New York: Parker Publishing Co., 1969.

A NOTE ABOUT THE AUTHOR

KATINKA MATSON is a literary agent, a former actress, and the author of *The Working Actor* (Viking, 1976).